American Indians, the Irish, and Government Schooling

Indigenous Education

SERIES EDITORS

Margaret Connell Szasz
University of New Mexico

Brenda J. Child
University of Minnesota

Karen Gayton Swisher
Haskell Indian Nations University

John W. Tippeconnic III
The Pennsylvania State University

American Indians, the Irish, and Government Schooling

A Comparative Study

Michael C. Coleman

UNIVERSITY OF NEBRASKA PRESS • LINCOLN AND LONDON

© 2007 by the Board of Regents of the University of Nebraska
All rights reserved
Manufactured in the United States of America
⊗

Library of Congress Cataloging-in-Publication Data
Coleman, Michael C.
American Indians, the Irish, and government schooling:
a comparative study / Michael C. Coleman.
p. cm.
ISBN-13: 978-0-8032-1563-4 (cloth : alk. paper)
ISBN-10: 0-8032-1563-0 (cloth : alk. paper)
ISBN-13: 978-0-8032-2485-8 (paper : alk. paper)
1. Indians of North America—Education.
2. Indians of North America—Government relations.
3. Irish—Education—Great Britain.
4. Irish—Great Britain—Government relations.
5. Education—Cross-cultural studies.
6. United States—Social policy.
7. Great Britain—Social policy. I. Title.
E97.C65 2007
370'.8997—dc22
2006032558

Set in Quadraat.
Designed by R. W. Boeche.

To those students whom I have taught, chatted with in the kahvio, sung with, played football with, become friends with, and learned from, in Finland, Ireland, and the United States since 1970; especially to students of the Department of Languages (English) at the University of Jyväskylä, Finland.

Contents

Illustrations

Following page 176

Maps

Acknowledgments

My major debt is to the Academy of Finland for its generous Senior Research Fellowship (*varttuneen tieteenharjoittajan apuraha*), which allowed me a full year of research in the Irish archives (1996–97). I also wish to thank colleagues and ex-colleagues in the Department of Languages (English) here at the University of Jyväskylä for their encouragement and support of my research ambitions, especially the present comparative venture: Liisa Lautamatti, Raija Markkanen, and Kari Sajavaara, in particular. Other Finnish scholars also deserve acknowledgment: Markku Henrikkson, Marjatta Hietala, and Olli Vehviläinen. As always I am grateful to the University of Jyväskylä for its generous policy of *virkavapaus* (leave of absence), and to its ever-helpful library staff—I sense that the Inter-Library Loan office had to employ extra personnel just to keep up with my demands.

I would also like to thank my students at the University of Jyväskylä, especially those in my seminar, and members of the Finnish National Graduate School for North American and Latin American Studies, all of whom have suffered my scholarly impositions with humor. They have read and commented critically on many of my efforts—and perhaps enjoyed seeing me fall into the very errors for which I lambasted them ("Did you not criticize us for being apologetic and for repetition and for using the passive voice?"). If teaching is learning, learning can sometimes also be teaching.

In Ireland I was treated most helpfully by the staffs of many archives and libraries: the National Library of Ireland; the National Archives of Ireland; the Main Library and Department of Irish Folklore, University College Dublin; the Berkeley Library and the Early Printed Books Library, Trinity College, Dublin; Marsh's Library, Dublin. A number of Irish scholars also encouraged my comparative ambitions: John Coolahan, Mary Daly, David Fitzpatrick, Marie Keane, Christóir MacCarthaigh, Bairbre Ní Fhloinn, Susan Parkes, and Deirdre Raftery. I also want to thank Maeve Bradley, Kenneth Milne, Melissa Newmann and Mike De Jong, and Diarmuid Ó'Gráda for their help. My late mother, Beatrice Coleman, also deserves credit, and not only for putting up with most of the Coleman family, Finnish branch, for an academic year; she and my late father, Michael Sidney Coleman, first stimulated my interest in history.

In my American publications I have already thanked individuals and institutions for their wonderful help over the last three decades of research and writing about American Indian history, and my scholarly debts will also be obvious from my notes. A number of individuals deserve explicit recognition, however: David Wallace Adams, Bob Bieder, Margaret Jacobs, Herbert Lewis, Francis Paul Prucha, SJ, Charles E. Rosenberg, Seetha Srinivasan, W. H. A. Williams, and Allan Winkler. As editor of *American Indian Quarterly*, Devon A. Mihesuah was brave enough to publish my first venture into Irish-Indian comparative history. Margaret Connell Szasz and Ferenc Morton Szasz deserve special thanks for interrupting their holiday and offering, then and later, powerfully useful criticism of the present manuscript. And, although the prospect of copyediting is often a terrifying one for the author, working with Jane Curran was an instructive and enjoyable experience.

Members of my immediate family also read and critically commented on chapters, and were not in the least constrained by respect for paterfamilias: my wife, Sirkka, and Donagh and Tiina Coleman. Markus Coleman read and commented in detail on the whole manuscript, losing whatever was left of his belief in parental omniscience.

All shortcomings are, of course, my own.

Buoichas daoibh go léir—thank you all—*kiitos teille kaikki.*

Abbreviations

ABCFM   American Board of Commissioners for Foreign Missions

AIC   American Indian Correspondence, Presbyterian Historical
        Society, Philadelphia, Pennsylvania

AR   Annual Report

ARCIA   Annual Report of the Commissioner of Indian Affairs

BFM   Board of Foreign Missions of the Presbyterian Church
        in the United States of America

BIA   Bureau of Indian Affairs (also Office of Indian Affairs,
        Indian Office)

CNEI   Commissioners of National Education in Ireland
        (also the National Board)

IFC   Irish Folklore Collection, UCD Delargy Centre for
        Irish Folklore and the National Folklore Collection,
        University College Dublin

NA   National Archives, Washington DC

NAI   National Archives of Ireland, Dublin

NLI   National Library of Ireland, Dublin

M   Microfilm

MS   Manuscript

PCUSA   Presbyterian Church in the United States of America

RG   Record Group (in National Archives: e.g., RG 75).

American Indians, the Irish, and Government Schooling

Introduction

As an Irishman specializing for over three decades in Native American studies, I have long felt strong "resonances" between Indian and Irish histories.[1] These "problem peoples" experienced centuries-long military and cultural assaults by more powerful expanding states. They suffered massive land loss and demographic collapse through disease, famine, population movement, and emigration. In myriad ways they also demonstrated resilience, adaptability, and manipulative pragmatism. Moreover, for centuries they faced sporadic attempts by missionaries, sometimes state-supported, to wean them from their supposedly uncivilized or disloyal ways. Most significantly—and the subject of the present comparative study—from the early nineteenth to the early twentieth centuries Indians and the Irish peoples confronted systematic, state-controlled, and *assimilationist* educational campaigns, as the United States strove to Americanize the Indians and the British government to Anglicize the Irish. These campaigns were designed to absorb supposedly deficient peoples into larger, dominant nations, leading not to cultural cross-fertilization but to the erasure of minority cultures and identities.[2]

From the early sixteenth century, as white colonists spread onto tribal lands in what would later become the United States of America, Catholic and Protestant missionaries began the formal schooling of Indian children. Missionary societies back in Europe sometimes aided these ventures, and the imperial and colonial governments also saw the usefulness of education for the "civilization," Christianization, and pacification of Indians.

To achieve an acceptably humane solution to its "Indian problem," the new United States immediately put its prestige, power, and increasing amounts of its money behind similar but far more ambitious efforts. In 1794 the nation made its first Indian treaty specifically mentioning education, and many more treaties would contain similar offers and even demands for compulsory schooling of tribal children. In 1819 Congress provided a specific "civilization fund" of $10,000 for the "uplift" of Indians, and the assimilationist campaign continued to employ legislation, treaty making (until 1871), and other expedients to achieve its goals. Initially the United States government, through its Office/Bureau of Indian Affairs (BIA), depended upon Christian missionary societies, but by the later nineteenth century the government dominated the educational effort, having established a loose system of hundreds of day schools, on-reservation boarding schools, and off-reservation boarding schools. BIA and missionary schools together worked to Christianize, "civilize," and Americanize Indian children: the rigidly ethnocentric curriculum aimed to strip them of tribal cultures, languages, and spiritual concepts and turn them into "cultural brokers" who would carry the new order back to their own peoples.[3] This approach persisted until the inauguration of more culturally sensitive Indian policies during Franklin D. Roosevelt's administration in the 1930s. If the assimilationist campaign began in earnest after 1819, the decade of the 1920s, then, marks a logical cut-off point for the American side of the present study.

When the Norman kings of what would later become England first established a claim to Ireland in the twelfth century, the country was broken into many competing subkingdoms and overkingdoms. Even by early modern times no native national state had developed, and so the new centralizing English Tudor state (1485–1603) more easily achieved a military conquest. While England became predominantly Protestant, most Irish people remained Roman Catholic, adding a further and deeply divisive element to an already bitter conflict of politics and cultures. There followed major Protestant plantations, in Ulster especially; the dispossession of most Catholics of their lands; and the firm subjugation of Catholics (and dissenter Protestants) to a minority Anglican Protestant ascendancy—which in turn remained firmly under the domination of Westminster. By the 1780s the colonial elite in Ireland, as in the American colonies, was seeking greater freedom within the British Empire—and similarly ignoring the claims of "native" peoples. By 1787 American colonists had broken completely with the British Empire. After complex and bloody rebellions in 1798, however, Britain decided to solve its "Irish problem" by fully absorbing the country into the United Kingdom through the 1800 Act of Union.

From the time of Henry VIII in the 1530s British governments had seen the potential of schooling for Anglicization of the Irish and their conversion to Protestantism, and later British governments gave some support to independent missionary societies. Yet by the early decades of the nineteenth century it had become obvious that a more systematic approach was needed to integrate a predominantly Catholic people into the Union. After a number of commissions reported during the 1820s, Parliament in 1831 agreed to fund an Irish elementary school system. Run by the Commissioners of National Education in Ireland (CNEI, also called "the National Board"), the new national schools would be open to all boys and girls. No child would be subjected to religious teaching by members of a different denomination. This toleration of local religious sensibilities did not extend to other areas of Irish culture. Until late in the nineteenth century all instruction was through English, although initially a high percentage of pupils were monoglot Irish-speakers. Like that of the BIA, the CNEI curriculum also ignored most "native" cultural knowledge and could have been suitable for any English-speaking populations.[4] The fact that most commissioners, inspectors, and teachers were Irish should not disguise the fact that they were working to assimilate Irish people into modern British life—to Anglicize, or perhaps we might say "Briticize," them—just as the white and Indian members of the BIA worked to assimilate Indians into American life. In each case successful assimilation would end a long-term ethnic "problem" and achieve an unblemished wholeness of community and polity.[5]

With the partition of the island into the Irish Free State (later Republic of Ireland) and Northern Ireland in the early 1920s, the National Board passed out of existence, also making this decade a logical cut-off point for the Irish part of my project.

Of course, there were also many differences between Irish and American Indian historical and cultural experiences that would produce discernible differences in policies, practices, and responses. If nineteenth-century Ireland was fragmented into class, urban/rural, religious, ethnic, linguistic, political, and regional divisions, these were hardly equivalent to the kaleidoscopic variety of Indian tribal cultures, many with distinctive cosmologies, spiritual beliefs, languages, social structures, and economies. By the 1830s close to seven million Irish people—about six million Roman Catholics and one million Protestants of various denominations—lived on the island. Approximately three hundred thousand Indians were even then a diminishing minority—incorrectly believed by many Americans to be vanishing—in areas claimed by the expanding United States. Further, what we might call the "cultural distance" between Irish people of whatever lifestyle and the English was far less than the "cultural distance" between most Native Americans and Euro-Americans. All communities educate their children, but by the 1820s few Indian children attended schools (more knew of this alien educational institution, however). There were over 11,000 schools scattered throughout the small island of Ireland then.[6] And although large numbers of rural Irish people lived at a "pre-modern" subsistence level not much different from many Indians, other Irish peoples lived in villages, small and larger towns, and in a few cities; there was a growing middle class (Catholic and Protestant).

Increasing levels of modernization were evidenced by, for example, mass po-
liticizations and mass movements. Thus, far more Irish people than Native
Americans had begun to experience the privileges and perils of modernity.

The historian must not elide such differences, but neither should the differences belie the many similarities in historical experiences, nor invalidate
comparative analysis. Indeed, scholars have recently shown that fruitful comparison can be made of similar educational processes, such as mass education, in different contexts. Peter N. Stearns has compared and contrasted the
rise of mass schooling in two Western nations, each with its own distinctive
educational traditions, the United States and France, and in a unique Asian
nation, Japan. More recently Edmund Burke III has drawn instructive comparison between the nineteenth-century French "civilizing mission" in such
culturally and religiously distinct areas as its own subregion Brittany and
newly conquered Muslim Algeria. Ann Laura Stoler specifically compared
American Indian schooling with Dutch colonial variants in the East Indies
and ended her essay with a ringing plea for comparison. "The incommensu-
rabilities between the North American empire and European colonial history
diminish when the intimacies of Empire are at center stage," she believes.
These "intimacies" include "colonizing the hearts and minds of women, children, and men."[7]

Indeed, current thinking among both American historians and scholars in
the broader multidisciplinary "field" of American studies suggest that comparative approaches are crucial to moving Americans away from a sense of
"exceptionalism." A critique of isolationist thinking, writes Rachel Adams,
has become one of the central concerns of American studies, which has
turned increasingly toward comparative, multicultural, and transnational
perspectives "as a way of combating the field's more traditional focus on a ho-
mogeneous national culture."[8] Michael Adas similarly critiques conventional, inward-looking historical perspectives. Serious comparisons, he writes,
"compel us to focus on clearly delineated processes and particular types of
institutions, social movements, or discourses"—schooling could surely be
counted under any of these headings. Both recurring and divergent historical
patterns, he believes, are proper subjects for comparative and international
history, as both challenge American exceptionalism. Contacts with indigenous peoples throughout the world are of special concern to Adas. Indian-
white relations and the frontier experience "underscore the ways in which the
history of the United States has been both integral to broader global developments and unquestionably distinctive but in no meaningful sense unprec-
edented or unique."[9]

European scholars have also seen the need to move beyond single nation emphases, as demonstrated by a number of recent studies focusing on the interrelated histories of England, Scotland, Wales, and Ireland—the nations of the so-called British Isles. Each has its own distinctive history, and many subhistories, yet there are obvious connecting and comparative issues worth exploring. And in the British journal History of Education issue devoted entirely to comparative study, editors David Crook and Gary McCulloch declare that "we need constantly to be reminded, as educational historians, of the value of adopting comparative approaches." This is especially true because much work in this field gravitates toward the particular case. Nevertheless "it is essential that we should go beyond the purely local and singular, and attempt to develop connections between phenomena and problems encountered in different countries and cultures."[10]

Irish experiences have been in ways distinctive, in other ways similar to those of very different peoples beyond Indians. "Whether or not they are aware of it," claims John Hutchinson, "most Irish historians are methodological nationalists since they tend to take for granted the nation as the proper unit of analysis." Nationalism is a global phenomenon "and cannot be explained in any one country by local peculiarities." In stressing the need for an international perspective in Irish historiography, he encourages scholars to employ, among other methods, comparative historical frameworks "to contextualize and explain the rise of nationalism in Ireland." A similar plea could be made for other areas of Irish studies, and Kevin Kenny has pointed to the need for both *transnational* studies (going beyond individual national histories) and *cross-national* studies (comparative studies of national developments) for better understanding of the complexities, continuities, and discontinuities in the Irish diaspora.[11] Scholars such as Joe Cleary, Cormac Ó'Gráda, and Ian Lustick have instructively compared aspects of Irish history to similar and different experiences in countries as diverse as Algeria, Finland, and Israel/Palestine.[12] Alice Scheper-Hughes, David Harding, Katie Kane, Nicholas P. Canny, and I have explicitly compared Irish and American Indian developments.[13]

In his impressive comparative study of the relationships between Britain and Ireland, France and Algeria, and Israel and the West Bank-Gaza, Ian Lustick calls for some "framework of analysis" when we attempt such comparisons.[14] My brief historical surveys suggest that, at its broadest, imperialism might be such a framework for Irish-Indian comparisons. I can, however, fine-tune things a little more. My framework for analysis is assimilationist mass elementary schooling. And my goal is *to compare, on the one hand, the assimilationist policies and practices of American and Irish government educators from about the 1820s to the 1920s and, on the other hand, the responses of Indian and Irish peoples to these campaigns.* I shall, of course, analyze differences in policies, practices, and responses. Yet the broad similarities, especially the ambitions of the educators, are clear in each country, leading to immensely complicated cultural and personal interactions and to forms of symbiotic interdependence of educators and educated. The once "new social history" of the later twentieth century may now be old hat, but its insistence that scholars examine the experiences of the "outs"—subject peoples, women, ordinary people till then relatively neglected by historians—is still valid and indeed central to my venture. So are postmodernist and postcolonial concerns about the (dis)empowerment of the "Other." I shall show how those-to-be-educated retained initiatives and sometimes succeeded in manipulating the new systems to their own advantage.

Peter Kolchin has made three major claims for the importance of comparative history, all of which I hope to validate in this book.[15] First, it should point to broader patterns and thus warn us against parochialism in our conclusions about any historical phenomenon—a function, as we saw, that may lead historians to further question traditional claims for American or English or Irish historical exceptionalism. The assimilationist schooling and "uplift" of American Indians has in recent decades been the subject of numerous studies.[16] So too has the assimilationist thrust of British educational policies and practices in Ireland.[17] This book thus goes beyond relatively well-studied but nationally focused concerns and places them in a comparative framework. Further, by drawing on the writings of scholars of mass education, such as Stearns, John Willinsky, David Vincent, Andy Green, and others, it places American and Irish variants of mass education within the context of one of the great modernizing revolutions of recent centuries. It further demonstrates the faith of elites in the power of education to transform "troublesome" subject peoples and suggests patterns of resistance/accommodation/negotiation on the part of the supposed beneficiaries, many of whom—for their own reasons—powerfully desired schooling for their children. Above all, by comparing relationships between educators and educated, comparative analysis can suggest something of the bewildering *variety* and *complexity* of such relationships in America, Ireland, and elsewhere.[18]

Second, in Kolchin's view, comparison allows us to test hypotheses and form historical generalizations. For example, Indianists have given much attention to the "cultural broker" or mediator between cultures. To what extent might this concept be applied to the Irish educational context? American and British language policies—only English must be used in instruction—certainly helped lead to the near-collapse of Irish and many Native American languages. Did such policies inevitably lead to the demise of local languages? Or was language loss also due to factors outside the schools? Why did these minority languages almost disappear in the nineteenth century under imperial influences, whereas others, such as Navajo and Finnish, survived and thrived? The present study cannot give definitive answers to these questions. By comparing United States and British government policies and practices, however, along with "native" responses to them, it can allow us to propose hypotheses and suggest that the loss/survival of languages and other cultural traits is contingent and by no means inevitable under imperialism.

Third, Kolchin believes that comparison helps us explain differences in developments. When we study American Indian educational history in isolation, it is too easy to make certain assumptions about assimilationist schooling. American government and missionary teachers generally demonstrated contempt for Indian religious and spiritual ideas; such "heathenism" was to be erased and replaced by variants of Christianity. The British government's earlier support of Protestant missionary societies in Ireland showed similar though not identical disdain for Catholicism. Yet by the 1830s Westminster's Irish educational establishment rigidly forbade religious proselytizing in its schools. This is but one of many differences that a comparative approach can reveal and perhaps explain; such developments, when examined in a single context, might lead the historian to assume their typicality rather than distinctiveness.

The present comparative study thus permits me to illuminate further the history of imperialist, assimilationist education. For centuries imperial/colonial authorities and missionaries presumed the right to instill alien cultural and educational ideals and practices into generations of children of "problem" cultures from India to Africa to Ireland to America. Colonial assimilationist schooling, writes John Willinsky, "was made to stand against family and community, against a culture that seemed to fly in the face of the ostensible rationality and enlightenment of the colonial power." Such schooling "turned the concept of learning into the acquisition of what and who one was not."[19] Although many scholars would broadly accept such generalizations, much remains to be said on both the similarities and the differences in the varied approaches pursued by governments and missionary societies from the United States, Britain, and elsewhere.[20]

The analysis that follows is based partly on my own archival research in both the United States and Ireland and on the publications that resulted. As is common in comparative analysis, I also draw freely on the published work of other scholars in both areas, and on the work of those who have examined broader issues of education and imperialism. In my own research I have extensively used Indian and Irish autobiographical accounts and reminiscences of schooling. Elsewhere I have conceded the problematic nature of long-term autobiographical memory for accurate recall. Yet I have simultaneously argued that if such reminiscences are carefully corroborated by other sources, they can be critically utilized by the historian.[21] Even if they are generally credible in their recall, I make no claim that ex-pupils and ex-teachers who later produced autobiographical account were representative of all their peers. I draw on their often-rich accounts for insights otherwise unavailable.

Before proceeding to the heart of my subject, I briefly outline the educational opportunities, formal and informal, available to Indian and Irish peoples up to about the 1820s (chapter 1). Then I sketch the policies and practices of American and British governments from the early nineteenth to early twentieth centuries, when both systematically exploited the school as a weapon of state in the struggle to assimilate "problem" peoples (chapter 2). The next six chapters constitute the core of the book, as they focus on the complex interactions between assimilationist educational policy and reality on the ground. Chapter 3 examines the responses of the local communities, Indian and Irish, to the new government programs of mass schooling. This chapter also suggests reasons for enrollment on both continents—full compulsory schooling was never effective during these decades, and thus subject peoples did have a measure of choice. The chapter also shows how divisive the school could become, especially for Indians, even in the same village or family: cultural background certainly influences attitudes to schooling, but it is never determinative. Chapter 4 takes us inside the school, examining the educational regimes and pupil responses to them. This chapter also focuses upon issues of initiation, discipline, and punishment, along with overall problems—and achievements—of pupil adjustment. It gleans the initial responses of children who often spoke no English to instruction only in that language. Chapter 5 examines the assimilative nature of the BIA and CNEI curriculum. On both continents it sought first to deculturate pupils, then to educate them in the knowledge and worldview of the dominant power: to transport them into a new universe. Chapter 6 focuses on teachers and other school staff, including students promoted to positions of authority. In Chapter 7 I move to consider peer relationships at Indian and Irish schools—how pupils abused or helped each other and often became "cultural brokers," mediating between themselves, the schools, and the local communities, and, sometimes, between the schools and the larger society. This chapter also examines kinds of sanctioned extracurricular activities that grew up at the schools and, especially, their influence on peer relationships. Chapter 8 focuses upon the many forms of pupil resistance or even rejection that developed within the schools. Chapter 9 broadly summarizes the immediate results of the BIA and CNEI campaigns and speculates on long-term results: what might have happened had the American and British governments not supported such educational campaigns? This chapter also suggests how individual Indian and Irish ex-pupils felt about schooling. Finally, in my conclusion I present the historical significance of my comparative findings and suggest potentially important areas for further research. Throughout, I hope to provide historical insights that can be gained only through comparative study. Or—to use Edwin Amental's formulation—I too ask: "What would be lost if there had been no comparative research in this area?"[22]

George M. Frederickson has claimed that comparative history should "jolt" historians into new ways of looking at a supposedly familiar past.[23] If the present study does not actually jolt its readers, I trust that it will provoke them to think in new ways about each of the campaigns and their significance in the history of mass assimilationist education.

1. Education in Native America and Ireland to the 1820s

In 1812 the Commissioners for Inquiring into the State of all Schools, on Charitable or Public Foundations, in Ireland admitted that while "the present establishments for the instruction of the lower orders [are] extremely numerous," they were "inadequate as a system of general education."[1] More commissions reported, and by 1824, according to the Commissioners of Irish Education Inquiry, there were 11,823 schools of all kinds, enrolling over half a million pupils out of a total population of about seven million.[2] Over 9,000 of these Irish "schools," however, were extralegal and impermanent "hedge schools." The far fewer and far more dispersed Indian mission schools in the United States—perhaps 32, enrolling less than a thousand pupils the same year—"served" one-third of a million tribal peoples.[3]

Thus a far higher percentage of Irish children than Indian children had some experience with the school by the early nineteenth century. However, combining figures from many different Irish educational organizations, churches, and societies, Graham Balfour estimated that by 1824 only about two-fifths of Irish children were enrolled in some school. He further convincingly claimed that "the extent of their attendance and the quality of their instruction may have amounted to anything or nothing." Indeed, as Peter N. Stearns writes about western Europe up to about 1800, "most children, after a few years of infancy, defined their lives in terms of work." Because of costs, parental goals, and widespread social inequality, the majority of children in pre-industrial Western societies did not attend formal schools at any point in their lives.[4]

By the 1820s, then, Indian and Irish experiences of the school were not as incommensurably different as we might expect. A major theme of the present book is that both groups were to converge in their experiences of this educational institution during the century under review. The present chapter sketches the educational experiences, traditional and school based, of Indian and Irish children into the early decades of the nineteenth century, when the U.S. and British governments began to systematically enter the field. I ask the following three questions: How similar or different were traditional—non-school—methods of education, for Indian and Irish peoples? To what extent

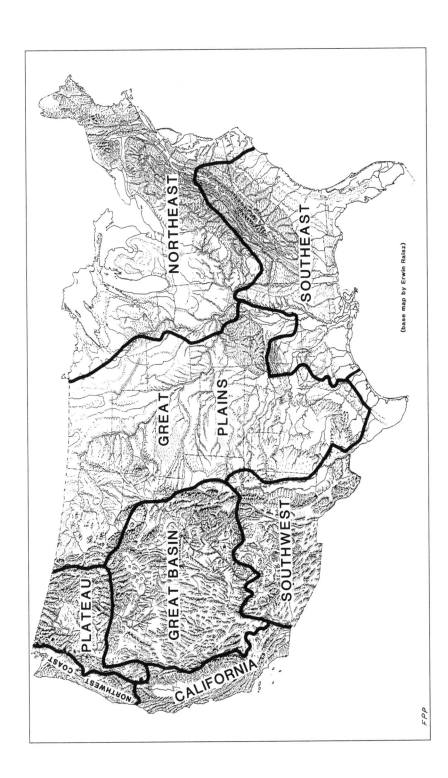

NORTHEAST

SOUTHEAST

GREAT PLAINS

GREAT BASIN

PLATEAU

NORTHWEST COAST

CALIFORNIA

SOUTHWEST

(base map by Erwin Raisz)

FPP

had children in the two areas experienced the kinds of education we in the West designate as schooling? How did these earlier experiences of education, non-school and school, influence Irish and Indian responses to BIA and CNEI campaigns in the century under review?

I

"The school is the only place for the Indian child to learn," wrote H. B. Peairs, superintendent of the BIA's Haskell Boarding School in 1896. "He learns nothing of value at home; nobody there is competent to teach. He learns nothing from his neighbors; nobody with whom he associates does anything better than he finds in his own home." Similarly reflecting the common Euro-American belief that "primitive" peoples lack education because they apparently lack the institution of the school, another educator generalized that the Indian girl's "mental attitude [was] a blank, her moral consciousness worse than a blank." And in a classic statement of prejudice, Capt. Richard Henry Pratt, the famous founder and first superintendent of the Carlisle Indian Industrial School in Pennsylvania, informed a group of Lakota adults in 1879: "You have no education."[5]

This ethnocentric assumption was also a product of another characteristic Euro-American perception, one that flourished from first contacts in the fifteenth century until—and beyond—the period under review: that Indian peoples failed to control their children. "No feature of native American child rearing evoked more criticism than an apparent lack of child discipline," writes historian Margaret Connell Szasz."[6]

Like peoples everywhere, however, Indians did indeed discipline and restrain their children, if in ways different from those prevalent in Euro-American societies at the time and since. F. Niyi Akinasso has contested the assumption that for schooling to exist, so must literacy. He has pointed to examples of formal learning among non-Western and non-literate peoples that together suggests the existence of kinds of schooling. Formal, institutionalized education implies that learning is organized to fulfill the specific purpose of transmitting certain values, attitudes, skills, and other kinds of knowledge (specialized, rather than practical); that such learning is separated from normal, daily routines and usually takes place outside the home

---

Map 1. American Indian Culture Areas. The many Indian groups living within each of these broad geographical and environmental divisions shared some adaptive cultural similarities yet also manifested great linguistic, cultural, and other differences. Reprinted from *Atlas of American Indian Affairs*, by Francis Paul Prucha, by permission of University of Nebraska Press. Copyright © 1990 by the University of Nebraska Press.

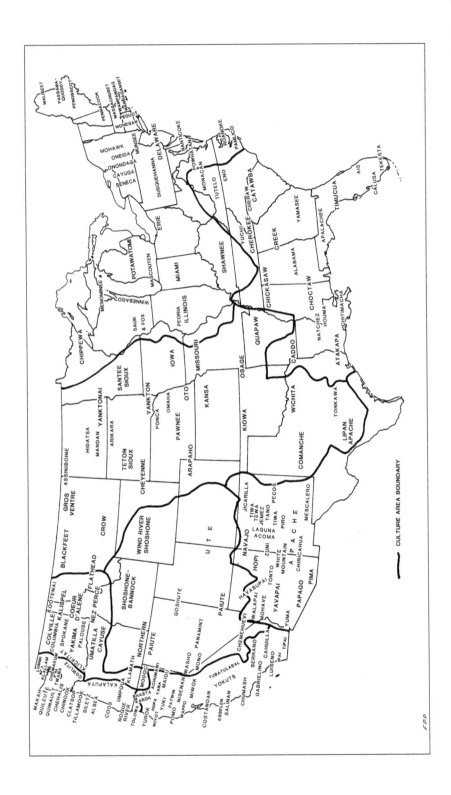

— CULTURE AREA BOUNDARY

(decontextualization); it is usually transmitted through language (even if orally) rather than demonstration or example only; it is institutionalized, in the sense that a professional elite such as administrators and teachers (rather than only peers and kin) accepts responsibility; it generally involves a shift from home or other nonspecific areas to a specialized scene of learning, a "school" (perhaps involving special clothing and rituals); it involves the accumulation of rules, regulations, and conventions; and it may also involve amounts of capital, money, or other kinds of wealth. All of this, Akinasso believes, "involves the incorporation of an elaborate ritual and symbolic order that sets apart the province of meaning [of formal, institutionalized education] from the paramount reality of everyday life."[7]

Whether or not diverse Indian tribal peoples exhibited all such elements of institutionalized "formal" education—institutions to which the Western term "school" could thus be applied—is not a crucial question here. Suffice it to note Akinasso's admonition against assuming the simplistic dichotomy of "Literate/schools versus non-literate/no schools" and to see such things in terms of a continuum rather than in absolutes. Schooling, he concludes, "is not a unique characteristic of Western literacy and the distinction between formal and informal learning does not depend on, nor is it isomorphic with, the distinction between literate and nonliterate."[8]

Certainly, if by education we mean "the transmission of a society's culture and worldview to succeeding generations," all Indian peoples educated their children to knowledge of and participation in community life.[9] Further, from 1500 on, Christian missionaries and others began to encourage Indians to send their children to Western schools. Therefore, while by the early 1800s most Indian peoples saw education in purely traditional—yet highly institutionalized and indeed formal—terms, many others blended such practices with the Western school. This section briefly outlines such traditional practices, moving on to sketch pre-1820 Indian experiences with mission and other kinds of white schooling.[10]

Many Western observers, along with Native American informants, testified to the importance of children to Indian peoples—they were, quite obviously, the future. Szasz has pointed to the three central and overlapping kinds of knowledge that tribal people needed to transmit to these children. First,

Map 2. American Indian Tribal Locations. The map shows approximate historical locations of selected Indian groups up to and, for some tribes, beyond the beginning of the period under review. Reprinted from *Atlas of American Indian Affairs*, by Francis Paul Prucha, by permission of University of Nebraska Press. Copyright © 1990 by the University of Nebraska Press.

(economic) training for survival, which, of course, varied greatly according to culture and environment: hunter-gatherer peoples such as the Nez Perces of Idaho and agriculturalists such as the Choctaws of Mississippi had different things to tell their children. As in Irish society, these and other Indian peoples generally demarcated life into complementary roles appropriate for males and females; the education for survival presented to boys and to girls thus varied according to gender. Second, knowledge of cultural heritage: stories of Coyote the Trickster or of Masaw were entertainment, but beyond that they also conveyed tribal knowledge, values, and models of correct and incorrect behavior. Third, spiritual knowledge: Indian cultures did not segregate life into the secular and the spiritual, so knowledge of the spirit world, and of how to attain help from spirit forces, was vital to success or even survival.[11]

Native American historian Donald L. Fixico notes that tribal life is one "where the metaphysical is more powerful than the physical world, and where certain ceremonies and important rites need to be performed for protection or blessing by those powers greater than all human beings."[12] Through stories, instruction, or participation in initiation ceremonies or the demanding trials of the vision quest, children and young adults thus learned that they lived in a world utterly permeated by and influenced by spirit beings, and—in some tribes—by a Great Spirit or Great Mystery.

Although the content of knowledge varied greatly, even among tribes living quite close to each other, all Native peoples devised methods—generally efficient methods—to inculcate knowledge in all these areas. Yet, in ways perhaps difficult to understand for members of twenty-first-century industrial societies in which knowledge, institutions, and elements of lifestyles are often highly segmented, Indian peoples saw education as a holistic enterprise, in which the economic, cultural, and spiritual blended together. Fabio Pittaluga tells, for example, how traditional Kiowas and the Kiowa Apaches of the Southern Plains, "provided their youths [of both sexes] with all the necessary means for functioning in the complex socio-cultural setting of adult life. Children received a pragmatic education in the totality of fields of human experience culturally meaningful to them." Native historian Henrietta Mann similarly notes how the Cheyennes "developed sophisticated concepts of education to prepare their children for satisfying lives in an adult world." As in other tribes, Cheyenne family members, elders, and the whole tribe were responsible for this education. When the child grew older, the teaching "became more formal, in that elders continually instructed her [and him] as to what was involved in being a Cheyenne: its language, ceremonies, value system, moral code, kinship system, tribal government, band structure, gender roles, traditions, customs, and economy." In this "holistic and well-developed curriculum," the young Cheyenne girl or boy "learned through observation and by intense instruction about everything that comprised Cheyenne life and made up its world-view."[13]

Therefore traditional education was, in George A. Pettitt's words, "an intense and lifelong affair" for Native American peoples. Szasz notes that the Indian child "was surrounded by expanding concentric circles of people who cared for him or her." These circles included kin such as parents, siblings, aunts and uncles (especially important in some tribal kinship systems), and—perhaps surprising to modern Westerners accustomed to discarding the aged as burdens on society—grandparents. When children grew older, nonrelated specialists such as shamans, skilled craftsmen and women, warriors, or others complemented the educational work of kin.[14] There was nothing haphazard about how adults performed their duties.

Although less so than in modern Western society—at least where the two-parent family still functions—Indian biological parents often did have a direct role in upbringing. Mann notes how the young Cheyenne girl "imitated her mother's every action." Luther Standing Bear claimed that, even while he still hung in his cradleboard, his Lakota (Sioux) mother had begun the task of training him for membership of the group. And until he went off to boarding school at age ten, he appears to have had a warm and instructive relationship with his father. Similarly, Irene Stewart's Navajo father was for her a major educator, especially after her mother died. And the Nakota (Yankton Sioux) Zitkala-Ša remembered—not without some degree of resentment—how through a systematic combination of observation, practice, and critical appraisal, her mother taught her the "female" craft of beadwork. Zitkala-Ša graphically conveyed the sense of tension and, finally, release involved: "Often after these confining sessions I was wild with surplus spirits," she wrote decades later, "and found joyous relief in running loose in the open again."[15]

Other close relatives, including uncles and aunts (especially the mother's brother and father's sister) often accepted major responsibility for upbringing. There was no implication that the biological parents had failed; indeed, many Indian kinship systems mandated the active involvement of such relatives. Polingaysi Qoyawayma remembered how in her matrilineal Hopi tribe, which traced descent in the female line, "children are advised, instructed, scolded, and sometimes punished by their maternal uncles." Similarly, among the Kiowa-Apaches, Jim Whitewolf's grown sister was taught beadwork by her mother's half-sister. Charles Eastman was one of the most famous of "educated Indians" in the later nineteenth and early twentieth centuries, as he became an author, lecturer, Indian spokesman, and medical doctor (Boston

University). He told how he acquired his traditional learning from his father's brother, who systematically instructed the young Dakota (Santee Sioux) to observe, name, and describe the things he saw each day. Later the uncle taught the boy about the habits of animals and instructed him in tribal ethics—such as generosity and respect for the aged—and in spiritual values.[16]

In many tribes across the continent, grandparents were especially important as educators and as constant companions of the young. Among the Kiowa and Kiowa Apache, writes Pittaluga, grandmothers played a fundamental role in the instruction of both girls and boys. They taught how to manufacture material items, transmitted moral standards of behavior, and introduced them to storytelling, to appropriate gender roles, and into respective social circles of fundamental importance in adult life. A grandmother might teach little girls how to make miniature tipis and how to cook; she might also bring a young boy to observe some of the men's "societies" (restricted membership groups within the tribe). James Kaywaykla, a Warm Springs Apache, recalled how his mother desired to be with her warrior husband and so handed the young boy over to his grandmother. "It is natural that you should love your grandmother best of the family," declared the mother. "She has taken care of you since you were a baby." Others such as Eastman and Allen James, a Pomo, similarly recalled the affectionate and educational role of grandmothers and even great-grandmothers.[17]

Grandfathers too could accompany and instruct. Jim Whitewolf's grandfather came to stay with him and taught him things a boy should know: how to get a wife, how to lasso dogs, and how to make and shoot blunt-edged arrows. "He told me not to shoot at anything but birds," and not to go crazy like some older boys. Whitewolf was not to swim with bigger boys, who might drown him. The older Kiowa Apaches also used to rouse the boy from sleep and helped him learn to ride horses. "Now," concluded Whitewolf significantly, "I have tried to teach my own grandson Willy some of the things that I learned from my grandfather." Other old men could simultaneously entertain and instruct. A Kiowa remembered how they not only provided stories but, by constant repetition, helped the boys learn them. We shall see how nineteenth-century American and Irish educators decried rote (memory) learning, but in oral societies this was a vital form of pedagogy, crucial for passing knowledge from one generation to another. "These old folks would tell stories at night, over and over and over," the Kiowa recalled. The young boys listening "finally got it down pat. That's the way they used to do it every night."[18]

Thus individuals in the various "concentric circles" systematically involved themselves in the child's education and enculturation. Further, what we might call "knowledge specialists," nonkin and kin, also stepped in at appropriate times to instruct. Forms of apprenticeship existed, and there was clear evidence of formalized educational patterns, if not fully fledged schooling in a Western sense. Anna Moore Shaw, a Pima from the Southwest, went as a young girl to live with a famous basket maker to learn her art. Jason Betzinez began his warrior training in the 1880s—with the Apache leader Geronimo. No young man could be trusted as a warrior, Betzinez claimed, without undergoing such an apprenticeship. Also through apprenticeship Mourning Dove sought to become a shaman to her Salishan people. Her adopted grandmother became the girl's tutor and actually rejected the validity of the girl's vision quest: a case of the teacher failing the pupil.[19] Not all tribes expected young women or young men to engage in the demanding vision quest, which could require arduous training followed by a period alone in the forest seeking a vision and spiritual adviser. But for those youths who so aspired, a tutor, related or unrelated, was vital to the enterprise.

Westerners have often stereotyped traditional cultures as "primitive" and thus "simple." However, the culture of even a single village was immensely complex, full of contesting views and always changing, even before contact with Euro-Americans. No child or even adult could know the whole of his or her culture—and indeed not all were meant to know the whole of it. Participation in some cultural activities required further education and initiation into its rites, or into full membership of a ceremonial or warrior "society." Such societies or sodalities, writes Pittaluga of the Kiowa and Kiowa Apache, "completed the children's instruction as far as warfare, hunting patterns, discipline, and knowledge of social hierarchies were concerned. [They] followed a well-articulated curriculum in preparing the children for their future duties." Younger boys might enter the Rabbit Society, for example, whose members learned by imitating the actions of the older age-group societies. Other Plains Indians such as the village-dwelling Omahas and the nomadic Cheyennes and Lakotas also evolved hierarchies of prestigious "societies," entry into which depended upon age or upon military, economic, or other kinds of achievement.[20] Some were gender-specific societies: a Cheyenne women recalled how she was instructed never to reveal the secrets of a women's society to men.[21]

Tribal education, then, was a long-term, indeed lifelong, affair, demanding much of kin and nonkin teachers. The complex process involved observation, hands-on learning, explicit instruction, and, of course, the educative wonders of storytelling. "To us," wrote Francis La Flesche, an Omaha who later worked for the Bureau of American Ethnology and became a major Indian spokesman of the early twentieth century, "there seemed to be no end to the things we were obliged to do, and the things which we were to refrain from doing."[22]

Of course, providing knowledge does not necessarily mean that it will be absorbed; tribal children were hardly more constitutionally prone to learning than Irish children. Thus Indian peoples devised incentives and punishments. On the side of incentives, many autobiographers confirm that love and respect for kin, especially for grandparents, generally did motivate children to learn. The giving of new names was especially important in many societies, both as stimulus and as reward for achievement. Although Hopi society discouraged individualism and thus shunned direct praise, Albert Yava received a new name upon entering the One Horn Society of the Hopis. Charles Eastman appeared thrilled to be renamed Ohiyesa (the winner) after success at lacrosse. Similarly, Luther Standing Bear described how, in Lakota society, a boy's first name was selected by parents or relations, "and this he keeps until he is old enough to earn one himself." After some act of bravery he "would then be privileged to take a name indicating what this worthy act was."[23] Similarly among the Shawnees, a child "might strive with all his power to win such praise," wrote Thomas Wildcat Alford.[24]

Girls did not generally compete for such public honor, but they too were encouraged by praise after an appropriate job well done. Kay Bennett recalled her initial resentment at the demanding standards imposed by her mother as the girl learned to weave rugs. Later, however, the Navajo developed a sense of pride in her achievement and began to show off the rug to family and neighbors. Among the Wishram, the old women would gather together when a young girl gave away her first gathering of huckleberries, thus initiating her into her role as provider. Girls, like boys, could also be given honorable names and later be admitted into women's societies.[25]

In these generally small, face-to-face communities, failure to measure up to group standards could incur punishments from the mildly irritating to the physically and psychologically devastating. As in most human societies, adult demands could produce deep resentments and thus require degrees of coercion. Humiliation, disdain, fear of worldly failure, and spiritual retribution were used in different ways among different tribes. Don Talayesva's Hopi grandfather warned him that it was a great disgrace to be called "kahopi" (not Hopi or not peaceable), and that such people would not survive long; those who lived by the teachings of the people could expect kindness and would reach an advanced age. Just how demanding these "peaceable ways" could be emerged in an interview that anthropologist Dorothy Eggan conducted with a forty-year-old Hopi woman. As a girl of six she had neglected to take proper care of her baby sister. For ten days her family ostracized her, insisting that she eat alone. "I was so ashamed all the time," the woman recalled. Noted the anthropologist, "she cried, even then, as she talked."[26]

A Shawnee might have his faults told to a visitor. Even more humiliating, Cheyenne girls might openly mock a young man who came home from an unsuccessful hunt or war party. "It was hard to go into a fight, and we were often afraid," recalled Stands in Timber with touching honesty, "but it was worse to turn back and face the women." Girls too had to strive to avoid shame. "Never be Lazy," the Pima mother told her daughter. "No one wants a lazy wife."[27]

The apparent willingness of Indian people to "spare the rod" led many whites to assume that they did in fact "spoil the child." Tribal societies often encouraged children—especially boys—to accept and even revel in physical pain, so its use as an educational punishment would have been counterproductive. Yet some tribes did employ "the rod" or variants thereof. Jim Whitewolf faced physical punishment that might have shocked even nineteenth-century Americans for its severity. The young Kiowa Apache's overuse of sexual talk brought a literally pointed adult response. "My mother went out and spoke to this old lady," he recalled, indicating how punishment could be inflicted by those beyond the immediate family to deflect resentment from the mother and father. She got a sharp piece of glass and "told me she knew I was always talking dirty. She grabbed me and threw me on my back. She cut my lip with a glass until it bled. Then she asked me if I was going to talk dirty anymore, and I said I wouldn't. They did that to a lot of kids who talked dirty." Edward Goodbird noted how his uncle so severely ducked him in a pail of cold water that the young Hidatsa thought he would drown. Don Talayesva was brought down into the underground *kiva* to be instructed, admonished, and—he expected—gently whipped by the Kachina spirits. But the young Hopi was totally unprepared for the beating he received. He took the first four blows of the whip without crying. But then the Kachina "struck me four more times and cut me to pieces. I struggled, I yelled, and urinated," wrote the Hopi in a stark and unflattering passage. "Blood was running down over my body . . . . I tried to stop sobbing, but continued to cry in my heart." Later, when he found out that these spirit beings were actually local men wearing masks and costumes, his resentment deepened. Ultimately, however, he felt the ordeal was a turning point in his life, drawing him closer to Hopi ways. After years of American boarding schools he would finally return to Hopiland.[28]

Tribal peoples lived in constant danger from enemies or from hunger; it is inconceivable that they would not have disciplined their children, either through incentive or punishment, and often through combinations of both. Asa Daklugie claimed that as young Apache warriors "we'd been trained more rigidly" than at the self-consciously rigid Carlisle School.[29]

All of this perhaps risks resuscitating a classic stereotype of Noble Savagery, of Indian peoples harmoniously balancing incentive and punishment to produce perfectly adapted Hopi, Apache, or Cheyenne adults. Tribal societies too could produce dysfunctionality. Indeed, Indian narrators themselves occasionally indicated that even as children they resented some of their tribes' methods. Many frankly recalled having disobeyed instructions. Two Leggings, an obsessively ambitious Crow, defied elders and went on war parties without the appropriate spiritual "medicine"—a sacrilegious and dangerous form of rebellion. Individual Apaches recalled similar intergenerational conflict. As a reminiscing adult, Mourning Dove regretted how she scornfully rejected the herbal knowledge her adopted grandmother offered, and how she quickly lost interest when she accompanied the old woman in the forest. Now, she admitted, that knowledge was lost to her forever. John Stands in Timber similarly regretted his youthful disregard for the wisdom of Cheyenne adults. And a Ponca man remembered how, while his father droned on with his adult wisdom, he himself wanted only to get started on the food.[30]

Demanding tribal work ethics drew negative comment. Kay Bennett recalled her mother rushing around exclaiming: "I must find work for them to do or they will become lazy"—almost as a matter of principle. And a Pima mother told her sons, "You never rest until you die." Asa Daklugie recalled the misery of morning dips into icy water, but he feared disobeying Geronimo, who was training the boys to hardness. Other older Indians admitted to deceiving adults, pretending to work while slacking off.[31] In a few particularly striking cases, adults remembered how they became skeptical of tribal values. A Navajo woman wondered why a man who ignored the proscribed exercises enjoyed wealth, while those who persisted in "doing the right thing" remained poor. And Kaywaykla admitted that some of his Apache people could question a particular tribal belief: "Like white Eyes, we had our skeptics among us."[32]

In general, however, tribal patterns appear to have successfully enculturated boys and girls, young men and women, and indeed adults into productive social life. Its patterns were inherently conservative, designed to preserve and extend the heritage of the people, but development of individual initiative was also central. What Anthony F. C. Wallace wrote of Northeastern peoples also applied to many other tribes. "Iroquoian children," he states in a memorable phrase, "were carefully trained to think for themselves but to act for others."[33]

This inculcation of heritage did not imply blind rejection of the new. Indian peoples quickly accepted and incorporated into their own systems such Euro-American "advances" as metal tools, the horse, and guns; some adopted and syncretized Euro-American thought patterns, such as versions of Christianity. As this book demonstrates, they also came to appreciate new kinds of educational institutions. Narrators could recall how older people, the supposed repositories of traditional tribal wisdom, could encourage them to attend school, to learn English and become literate—and above all to adapt to the new way. Sanapia, a Comanche medicine woman, told how her grandmother quickly saw the utility of writing to preserve the old traditions: "She tell me that I should write it down, but at the time I didn't even know what writing is, but my grandma did." Rosalio Moisés, a Yaqui, recalled how his father got him to transcribe family and tribal history to better preserve this heritage. Jim Whitewolf's Kiowa-Apache grandfather encouraged him to take care of his horses so he could farm with them, rather than fight; he also taught the boy how to use a .44 Winchester rifle. Pittaluga has convincingly shown how the latter people adapted their educational practices and traditional stories to changing circumstances. For example, as contacts with whites intensified in the late nineteenth century, stories of Saynday the Trickster began to reflect this reality. In a later story Saynday meets and deceives a white trickster, ending up with the latter's boots, shirt, and gun. Among the Cheyennes, stories of Ve'ho'e, the spider, were also adapted to incorporate increasingly problematic white contact. Such "myth revisioning," to use Peter Nabokov's term, does not imply abject surrender to the new but was part of a creative reformulation of ethnic identity.[34] Indian peoples, then, could combine a powerful reverence for the past with an equally powerful adaptive pragmatism. Significantly, it might be the older guardians of tribal heritage who encouraged the young in the new way—a process similar to what was happening in Ireland during this same period.

II

Whatever their attitudes toward white society, before and during the period under review tribal adults faced increasing educational competition, as Euro-Americans set out to Christianize and "civilize" Indian peoples through the schooling of their children. In northeastern parts of the present United States and Canada, for example, and in the Spanish Southwest, Roman Catholic Jesuit and Récollet (Franciscan) missionaries, along with Ursuline nuns and other congregations and orders, established far-flung missions during colonial times, some employing schools, some sending Indian children to live with white people.[35]

"Come over and help us," pleaded the Indian on the seal of the Massachusetts Bay Colony. Indian evangelization became part of the English public rationale for American colonization—just as Protestant ideology would underpin contemporaneous English colonization in Ireland. Yet, despite funding support from a number of home-grown missionary societies and support from the Imperial and colonial governments, only a small number of dedicated individuals actually set out to answer what they believed to be the American Native's plea for help.[36] "The Apostle of the Indians," seventeenth-century Puritan missionary John Eliot, established fourteen "praying towns" across New England. As with Catholic efforts in Canada, schools were central to his mission. Quarantined from their "savage" family backgrounds, young Indians would first be saved themselves. They would then return as "cultural brokers"—mediators—to carry the Gospel and English civility back to their peoples. Some colonists sent tribal children to England; some, like the French, took them into their homes. A number of young Indians actually attended Harvard and other colonial universities and colleges.[37]

In other regions of New England and in Georgia and the Carolinas further experiments were afoot. The eighteenth-century Enlightenment era also witnessed outbursts of religion of the heart—the Great Awakening—and this complex period saw, in Szasz's phrase, "a flurry of experiments in schooling for Indian youth." Perhaps the most important of these experiments was Moor's Charity School, at Lebanon, Connecticut, founded by Eleazar Wheelock in 1754, who also founded Dartmouth College in New Hampshire. Almost ninety Indian boys and girls attended the former institution, a number of whom have left behind writings from which we can glean their sense of achievements and deep frustrations as cultural mediators.[38]

In these and other ventures different denominations participated: Roman Catholics, as well as Congregational Puritans, Moravians, and Quakers and other dissenters. By the time of the American Revolution, according to James Axtell, perhaps only about 500 Indians—adults along with children—had crossed the cultural divide to become Anglicized Christians. Yet we have no way of telling the extent to which such people syncretized or partly adopted Christian and English ways. Axtell concludes that the many schools and educational experiments "notoriously failed to turn Indian children into English adults." Szasz notes just how difficult it is even to establish agreed-upon criteria according to which we might judge the success or failure of these many ventures. For my purposes, we can say that during the colonial centuries (1500–1780s) small numbers of Indian tribal children and their kinfolk became acquainted with the school as an educational institution; and we must remember that, at this time, only a small number of white American colonial children or Irish or other European children attended school for any length of time.[39] Of course, many white colonists regarded schooling as a relatively inexpensive way of pacifying Indians, and of removing them from their lands. Indians quickly learned the game of counter-manipulation, seeing schooling of their children as a tactic for individual and group survival in the rapidly changing colonial world.

The British colonial missionary enterprises, especially, established patterns for assimilationist Indian schooling that persisted throughout the nineteenth century and into the early twentieth century. Protestant colonial missionaries, their nineteenth-century counterparts, later U.S. government officials, and "friends of the Indian" fused versions of Christianity and an idealized Euro-American lifestyle into an all-embracing, messianic vision. This "Christian civilization" was locked in a deadly struggle against "heathenism," "savagery," and all such supposedly deficient cultural states. Colonial missionaries and later educators generally combined an egalitarian and nonracist conviction in the capacity of Indian peoples, with a near-absolute ethnocentric conviction that Indians must leave all their old ways behind and accept all the new ways. (The more culturally tolerant French Jesuit missionaries were less ethnocentric in their demands for changes not immediately religious). The school thus became a panacea: many Indians were too old and set in their ways to change; therefore salvation, spiritual and secular, would come through the children. Like Eliot with his quarantining "praying towns," later generations of missionary and U.S. government educators similarly struggled to separate children from their supposedly corrupting tribal environments, sometimes in large off-reservations boarding schools.

The nineteenth century has been called "the Great Century" of Protestant missions to the world. As a result of a turn-of-century outburst of religious revivalism—the Second Great Awakening—many new missionary societies were established and began to send their members to "the heathen"—including Indians—throughout the world.[40] The American Board of Commissioners for Foreign Missions (ABCFM) began life in 1812, and this Congregational and Presbyterian organization was soon heavily involved in Native American education among peoples such as the Cherokees and Choctaws (two of the "Five Civilized Tribes," the other three being the Creeks, Chickasaws, and Seminoles). By around 1820 ABCFM schools were teaching mostly in English, but also utilizing the Native languages, at least initially. The ABCFM then stretched its reach right across the continent to the Pacific Northwest, where it established missions among the Cayuses and Nez Perces. Indeed, Indians themselves may have been the instigators of these Northwestern missions; a number of them traveled to St. Louis in 1831 to ask for missionaries—we cannot tell the extent to which they understood the whole missionary venture and ambition.[41]

Therefore by the 1820s, Catholic and Protestant missionaries, French,

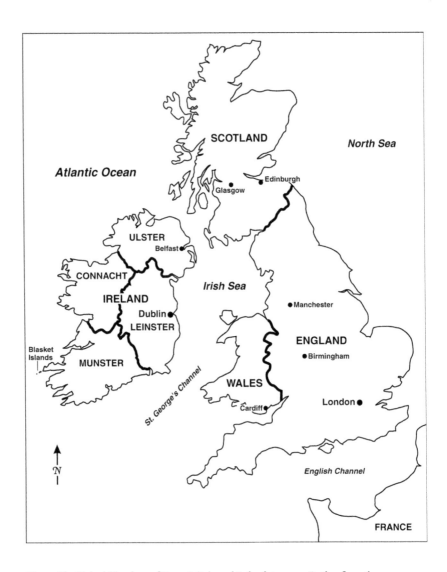

Map 3. The United Kingdom of Great Britain and Ireland, to 1922. By the 1820s there were over 11,000 schools of all kinds on the small island of Ireland. The vast majority of these, however, were extralegal and impermanent "hedge schools." By 1919 there were approx. 8,000 national schools, claiming an enrollment of 700,000 pupils.

English, and Spanish (in the Southwest), had established hundreds of missions and schools in many of the major regions of the present United States and Canada. Even among peoples who did not directly experience these developments, the knowledge of such different educational institutions must have permeated; as the nineteenth century wore on, always pragmatic Indian adults would become increasingly interested in, if ambivalent about, schooling for their children, to complement rather than displace traditional forms of education. By the beginning of our period of study, however, it is likely that the vast majority of Indian peoples had no personal experience of the school or schooling. But then, neither did large numbers of Irish people at that time.

III

Despite powerful alliances among some of its native leaders and help from Catholic Spain, the old Gaelic order was no match militarily for the new English Tudor nation state. Although a full cultural and religious conquest did not take place, the Battle of Kinsale in 1601 sounded the death knell of many older and "less civilized" Gaelic patterns. Around the same time began the Protestant plantation of large areas of northeastern Ulster that would so deeply influence later Irish history. In this political, cultural, and religious assault, Celtic educational institutions did not remain unaffected. The famed bardic schools and monastic schools of Ireland were repressed or gradually fell into disuse. These, however, never aimed at mass elementary education—rather the opposite, as their goals were the training of small cultural and ecclesiastical elites.[42] Although the Tudors and later English/British regimes sporadically sought to use the school as an instrument of policy, for over two centuries these meager efforts would have little effect on the educational experiences of the majority population. As we have seen, by 1824 perhaps only two out of five Irish children were enrolled at any school.

Indeed, it is difficult to tell how most ordinary Irish people educated their children during the seventeenth and eighteenth centuries. As John Logan has noted, compared with the history of schooling in Ireland, education within the household has been neglected by historians. Logan has shown how a tiny minority of Irish parents provided their children with the services of tutors, governesses, and wandering scholars from around 1700 to 1880. Neither in this useful study nor a later work do we learn how ordinary people, like contemporaneous American Indians, educated generations of children outside of school or tutoring; nor do we learn this from Antonia McManus's more recent study of the famous Irish hedge schools of the eighteenth and early nineteenth centuries.[43] Obviously the great majority generally did so without

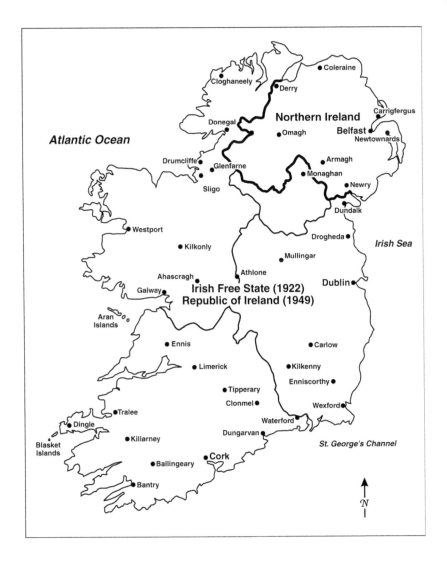

Map 4. Ireland after 1922. From 1831 to 1922 individuals whose experiences are featured in the present book attended national schools or National Board model schools in or near many of the cities, towns, and villages shown here.

the school or the private tutor. Their methods were probably similar to those used by Indians: observation, on-the-job training, oral instruction and story-telling—vital in nonliterate cultures—and various kinds of informal and formal apprenticeships, involving learning from adults within or outside the family. As in tribal societies, Irish girls and boys would have received partly similar and partly different forms of instruction appropriate to their future roles—as wives and mothers, or as farmers or fishermen.[44]

Micheál O'Guiheen remembered on the Blasket Islands off southwestern Ireland his father told him that when gannet birds dived into the sea the mackerel season was at hand: "The boats will be filled with them tonight." His mother instructed him on personal and religious values, on the dangers of envy, and on the importance of faith in God—her "good advice" combined conventional wisdom and Catholic devotion and would have complemented the more formal school religious instruction. She hoped that none of her family would go astray so that "we would all be in one company in God's Kingdom, the way we were in life"—a powerful blending of family and religious values. "In the long-term perspective," writes Colin Heywood of broader patterns that surely also applied to Ireland, "it is worth remembering that for most people in the West, right up until the nineteenth century, the family fulfilled many functions. It had to provide for the subsistence of its members, plus their education, vocational training, health, entertainment and old age."[45]

Other Irish narrators remembered stories of non-Christian traditions that persisted orally in Ireland alongside a supposedly exclusive Catholicism: family and other adults told them about fairies, ghosts, and strange and sometimes dangerous forces about in the land, especially at night. Patrick Bradley and his childhood friends awaited the visit of the *seanachaidhe* (storyteller). "Looking so far back now," he wrote as a reminiscing Indian might have, "it seems hard to realize the fascination these stories exerted on our youthful minds." Some people doubted the veracity of the stories. "As for myself, having heard from early childhood, round the winter fireside, tales of ghosts, fairies, leprechauns, pookies, and banshees, it will be readily understood that I was not one of the sceptics." Indeed as a youngster Bradley was so afraid of such beings he was loath to go out alone in the dark. Similarly R. B. Robson believed that "the effect of well-told stories on the young mind is wonderful." Writing about Protestant—and more self-consciously modern—Ulster, he claimed that "whether we admit it nor not . . . a considerable number of our Northern [Irish] folk are influenced more or less by superstition." William O'Malley more critically remembered how he "lived on Fairy stories and in an atmosphere of the grossest superstition" when he was a child. The stories he heard were also frightening, about "real Ghosts and of various tales of the

supernatural." Obviously a modernizer, he saw it as progress that such storytelling was dying out. "An improvement in the condition of the people and
the spread of Education" were, he believed, dissipating the faith "in Fairies
and hobgoblins."[46]

When undertaken regularly by kin or other assigned members of the community, education in the ways of fish, faith, or fairies, or in the demands of
farming or housekeeping was both formal and institutionalized. As Heywood
reminds us, European peasants and laborers who had little or no schooling
"were far from being ignorant, depraved, culturally deprived, or even illiterate." In a striking passage, one that recalls Francis La Flesche's account of how
much Omaha children had to learn, a French Breton man who also became
an anthropologist remembered the comprehensiveness of his nonschool but
systematic and demanding early education:

I began . . . by learning to use all the resources of the countryside: the trees, the plants,
the stones, the birds, the winds, and water in all its guises; by learning not to waste
the slightest thing. . . . [I] took the steps necessary for becoming proficient at doing a
peasant's job . . . [which] consisted above all in knowing everything about the surroundings, including all the traps that were to be set, and into which you were bound to fall if
you were a novice. It was thus that you adapted yourself to nature and occasionally held
it in check at the same time as it satisfied your basic needs.[47]

No doubt, the nonschool education of most young Irish boys and girls followed similar patterns. They learned the economic, cultural, and spiritual
values—to again employ Szasz's formulation for Indian children—vital for
survival or even a degree of prosperity in their immediate families and rural
communities.

As the advantages of speaking English and of literacy became more and
more obvious, Irish people, like Indians, began to see the practical value of
schooling. "The inability of most adults to read and write [was] one of the more
striking features of late eighteenth century [Irish] society," writes Logan, and
this "ensured that if children were to acquire literacy, it would not be from
their parents"—unless these were of the more privileged classes.[48] Or unless,
like the young Peter O'Leary, they were fortunate to have a mother educated
enough to tutor her children at night, after daytime work on the farm. Or to
have a helpful neighbor: Irish-speaking Michael MacGowan learned nothing
from an English-speaking teacher in the local national school. Luckily an old
man taught him the alphabet using shapes such as the gable end of the house
("A") to illustrate the letters. For some Irish children, both nonschool and
school learning could complement each other. "It all depended on the parents whether [children] got any learnin' before they started school," declared

an informant of the Irish Folklore Collection. "Not many parents were fit to learn their children anything, because they couldn't read or write." This informant had obviously internalized the official view that nonschool learning was not education. Luckily his father "learned us the alphabet and put us in the first book."[49]

IV

Long before the era of mass schooling, however, the rulers of an expanding English "Pale" around Dublin (the English-controlled area around the city)—like contemporaneous authorities in the American colonies—realized the importance of the school as a cultural and religious weapon. Indeed, with its bitter intertwining of national, political, and religious issues, education has always been a battleground in Ireland.[50] Certainly the Educational Commissioners of 1824 retrospectively saw things this way, referring to the act passed almost three centuries earlier in 1537 by the (English-controlled) Irish Parliament in Dublin (28 Henry VIII) as the first to relate to "the existing State of the Education of the lower Orders in Ireland." Although the act attempted to establish parish schools to preserve English culture and the Protestant religion, initially its ambitions were defensive and limited. According to Raymond Gillespie, "a state-sponsored national educational system was not in the minds of [the act's] drafters. It was principally directed at . . . the increased 'Gaelicisation' of the Anglo-Irish inhabitants of the Pale." Few such schools were actually established, and fewer still were the concrete results of the 1537 act. In other words, these parish schools had little effect on most Irish children. "The Irish Language, Habit, and Order continued to prevail [outside] the English Pale," concluded the 1824 Commissioners with obvious disdain, "and could with Difficulty be restrained from encroaching within its limits." By the early nineteenth century, according to the Commissioners, there were 782 parish schools in Ireland, enrolling 36,498 children (21,195 Protestants, 15,303 Catholics)—a small fraction of school-age children.[51]

In 1570 the Irish Parliament passed an act for the "Erection of Free Schools" (12 Elizabeth I) in every shire town, the preamble of which complained about the heinous offenses committed by an Irish youth uneducated in English ways. The master of every such "free school"—actually a kind of grammar school teaching higher subjects than the parish schools—was to be a Protestant Englishman. Few of these "diocesan schools" were built, and by 1800 only two or three were actually admitting students free of charge. They had become, according to the 1824 commissioners, "applied solely to the Education of the higher and middle Orders."[52] During the Stuart period in the early seventeenth century "Royal Schools" were established, as a part of the

Ulster plantation and elsewhere. However, they too remained few in number. By 1831 such schools enrolled a total of only 343 scholars. These parish, diocesan, and royal schools were created by legislation and endowed through government grants.[53] Other kinds of unendowed schools, or endowed institutions such as the Erasmus Smith schools, also functioned at various periods. Many schools were run by the (Anglican) Church of Ireland for its own children (a small minority of the total population); indeed this state church saw itself as the guardian of morality and political loyalty for all the people of Ireland from the later sixteenth century until its disestablishment in 1869. Of course, in the heavily Presbyterian regions of the country, especially in Northern Ireland, members of this intensely education-orientated denomination arranged the schooling of their own children. Therefore, not all Protestant schools in this period were primarily proselytizing.[54]

There was no systematic government policy of educating the natives during the remainder of the seventeenth and eighteenth centuries. Yet, as in the American colonies, a number of Protestant missionary societies and other private organizations set up schools in Ireland, sometimes with government help. For example, the Baptist Society for Promoting the Gospel in Ireland, the London Hibernian Society, the so-called charter schools, and the Society for the Promotion of the Education of the Poor in Ireland (more commonly known as the Kildare Place Society). The last of these organizations magnanimously defined its goals thus: "for the accomplishment of the great work of educating the Irish poor, schools should be set up upon the most liberal principles and should be divested of all sectarian distinctions of Christianity." Catholics initially supported the organization, but by the 1820s, as it distributed grants to large numbers of explicitly missionary Protestant organizations, representatives of the majority religion turned against it. In Akenson's vivid phrase, they "helped smash the Kildare Place Society with considerable vigor and tactical shrewdness." By 1831 the government had withdrawn financial support from the Kildare Place Society and other such missionary educational societies, in order to establish a state-controlled elementary system.[55]

Even had they been successful beyond all initial hopes, such Protestant missionary enterprises were too few in number to have converted and Anglicized the Catholic population. "Predictably," writes McManus, "all of these bids at rescuing the Irish from being Irish failed." The vast majority of the expanding and predominantly Catholic Irish people had little sustained contact with such forms of schooling, in other words. However, "the belief persisted in government circles that it was through education that the Irish would be socialized and politicized along loyal, law abiding lines."[56]

On the eve of the establishment of a state-supported national system of elementary education, the 1824 Commissioners noted that of their reported total of 11,823 schools with a daily attendance of 560,000, about 2,500 schools were dependent upon charitable or private foundations or connected with the state-aided Protestant education/missionary societies. The other 9,300 or so were independent "pay schools" receiving no aid whatsoever, conducted by private individuals for their own profit or at their own risk in a generally poverty-stricken country.[57] The vast majority of these "pay schools" were in fact "hedge schools," a response to the infamous Penal Laws of the later seventeenth and eighteenth centuries. The 1824 Commissioners conceded the anti-Catholic intolerance of this cumulative body of legislation. One of the statutes rendered it "highly penal to receive any other than a Protestant Education." Further legislation decreed that Catholics could not establish or run schools, nor could they travel abroad to obtain a Catholic education. By the late eighteenth century many of the most onerous provisions of the Penal Laws had been repealed, and there is controversy among scholars on the extent to which the any of them were rigidly enforced. Akenson notes ironically, however, that their very nature, their declared intention to deprive Catholics of almost any kind of education unless it be Protestant, only intensified the desire of the majority to seek, "with a tenacity born of desperation," some more acceptable form of schooling for their children, illegal or not.[58]

In what Akenson further calls "a quiet but widespread conspiracy," large numbers of such people patronized the hedge schools, established and run by sometimes peripatetic scholars in the shade of hedges or in available rooms, who charged whatever fees the local population could pay.[59] The 1824 Commissioners complained that "Papists keeping Schools was One great Reason of many of the Natives continuing ignorant of the Principles of True Religion, and strangers to the Scripture." This criticism was probably accurate in terms of religion. But ironically, and not withstanding their honored position in Irish nationalist hagiography, the hedge schools increasingly taught in English rather than Irish—thus preparing large numbers of pupils and parents for the new national school ethos. Individual teachers attempted to use Irish and preserve its literature. Yet parental pressures, along with the growing tendency of the Catholic Church to use English, and the association of Irish literacy with some Protestant missionary organizations that strategically exploited the vernacular—all militated against the greater use of Irish in the hedge schools. These schools also probably contributed toward a slowly rising literacy; by the time of the 1841 census perhaps 47 per cent of Irish people over the age of five possessed some degree of literacy, or at least claimed to be able to read. This was literacy in the new language rather than the vernacular. Thus these home-grown Irish educational expedients—established by Irish teachers, attended by Irish pupils, and supported by Irish parents—made their own contribution to the weakening of the vernacular even before the national schools and other forces of modernization came close to obliterating the Irish language.[60]

Individual folklore informants and narrators leave us with occasional but valuable firsthand evidence on the hedge schools. "There was no inspector over us like [in] the National School," recalled a man who attended a late-surviving school during the 1860s, "and we took holidays when we liked." A woman told of entering such a school at around the age of nine, perhaps during the same decade. As the master owned no house, he accepted a form of room and board from different families, who gave him a few shillings at the end of the year. He taught in a shed during the winter and outdoors during the summer. "We had no desks or seats." The first arrivals for the day would sit on turf sods or stones. "The rest of the class would have to stand or take in a few sods of turf with them to make a seat." Upon arrival the master would instruct pupils to fetch his stool. In cold weather they had a fire, "and that was a troublesome fire," she remembered. "There was no chimney in the botháin [shed] and sometimes you couldn't see to put your fingers in your eyes with smoke. Our eyes used to be running with the cut of the smoke." During night class two boys would stand each side of the master, "a splinter blazing away and they holding them up," so he could see. Then there was even more smoke than during the day. They had no books, only slates, and pupils had a free day a month to look for stones to write on the slate. Reflecting the one-on-one teaching often used in the hedge schools—as distinct from the graded system used from the early decades of the nineteenth century, in which a teacher worked with a full class—the master called individual pupils to the top of the room. They would kneel in front of him, "and he'd show us our lesson and he pointing out the letters with the stem of his pipe, he was for ever smoking. Most of his time 'twas telling us about foreign countries he was." He never taught them to write, "but we could spell anything for you after him." Significantly, although he could speak Irish and actually used it with the pupils, the master never actually taught a word of the language. In all, it is a sharp but affectionate account of the man and his school, told decades later. "We were lonesome after him when he died," the informant concluded.[61]

The makeshift, indeed pathetic, nature of some hedge schools is also conveyed by Dr. Mark F. Ryan, who describes a school held in a barn rented from a local farmer. The fifteen or so pupils paid a few pence a week to the teacher, who instructed them in English and used a strap to maintain discipline. Pupils each brought a sod of turf to school, and although instruction ran from 10 a.m. to the mid-afternoon, they had no food until they returned home. "The teaching was very poor," concluded Ryan, but he remembered how the pupils delighted in memorizing polysyllabic words that they hardy understood, but that impressed their parents. One boy told them that he had learned "Orthography, etymology, syntax, prosody agus [and] hieroglyph-ics!" At another such school Ryan attended, in a locally built church, they made a turf fire on stones (to protect the mortar floor). Again, they could hardly see each other until the smoke had cleared away.[62]

At least these hedge schools were in buildings. Lombe Atthil, another doc-tor, came upon what we might term a classic version of the type of school around midcentury: "I saw some five or six boys sitting around an old man, under a tall hedge by a roadside, not a mile from my house." The teacher ap-peared to be "a great sufferer," and Atthil brought him to his dispensary and gave him temporary medical relief for his ailments. Then the teacher

told me what indeed I knew—the condition of the men of his class; that he rarely received any money; that he had spent his life wandering from place to place, teaching when he had the chance the children of the poor the rudiments of learning. This he did in barns, sheds, or by the roadside, receiving in return such scanty food as they had to give, seldom sleeping in any dwelling-house, but in some dilapidated barn or uncleanly shed.

Earlier, the hedge schoolmaster claimed, things had been a little better. But by then, with the national schools "springing up everywhere, he was no longer wanted."[63]

Thus, the educational level in many hedge schools must have been abys-mal, even by early-nineteenth-century standards. The schools were, writes historian J. R. R. Adams, "totally independent of any kind of authority other than market forces and the ire of the parents." Yet Adams himself, Akenson, J. P. Dowling, and McManus all argue that the overall influence was deep and highly positive in providing a kind of schooling, at times a high level, for up to 400,000 mostly Catholic children by the mid-1820s—whose parental reli-gion would otherwise have deprived them of any. Above all, writes Adams, the hedge schools testified "to the strong desire of ordinary Irish people to see their children receive some sort of education." And McManus similarly claims that there "can be little doubt that Irish parents set a high value on a hedge school education and made enormous sacrifices to secure it for their children"—despite chronic poverty. Indeed these people came to regard the hedge schoolteacher as "one of their own"; he and they shared so much in terms of culture, music, song, and poetry. And considering how few children the various other schools taught, the growing literacy in English by the early nineteenth century is an indication of the reach of the hedge schools, despite their precarious nature. McManus has shown the wide variety of readings, from the moralistic to the horrific, utilized by the masters.[64]

As the eighteenth century wore on and the Penal laws were repealed or fell into disuse, the Catholic Church began the massive task of catechizing the people through establishing parish schools. By the second half of the eighteenth century there was a system of such church-controlled schools throughout the country. Due to a shortage of priests the church sometimes had to work with hedge schoolteachers to fulfill its mission. Often the local parish priest exercised the right of supervision over such hedge schools—the masters needed priestly approval to survive in a community and might in turn assist the priest as a kind of parish clerk. Indeed, claims McManus, a symbiotic relationship grew up between the Catholic Church and the hedge schoolmasters, at least until the early nineteenth century.[65]

In addition, various Catholic orders and congregations such as the Jesuits also began to open schools, as did orders of nuns, such as the Ursuline Sisters, the Sisters of Mercy, and the Poor Clares. By 1800 there were about 120 nuns in 18 houses belonging to 6 orders; by 1900 their number had increased to 8,000 nuns in 368 convents of 35 different orders. "By the end of the [nineteenth] century," writes Mary Peckham Magray, "women religious had created an immense network of institutions that had become indispensable to the functioning of the Irish church and Irish society." However, by around 1830 nuns were reaching relatively few of the Irish population.[66]

Established by Edmund Ignatius Rice in 1802 to provide elementary education for poor boys, by 1831 the Christian Brothers order had grown to only 45 brothers and could not have educated more than a few thousand children. By 1900 the number of brothers had increased to 1,000, in a smaller total Irish population, and they taught about 27,000 male elementary school pupils, thus also achieving far greater influence upon the Catholic population by the end of the period under review. Initially the brothers worked within the new national system established in 1831 but soon withdrew to provide unambiguously denominational schools for their boys.[67]

V

By the 1820s, then, American Indian and Irish peoples had different yet partly similar experiences of nonschool education and of schooling. In terms of nonschool education—the lot of the majority in both areas—there were perhaps surprising similarities. Responsibility fell mostly on kin and the local community. Further, and also related to the general lack of schooling, most education was oral in nature. Few Indian languages had by then been put into writing. Nor, despite the existence of manuscript and published sources in

Irish, were native speakers generally literate in this language, still spoken by around three million Irish people in 1800.[68]

We must concede, nevertheless, that compared to American Indian children, Catholic and Protestant Irish children in 1800 did have much more experience of formal elementary schooling in the Western sense of the term. However, we should not exaggerate the extent or regularity of that experience. Very limited numbers of Irish children attended the charter schools and other Protestant missionary institutions, or Catholic parish schools, and the Catholic teaching orders were still quite small in personnel at the beginning of our period. It is likely that attendance at hedge schools—even when a local school met regularly—was sporadic. Irregular attendance would plague the far more systematically organized national schools throughout the period under review; it is unlikely that the hedge schools fared better in this regard.

Indians and Irish people would thus bring diverse yet partly similar historical and cultural experiences into the nineteenth century.[69] Some of these experiences—their general ignorance of English and literacy and of systematically organized, daily schooling—ill-prepared them for the campaigns of mass education and later compulsory education they would face. Yet traditional forms of education, along with sporadic missionary and hedge schooling, were in some ways surprisingly compatible with the demands of mass schooling: memorization of stories at home would help some adjust to the rote learning common in both systems; some Indian and far more Irish children were beginning to learn English; the very idea of the school, as a place set apart for education, was becoming more and more familiar, especially in Ireland, but even among Plains and Far Northwestern Indian peoples too. Although the content varied from tribe to tribe and from Indian America to Ireland, and indeed within Ireland, boys and girls were educated to different gender roles. Traditional Indian and Irish constructions of gender were thus in principle compatible with the policies and practices of missionary organizations, the BIA, and the CNEI, all of whom assumed without question that the sexes should be educated to different future roles in life.

2. The School as Weapon of State

Until the nineteenth century, writes Colin Heywood, "the idea that the state should intervene between parents and their children was almost unthinkable."[1] Earlier British and American colonial governments had sporadically supported education to pacify and control subject peoples. Yet it was only in the early 1800s that schooling became a systematically wielded weapon of the state throughout the Western world. And it was only then that Britain and the new United States acknowledged national responsibility for the education of "difficult" subgroups and actually began to establish, support, and physically build national and later compulsory elementary educational systems to Anglicize and Americanize these subgroups.

The United States became a nation in 1787 and built on British Imperial and colonial policies toward Indians, including cooperation with missionaries. For decades more the BIA performed this duty in a less-than-systematic way; at one point the government attempted to slough off its responsibility, parceling out the tribes to various Catholic and Protestant missionary organizations. Yet by the later part of the nineteenth century, with the establishment of government day schools and boarding schools (on and off the reservations), the BIA had pushed the missionary societies to the margin. Indeed, from the beginning of its existence the United States had staked out its responsibility for "civilizing" and Americanizing Indian peoples, whose "savagery" and "heathenism" were affronts to the new Republic.

Responding to Roman Catholic complaints and to the critical findings of a number of educational commissions, and realizing the inadvisability of continuing to subsidize Protestant missionary ventures in a predominantly Catholic country, in 1831 the British Parliament agreed to establish and finance the new elementary school system for all Irish children. The British state, like the American, thus embarked on an ambitious program of mass education for a supposedly problem people, but from the beginning the British did so more systematically. The Irish national school authorities no longer worked with mission societies, for example.

At that time neither the U.S. government nor its British counterpart felt the need to provide national, state-supported elementary school systems for "ordinary" Americans or English children. The Indians and the Irish *were* different. Indeed historian John Coolahan has noted how the Irish national school system could be seen as a kind of laboratory for later developments in England itself.[2] Both educational campaigns were unabashedly assimilationist: the goal in each case was to absorb troublesome subgroups into the larger polity, thus finally solving both "the Indian Problem" and "the Irish Problem."

I

Large numbers of nineteenth-century Americans cared little whether Indians survived or vanished, as long as they vacated their lands for white settlement. Many U.S. government officials, however, along with missionaries and other concerned citizens (later to be called "Friends of the Indian") sought acceptably humane and Christian methods for dealing with the "Indian Problem": for both freeing "surplus" Indian lands of their inhabitants yet preserving Indian people as future citizens of the Republic. These white Americans believed that through the schooling of tribal children, Indians could be raised into Christian and civilized society and thus be saved both in this life and the next.[3] As in colonial times, such goals effortlessly blended a withering contempt for Indian lifestyles with an equally powerful belief in the capacity of Indian people to rise into the privileges and responsibilities of American citizenship: ethnocentrism and racial egalitarianism inextricably fused. The offer of civilization and Christianity would amply repay Indian peoples for the loss of mostly "useless" tribal lands; thus "uplifted" they would practice American-style agriculture and be absorbed into the population of the Republic.

This commitment to Indian schooling drew from broader developments in mass education throughout the Western world. Prussia lead the way in establishing nationwide, standardized, age-graded school systems, and other nations followed. Mass education had become a powerful cultural weapon, especially for those nations striving to indoctrinate the masses into a whole and unblemished body politic.[4] The commitment also arose out of specific American developments, especially the arrival of increasingly diverse white immigrants. The school would become the great unifier, creating one nation from many, in thousands of nearly identical classrooms across the expanding nation, presenting nearly identical curricula to children of different ethnic groups. From the Revolution on, writes Andy Green, "education was held to be uniquely important for the cultivation of national identity, for the maintenance of social cohesion, and for the promotion of republican values, especially in a country of dispersed and heterogeneous communities and in the early years of a new and fragile republic." Barbara Finkelstein has noted how the school became "a formidable structure of persuasion" that would inculcate American values, self-control, and Protestant Christianity into all groups. American advocates of the common school believed that "education would be the key to creating the good society," concurs Joel Spring.[5] Thus transformed, young "cultural brokers" of all ethnic origins would return to their communities to help instill American values into often still-deficient adult members.

Emerging from such a heady mix of idealism, social anxiety, and pragmatism, the 1819 "Act making provision for the civilization of the Indian tribes adjoining the frontier settlements," often called "the Indian Civilization Act," was sweeping and yet explicit in its goals. Building on colonial precedent and, as we shall see, on previous decades of treaty making, the act was introduced "for the purposes of providing against the further decline and final extinction of the Indian tribes . . . and for introducing among them the habits and arts of civilization." It empowered the president, where practicable, "and with their own consent," to embark on Indian schooling. He was "to employ capable persons of good moral character to instruct them in the mode of agriculture suited to their situation, and for teaching their children in reading, writing, and arithmetic." Most significant then and later, an annual sum of ten thousand dollars was appropriated to carry out the provisions of the act. Further, "an account of the expenditure of the money, and proceedings in execution of the foregoing provisions, shall annually be laid before Congress."[6]

The legislature discontinued this specific "civilization fund" in 1873—over half a century later. Yet Congress continued to appropriate money for Indian education. By 1882 the annual sum had risen to $150,000, and by the end of that decade to about $750,000. By 1900 the figure was $3 million—about 300 times the initial 1819 fund, a massive increase in expenditure, even accounting for inflation.[7] The 1819 act, then, was not a one-time measure but a commitment to permanent involvement, and to permanent accounting, in Indian education. Further, from 1837 government agents were given increasing responsibility for the oversight of Indian schooling and could actually close schools in their jurisdiction; and in the 1870s and 1880s an inspector and later a superintendent of Indian schools was appointed.[8] As the British government would soon do in Ireland, the United States government had gotten itself into mass elementary schooling, but not for its primary population.

The Constitution of the United States assigned responsibility for Indian affairs to the federal government, rather than to individual state governments. At the time of the "Civilization Act" the War Department exercised oversight of Indian affairs, and in 1824 Congress established a unit within it called the Office of Indian Affairs, later referred to as the Bureau of Indian Affairs (hereafter BIA). Headed from 1832 by the commissioner of Indian Affairs, the BIA was in 1849 transferred to the Department of the Interior, where, despite some attempts to return it to the War Department, it has remained to this day.[9] In the first few decades of its existence the new BIA used the civilization fund to subsidize existing missionary efforts among the tribes, rather than to plunge into new school-building ventures. By 1824 there were thirty-two such schools in operation, enrolling over 900 tribal children, and this relationship continued to develop throughout the nineteenth century. Indeed a later Indian commissioner, Francis E. Leupp, admitted in 1905 that for the first hundred years of the Republic (until about the 1880s, in other words) the education of tribal children "was practically in the hands of the religious associations."[10] This occurred despite the ideal of church-state separation supposedly so central to American republican ideology. Irrespective of the apparent willingness to surrender some of its prerogatives to religious organizations, however, the federal government had become inextricably involved in both the subsidizing and policing of Indian schools—and it would later begin to build and staff such institutions.

Treaties too were crucial to Indian schooling. According to the Constitution, the making of treaties was a federal responsibility: the executive branch negotiated a treaty, the legislative branch (through the Senate, the upper house) ratified or rejected it.[11] In a comprehensive study of the process Francis P. Prucha concedes that treaties "were the legal instruments by which the federal government acquired full title to the great public domain stretching west of the Appalachian mountains." They were also "to a remarkable degree . . . instruments intended to transform the cultures of the tribes," especially by encouraging Indians to become agriculturalists (which some already were). Aside from farming, "formal schooling was the principal vehicle for modifying Indian cultures."[12]

As early as 1794 the United States made its first Indian treaty that mentioned education. The treaty with the Oneida, Tuscarora, and Stockbridge Indians mandated the establishment of mills and the instruction of some young men "in the arts of miller and sawyer." A decade later in 1803 the treaty with the Kaskaskia Indians of Illinois noted that the United States would provide $100 annually over seven years toward the support of a Roman Catholic priest, who would "engage to perform for the said tribe the duties of his office and also to instruct as many of their children as possible in the rudiments of literature." The 1857 treaty with the Pawnees dealt, of course, with the ceding of tribal lands but was also specific in its educational goals. "In order to improve the condition of the Pawnees, and teach them the arts of

civilized life," the United States agreed to establish "for their use and benefit, two manual labor schools, to be governed by such rules and regulations
as may be prescribed by the President," who would appoint the teacher. The
schools would teach "the various branches of a common school education,
and, in addition, the arts of agriculture, the most useful mechanical arts, and
whatever else the President may direct." The treaty, as others, also contained
compulsory stipulations and penalties: unless children from seven to eighteen were kept at school nine months per year, parents or guardians would
lose annuity money provided by the treaty. The treaty left no doubt as to who
was in control: if not satisfied that the tribe was carrying out its side of the
educational bargain, the president might "at his discretion, discontinue the
schools in whole or in part."[13]

The 1863 treaty with the Nez Perces of the Far Northwest obligated the
government to pay $10,000 for the erection of two school buildings, "to be
conducted on the manual labor system as far as practicable." The government
would also employ two matrons for the boarding schools and two assistant
teachers. The last treaty made with Indians, that of 1868 with the same people, stipulated that money set aside in the 1863 treaty to be used for education,
but since then "used for other purposes," should be reimbursed to the tribe,
and invested in United States bonds. Then it stipulated that "the interest of
the same to be paid to said tribe annually for the support of teachers."[14] Three
years later (1871) the treaty-making phase of Indian relations ended—the
United States would no longer recognize tribal peoples as sovereign nations
in the Western sense of the term—but the stipulations of ratified treaties remained on the book. Congress "could not disregard the sanctity of treaties
already signed and ratified," writes Prucha, "and confirmation of those treaties appeared side by side with the prohibition against making any more"—a
confirmation vital to Indian educational developments then and since.[15]

Native peoples, or at least specific individuals and groups within tribal
communities, often saw the adaptive use of schooling for personal and group
advancement. Leaders of part-white ancestry among, especially, tribes such
as the "civilized" Cherokees and Choctaws utilized treaty funds to subsidize
American missionary education for their peoples.[16] Actually in the pre-Civil
War decades direct government aid, important though it was, amounted to less
than 10 percent of the money being spent to "civilize" Indians. The mission
societies raised some of the rest, and Indian treaty money provided the bulk of
it.[17] Thus the government, the missionary societies, and tribal peoples became
tied into complex and indeed highly symbiotic educational relationships—but
increasingly the BIA would call the tune, at least on the white side.

Partly federally financed and treaty subsidized, the schools of the

American Board of Commissioners for Foreign Missions (ABCFM) among the Cherokees of the Southeast had become by the 1820s, in the words of William G. McLoughlin, "an international showpiece."[18] At such ABCFM schools, and at those run by other Protestant (and Catholic) missionary societies, the regimen and curriculum drew on colonial precedents and became characteristic of missionary and government education throughout the period under review. Combining literary and vocational instruction (the "half and half" curriculum) with Christian ideals of morality, it was relentlessly assimilationist, almost totally ignoring tribal cultural values. Although missionaries sometimes initially used tribal languages, teaching at government schools was in English, irrespective of pupil ability or total inability in this strange tongue.[19]

Thus imbued with "civilized" and Christian values, the children would return to spread the word among their own peoples. "Soon [Cherokee pupils] will be mingling with their countrymen," declared the ABCFM in 1821 in a classic description of the "cultural broker," "imparting their acquired character to others, and they to others still, in a wider and wider range." As historian Clyde Ellis notes, schools "could act as the most powerful engine of all in the cultural transformation that policy makers devised for Indians." The school was targeted at tribal children, "the most vulnerable and least able to resist, at least in theory," and thus "the logical targets of a policy designed to erase one culture and replace it with another."[20]

Missionary efforts in the Southeast, especially those of the ABCFM, were badly disrupted by the Removal Crisis of the 1830s. Despite protests from many missionaries and other Friends of the Indians, and despite an apparently sympathetic Supreme Court decision of Judge John Marshall that the Indians were "domestic dependent Nations," most remaining Southeastern Indians were forced along the infamous Trail of Tears to the Oklahoma Indian Territory.[21] Missionary activity took up again there, and the ABCFM and other societies continued their educational enterprises in the new land. The Indians' own adaptive capacity also reasserted itself, and many of these tribes continued to build partly treaty-supported school systems. In addition, missionary-government educational activities elsewhere in the nation and even in distant areas claimed by the United States continued during this decade of crisis for the Southeastern Indians. By the eve of the Civil War Protestant and Catholic missionaries, broadly in cooperation with and under the protection of the U.S. government, had also set up missions and schools among tribes as widely separated as the Omahas of the Midwest and the Nez Perces and Cayuses of the Far Northwest.[22]

After the 1861–65 Civil War, however, the federal government attempted temporarily to divest itself of its educational responsibilities for the tribes. Perhaps as a result of the exhaustion brought on by the war and by attempting to reconstruct the defeated South, and also out of a growing conviction about corruption in the Indian Service, the government sought to hand over—or, we might say, hand back—Indian schooling to the missionary bodies. Through its Peace Policy, the administration of President Ulysses S. Grant first invited the Friends (Quakers) to suggest church members as federal agents and teachers to the tribes—a further extraordinary blurring of state-church relationships. In 1870 Commissioner Ely S. Parker (himself a Seneca—a highly unusual early example of Indianization of the BIA) noted the goal of achieving "a greater degree of honesty in our intercourse with the Indians." He declared that the experiment had been such a success that other denominations would similarly be called upon. The fused secular and religious goal, according to Parker, was "to combine with the material progress of the Indian race, means for their moral and intellectual improvement." The whole plan, he believed, was "obviously a wise and humane one." He conceded that Indians tended to pick up the vices rather than the virtues of whites, a common nineteenth-century belief, here regurgitated by a highly acculturated and "successful" Indian. Yet Parker maintained that through the new policy the president "wisely determined to invoke the cooperation of the entire religious element of the country." Christians would help "to bring about and produce the greatest amount of good from the expenditure of the munificent annual appropriations of money by Congress, for the civilization and Christianization of the Indian race."[23]

By 1872 the Friends had been given sixteen agencies with a missionary and educational responsibility for 24,322 Indians; Presbyterians got nine agencies with 38,069 Indians; and Roman Catholics received seven agencies with over 17,856 Indians. This crass parceling out of peoples produced much resentment among the denominations and achieved little obvious "uplift" of the tribes; nor did it produce greater peace on the frontier. By the early 1880s the ambitious policy had petered out. Although the federal government appeared to have attempted to divest itself of Indian schooling, in reality this was not fully so. Even during the Peace Policy, congressional money still subsidized missionary educational ventures, and ultimately the government validated the programs of denominations. It was also the government that belatedly decided upon the failure of the policy. The whole program, as Commissioner Parker noted, was established to achieve "the desire and purpose of the Government."[24]

The collapse of the Peace Policy and the ending of treaty making in no way weakened the government commitment. Indeed, before the late 1870s the

BIA was moving much more forcefully and directly into Indian schooling and within a few more decades would push the Protestant and Catholic missionary societies to the margins. Some historians also see an intensification of overt American patriotism at the expense of explicitly Christian proselytization at this time.[25] Yet, just as the British-provided national schools from the beginning worked to anglicize Irish children of all faiths, so American government officials and missionaries strove not just to Christianize but also to Americanize their charges. These educators were often acutely embarrassed by the un-Christian example of individual white Americans. Yet such sinners in no way invalidated the greatness of the nation or the importance of the goal. Above all nations, including even Britain, the United States embodied the Christian Civilization.

Educators could express these nationalistic convictions in stark and strident language. It was of prime importance that a fervent patriotism should be awakened in the minds of tribal children, declared Indian commissioner Thomas J. Morgan in 1889. "They should be taught to look upon America as their home and upon the United States Government as their friend and benefactor. They should be made familiar with the lives of great and good men and women in American history, and be made feel a pride in all their great achievements." They should hear little or nothing of the "wrongs of the Indians" and of the injustice of the white race. "If their unhappy history is alluded to," Morgan decreed, "it should be in contrast with the better future that is within their grasp."[26]

As the century wore on and the BIA increased its involvement in tribal education, most Friends of the Indian agreed on broad goals, but disagreement sometimes arose over methods. Which form of school would most effectively Americanize Indian children: the local day school that many then attended or the distant boarding school? Situated on the reservation, the day school was obviously cheaper to maintain, but by only temporarily removing children from their homes, it allowed continuous contact with kin and culture and thus dissipated the civilizing message of the teachers. The boarding school, especially the off-reservation boarding school, hundreds or even thousands of miles from tribal lands, far more securely quarantined children and to many educators was well worth the extra expense. Actually, both kinds of institutions, along with an intermediate form, the on-reservation boarding school, persisted from the 1870s until the 1920s, and beyond. Yet in the decades around the end of the nineteenth century the large, off-reservation boarding school seemed to be the most promising tool for Americanization.

Although missionaries had built boarding schools before and throughout the period under review, the new wave of government boarding schools was a product of the vision and energy of Captain (later General) Richard Henry Pratt. In 1879 he founded the Carlisle Indian Industrial School in Pennsylvania. An extraordinary man, combining powerful cultural intolerance with a deep sensitivity to Indian needs as he perceived them, Pratt was convinced that only by removing children from the supposedly corrupting tribal environment and by schooling them among white people could they assimilate into American life. Until its closure as an Indian school in 1918, Carlisle became a home away from home to thousands of Indian boys and girls from hundreds of different tribal groups.[27]

Pratt's example stimulated the opening of many more BIA off-reservation boarding schools. By 1900 there were twenty-five, with an average yearly attendance of about 6,000 students, at widely separated locations such as Chilocco (Oklahoma), Phoenix (Arizona), Santa Fe (New Mexico), Flandreau (South Dakota), and Lawrence (Kansas).[28] Each school developed its own version of the half and half curriculum of literary and vocational education. Many also followed Pratt's idea of "outing" students: sending them out to work on local white farms during the summer months or even to urban environments. Thus near-total immersion in "civilized" society was achieved: first separation from kin and culture; then further separation from *all* Indians, even fellow pupils, for at least a few months each year. In rigidly polarized language, the superintendent of the Haskell Boarding School expressed the urgency of the task. Confronting "the invincible march of civilization," the Indian had few alternatives: "civilization or annihilation, absorption or extinction."[29]

During the nineteenth century, according to Heywood, families in the Western world came under "an increasing barrage" of advice from new experts "eager to pontificate on child-rearing." If a poor Western home was inadequate to properly train children, how much more so was a "savage" Indian one. American educators thus made no apologies for tearing tribal children from the bosom of their family and sending them to often-distant boarding schools—a separation spared most Irish elementary school children. Many educators shared Pratt's conviction that Indian kin arrangements did not merit the sacred appellation "home." With astounding insensitivity, the teacher at a Catholic mission school declared in 1862 that pupils "must become as orphans, that is they must forget their parents as far as possible." The following year Commissioner William P. Dole claimed quite characteristically that Indian children who attended only day schools on the reservations retained "the filthy habits and loose morals of their parents, and acquire[d] only a limited knowledge of the simpler branches [of the curriculum]." In a boarding school, however, the children were "*under the entire control of the teacher* [emphasis added]; they are comfortably clothed; fed on wholesome diet . . . in fact, they are raised and educated like white children and on leaving school are found to have acquired a knowledge and taste for civilized habits." A decade later in 1873 another commissioner was equally forthright but more detailed in his belief that except for children "already far along in civilization," the reservation day school was clearly inadequate. "Indian children cannot come from the wigwam suitably clothed for the school-room," he believed. "The habits also of wigwam life are entirely irregular." The Indian "has no regular habits or hours. He eats and sleeps when or where he will or can," and regular attendance could not be relied on. It was also, he claimed with a degree of validity, "well nigh impossible to teach Indian children the English language, when they spend twenty hours out of the twenty-four in the wigwam, using only their native tongue." The boarding school, obviously, "takes the youth under constant care, has him always at hand, and surrounds him with an English-speaking community, and above all, gives him instruction in the first lessons of civilization, which can only be found in a well-ordered home."[30]

Not only control was sought, however.[31] Such educators sincerely hoped that, at their best, the boarding schools really could become substitute homes for their charges, providing not only civilized learning but firm and fair discipline, adequate food, and professional yet loving teachers. Perhaps surprisingly, considering the disdain of white educators for Native traditions, some Indian boys and girls did find such "homes" at the schools.

As historian Frederick E. Hoxie notes, this educational campaign constituted "a unique level of federal activism on behalf of a non-white minority"[32]— just as the Irish national school system was established decades ahead of a similar system for English children. In 1877 there were only 300 BIA schools, mostly day schools, enrolling about 5,000 children. By 1900 the educational reach of the federal government had dramatically extended. Along with the 25 off-reservation boarding schools referred to above, the BIA supported 81 on-reservation boarding schools (with a claimed attendance of 8,000 pupils), and 147 day schools (with a claimed attendance of 3,500 pupils). Indian commissioner William A. Jones proudly declared that these institutions were "all under complete Government control." There were also about 30 schools subsidized through contracts with the government. Further, the BIA still assumed "supervisory care" over mission schools with an enrolment of just under 3,000 pupils. Indeed, a decade later Commissioner Robert G. Valentine could describe the Indian Service as "primarily educational," in the broadest sense that it aimed at the transformation of all Indians, young and old. It was, he declared in 1909, "a great indoor-outdoor school, with the emphasis on the outdoor. The students in this school are 300,000 individuals, ranging in age from babes at the breast to old men and women of the tribes, and with a range of characteristics which is indicated by no one fact perhaps better than that these 300,000 individuals speak about 250 fairly distinct dialects."[33]

It was still a loose kind of control that the BIA exercised; there was no centrally imposed hierarchy of schools or standardized examinations. In the late 1880s Commissioner Morgan had attempted to bring greater order through establishing a uniform curriculum, standardized textbooks and forms of instruction, and a merit system for teachers. He also attempted to inaugurate a graded system of schools through which students would progress: from day school (elementary education) through on-reservation boarding school to Carlisle or other off-reservation boarding school (vocational high school). Although he brought greater coherence to the "system," few of even the most ambitious boarding schools could claim to have been anything more than elementary schools. Indeed, as late as 1928 the commissioner admitted that although at six government institutions Indians could receive "a high school education," there was not an Indian school that was "strictly a high school." Despite the hopes of visionary white educators, we are here dealing with *elementary* systems of education.[34] Further, it was highly difficult to bring order to what was a loose collection of schools, scattered over the vast distances of the United States, catering to children of highly diverse tribal cultures, who often spoke no English and a variety of tribal languages upon entering school.

By the early twentieth century a new phenomenon had begun to manifest itself: more and more tribal children attended local state public schools, often with BIA assistance. At the beginning of the century only 246 did. By 1930 this number had exploded to almost 38,000—more than half of all Indian children in school. As almost all of this latter development took place at the very end of my period of study, and as my focus here is upon explicitly "Indian schools," I have not attempted to examine it.[35] Whether at BIA, missionary, or state public schools, the goal for the government was the same: kill the Indian to save the man or woman trapped within tribal culture. "Give the Indian a white man's chance," wrote Commissioner William A. Jones in 1903. In a passage that powerfully combines cultural intolerance with egalitarian pragmatism, he continued:

> To educate the Indian in the ways of civilized life, therefore, is to preserve him from extinction, not as an Indian, but as a human being. . . . Educate him in the rudiments of our language. Teach him to work. Send him to his home, and tell him he must practice what he has been taught or starve. It will in a generation or more regenerate the race. It will exterminate the Indian but develop a man.[36]

Frustrated by attendance problems, coincidentally during the 1890s authorities in both the United States and Ireland passed general compulsory education laws. Individual Indian treaties had sometimes included clauses allowing for compulsion—reflecting what Joel Spring calls "the mania that developed among nineteenth-century educators over [American] student attendance and punctuality." Congress had earlier passed a number of laws allowing the BIA to compel school attendance on particular Indian reservations. In 1891 the legislature for the first time authorized the commissioner to "make and enforce by proper means such rules and regulations as will secure the attendance of Indian children of suitable age and health at the schools established for their benefit." By 1893 Congress allowed the withholding of rations and annuities (owed to tribes according to treaties) from parents and guardians refusing to send their children to school. The next year Congress partly backtracked and forbade the sending of children to off-reservation boarding schools without parental or kin consent. Congress passed other compulsory laws, and authorities on many reservations tried to coerce parents into sending children to school, even employing agency police to round them up. The whole question of compulsion remained controversial even among educators and officials, however, and a proportion of Indian children remained unschooled—though not uneducated—through the 1920s.[37]

Yet by the end of the period under review, the vast majority of Indian children—like their Irish counterparts—attended some kind of school: about 34,000 in government schools, 6,000 in missionary schools, and 38,000 in public schools. Thus *convergence* from very different beginnings is a major theme of this comparative study. Indeed, individual Indian schools experienced problems of overcrowding. Statistics suggest, writes Szasz, that education was thus one of the most successful programs of the BIA. Indian narrators and later historians have shown how tribal peoples could indeed become highly possessive about "their" local boarding schools, even rejecting their closures.[38]

Some historians claim that by 1900 the culturally intolerant but racially egalitarian policies of the government began to change. Officials, according to this argument, became more tolerant of tribal cultural traits but simultaneously more convinced of Indian racial limitations. The schools were thus to lower their sights: to train tribal children for work more appropriate to their future condition in life, mostly as lowly farmers, manual laborers, or, if girls, farmers' wives or domestic servants for whites. Indians would become citizens, yes—but they would simultaneously remain wards of the government, forever trapped in this legal limbo, forever "proletarianized" and limited by their racial "blood." Other historians, myself included, see far more continu-

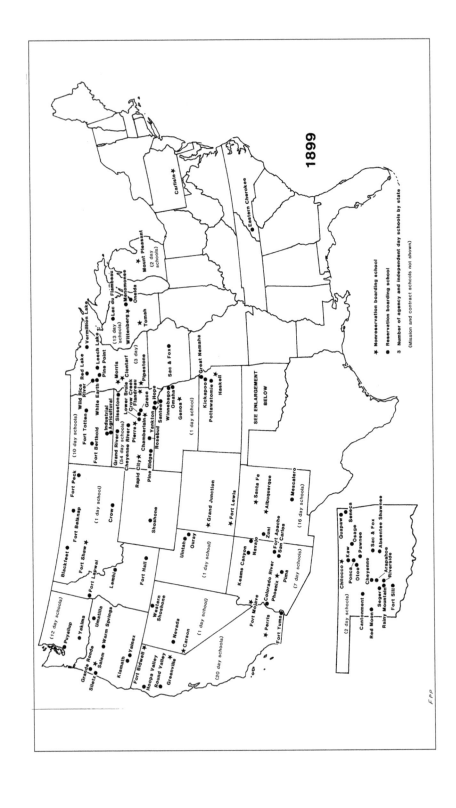

ity in practice at least, regardless of policy. The New Course of Studies (the more vocationally orientated curriculum of 1901) and apparently racist statements by Indian commissioners and other educators can be read in many different ways and can indeed support either argument. Accounts by Indian narrators who attended BIA schools into the early twentieth century suggest that despite changes in policy, those at the receiving end noticed few of them. Schools continued to be as culturally intolerant and teachers as humanly varied as ever, but not more explicitly racist in their treatment of Indian pupils. Whether working with missionaries or building its own school system, the major BIA goals remained unchanged: school them, civilize them, Christianize them, and assimilate them.[39]

And the goal of citizenship remained consistent. In 1892 Commissioner Morgan powerfully linked citizenship to individuality, supposedly lacking in tribal society. "Citizenship," he wrote, "accompanied by allotment of lands [into private farms], necessarily looks toward the entire destruction of the tribal relation; the Indians are to be looked upon as individuals and not en mass; they are to stand on their own personal rights and be freed absolutely from the trammels of the tribe and the limitations of chieftaincy." Over a decade later in 1905 Commissioner Leupp, who strongly argued for a less academic and more "relevant" curriculum, still believed that Indian children should have all the chances "for intellectual training" that were available to "the young Caucasian." And he accepted that government policy should lead Indians to assume "the responsibilities of citizenship." His successor in 1908 claimed that all his work was "guided by my general aim of preparing the whole Indian establishment [BIA] for going out of business at no very distant date"—implying the complete blending of Indians into American society. The following year Commissioner Robert Valentine gave another ringing declaration of BIA policy. "Whether in the schoolroom or on the irrigation ditch," he declared, "whether in leasing part of an allotment or in the issuance of a patent in fee or in the use of individual or tribal funds, the one test to be brought to the business aspect of the case is, will doing this and the way of doing it educate the child or the woman or the man for citizenship?"[40]

Map 5. U.S. Government Indian Schools in 1899. By the end of the nineteenth century the commissioner of Indian Affairs claimed that these schools enrolled over 20,000 pupils. Contract schools receiving government support enrolled another 3,000 pupils, and mission schools over 1,000 pupils. State public schools then enrolled only ca. 300 Indians. After removal to Oklahoma in the 1830s, the Five Civilized Tribes (Cherokees, Chickasaws, Choctaws, Creeks, and Seminoles) built their own school systems, which were taken over by the U.S. government in 1906. Reprinted from *Atlas of American Indian Affairs*, by Francis Paul Prucha, by permission of University of Nebraska Press. Copyright © 1990 by the University of Nebraska Press.

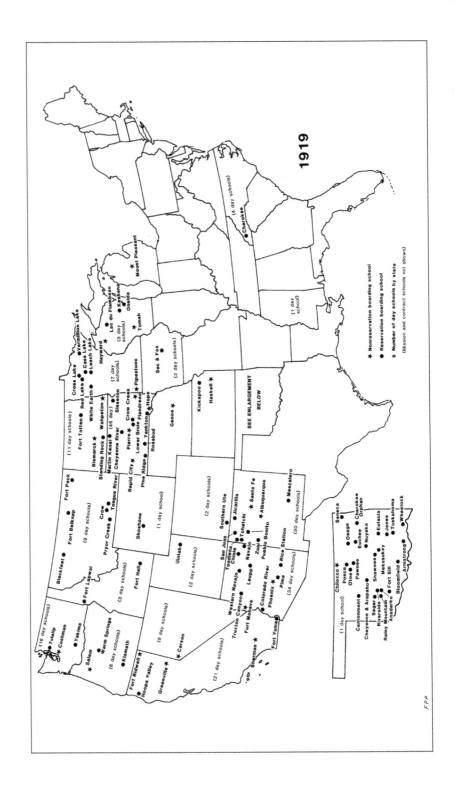

1919

★ Nonreservation boarding school
● Reservation boarding school
6 Number of day schools by state

(Mission and contract schools not shown)

FPP

By the 1920s influential groups of mostly white reformers had begun to focus their attentions on Indian policy, and specifically on Indian education. Rejecting the ethnocentric yet optimistic tenor of official reports, and reflecting a growing anthropological appreciation of non-Western cultures, groups such as the American Indian Defense Association assailed the wisdom of a century in Native American affairs. This mounting criticism received powerful expression in *The Problem of Indian Administration* (1928), generally known as The Meriam Report since it was produced by a team—including the Winnebago Indian Henry Roe Cloud—under the directorship of Dr. Lewis Meriam. The carefully researched report devoted over 800 pages to telling the secretary of the interior—to whom the BIA was responsible—just what was wrong with Indian administration. W. Carson Ryan, from 1930 to 1935 director of Indian education in the BIA, wrote the section on education. Rejecting the "civilize or die" maxim, he instead insisted that Indians should be allowed to adapt at their own pace to American ways. Almost every aspect of Indian schooling came in for criticism, from its ethnocentric and rigid curriculum—the vocational side of which often degenerated into the exploitation of pupil labor to help support the schools—to the severe health hazards faced by pupils. Influenced by the so-called progressive education movement, the report advocated more sensitive and community-centered education, the kind that would encourage creativity and help produce adults capable of living full lives in the community of their choice.[41]

The Meriam Report was massively influential. Franklin D. Roosevelt's choice of reformer John Collier as commissioner of Indian affairs in 1932 led to radical—if not fully permanent—reform of many areas of Indian policy and practice. Bringing a passionate and even mystical appreciation of Indian cultures (as he perceived them) to the job, Collier wrought changes especially in education. Here he drew upon his own experiences among Indian peoples (actually quite limited), openly utilized the ideas of anthropologists, introduced further progressive ideas, and attempted above all to foster rather than destroy Indian cultural values. It should be the aim of Indian education at least for the next generation, he wrote in 1935, "to deliver Indian adolescents fully and practically prepared to make the most of their available resources"—a goal with which few previous commissioners would have quarreled. But his

Map 6. U.S. Government Indian Schools in 1919. In 1918 the government closed the famous Indian Industrial School at Carlisle, Pennsylvania. By then government schools claimed an enrollment of over 25,000 pupils. Mission and contract schools enrolled over 5,000 pupils. State public school enrollment exceeded 30,000 Indian pupils. Reprinted from *Atlas of American Indian Affairs*, by Francis Paul Prucha, by permission of the University of Nebraska Press. Copyright © 1990 by the University of Nebraska Press.

next words indicated the degree to which his thinking differed from past approaches. The tie that bound such adolescents to their homeland should "be strengthened rather than broken, [they would be] Indian youths with wide horizons, bilingual, literate, yet proud of their Indian heritage, [able] to become completely self-supporting, even though going without some of the mechanical resources of the present day."[42] By the end of the Second World War Collier had resigned, and the pendulum in Indian education would again swing back—but not completely—toward older forms of assimilationist thinking. By the 1960s and 1970s it would swing again toward increased appreciation of Indian culture and increased faith in Indian "self determination."[43]

The Indian New Deal thus marks the most radical break in thinking on Native American education since the 1820s—indeed since 1492. And so the 1920s makes a logical cut-off point for the American side of this study.

II

"We have applied our efforts," declared the Commissioners for Inquiring into the State of all Schools, on Public or Charitable Foundations, in Ireland (1812), "to the framing of a system which . . . shall afford the opportunities of education at every description of the lower classes of the people." By the early nineteenth century critics of British educational policy in Ireland—if haphazard support of Protestant missionary organizations could be termed a "policy"—included not only Catholic clergy and laity, but even supposedly disinterested government commissioners. The leading principle of any acceptable new system, the 1812 Commissioners reiterated, was "that no attempt shall be made to influence or disturb the peculiar religious tenets of any sect or description of Christian." This stipulation was not a product of rising British appreciation for the religion of the vast majority of Irish people. "Constitutionally," writes Sean Farren, "the United Kingdom of Great Britain and Ireland was a 'Protestant' state and still, in the early nineteenth century, suspicious and at times openly hostile to Roman Catholicism." The stipulation was, rather, a pragmatic awareness of demographic realities in Ireland. By 1812 about five of the six million people were Catholic; large numbers of Ulster people were dissenter Protestant; only a small number were actually members of the Established Church, the (Anglican) Church of Ireland. Therefore to achieve the integrationist goals of the 1800 Act of Union and to effectively Anglicize the fast-expanding Irish population, a new, more realistic approach was necessary. This had to provide mass elementary education in a way that would win the hierarchy of the Catholic Church in Ireland and the lower orders, and also major dissenting Protestant churches such as the Presbyterians. Employing language similar to that used by American educators to depict Indians, the Irish 1812 Commissioners decried the supposed defects of earlier educational efforts, especially hedge schools. The minds of poor children educated in such schools were "corrupted by books calculated to incite lawlessness and profligate adventure, to cherish superstition, and to lead to dissension and disloyalty." In order "to substitute for the ill-taught and ill-regulated schools," the commissioners believed that "a systematic and uniform plan of instruction" was vital, one that would "gratify the desire for information which manifests itself among the lower classes of the people of Ireland." Such a plan would also "form those habits of regularity and discipline which are yet more valuable than mere learning."[44]

These 1812 Commissioners further recommended that a permanent board of educational commissioners be established to run this new system. Such a board should have very wide powers and duties, making it responsible for, among other things, the selection of proper locations for schools, "(for) prescribing the mode of education to be pursued, and for the general superintendence of them." Reflecting the growing belief in the importance of a state role in elementary education that also impelled American educators, the 1812 Commissioners explicitly noted that a new board should "have a general control over the whole of the proposed establishments for the instruction of the lower classes.[45]

This, then, should be no stopgap measure. Like legislators who inserted educational clauses into Indian treaties and who drafted the Indian Civilization Act in 1819, these commissioners were strongly advocating that the national (British) government become permanently and systematically involved in Irish education—also in the education of a troublesome subgroup, rather than of the "normal" English population. Time was not fully ripe for such recommendations in 1812, however, and it would take mounting criticism in Ireland and further major commissions, working in 1824–27, 1828, and 1830 before such advice was taken up by Parliament.[46]

The Commissioners of 1824–27 included four Protestants and—notably— one Catholic and produced nine reports. The First Report of the Commissioners of Irish Education Inquiry (1825; hereafter First Report) actually began by quoting a long petition from the prelates of the Roman Catholic Church in Ireland, to the effect that present educational arrangements were totally inadequate if not offensive to their members, and that the recommendations of the 1812 Commission still had not been met. To the extent that the majority population received any education, it was mostly through the hedge schools. The critical First Report also recommended the setting up by the government of a board to superintend "schools of general instruction" and recommended, among other things, the instruction of Catholics and Protestants together for "literary instruction" (secular learning and even learning of a moral nature not denominationally sensitive) and separately for religious instruction. The new board should be able to hire inspectors and should have complete control over all monies supplied for education, over the appointment and dismissal of teachers, and over the selection of books for the new schools.[47]

By late in the 1820s, then, a strong feeling had built up among British and Irish educators, politicians, and church leaders that Ireland needed special educational treatment to achieve greater justice and also greater integration into the Union. Ultimately it was a letter that established the new system.

In 1831 Lord Stanley, chief secretary of Ireland under the lord lieutenant—the highest representative of the British monarch in Ireland—sent this letter to the Duke of Leinster. Explicitly referring to the recommendations of earlier commissions, Stanley noted that Parliament had sanctioned funds "as an experiment," and invited the duke to become "President of the New Board." Declaring that in the future parliamentary funds for Irish education would be channeled through a board rather than through voluntary (and missionary) societies, Stanley perceptively admitted that the latter, denominationally partial approach "could not become one of National Education." The new system would be one "from which should be banished even the suspicion of proselytism, admitting children of all religious persuasions, [and] should not interfere with the peculiar tenets of any." By combining literary education with separate religious instruction, it would become "so far adapted to the views of the religious persuasions which divide Ireland, as to render it, in truth, a system of National Education for the lower classes of the community.[48]

This letter, then, rather than individual treaties and the Indian Civilization Act in the United States, would become the foundational document of the Irish national schools until independence and partition in 1922. Stanley advocated that members of the new board—later to be collectively referred to as the Commissioners of National Education in Ireland (CNEI or the National Board)—were to be men of high personal character and of different denominations. They "should exercise a complete control over the various schools which may be erected under [their] auspices." Although Parliament would supply funds, local initiative would also be necessary—recall how Indians too were expected to partly pay for schools through "their" treaty money. Therefore some of the expenses, for teachers' salaries and maintenance, should be raised locally. As earlier commissions also suggested, the CNEI would have control over textbooks, inspection, and disbursement of all funds. Initially seven commissioners were appointed: three from the Church of Ireland, two Catholics, and two Presbyterians; the Duke of Leinster, a Protestant, became president or chairman. Although the appointment of these two Catholics was almost radical, it should be remembered that in 1831 Catholics vastly outnumbered Protestants of all kinds. Similar to the accountability requirement of the Indian Civilization Act—Congress should receive annual reports on expenditure—the CNEI should also "submit to Parliament a Report of their proceedings."[49]

The CNEI thus appeared to control the new system, yet final authority resided with the British Parliament, which, subject to Treasury oversight, supplied the funds.[50] The lord lieutenant appointed the board members. He could also dismiss any member—a right never exercised in the almost century-long life of the CNEI. Indeed, until Parliament granted them a charter of incorporation in 1844, the commissioners actually existed at the whim of the lord lieutenant.[51]

The Irish were nevertheless more "equal" in this arrangement than were the Indians in the United States. There was never a block of Indian representative in Congress, but 100 Irish members sat in the House of Commons after 1801 (out of approximately 500), and 32 sat in the House of Lords. Akenson claims, however, that Ireland still experienced a quasi-colonial relationship with London. The Irish executive, headed by the lord lieutenant, remained an adjunct to English politics. After the Union, as before, "Ireland was governed by men of a colonial stripe"—who could oscillate between coercion and programs designed to better the economic, social, and educational conditions of the people. In a later work R. F. Foster sees a similar paradox in Ireland's equality within the United Kingdom. Although supposedly "as British as Yorkshire (or Finchley), the Whitehall or Dublin Castle practice brazenly admitted the opposite. . . . Economic or political exploitation formed the basis of its operation, whether that had been the original intention or not." In a more recent study that questions the applicability of colonial and imperialistic models to nineteenth-century and later Ireland, Steven Howe still accepts a degree of paradox in the country's somewhat hybrid position within the United Kingdom. "Ireland under the Union," he writes, was "quite unlike any other part of the subject Empire in that it was represented—on the whole fairly represented, proportional to population—in the Imperial Parliament." Yet Ireland was "unlike any other part of the Kingdom in the presence of 'colonial' institutions headed by the Lord Lieutenant." Whatever the legal situation, the everyday running of the new educational system involved complex and changing power relationships between the board, Irish clients, government representatives in Ireland, the Treasury, and Parliament; and the government in London finally called the shots.[52] Also, no matter who controlled things, the CNEI goal, like that of the BIA, was to assimilate a problem population into a larger cultural and political entity.

Soon the board was augmented by the appointment of a resident commissioner, a position analogous to that of a government departmental secretary.
A peculiar central-local allocation of powers and responsibilities grew from
the 1831 decision. Parliament stood at the top of the pyramid, holding—like
Congress in the United States—all authority and granting yearly funds, even
if Irish educational affairs received little attention at Westminster. Under this
came the so-called Irish government, the lord lieutenant and chief secretary,
who together formed a liaison with Parliament, appointed members (commissioners) to the board, and approved its rules. The board, and thus CNEI,
was the operating authority in Ireland, distributing funds, approving school
schemes, setting rules and regulations, and controlling the curriculum and
the selection of textbooks, the suspension of teachers and the removal of
local managers—and, especially significant, the appointment of inspectors
who would become the enforcing agents and the terrors in the lives of many
teachers. A local patron had to suggest the building of a national school in a
particular area and appoint a school manager who in turn had great power in
hiring and firing teachers and in generally overseeing the work of the local
school. The raising of contributory local funds never worked to the satisfaction of the British Treasury.[53]

The goal of the system was to achieve greater harmony between the religious
groups in Ireland and thus ensure greater loyalty to the Union. Lord Stanley's
letter emphasized that the new board would "probably look with peculiar
favour" upon multidenominational applications for school funds—from
mixed groups of clergy in a parish, from a clergyman of one faith along with
parishioners from another, or from mixed groups of parishioners. Hopefully,
such applications would lead to real interdenominational schooling for all
curricular subjects except those explicitly denominational. But things did
not work out quite that way. By the middle of the century the system had in
fact fragmented into blocks of Catholic, Presbyterian, and—later—Anglican
schools. Children from local minority faiths sometimes ended up being
educated with the local majority. Nevertheless, the national school system
rapidly metamorphosed into a peculiar hybrid, a state educational system
run by the churches. "Denominationalism," writes Farren, "was to prove too
hardy a plant to smother under any scheme for 'united' education." Social and
religious realities in Ireland forced the government to compromise, leading
to "a system that became more and more explicitly denominational over the
course of the following decades."[54]

The Presbyterians of Ulster first forced changes in the system to bring it
closer to their needs and by 1840 had come to accept it, leading to a block
of Presbyterian national schools, mostly in Ulster. The (Anglican) Church of

Ireland resented the weakening of its role as the Established Church for all the island's people and initially rejected the national system. In 1839 it established its own school organization, the Church Education Society. Gradually during the century, and escalating after the disestablishment of the Church of Ireland 1869, pupils of this denomination more and more gravitated toward the national schools; by 1880 10 percent of all national school pupils were from this church, although some Church of Ireland children still attended its own schools.[55]

Leaders of all the major denominations would have preferred state funding of explicitly denominational systems, none more than the Catholic bishops. There were divisions within the Catholic Church on many educational issues, but the leadership realized that the CNEI was a vast improvement on earlier state support of Protestant missionary societies and on the hedge schools; and whatever its misgivings, it also went along with the national schools. By the middle of the century its bishops were patrons for schools in predominantly Catholic areas, and its parish priests were often the local managers of individual schools.[56] Each denomination thus jealously guarded its educational prerogatives for "its own" children. The vast majority of the national schools, both before and after the Great Famine of 1845–48, were thus obviously Catholic in terms of local control and pupil composition.

Catholic resentment increased when, in the 1840s, the CNEI set up a number of model schools and teacher-training establishments, directly under its control, rather than local control. Insisting on the importance of a Catholic ethos for training its teachers, the Catholic hierarchy never accepted such schools, nor could any member of the church attend them. In the later decades of the century Catholics and Church of Ireland authorities gained permission to open state-supported and independent teacher-training establishments. By then the Catholic Church more and more fully accepted and indeed manipulated the national school system to its own advantage and had won themselves ten of the twenty board memberships, a dramatic change from the original two out of eight.[57]

Even the CNEI admitted that daily attendance figures rarely matched enrollments, yet historians generally accept that, like the BIA system, the Irish national school system did expand dramatically during its ninety years of life. According to the CNEI's annual *Report*, by 1835 there were 1,106 national schools, with 145,521 pupils. By 1839, after close to a decade of operations, there were 1,581 national schools, claiming an enrollment 192,971 pupils. By the end of 1849 there were 4,321 schools with 480,000 pupils on the rolls. And by 1900 there were 8,684 schools claiming 770,622 as the "average number

of pupils on the rolls." The religious breakdown at the beginning of the new
century, according to the CNEI, was the following:

Roman Catholics: 559,520, or 75 percent
Church of Ireland: 88,675, or 11.9 percent
Presbyterians: 83,254, or 11.2 percent
Methodists: 8,600, or 1.1 percent
Other: 5,812, or 0.8 percent[58]

The initial Parliamentary grant was £30,000; by 1870 this had risen to close
to £400,000, and by 1900 to £1,145,721.[59] Because of poor attendance, especially during the harvest time and other occasions when parents needed their
children's labor, CNEI officials—like their American counterparts—often
complained of the need for some form of compulsory measures. Also in the
1890s, the British government introduced compulsory legislation for Ireland,
although the 1892 Act was limited to municipal boroughs and towns and
townships under commissioners.[60]

At the beginning of the twentieth century, then, the national school system dominated the Irish elementary education scene; it had become, in
Coolahan's words, "a landmark institution in the life of the Irish countryside, so much so that by 1900 every parish and many townlands could boast
of having their own national school." Some groups still remained outside,
such as the Christian Brothers (Catholic) and some orders of nuns, enrolling
around 150,000 pupils.[61] The total figures for (CNEI) enrollments are massive compared to the Indian effort (700,000 Irish pupils compared to about
20,000 Indians by 1900). But recall that by the turn of the century the BIA
almost totally dominated Indian schooling; it was only at the very end of our
period, in the 1920s, that large numbers of Indian children began to attend
state public schools. Despite the greater exposure of Irish children to the
school in the early nineteenth century, by the end of our period convergence
had taken place: the vast majority of Irish *and* Indian children were attending
some school.

The CNEI's loyalty to Britain is demonstrated decade after decade, over thousands of published pages in its yearly *Report*, all in English (although, during
the early decades of its existence, large numbers of its pupils and their parents
only spoke Irish). Each *Report* was directed to the lord lieutenant and through
him to Parliament. All members of the CNEI were employees of the British
state and were expected to extend its benefits to Irish children, thus assuring
their loyalty. "We accepted the commission with which we are charged," declared the board in 1836, "in the hope that it might enable us to pour oil on the

troubled waters of Ireland and to allay those dreadful dissensions which divide and distract her people." The board had "no sordid object to accomplish,
no factious purpose to serve, no bigoted passion to gratify." Rather it was

*endeavouring to give a new stamp to the rising generation of the country; to bring chil-
dren of all denominations together, from their infancy, in feelings of charity and goodwill, to make them regard each other, not as belonging to rival sects, but as subjects of
the same King, and fellows of the same redemption.*[62]

Two decades further on, in 1855, Patrick J. Keenan, then the inspector
and later the resident commissioner, noted how the system was *national* (his
emphasis). It prepared Irish children "to be good citizens, to be loyal to the
Sovereign, to be obedient to the laws," and it taught them "to nurture love
and devotion for our country"—implying Ireland within the larger Union.
Half a century later the board frankly conceded that although it enjoyed a
high degree of autonomy, "no fundamental Rule should be changed without
the sanction of the Lord Lieutenant."[63] After the "deplorable occurrences" at
Easter 1916, when a few thousand revolutionary nationalists staged a military
rising against British rule, the CNEI assured the government that it was doing
all possible "to prevent seditious teaching in its schools." Board inspectors
found that even in districts where disaffection might have been expected,
"distinctly loyal ideas have been encouraged by teachers." Staff who joined
the nationalist Irish Volunteers had been forced to leave that organization or
resign their positions. The *Report* noted the board's prohibition of the wearing of "seditious and political badges" by pupils and continued: "From the
very beginning . . . the Commissioners have forbidden national teachers to
take any part in political agitation and we are glad to be able to bear witness
to the general loyalty with which our injunctions have been observed by the
great majority of the teachers."[64]

Like the BIA, the CNEI also saw its goal as assimilation: not to enculturate
Irish children into the knowledge of Gaelic culture and language, or even into
the other varieties of Irish subcultures, Catholic and Protestant. The goals
were to overcome disloyalty, "backwardness," and religious divisions, and
to Anglicize and modernize these children (without giving them ideas above
their station); to make them, in Thomas A. O'Donoghue's words, "British-
minded and English-speaking."[65] For most of the period under review, the
CNEI curriculum, enforced by constant inspection, was almost devoid of
material relating to Irish life and culture; until late in the board's life, history of any kind could not even be taught in the schools. Initially all instruction was in English, even to masses of uncomprehending pupils. From 1879,
however, the Irish language could be taught, first as an extra subject and as a

foreign language; beginning in 1884 teachers could use the vernacular where necessary; then, in 1904, the board established a full bilingual curriculum in certain areas.[66] By the later decades of the nineteenth century, therefore, the CNEI curriculum did begin to reflect slightly more of Irish culture. Such changes were slow, grudging concessions to revivalist groups like the Gaelic League. As John Coolahan has written: "The system was conceived in support of the cultural assimilation and socialisation policy of post Union politics." Until later in the nineteenth century the CNEI curriculum, and the books it produced or sanctioned, could have been intended for any group of English-speaking children in the Empire—or even for young Indians in the United States. Indeed, in its early decades, the CNEI produced a series of schoolbooks that were so pedagogically successful yet so locally unspecific that they sold well throughout the British Empire.[67]

The CNEI even developed its own version of the half literacy and half vocational education curriculum in use at Indian schools: it first established a model farm, then a number of model agricultural schools, and some of its ordinary schools also had farms attached, the better to teach vocational skills and proper attitudes toward work.

From 1872 to 1899, as a result of yet another British government commission (the Royal Commission of Inquiry into Primary Education, the so-called Powis Commission of 1868–70), the Irish national schools began a "payment by results" scheme that lasted for three decades. According to this, a teacher augmented his or her salary according to the success of pupils in examinations administered by CNEI inspectors—a system that had no counterpart in BIA schools, although there too teachers were at the mercy of agent and other kinds of inspections.[68]

Always the butt of controversy, the CNEI nevertheless survived from 1831 until the early 1920s—close to a full century of contention, tragedy, rising national awareness, and even violent revolution in Ireland. There are a number of reasons for such longevity. Just as BIA teachers and missionaries worked under the umbrella of rising U.S. military and economic power, so the CNEI basked in the continued support of the greatest power on earth during the nineteenth century and into the twentieth. For all its essentially conservative goals (in a social sense of producing a loyal working class, educated to, but not beyond, a certain level) the board showed an impressive adaptive capacity, managing to ride out problems and satisfy most of the needs of the major churches—hardly unimpressive, considering the often bitter nature of Irish denominational rivalries. Much as it advocated and implemented an English language and Anglicizing program, the CNEI also balanced assimilative tenacity with grudging but effective flexibility. Around the time that the BIA was explicitly declaring an English-only policy in all its schools, the CNEI was slowly making more room for the Irish language in its schools. Irrespective of the board's Anglicizing mission and irrespective of its teaching through English—indeed partly because of these goals—increasing numbers of Irish parents sent their children to the CNEI schools and experienced no sense of treason or national betrayal in doing so. Like American Indians, Irish people displayed an unsentimental pragmatism when it came to the education of their children, and the CNEI tapped into this pragmatism.

Yet just as the decade of the 1920s was to mark the end of uncompromising assimilationism in the BIA, so that decade marks an endpoint for the Irish side of this study too. The Anglo-Irish War of 1919–21 and the Ireland Act of 1920 together produced the partition of the country. In 1922 the predominantly Catholic areas outside of northeastern Ulster became the Irish Free State, a dominion within the British Empire until becoming an independent republic and withdrawing from the Commonwealth in 1949. Six of the nine counties of Ulster, heavily planted by Protestants in the seventeenth century, became Northern Ireland, which gained a subordinate parliament of its own but remained within in the United Kingdom. By 1923 the Department of Education of the Irish Free State and the Ministry of Education in Northern Ireland had absorbed the activities of the National Board, and the CNEI passed out of existence.[69]

III

Obviously there were differences as well as similarities in how two states used mass elementary education as a political and cultural weapon, and it is the task of this book to further examine them and point to their significance. One obvious difference relates to the more systematic approach of the British government to Irish education from 1831. Despite treaty and legislative commitment, the BIA continued to work primarily through missionary societies until well after the middle of the nineteenth century. Further, the different approach to teaching religion requires greater comment later in the book: the CNEI's obsessive respect for the home religion of each student contrasts sharply with the BIA and missionary contempt for Indian "heathenism" in all its forms. The BIA, however, carefully respected the Christian beliefs of teachers and individual pupils and, like the CNEI, strove to avoid denominational favoritism.

Although we are dealing with elementary education on both continents, there were also differences in the kinds of school provided, and thus in the experiences of the children. Although large numbers of Indian children, like almost all pupils of the Irish national schools, attended local day schools, many Indians later attended boarding schools, some of them vast distances from home. Numbers of such Indians attended voluntarily; others were quite literally dragged from their homes. We must examine the extent to which all this changed the nature of assimilative experience. I argue that although boarding schools implied a far more disruptive removal of the tribal child from home and provided a more intense immersion in the new culture, their assimilative goal was not essentially different from that of the day schools. In all cases the schools sought not to enculturate but to *deculturate* first, and then absorb the children into the dominant culture or polity.

Another difference relates to what we today call "indigenization." Although Parliament and the lord lieutenant were the reigning authorities, from the beginning the national school system at every level was staffed by Irish men and women. Almost all the commissioners were Irish, as were the inspectors, teachers, and administrators. Indigenization of the CNEI was close to 100 percent, in other words. The situation was different—but not totally so—in BIA and mission schools, where the vast bulk of teaching staff, government officials, and Indian commissioners (Ely S. Parker excepted) were non-Indian during the period under review. As the century wore on, however, Indian indigenization increased: at many schools pupils were recruited as disciplinarians and "officers"; later many Indians served as teachers. By 1899, 45 percent of the BIA was Indian, but this figure later temporarily decreased.[70] So we can say that indigenization was far greater in the CNEI than the BIA and American missionary societies.

This leads to another major difference, a difference of "representation." In the *Annual Report of the Commissioner for Indian Affairs* (ARCIA 1850–1930) white educators employed a dichotomizing language of "civilized/savage," Christian/heathen, to represent Indian people. As late as 1920, for example, Indian commissioner Cato Sells characteristically denounced Indian tribal culture. "Nothing is plainer," he exclaimed, "than that the old order—or rather disorder—is rapidly changing . . . the old barbarous customs and degrading influences with their pagan dances, their superstitious medicine men, and all the feathered and painted heraldry of wild indolence are giving way to the sure beginnings of initiative, industry, and thrift, and to the desire of their children's education and social betterments." Here we have the classic dichotomies of "othering": disorder, barbarous, degrading, pagan, superstition, wild, indolence—all in explicit or implicit contrast to order, civilized, uplifting, Christian, scientific, disciplined, initiative, thrift, education.[71]

Little such ethnic "othering" exists in the annual *Report* of the CNEI. The effect here is of a "normal" educational venture among our own people, if a lower class. But of course! As almost all the members of the CNEI, from the commissioners down, were themselves Irish, so we would not expect them to brand their own people as "savage" and "uncivilized." Yet the "othering" in BIA reports and its lack in CNEI reports both flow from the same need—the need to transform a people, to Americanize or to Anglicize them. The Indians were so culturally (and for some Americans, so racially) different, that they appeared shockingly "other"; to denigrate their cultures in no way implied failure in American civilization. For the CNEI to have thus "othered" Irish people, however, would have been to associate itself with backwardness and disloyalty. BIA/missionary representations of traditional Indians were characterized by *contempt*, whereas CNEI representations of Irish people were to some extent a product of *shame*. The very fact that CNEI members were Irish made them less likely to highlight differences in British and Irish cultures or politics and, indeed, made them ashamed of such persisting differences. To do its job the BIA had to convince Congress of the terrible "otherness" of Indian life. To do its job the CNEI had to convince Parliament—and itself— that Irish people were almost "normal" and British and were well on the way to full Anglicization and loyalty. Thus two very different representations could spring from similar goals and needs, and from similar understanding of the nature of the problem. Although Irish and Indian cultural variants and historical experiences were strikingly different, and thus some educational policies and practices in both areas were different, the imperatives for BIA and CNEI educators were highly similar: each organization strove to absorb deviant peoples into a dominant culture and polity. To employ the metaphor of a journey, the assimilationist destination was similar for both groups, but most Indians had a longer road to travel than most of the Irish.

Whether Indian and Irish peoples and their children even began to travel that road, however, and how far along it they progressed—all depended on the responses of thousands of local communities to the new schooling systems. We now begin to examine those responses.

3. The Local Community and the School

"The drive to mass elementary education," writes David Vincent of nine-teenth-century efforts by European national states to school the people to literacy, "was founded on a dismissal of all that the home could teach the child." Left to its parents, authorities believed, "the growing boy or girl would gain the wrong lessons in conduct, and at best an undisciplined command of literacy."[1] The rejection of the "savage" or backward local community has already emerged in references to the "Praying towns" American colonials built to quarantine Indian converts and in the push for BIA boarding schools. To a lesser but still real degree it also characterized the CNEI campaign to Anglicize and modernize the Irish. Writing of women's religious orders, many of whom worked within the national school system, Mary Peckham Magray notes how nuns "not only assumed the right to supervise but also to control their charges. In many cases, this authority challenged that of their own parents."[2] Yet kin and local community were vital to the success of the campaigns, and in this chapter I compare and contrast the ways in which Indian and Irish adults responded to systems of mass elementary education aimed at them and their children.

I

Educator derision of local Indian kin was born of endless frustration, as children failed to attend, or fled the schools, or attended on whim—"irregular-ly." In 1895 Edward E. Reardon, teacher at the day school to the Sac and Fox Indians of Iowa, reported to the United States agent that although there were 120 children of school age under agency jurisdiction, only about 10 attended on average. There was "no organization, no regular hours for school work," he complained. "No discipline can be exercised, nor authority executed." The Indian children "come when they please, do about as they please, and go when they please." When corrected or reprimanded, "they answer you in the Indian language, drop their work, and disappear 'to return no more.'" As the school was held in the mission building, mothers and other adults wandered in and out of the classrooms, "interfere[d] with the work," spoke in the vernacular, and even took the children from class. "If we had a boarding school of our own," he bluntly noted, "these obnoxious intruders" could be kept away, away, and the mission workers would have "a clear field to accomplish good."[3]

Examples could be multiplied of such thinking. The same year J. M. Cataldo, S.J., superintendent of the St. Xavier's Mission Boarding School on the Crow reservation in Montana, expressed similar frustration, without quite descending to such invective against kin. "One of the great obstacles to the educational advancement of these children is the opposition of their parents, who are really ignorant of their duties towards their children," he complained. While the teachers tried to instill "a love of education, patriotism, industry, and good morals, the poor benighted parents act in a contrary direction, by trying to have them at home engaged in their old manner of living." Five years later, in 1900, the Indian commissioner himself was urging that some law be passed "which will take from ignorant parents the privilege of continuing their children in a state of savagery and will bring the children into contact with the highest types of civilization."[4]

Perhaps nowhere in these sources did the denigration of the Indian family reach lower depths than in the 1888 report of C. Robinson, superintendent of the Haskell Institute at Lawrence, Kansas. Even the best boarding school was inadequate to shield children from the old ways," he wrote, "because, sooner or later, students must leave these schools, and like the swine return to their wallowing, filth, and barbarism" (emphasis added). Robinson's own "great nation" had "to go on its knees to its wards," he fumed, and beg them to send an odd child to school." In line with his inflammatory language, Robinson recommended that the government take every Indian child between five and seven years, "send it to school and keep it there till 18 or 20 years of age, or until he or she had learned enough to become self-supporting, and then there will be a speedy end to complaints of returning to blankets and barbarism."[5]

Not all American officials or teachers wished to quarantine children from parents for a decade, but Robinson's approach was unusual only in its vehemence.[6] Many American agents and superintendents advocated compulsion and were only too willing to use force, in the form of agency police (themselves Indians) to remove children from their families—increasingly to remove them to distant boarding schools.[7] If tribal adults clung to savage ways, then the United States and its representatives claimed to stand in loco parentis—a development similar to that taking place during the nineteenth century in many Western nation-states. Such thinking was realized in the enactment of different forms of compulsory elementary education.[8]

II

Representatives of the CNEI rarely wrote with such bitterness or revulsion about "traditional" Irish family life. Yet inspectors and others continually lamented the unwillingness of parents to send their children to school, or their insistence on taking them away during harvest times or when extra hands were needed at home, and also advocated forms of compulsory education. Agents of bourgeois values as well as Anglicization, CNEI inspectors too could write in deeply patronizing language. If not quite "savage," many Irish families clearly lacked appropriate attitudes toward education and were certainly "other" in terms of class and backwardness, if not culture or race.[9]

In 1861, for example, inspector Dr. Newell claimed that "The great difficulty in teaching reading is to rid the pupils of the imperfect manner of speaking they have learned at home." A year later another inspector complained that the pronunciation of some children was "extremely vulgar."[10] And in 1892 inspector J. Brown unselfconsciously paraded his class prejudices to absolve the children and justify the mission of the CNEI. "There is a great deal of honest work done in our schools," he wrote. Yet too little attention had been given to improving the school environment so that it should impress the children "who, for ten years of their lives, and those the most impressionable, scarcely see anything more orderly or more tasteful in their own homes."[11]

Mr. Downing, inspector for the Galway district in the west of Ireland, admitted that the poverty of the people often prevented their sending all children to school. In 1884 he, like BIA educators, advocated separation of children from family as a last resort. Parents were often "influenced by dread lest the children when educated would rebel against the drudgery which is their pitiful portion" in future life, and were "almost without exception, wholly illiterate, and cannot, therefore, appreciate education." If all forms of compulsion failed, he believed, "even though it were merely through the inability of parents to provide clothing, the children should be removed from their unhappy homes to be properly reared."[12]

In the early twentieth century inspector J. P. Dalton waxed poetical about the potentially uplifting influence of well-run schools. They would send, he exclaimed in words a BIA employee might have written, "a sweetening influence, like a beam of warm sunlight, through the personal habits of the children who attend them, and thus help forward the cause of domestic refinement and of physical well-being among the rising generation." The poorer and more squalid the home surroundings, "the more indispensable becomes the duty of the school to concentrate every resource of precept and every agency of example on an untiring crusade against the unwholesome and degrading practices that have been established by usage." Therefore, a national school had to be "a good one if it is to succeed in refining the taste and raising the tone and habits of children nurtured in such surroundings." Also expressing this class prejudice, inspector Beatty informed his employers in 1903: "At present the teacher in this country fights single handed in the work of civilization and is only too glad, if his work is not daily undone in the homes."[13]

III

Vincent is probably right to claim that parents had little voice in what their children learned or how they were treated.[14] Still, at both the local level and on the larger national scene (especially in Ireland), it was good politics and good pedagogy to try to win over the supposedly unenlightened hearts and minds of the people. Most of his Irish colleagues and his counterparts in the BIA and missionary societies would have agreed with the observations of a writer in the CNEI's Report of 1870: "No system of education can possess the elements of permanent popularity and ultimate success which does not command the sympathy and co-operation of that part of the community for whom its benefits are more especially intended."[15]

The school was somewhat less alien to many Irish people than to Indians by the 1820s. So, despite the anti-local nature of the curriculum, and the small fees demanded of those who could pay them, large numbers of Irish parents immediately sent their children to the new national school "down the road." By the beginning of the twentieth century, as we have seen, the CNEI claimed that over 700,000 children were annually enrolled at its schools.

More gradually, many Indian parents and kin also began to respond positively to the school despite its assimilationist cultural agenda, even more alien to them than was the agenda of the national schools to the Irish. Compulsory laws were never fully effective during these decades, so the people did have a degree of choice. By 1930 the vast majority of Indian adults chose to send their children to school. From the BIA and missionary perspective, these parents were well along the road from darkness to light. From the perspective of the historian or anthropologist, tribal adults had once again pragmatically recognized the reality of the situation. Although they would continue to impart their own traditions and cultures to their children, only the school could offer the skills needed for personal, kin, and community survival in the new world growing up around them.[16]

By 1900 roughly half the BIA schools were day schools on the reservation, and kin could divide on whether to enroll children; some were forcibly removed by agency police even to such local schools. Yet increasingly large numbers of Indian parents had a far more difficult decision to make—one spared most Irish kin. Should Indian adults surrender children to white officials who would transport them hundreds or even thousands of miles away to mysterious boarding schools where, according to stories seeping back to the reservation, many of them suffered terribly and even died? Some Indian kin resisted, but by the 1920s thousands of young Indians had been removed from their homes and were attending distant boarding schools, often with the consent of their parents.

Despite this far more wrenching decision often facing tribal kin, then, by the end of the 1920s there was thus a high degree of *convergence* between Indian and Irish responses to the school—a major theme of this study. If the statistics of the BIA and the CNEI are even partly credible, a similar percentage (close to all school-age children) of Indian children and Irish children were attending all kinds of schools by the end of the period under review, despite the far greater cultural distance between Indians and white educators, on the one hand, and the Irish and their educators, on the other.

IV

Why did these target peoples generally come to accept not just the school but the whole concept of state-provided and state-controlled elementary education? Of course, there was nothing unusual in such responses. Historians of education have for decades been examining "the rise of the schooled society" in the West and later throughout the world. Many of the reasons for acceptance by Breton-speakers in France or Africans or others were shared by the Irish and American Indians. There were also similar reasons for resistance or rejection, such as the need for child labor in the home and on the farms. But why did Irish and Indian communities, specifically, converge in their gradual acceptance of schooling?

Because, goes the short answer, the CNEI and the BIA were often wrong-headed in their stereotypical representations of these peoples. Tribal Indians were not mindlessly "traditional" and culturally static, nor were the Irish peasantry afflicted by misty-eyed romantic anti-utilitarianism. Both Indians and rural (not to speak of small-town and urban) Irish were *highly pragmatic* in their response to all contacts with outside cultures, especially to new educational systems. Many of them did not see schooling in terms of loyalty/disloyalty to some sort of tribal or national ideal. For an increasing number of Indian kin, it was not "treason" to send their children to the white man's school.[17] Similarly in Ireland, parents who sent their children to the national school and deliberately stopped using the Irish language in front of them might simultaneously support radical nationalist or Home Rule agitation against the Union with Britain. Although the Gaelic League labeled the national schools as anti-Irish, and the nationalist and educator Patrick Pearse memorably called the system "the murder machine," the vast majority of Irish people came to see schooling as a practical matter, to be milked for personal and family advantage.[18]

Unfortunately the voices of ordinary Irish people (apart from CNEI staff) rarely appear in the official publications. In 1854, however, the yearly CNEI *Report* contained a letter, in quotation marks, purportedly from "the parents of the pupils and the friends" of the Athy Model School, a CNEI institution that taught pupils and also helped train prospective teachers. The letter was signed "on behalf of the parents, etc., present," by a number of local worthies, including the Presbyterian minister—hardly a group of lowly peasants. So there is little reason to doubt the enthusiasm of those parents who expressed their pleasure at attending a public examination. This was "conducted in a most efficient manner. . . . embraced almost all the branches of a complete English education, together with an outline of agricultural science." In general the answering "was highly creditable to the Teachers, while, on the part of the pupils, it manifested a degree of attention and proficiency truly gratifying." The parents also expressed appreciation for the fact that music was now a part of the curriculum, and hoped that the classics would soon become so too—an indication of the middle-class nature of the group. "These schools appear to be in a flourishing state," they believed, "and whether we take into account the increase in the classes, or the appearance of the pupils, or the attention and urbanity of the officers, or the instruction imparted, we have much reason to record our conviction of [the school's] efficiency."[19]

A quarter of a century later in 1880 inspector P. Connellan recounted an episode that confirmed for him the desire of even the poorest rural people for education. Many of the children in his district actually came to school barefoot in cold weather. Further, during "terribly severe snow storms" one of three sisters died. The following day, "although the mother was mourning over the dead body of her child," she sent the other two children to school for examination by Connellan. "Every thoughtful mind will draw conclusions from this fact," noted the inspector, but his own were explicit: this was an illustration "of the thirst of the Irish people for knowledge, and their gratitude for those who impart it." If such people were less poor, "laws *compelling* them to send their children to school would hardly be necessary"(emphasis in original).[20]

Autobiographical narrators add anecdotal but impressive support "from the bottom up" to such claims. Indeed, in about forty autobiographical accounts, the overwhelming impression is that, no matter how poor, Irish parents generally supported the national schools. Michael MacGowan and Peter O'Leary remembered how adults had begun to educate them in English and other subjects even before they began school, or alongside it. When Jeremiah Murphy's education was curtailed because of the 1916 Rising, his father insisted that he study at home. The older man prescribed a course of English grammar and vocabulary: "He examined me once a week, and after incurring his wrath a few times I soon found out it was much safer to study than neglect it." Conveying a sense of extended family responsibility, his uncle provided him with an arithmetic book and introduced him to equations and trigonometry.[21]

Tomás O'Crohan from the remote Blasket Islands off southwestern Ireland, left a telling vignette of how carefully his mother prepared him for the first day at school: "I thought she wouldn't leave a trace of skin or nose on me, she gave me such a scrubbing." A folklore informant remembered little except that she got "special new clothes, and a nice pinafore," and her mother brought her to school. Patrick Shea, son of a policeman in the Royal Irish Constabulary (RIC, the national police force under British rule), corroborated such accounts: "like many Irish parents of their generation," he wrote, his "were very ambitious for their children. Father had almost an obsession about security; for him the first test of a career was that it should be permanent and pensionable. . . . The penalty for failure was the workhouse." And in similar vein Sean O'Faolain, later one of Ireland's most famous writers, told how his mother "shared my father's ambition for her children. She expressed it in a phrase she dinned into us day after day: 'Rise in the World!'"[22]

Kin awareness of the need for children to learn English—and to read and write it—reverberates through the literature in both areas. Even CNEI inspectors sympathetic to the teaching of Irish noted how parents themselves often opposed the use of the old language in the schools. Ex-pupils remembered such attitudes in their own lives. On the eve of the Great Famine in the 1840s, close to three and a half million (out of eight and a half million) spoke Irish, mostly in the northwest, west, and southwest of the country. By 1851 that number had dropped to just over one and a half million, about 23 percent of the dramatically reduced population. Perhaps a third of a million of the latter figure were monoglot.[23] In the 1850s Patrick J. Keenan, then head inspector, acknowledged that through its curriculum and English-only policy, "the National Board is every year diminishing this number [of Irish-speakers]." Although he strongly advocated mastery of English as the final goal, he also spoke warmly of Irish and of the advantages of bilingualism. Keenan, then, was no simple-minded opponent of Irish. Yet, like colleagues before and after him, he pointed to the increasingly apparent fact that even on the remote Western islands, the people themselves were giving up the old language. In 1856 Keenan claimed that one Irish-speaking teacher not only punished pupils who spoke that language, but he also "instituted a sort of police among the parents, to see that in their intercourse with one another, the children speak nothing but English at home. The parents are so eager for the English, they exhibit no reluctance to inform the master of every detectable breach of the school law." Keenan wrote of how their "strong passion" for education could be traced to "the desire to speak English." Then he launched into an explanation that could have been applied to many Indian peoples too. Whenever a stranger visited the remote Atlantic islands the peasants there see

that prosperity has its peculiar tongue as well as its fine coat . . . that [fishermen and others] count [money] out in English; and if they ever cross over to the [Irish] mainland for the "law," as they call any legal process, they see that the solemn words of judgment have to come to them second-hand through the offices of an interpreter. Again, English is spoken by the landlord, by the stray official who visits them, by sailors . . . and by the schoolmaster himself; and whilst they may love [the Irish language] . . . they see that obscurity and poverty distinguish their lot from the English-speaking population.

Thus, he claimed, to these people "the key-stone of fortune is the power of speaking English, and to possess that power" there was "a burning longing in their breast that never varies, never moderates." It was, wrote Keenan perceptively, "the utilitarian, not the abstract idea of education" that motivated them, and "the knowledge for which they thirst for in school is, therefore, confined to a speaking use of English." Keenan talked to a Tory Island man, who himself spoke English well but who was ashamed of his companions who spoke only Irish: "'they stood like dumbies [sic]; the cattle got on as well as them.'"[24]

Thirty years later CNEI inspector Downing concurred. This inspector also claimed—validly, according to the work of later historians—that the people themselves, along with the Catholic Church, had turned against Irish even *before* the establishment of the national schools. Noting that his own prejudices "were and are in favor of the vernacular," Downing pointed out that the pupils in an Irish-speaking area did not speak Irish in class, nor did even Irish-speaking teachers use the language. "The parents in these localities evince no desire to have Irish taught [,] quite the contrary." It was noteworthy, he believed, "that in the private adventure schools [hedge schools] . . . whilst the people had all in their own hands, no Irish was taught or tolerated." Of course such views are never innocent, and the inspectors served masters whose goal was the Anglicization of the country. Yet Downing, Keenan, and other inspectors publicly spoke out for Irish, or at least for bilingualism. Downing, in particular, lamented the lack of parental interest. "Whenever I saw any desire amongst the people for the teaching of Irish to their children," he concluded, "I gave the movement every encouragement."[25]

In 1906, as the National Board had begun to allow a program of bilingual teaching in Irish-speaking areas, inspector Dr. J. B. Skeffington, who also appeared sympathetic to the vernacular, similarly claimed that "especially in the more Irish parts, the parents are frequently opposed to its being taught." Ironically, it was taught on occasion "*against* the wishes of the parents*," some of whom, although they knew Irish, "do *not* speak it to their children" (emphases in original). The same year inspector Dalton perceptively noted the process taking place. The grandparents, he believed, generally spoke Irish and that alone, "fluently at command." The parents were "more or less at home in either language," but significantly, "unless when in conversation with their elders, will learn to use English." The children understood the language, but "with less and less comprehension," and "will but rarely use an Irish phrase themselves, and then only when they cannot help it." He also pointed to a fatalism in many people: by then, few wanted the bilingual system, and each was resigned to the demise of Irish—"as if its extinction were the fulfillment of an inevitable doom."[26]

Dalton thus outlined a sequence in language loss that, according to David Crystal, seems to be universal. First, immense pressures build against the old language, both "top down," from authorities and dominant groups, and "bottom up," from the people themselves. Second, there is a period of temporary bilingualism. And third, as in Dalton's account, the younger generation becomes more proficient in the new language, and ceases to use the old. The process, Crystal continues, in a broader generalization that certainly applies to both Irish and many Indian tribal situations, "is often accompanied by a feeling of shame about using the old language, on the part of the parents and the children," with the parents using it less and less to the children. Soon, writes Crystal, employing a similar term to Dalton's, bilingualism "gives way to the threat of *extinction* of the old language." Although British imperialism was the context, what happened in Ireland, then, was less "language murder" than a form of "language suicide."[27]

These views are given further weight by narrator recall. Michael MacGowan remembered the characteristically pragmatic approach of his parents, as "utilitarian" as those described by inspector Keenan and other CNEI employees. "Older people had been going to and from Scotland [for seasonal work] for years," MacGowan recalled, "and they were always complaining that they were looked down on because they had neither education nor English. So I was sent to school." A number of narrators also noted how Irish-speaking parents spoke English to the children. One folklore informant noted that "they did what they could to see that we wouldn't know [Irish]." Another informant claimed that in his district around 1880 parents discouraged the speaking of Irish, for "they reckoned that it was just "*a slave's gibberish and a useless load*" (emphasis added). He had been "bitterly blamed" for attempting to speak it at home, and claimed that teachers and national school managers regarded speaking the vernacular as "downright bad manners and quite vulgar."[28]

Not all Irish adults turned against the old language. By 1900, however, despite heroic efforts by revival groups such as the Gaelic League, there were only a few hundred thousand Irish-speakers left—about one tenth of the 1845 pre-Famine number—themselves an ever-diminishing minority. Perhaps 75,000 national school pupils spoke the language.[29] A major motivation of many Irish people for supporting the national schools, then, was that their children should learn English—to speak, read, and write the language—and English alone. I suspect that by 1900 there were few parents, no matter how wedded to the old language and culture, who wanted their children to remain monoglot Irish speakers. Should they migrate to Dublin, or emigrate to Britain or its empire, or the United States, the need for English would be even greater than in local areas.[30]

Not all of this broad interest in education benefited the National Board—some Catholic children attended Christian Bothers schools or convents not under the authority of the CNEI. Also, Irish parents, like Indians, could be highly selective and ambivalent in their approach to schools, often pulling out their children to work on the farm or for other "backward" reasons. Nevertheless, by the beginning of the twentieth century or earlier, the vast majority of Irish parents had been won over to the national schools, despite their often antinationalist policies and curriculum. Like national systems in other parts of Europe and the United States, the CNEI made little effort to listen to the voice of the people—mass education was very much imposed from above. Yet its impressive growth was in part a result of the selective interest of those for whom it was often patronizingly intended.

V

When we ask why Indian kin grew to accept white schools, we come to similar conclusions. Many tribal adults—we can never know the exact numbers or percentages—sent their children to school to learn the new language along with other aspects of white civilization that appeared vital for personal and community survival in a new and alarmingly changing world. Indian commissioners and others involved in the educational campaign, including teachers at many BIA and missionary schools, openly admitted the difficulties they faced in attempting to entice tribal adults to enroll their children. Yet white American educators, like their CNEI counterparts, were only too happy to report and offer explanations for what they saw as growing Indian enlightenment. In 1880, for example, the commissioner strongly denied that Indian children were being taken against their will to Hampton Institute in Virginia and Carlisle School in Pennsylvania. On the contrary, he countered, "Indian parents have urged upon the Bureau more children than it was ready to receive." Despite the fact that such children faced journeys of hundreds or even thousands of miles away from their tribal areas, "the [BIA] has repeatedly been obliged to deny the earnest request of parents that their children might be educated in the East." If funding sufficed, he claimed, the bureau could immediately double attendance at both schools.[31]

What better way to demonstrate the truth of such claims, and the motivations of "progressive" Indians, than to quote from the letters of kinfolk. "Learn all you can; it will be for your own benefit," wrote an Indian mother to her child at Hampton. A father hoped that some of the pupils would become teachers so that "when they come back they can teach the boys and girls"—an Indian encouraging tribal children to become cultural brokers. "I am going to write you a letter again," declared a father to his son. "I want you to write letters to me often. I am glad that you are trying to learn. Don't run away from school. It will be your own good if you learn. Do all the work they tell you to do and learn to be a carpenter and a blacksmith. I would like to see how the Indian boys learn." Then, broadening the picture from his own desires to those of his people, the man pointed out that the fathers of other boys "would like to go down and see them. Then they would come back and tell other Indians. Then they would like to send all their children." The unnamed correspondent ended with the signal words: "Learn to speak English; don't be ashamed to talk it."[32]

As in the case of client voices occasionally quoted by the CNEI, it is difficult to know how to credit such earnest and poignant correspondence. However, in her study of the Flandreau and Haskell boarding schools, Brenda J. Child, an Ojibwe, has discovered original copies of many such letters in BIA archives, similar in tone and detail to those quoted here. Her powerful argument is that the boarding schools became family concerns, generating a constant three-sided correspondence between children, parents, and authorities. Indian people sometimes visited the schools. This could lead to teacher frustration; yet authorities encouraged such visits to impress adults with the wonders of American civilization.[33] Whether or not they visited the schools, many Indian parents were obviously impressed.

Ex-pupils sometimes recalled words of encouragement from tribal adults who insisted that children needed to learn the new way to survive. Francis La Flesche attended a Presbyterian missionary school in Nebraska in the 1860s, and his part-Omaha father's demanding words emphasized the importance of all learning. That the boy might "profit from the teachings of your own people and that of the white race, and that you might avoid the misery that accompanies ignorance . . . I placed you in the house of [the missionaries] who are said to be wise and to have in their books the utterances of great and learned men. . . . Am I to be disappointed?" These words do not imply total rejection of Omaha ways, merely the need to supplement traditional learning with the new and obviously powerful knowledge, especially book knowledge. Similarly, Thomas Alford remembered how Shawnee chiefs sent him and another boy to school. "They told us of their desire that we should learn the white man's wisdom. How to read in books, how to understand all that was written and spoken to and about our people and the government." Later the chiefs specifically referred to treaties and to legal problems facing the people, and of the importance of knowing how to deal with such issues. Their goals for the younger Shawnee were also highly, even cynically utilitarian: use schooling to the advantage of the people.[34]

Two Choctaw girls recalled how their mother hoped that "we would have some educational advantages [at the Chilocco School] that we could no longer have at home." The older woman was not impressed at the results, they wryly admitted. "'I thought I sent you kids up there to be educated, get civilized,'" she complained when the girls came home singing Indian songs and doing Indian dances (permitted late in the period under review). Although from a modern perspective this sounds like a treasonous rejection of Native cultural values, it appeared quite different from the Indian mother's point of view: Why send children far away to school if they only learned what could be had at home?[35]

Many scholars emphasize both resistance to and manipulation of the BIA and missionary school, yet these scholars also strongly concur with the vignettes presented above. A major theme of Clyde Ellis's study of the Rainy Mountain Boarding School in Oklahoma, for example, is the desire of Kiowa adults for the education of their children at what became "their" school. Scholars do not see Native peoples as monolithic or as passively surrendering to the power of white America. Indians, like the Irish, responded in highly diverse and creative ways to the challenge of the new. Tribal individuals and subgroups selected out aspects of white civilization that they found useful, and understood schooling in terms of their own clan and group needs, rather than fully accepting the BIA or missionary rationales.[36]

Apart from long-term reasons for sending children to school, Indian kin also responded to more immediate needs. In Ireland local day schools did not have kitchens, but Indian boarding schools provided food and clothing for children of tribal people who sometimes lived on the edge of physical survival. Significantly, Helen Sekaquaptewa remembered how the year she was home from boarding school, she and her Hopi family "never did have enough food." Cyrus Beede, agent to the Osages of Oklahoma, admitted in 1877 that it had "been found difficult to create sufficient interest in education alone to induce many parents to part with their children for any considerable length of time." Nevertheless, "partly on account of clothing furnished, and partly to insure a better supply and quality of food . . . the tribe has responded to my demand for children to about [equal] the capacity of our school building." And twenty years later A. H. Viets, superintendent of the Santa Fe Indian Industrial School, trenchantly noted that "Indian parents demand three things of the school, and three things only . . . (1) My boy must be fed; (2) he must be well clothed; (3) He must not be punished."[37]

Indeed, according to Scott Riney, by the 1920s boarding schools had become "welfare providers of the last resort" for Indian peoples. The multitribal Rapid City Boarding School in South Dakota "remained overcrowded not because its superintendent wanted to put every last Indian child on the road to assimilation, but because Indian parents and reservation officials enrolled children who could not be fed, clothed, and housed anywhere else." In addition, Rapid City and other schools began to provide Indian people with employment at many levels from clerical to manual to teaching positions. This development would not have been obvious early in the period under review, but became more important later. When the Rapid City school closed in 1933, it also deprived Indians in the area of employment resources, and the same was true for other schools around the nation.[38]

Therefore, notwithstanding the role of Indian schools in an essentially imperialistic campaign of cultural conquest, Indian peoples quickly came to see their uses. As much as they could within an obviously unequal power relationship, Indian individuals and groups, like the Irish, made their peace with this intrusive educational institution and began to exploit it for all it was worth.

VI

Thus a complex and strongly ambivalent quality characterizes community responses in BIA, missionary, and CNEI reports and from autobiographical narrators. Irish and Indian kin gradually came to accept the need for schooling—but not uniformly enough or wholeheartedly enough for authorities. Perhaps the term "irregular attendance" best sums up the problem, from official perspectives, on both continents. Local communities simultaneously accepted, manipulated, and resisted the best efforts of educators to mold them into literate, loyal, obedient subjects or citizens.

Authorities in both areas struggled to explain family influences on the frustrating half-success implied by irregular attendance. At times, as we saw, they resorted to simplistic denigration of Indian traditions and Irish peasant ways to explain the problems. Some observers perceptively avoided such stereotyping, however. CNEI inspectors were often acutely aware of the terrible burdens of poverty that stymied even parents who would otherwise have sent children to school. Writing in 1851, inspector McCreedy noted that only 54 percent of those on the rolls attended regularly, and he then launched into a long attempt to explain this "monster evil of our present position." He blamed, as would others of his colleagues, "the extreme poverty of the great masses of our people, which makes them dead to everything but the most urgent causes of their physical nature. . . . the 'flesh' wages a deadly warfare against the 'spirit', and soon triumphs over it, quelling and stifling, if it do not extinguish, all the nobler desires of their natures." The people should not be blamed for this, or for grasping at charity. "It is 'their poverty and not their will consents' to this woful [sic] intellectual destitution of their children," whose terrible deprivation and exploitation as cheap labor he proceeded to describe.

McCreedy then hit on a further aspect of the problem—the inclination of many less-than-destitute parents to withdraw children for annual farm labor or work in the home. They were interested in only "what admits of the most direct, palpable, and practical applications in what may be called their work-day world." They might need "a little reading" to use their favorite Almanac or shop advertisements, and enough writing to sign their names or draw up a bill or promissory note, or to write to friends in America. They of course needed some arithmetic to conduct business. Therefore they might sacrifice a little to give their children some schooling, as long as there was no harvesting or other work to be done. But these people had no notion whatsoever "of the intrinsic worth of education, *as such*" (emphasis in original). So they allowed their children to school until they had achieved a basic instruction in "the three arts," but no more, and they regarded any attempt by the teacher to stimulate interest in learning as "mere idle display." The children of such parents technically attended school, he believed, but in an irregular manner between stints of field labor, and hopelessly failed to reach appropriate levels.[39]

Repeatedly CNEI inspectors offer such explanations, especially poverty— thus partly exculpating the parents for poor attendance of their children. The homes of many poorer pupils, wrote inspector Keenan in the decade after the Famine, were "filthy and wretched," which was "the effect of poverty and misfortune, wherein the struggle is to defeat starvation and to secure an existence." Half a century later in 1892 inspector J. O'Riordan noted how the people lived on tiny plots "of very mediocre land." The men often had to migrate to England for work, sending back money and returning near Christmas. Those who did attend school came "thinly clad, and one marvels how it is that they escape colds and other serious ailments during the winter season." Their "thin, pale faces were evidence of the lack of nourishing food—hardly ideal circumstances for learning." O'Riordan was nevertheless impressed with their "natural sharpness and adroitness of intellect," which may have been the result of the struggle for existence they experienced; the teachers too were active and energetic. Thus the circumstances were anything but favorable for schooling, and lack of enthusiasm was not always the fault of the people themselves.[40]

Although it was obviously in the interests of CNEI personnel to report full schools, some inspectors insightfully warned *against* imposing compulsory education on people too poor to obey such a law. Inspector Eardely highlighted a problem growing out of the poverty of the people: the prevalence of infections such as measles, scarlatina, and diphtheria. Some of the recent outbreaks had been so virulent as to cause deaths in his district and to necessitate the temporary closing of schools. Further, in an area inhabited by small farmers, the work demanded all family hands, leaving only the infants unemployed. "I do not see," he wrote with some sympathy for the predicament of the people, "how legislation could remedy such a state of things which is one of absolute necessity." From everything he had observed, the state of attendance was "nearly as regular as the circumstances of the country will admit." There were, he conceded, some "indifferent parents" (as well as some children with a complete aversion to school), but obviously he felt that it was poverty rather than obstinacy that kept many children at home, or kept them from continual attendance.[41]

Autobiographical narrators sometimes corroborated such official accounts. Peig Sayers was the author of a famous autobiography of life on the Blasket Islands, off southwestern Ireland, in the late nineteenth century. She remembered bitterly how, just when she was enjoying school, her parents took her out and put her into domestic service. Dan Breen, later leader in the Anglo-Irish War, left school at fourteen: "I had to go out and earn my bread." A folklore informant remembered how his father took him out for seasonal fieldwork. "I used to go in the winter after that," he recalled, "but when the work 'ud [would] begin the Spring I was to stay at home again." There were plenty like himself, he believed, and many went on to seasonal work in England. Another informant told her interviewer how in the old days the people "did not take the matter of sending their children to school too seriously. So long as they knew enough to be able to catch the sprong [?] and the shovel many of the parents were quite satisfied . . . they believed that too much education will spoil a farmer." Yet she also suggested adult ambivalence: once children actually attended school, the parents insisted on high standards. If they were not raised to a more advanced class each year, parents "kicked up rows with the teachers and leathered the children for their stupidity." This informant's father withdrew her at age twelve. When the teacher objected, asking what use a child that age would be around the house, the father replied that "she would be all right to blow the fire while her mother was feeding the pigs."[42]

Another folklore informant humorously remembered the same problem of irregularity. A boy in the locality attended school for only a single day: "The poor man wouldn't know an 'A' if 'twas as big as his head." Once the national schools came into the area, and for a long time after this, many pupils only attended now and then, some going perhaps three days a week. During the winter months when there was no work on the farm, the attendance would rise. Some of the pupils would be grown men, "as big as the master, and they having [writing] slates in their hands." Apparently they paid great attention—until the weather changed, and they were off out working again.[43]

Most Irish people wanted education for their children, then, but of a limited duration, and if it did not interfere too much with work on the farm. For the very poor, irrespective of desire, the brutal necessities of life came first. And to be fair to CNEI inspectors, they sometimes saw past stereotypes of benighted people to the real difficulties many of them faced.

VII

By the 1920s it is likely that most Indian kin were pleased that most of their children were at school. Yet the BIA and its missionary allies also confronted irregular attendance, not to speak of non-attendance. More so than in the Irish case, American school authorities were plagued by the problem of "runaways"—children who fled the schools, sometimes to the frustration of Indian parents too. In this chapter, however, I focus on the adult side of the issue; later I take up the issue of pupil response and resistance.

In words very similar to those of CNEI inspectors, the teacher at a Catholic mission school in Sault Ste. Marie reported in 1852 that during winter the school had "been pretty carefully attended." In summer, however, activities such as haymaking and fishing were a distraction for Indian boys and their relatives; the fishing habits of the families especially scattered the children, moving them away from the influence of school. The teacher did not doubt pupil capacity, but their "want of constancy." How could things be otherwise, he wondered, "when parents seem for the most part careless themselves whether their children be educated or not." Similarly, when semi-sedentary Omaha people went off on their annual buffalo hunt in the 1860s, pupils who stayed at school were so disturbed that the work suffered; indeed, some temporarily fled the school to follow the hunt.[44]

Half a century later the superintendent of the Navajo agency reported parental refusal to surrender *all* school-age children, and to pick the students according to—from BIA perspective—mundane family needs. "It is unfortunate that so few parents can be induced to bring in the girls," he complained—suggesting sometimes different parental treatment of the sexes—because parents marry them off early "for a few sheep or ponies," rather than waste schooling on them. This man also claimed that there was a tendency to bring in the physically weaker children, while keeping the strong ones at home to work. The school staff had tried to explain that the weaker needed some outdoor work and the stronger some indoor schooling, and apparently the situation was now improving.[45]

In the same decade William B. Dew, superintendent of the Fort Lapwai School in Idaho, spoke very positively—if in language characteristic of the period—about the Nez Perce Indians of that Far Northwest region. "Racially speaking" they had "far the brightest mind" he had found among the Indians. This people had advanced as much in two years as the average tribe in three, "and when they can be held in school are thoroly amenable to discipline." A problem existed, he wrote, conveying a similar sense of "progress but not enough," as the Irish officials. "There seems to exist an innate objection to regular attendance." Because they were citizens, there was no existing law or authority sufficient to force attendance. "Children were enrolled in late April, some of them from the best elements of the tribe . . . [but] there is always some reason for taking them home again." The parents or near relatives, he claimed, "continually affected severe maladies, requiring that the children return [and so] the work of course suffered."[46]

Other BIA officials became especially upset when basically cooperative Indians appeared to be manipulating the schools, or when they demonstrated inadequate gratitude for the gift provided. William S. Kelly, superintendent of the Indian Industrial and Training School at Sitka, Alaska, was both complimentary and scathing in his comments. Some Indians, he wrote in 1887, were slowly "beginning to feel that it is a privilege to be permitted to place their children in schools for gratuitous care and instruction." However there were other "benighted parents who think *they* ought to be paid for giving their children a chance to be taught the white man's way of living and learning." The "crude ideas of such Indians were so vague," he fumed, "that *they think they are doing us a great favor and placing us under lasting obligations by giving us a child to support and educate*" (emphasis added). Obviously, complex mutual manipulations were taking place. A compulsory education law, according to superintendent Kelly, was "the only salvation for thousands of helpless heathen children in Alaska, who in their primitive state are as the beasts of the forest."[47] A similar petulance characterized the comment by the Indian commissioner a few years later in 1890, one reminiscent of an Irish informant's claims that parents casually withdrew children yet simultaneously expected the schools to achieve great things for them. A major hindrance to Indian education, claimed Commissioner Morgan, was "the failure of parents and children alike to appreciate the nature and importance of education." They "either ignore the school entirely or expect it to accomplish miracles in a brief period!" Yet he felt that both parents and children were becoming more interested in schooling.[48]

Although Navajo parents promised at the end of one term to return their children for the new session, not all did, complained the school superintendent in 1901—at least not promptly enough. They also thought that "they are conferring a great favor upon the whites by bringing their children to school, and that they ought to be compensated for this favor." The generosity of the government had been explained many times, yet "they still do not properly appreciate the efforts made in their behalf." Again, a complicated picture emerges: there had been improvement—a higher percentage of pupils than the previous year—yet the work was "very trying," and "the prospect of making valuable citizens [was] not very brilliant." The writer also noted the prevalence of sickness at the school, and that six children had died there during the year. However, he made no attempt to draw conclusions from this relating to Navajo attitudes, either about the safety of their children—or about their fear of chindi, the dangerous "ghosts" that might persist about the place in which people died.[49]

Some authorities, like their CNEI counterparts, were less judgmental. An agent perceptively recorded the valid objections of Sac and Fox people. They were not, as a rule, averse to schooling, but they objected "to having their children taken away from them while they are so young and sent 'away off' to [boarding] school before they are able to properly take care of themselves." Rather than berate savagery, he accepted that their objection was "surely prompted by parental love," and he blamed those who turned local schools into veritable "kidnapping institutions" for more distant schools. If local schools respected parental wishes, they could function better and provide students for the more distant schools without aggravating the people.[50]

VIII

Other white observers and Indian narrators described just how divisive schooling could become for Indian families and communities. His Dakota father and more traditional grandmother differed over whether the young Charles Eastman should attend a white school. Similarly, Irene Stewart recalled how her Navajo father and grandmother contested one another on the same issue. And for three years the argument over whether Max Henley should attend school swung back and forth between his traditional Navajo grandmother and his uncle who wanted him to learn English, get a job, and earn money. He himself wanted to begin school, and finally he did.[51]

White observers also commented on such divisions. In 1878, for example, Omaha agent Jacob Vore made the oft-repeated distinction between "progressives" and their opponents. Not unusually, power-hungry "chiefs" were depicted as being the latter, although Joseph La Flesch, who so strongly recommended schooling to his son Francis in the 1860s, had then been an Omaha "chief." Vore believed that "the more intelligent" sought "their general advancement towards civilization, by abandonment of their tribal relations and aboriginal customs." The chiefs, however, were "reluctant to yield their positions and influence over their followers, and are, consequently, an obstacle to the advancement of the tribe in civilized customs." Despite such opposition, the people had been supporting the schools well the previous year, encouraging their children to learn English, even visiting the school and expressing satisfaction at their recitations in the new language. Half a decade later the agent at the Fort Apache School made a similar complaint, noting that "The Indians who are most influential are generally opposed to the education of their children."[52]

In the late nineteenth and early twentieth centuries such divisions reached crisis proportions among the Hopis of Oraibi pueblo, Arizona, a people by then renowned for their peaceful ways, who split into groups called Friendlies and Hostiles, on education, among other issues. The conflict attracted widespread attention ("so much has been said in the public press"). Some of the Hostiles actually went to jail rather than enroll their children at the new schools. Claiming in 1906 that "a factional warfare" had existed among Hopis for a number of years, the commissioner perceptively claimed that its origins "grew wholly out of internal political dissensions," and that the Friendly group attempted to manipulate white Americans. To prevent the spread "of the spirit of defiance," the commissioner felt the government might soon have to show "its strong hand." He himself had tried to convince one of the Hostile chiefs of the importance of civilization, especially of "the little day school at the foot of the mesa," and—again—of "how much his people really owed the Government." Such persuasion was to no avail. "With a sneer," the chief threw it all back in the commissioner's face, claiming that "their fathers had warned them not to let their children go to school and learn white ways." Finally the official declared that "even their parents had no right to deprive the young people of what was a practical necessity in their lives." The commissioner got little more satisfaction from the Friendly chief, who accused him of being ignorant of affairs in Hopiland. Then this man laughed in the face of the official representative of the U.S. government to the tribes.[53]

The two factions actually came into physical conflict a short time later, although all agreed not to use weapons. Yet in the same annual report the Hopi school superintendent claimed that, with one exception, the schools were actually "quite satisfactory." The following year the commissioner reported how schools at Oraibi had reopened, and that the people had a choice of whether to send their children to day school or boarding school. He ordered that the ringleaders and Hostile offenders be sent to jail for periods of hard labor. Some leaders were publicly deposed, and regular troops were sent temporarily to Oraibi to preserve order. The commissioner tried not to impose "unnecessary hardship" even upon the Hostiles, who were, after all, "poor, benighted creatures." In a classic expression of the century-long campaign of assimilation, the commissioner declared: "Indians must conduct themselves reasonably like white people, or be treated like white people are treated who are forever quarreling and fighting among themselves." It was, he ruefully concluded, a "whole complicated business."[54]

Despite the marked ambivalence of many Irish families to schooling, there is little evidence of the kind of factional community divisions that erupted in Indian societies. Perhaps this was because such tribal societies were more isolated, culturally distant from the educators, and more self-contained than local Irish communities. Indians too would later become less divided on these issues. Because of earlier hedge and missionary schooling, Irish parents more quickly saw the school as a method of advancing their children into somewhat higher levels of society, through teaching or civil service jobs—or through emigration. Also, few Irish parents faced the removal of young children to distant boarding schools.

IX

Why did individual Indian and Irish boys and girls begin school? There was plenty of generalizing by BIA and CNEI officials, some perceptive, some stereotypical—but, not surprisingly, little attempt to seek the views of those most directly on the receiving ends of the educational campaigns. To suggest answers I draw upon autobiography and reminiscences: about one hundred Indian accounts, but only about forty Irish accounts, not enough to claim as representative, but enough to offer the historian some further insight into this issue.

In the Irish case the question is more simply answered. Both CNEI literature and autobiographical accounts agree that Irish children had little choice in the matter: if their parents were uninterested in education, they might avoid school; if sent there, they might "mitch" (play truant) or resist. If parents wanted them to get an education, however, they almost certainly went to school. Peig Sayers of the Blasket Islands remembered being allowed to choose *when* to begin, as a mere four-year-old, but from her account there is little doubt that sooner or later she would have been sent.[55] Despite parents' somewhat cavalier attitudes to regular attendance, by late in the period under review elementary education had become the expected reality of modern life for the Irish child, urban or rural.

By the early twentieth century this was true for most Indian peoples too, but the development of such an attitude was somewhat slower. In my earlier research I worked out a rough statistical breakdown on school enrollment for Indian autobiographical narrators. Of about one hundred accounts, sixty-nine gave indications of why they began schools:

Compelled by "authorities" (agents and tribal police):   17
Sent by tribal members (no immediate BIA compulsion):   33
Overlapping influences: 9
Personal choice: 10
Total number supplying information (of 102 narrators):   69

We cannot validly extrapolate such figures to tens of thousands of Indian children over a century of schooling campaigns. Indeed I suspect that on this issue too by 1930 there was far greater convergence between Irish and Indian experiences: fewer and fewer Indian children were being allowed real choice. Yet the figures may offer evidence for the argument made by white observers—often derisively—that Indian children sometimes enjoyed a measure of freedom of choice.[56]

Almost one third of Indian narrators giving information remembered how white authorities allowed them little choice in the matter. After the "last Indian war," the Geronimo campaign of 1886, U.S. Army officers selected out Jim Kaywaykla and other young Apaches to attend the Carlisle Indian School. Another Apache, Jason Betzinez, similarly remembered how Captain Pratt "volunteered" him for Carlisle although he was at that time twenty-seven years old. These instances took place before compulsory schooling legislation of the 1890s. Fred Kabotie's family, of the Hostile Hopi faction, opposed schooling, but he and other such children were rounded up by tribal police. Helen Sekaquaptewa, another Hopi from a Hostile family, vividly described how her parents tried to hide her from the agency police—actually Navajos, which added insult to injury. They finally found her and, after a ritual protest by her mother, brought her to school, which she greatly enjoyed.[57] Accounts by government teachers and agents on the Hopi reservation help bolster the credibility of these accounts by ex-pupils. Boarding school superintendent C. E. Burton described how he used agency police to take pupils "under guard" to school—the police even resorted to drawing their guns in the face of Hopi protest. Indians from other tribes also faced coercion. Perhaps to exorcise such bitter memories, at the fifty-eighth anniversary of the Wahpeton Indian School in 1958, the pageant included re-enactment scenes of the agent and police taking children to school.[58]

Many autobiographical accounts (about half, in my sample) lend weight to claims by white officials that, for varied reasons, Indian kin insisted upon schooling. Charles Eastman recounted a harrowing episode from the 1870s, when a young Dakota girl went screaming to her parents, begging them not to leave her. They, and not the teacher, led her back to school. Asa Daklugie, an Apache, remembered how Geronimo insisted that some of the boys and girls should attend school to learn the ways of the whites for the good of the people. Much to his disgust, Daklugie was one of those chosen. According to Jim Whitewolf, in 1891 a Kiowa Apache chief asked the agent that those parents who did not send their children to school should be deprived of government-supplied rations. The Hidatsa grandfather of Edward Goodbird expressed a truth being accepted then by many tribal peoples: "It is their books that make the white men strong."[59]

About one tenth of my Indian sample, unlike any of the Irish narrators whose accounts I read, enjoyed a degree of choice on whether or not to enroll. Some voluntarily began school, either with or without parental consent. To avoid being caught by the agency police, Don Talayesva did so. In his vivid and funny account the Hopi—like other "volunteers"—conveys a sense of deep childhood curiosity about the new institution, the new clothes, and a sense of deep aversion to the demanding tribal work ethic. Individual Navajos also recalled heading for school to get away from family demands. Luther Standing Bear, a Lakota Sioux, was also tempted by curiosity—a curiosity deliberately stimulated by special recruiting groups sent west by schools such as Carlisle. These groups consisted of teachers and uniformed Indian pupils, who attempted to convince both parents and peers of the worth of white education. Standing Bear was convinced, and he would later return to the reservation as a recruiter. He also believed that by enrolling he was satisfying his father's desire that he distinguish himself in a new kind of adventure. Zitkala-Ša

(Gertrude Bonnin) conveys a similar sense of wide-eyed wonder about the strange place in the East to which she would travel—an account made more credible by the fact that she later grew to detest much about her boarding school experiences.[60]

In the literature of Indian schooling the "runaway" holds a special place— a hero, perhaps, to many fellow pupils, a scourge to teachers and even at times to fearful or acculturating Indian parents. However, individual narrators remember running *to*, rather than *away from*, school, or at least insisting on the right to attend, despite kin attitudes. A number of Navajos did so: Ernest Nelson followed his student brother, as did Kay Bennett, impressed by the stories of her school-going siblings. Her reluctant mother finally let Kay go, but the decision at that point was the child's. Polingaysi Qoyawayma (Elizabeth B. White) heard from the Hostiles that Hopis became white at the white man's school. Yet curiosity, an interest in school-provided clothes, and the lure of extra food propelled her from the mesa to the strange new building—despite bitter criticism from her mother, who accused her of taking "a step away from your Hopi people," a very serious accusation in such a small, face-to-face society.[61]

A sadly memorable account of the desire for schooling comes from Ashie Tsosie, a Navajo who never got there. "Now I am what I am," he declared decades later, speaking through an interpreter:

An uneducated man who does not know a word of English and who never has used a pencil. . . . if I had been permitted to go to the school and to have been well educated I might have been a teacher or a person sitting in an executive's chair as a director. . . . I would teach my children at home. . . . I always will blame my father for my being held down in life.

When Tsosie went to the store or the school, and teachers tried to talk to him he—like Irish peasants described by Keenan—"could only stand dumb because I do not understand them." The best he could do was "just to smile." Of course Tsosie may have been projecting adult inadequacies back into childhood, but the whole tenor of the piece suggests life-long disappointment.[62]

Thus, because of differing child-rearing practices, and different levels of familiarity with the school as an institution, a small percentage of Indian children appear to have enjoyed the privilege of deciding whether to attend. By the end of the period under review, however, they were probably just a few paces ahead of the agency policeman—or of anxious parents. Like the Irish, but facing more demanding challenges, Indian kin and communities had also made their peace with the school.

4. Regimentation

My folks tole me I must go to school but I don't like to go. . . . So my father
took me to the school. When my father went away I was not feeling good. I
didn't talk to anyone because I don't know these children. . . . Some of them
is mean to me sometime, too, and make me cry. By and by I got a friend,
and now I'm happy with him.

The teacher was trying to talk to me. I didn't say a thing because I don't
understand them what they mean. In the school was very hard lesson for
me. When my teacher try to make me read, I won't do it, and so she some-
time whip me . . . I was scared, and when we have vacation, I went home
and tell my folks all about how I was doin in school.

Charlie Tallbear, essay to BIA teacher,
early twentieth century

The first reminiscences of school, writes Susan Douglas Franzosa, "are retold
as a terrifying entry into an alien culture presided over by towering adults
who . . . expect their charges to act in incomprehensible ways." The place is
often evoked "through meticulously sensuous detail, now familiar but distant, then strange but clear."[1] If the experience can shock twentieth-century
Western children, how much more challenging must have been the first day
for nineteenth-century Indian and Irish children, many of whom spoke no
English and began early in the age of mass elementary education, when the
very idea of schooling was new to them and their peoples.

Although educated to participate in their own communities, children living in remote parts of western or southern Ireland were almost as unused to
the school as Indian children. Irish autobiographical narrators recalled, for
example, that their families did not possess clocks, and they had never even
seen spectacles, let alone experienced a systematically organized curriculum that segmented approved knowledge into half-hour periods, regularly
dispensed in custom-built establishments.[2] Supportive kin could prepare
the child; older siblings or mates could help adjustment. But, whether in
Dunquin, County Kerry, or at the Presbyterian boarding school in Nebraska,

the young boy and girl encountered the school—with its new physical environment, often incomprehensible language, regimentation, and its severe
punishments—in some sense alone.

I

"All the children trooped in and each class sat on its own bench," wrote Peig
Sayers of her first day at school on the Great Blasket Island off southwestern
Ireland in the late 1870s. When the master finally arrived the "clatter or noise"
made by the pupils ceased abruptly, and Peig held onto an older friend's hand
"with the grip of a drowning man." Then, in a passage that powerfully conveys the awed ambivalence of many of these accounts, she remembered: "my
two eyes were as big as bowls with fear and wonder . . . [and they] darted here
and there taking in every single detail." Although she was a monoglot Irish
speaker, and the class activity was in English, Sayer's first day went well. More
experienced pupils looked out for her. The teacher, a near-relative, presented
her with a book because in those decades of "payment by results" he wanted
pupils to attend regularly and learn well. The girl's initial ambivalence dis-
solved as she came to thoroughly enjoy her schooling.[3]

Micheál O'Guiheen, Sayer's son, also remembered a gift: "My heart was
pounding in my breast with delight when the master gave me a new book,"
he wrote. "I didn't let go of the book but was looking at the nice pictures until midday"—a child's thrill of ownership and fear of loss. "I loved being at
school," he recalled. "All the small children were there and we had great company," and the teacher too had been pleasant and gentle with him. Maurice
O'Sullivan, another Blasket Islander, similarly recalled his sense of fear being
immediately transformed into joy by the gift of sweets and—of course—a
book. After that "I saw a sight which put gladness into my heart," he recalled,
"sweets in the shape of a man, a pig, a boat, a horse, and many another. . . .
So there I sat contentedly looking at the book, while not forgetting to fill my
mouth." That O'Sullivan later grew to dislike school lends credence to his
retrospective account in that he admitted some positive aspects among the
negative.[4]

Not all Irish narrators were so positive in their recall. Along with fear
and joy, O'Sullivan remembered fellow pupils making "a power of noise."
Noise also impressed Patrick Shea at his first school in the provincial town
of Athlone. "[Silence], even for one moment, was unknown," he wrote. "All
through the day the teachers explained, ranted, interrogated, swung their
canes; boys shouted out answers, read set pieces or recited prayers. Every half
hour the sitting and the standing classes exchanged places with a shuffle and
a clatter that made the floor quiver." A sense of organized noise from rote

memorization struck Peter O'Leary. "I was amazed," he wrote, "when . . . I saw for the first time young people learning, reading, and speaking words and then telling what their meanings were, while they hadn't got the slightest idea as to the meaning of the words or the meaning of the meaning!"[5]

The incredibly early age at which some Irish children began school—along with the crude effectiveness of rote memorization—were conveyed by an informant for the Irish Folklore Commission. Enrolled at the age of *two and a half* to keep her out of trouble on the farm, she was wrapped in a shawl and left all day on the school bench. When she later got sick and became delirious she claimed that she shouted out words such as "past tense" and "indicative mood." Naturally this informant provides us with little else on her early school experiences. Her account, nevertheless, suggests once again how parents pragmatically exploited the new state-provided institution to their own ends.[6]

Perhaps because even the poorest Irish pupils lived in some form of western housing, individuals noted—at least in retrospect—the physical failings of the schools. The first national school in a folklore informant's area of Limerick was an improvement on a previous hedge school but still had only a mud floor, a thatched roof, and small windows. Initially there were no desks, and the pupils used slates. Unlike in the hedge school, however, there was a blackboard, and a chimney allowed smoke to escape. Many schools lacked any sort of playground. Shea was particularly critical of his, in the relatively prosperous town of Athlone: "Even by the Spartan standards [of c. 1900]," he wrote, "this must have been one of the worst-provided schools in Ireland." At the back "through a wasteland of nettles, a muddy path lead to the malodorous 'toilets,' the creation of some long-forgotten handyman whose skills did not include plumbing." Most Irish schools were heated by open fires, for which pupils often brought a sod of turf. At Shea's school the classes took turns standing around this fire. Sean O'Faoláin's school in Cork, third city of Ireland after Dublin and Belfast, was larger, but even less suitable for education: "I do not know what it was originally: it may have been a factory, or a barracks, or a poorhouse, or it might have been a madhouse, or it might have been some eighteenth-century lunatic's idea of how a school should be built." It included a "black hole where chronic criminals were flung to whimper among the coals and the rats." A slim, graveled yard running along each side of the building sufficed for a playground, and its outside toilets were also "malodorous."[7]

Officials corroborated such accounts. According to a CNEI inspector, the weather in the previous October had been "excessively wet and inclement." Yet at sixty schools he visited only three had fires. In a depressingly apt phrase, another inspector noted how in "the weeping climate" of Ireland, the dampness of the walls tended to badly effect maps. How must it have affected children, especially if there was no fire, or only a single fire, with most its heat going up the chimney?[8] In 1904 CNEI inspector Dewar wrote of "wretched hovels" that were "unwholesome and unhealthy, and act injuriously on the mind as well as the body, and they oppose a barrier to the best and most elevating influences." Also around the turn of the century head inspector A. Purser actually expressed relief that "compulsory education is still merely nominal" after he visited a school on what he believed to be the wettest day of the year:

I shudder to think of . . . tens of thousands of children who would otherwise be compelled to trudge imperfectly clad to school to find themselves in a cold, bare apartment without a fire, or with a fire only just kindled, and as yet giving out practically not a particle of heat; the children's scanty muffling all thrown into a heap in the corner where wet soaks from article to article until the whole becomes a mass of reeking moisture.

No other ex-pupil, not even famed authors such as Frank O'Connor and Sean O'Faoláin, matched Purser in conveying the cold dampness of Ireland and the state of some national schools into which parents placed their children.[9]

II

The boarding school has assumed classic resonance in the history of Indian education. Yet many tribal boys and girls, like most Irish children, also began and continued their schooling at local reservation day schools, the Indian equivalent of "the school down the road." By 1900 about one in four of around 20,000 pupils at government schools were in day schools—and it is likely that many of the boarding school pupils had earlier spent some time in local schools.[10] Their memories of the first days could be highly similar to those quoted above. Polingaysi Qoyawayma (Elizabeth Q. White), who braved Hopi family disapproval to enter a nearby school, used language like that of the Blasket Islanders. The girl's heart "beat like a Hopi drum" as the red-faced, whiskered teacher spoke to her in language she did not understand. Nothing her sister told her about school prepared Qoyawayma for the indignity of a forced bath or for the trial of copying strange marks from a board on the wall. On his voluntary arrival at a local school, Don Talayesva actually got into a bath and began to scrub himself. Mistaking a teacher's surprised gestures for anger, this young Hopi fled the school. Later he returned to praise in words he did not then understand. The disorientating experiences continued. He was initially afraid to sit on a toilet: "I thought something might seize me, or push me from below."[11]

For Indian boarding school pupils the disorientation and sense of long-term removal from a known environment were greater, even if they attended an "on-reservation" school. "My first day at [boarding] school was near my home," wrote a third-grade Indian pupil in an essay to his teacher. "Mother took me to school and I was homesick in a week." He announced that he was returning to his family, but the matron forbade him to leave. "And I told her I was going to tell my mother and she is going to *gift you with a black eye* if you don't let me go home" (emphasis in original).[12]

For those tribal children who traveled some distance to a boarding school, the challenge of adjustment was often greater still.[13] In an essay a young girl told how initially, "I was afraid to lay on that high bed, because I might fall off in the night." Even during the day she faced problems: used to eating with her hands, she could not use a knife, fork, or spoon. Although a Kiowa woman attended in the late 1920s when things should have been better, she remembered big, cold dormitories, housing twenty to thirty pupils, and the frightening trips to the toilets, as problematic as some in Irish schools. "Imagine a little girl walking through the dark to downstairs," she told her interviewer, "for years I would have nightmares of those restrooms; they were constantly running over, and all those things, and I think it just gave me such a terrible distaste for school."[14]

Irene Stewart's arrival at the Fort Defiance Boarding School in Arizona was a shocking experience: "From a primitive, wild Navajo life into a strange place with strange people, food, clothing. I was homeless. No one cared for me as my old home folks had. I feared everything, especially the people and the strange facilities." When an older student attempted to force her into a bath, Stewart screamed and fought but had to endure a scrubbing and hair combing, along with the forced donning of strange, uncomfortable clothing and heavy leather boots. Stewart later came to like school, but her account of the first day at boarding school is typical of many Indian experiences.[15]

Zitkala-Ša, a Nakota (Yankton) Sioux later became a major spokesperson for early-twentieth-century Indian peoples. She also remembered vividly her arrival at school—especially the glaring electric lights and the noise of hard shoes upon a bare wooden floor. Her disorientation was intensified by being thrown into the air by a well-meaning if insensitive teacher. The young girl's mother had never treated her in so undignified a manner: "Remembering this I began to cry aloud." In the midst of her misery she noticed something strange: boxes apparently piled one on top of another, but sloping away from her—an Indian child's perception of a staircase.[16]

Both part-Indian parents of the young Lucille Winnie already worked for the BIA, but this did not cushion the arrival for her. Although she would grow to like Haskell Boarding School in Kansas, her first days were "a never-to-be-forgotten experience." Ironically, being used to western-style clothes, she

was as ill-prepared as more traditional Indians for the rough and unattractive
military-style uniforms worn even by the girls. Although older Indian pupils
often helped beginners, in Winnie's case the student "officer" threw a bundle
of what "looked like prison garb" at the poor girl and refused to exchange ill-
fitting shoes for a more suitable pair.[17]

Also relatively experienced in Anglo-American ways when she began the
same boarding school, Esther Burnett "Essie" Horne, of mixed white and
Shoshone ancestry, had actually attended white public schools before beginning at Haskell. She spent time as a student, an "officer," and later as a
teacher at a number of BIA boarding schools, so her multiple perspectives
are particularly valuable to the historian. She too vividly recalled the sense of
apprehension when she, her sister, and her brother took the train all the way
from Wyoming to Kansas. "As we clung tearfully to our mother" before leaving, the older woman warned them that if they ran away from school, "'you'll
go back faster than you came home'" (emphasis in original). Horne also conveyed the sense of isolation and loneliness, intensified in her case by special
associations. "We were worn out and disheveled from our travels and leery
of what new changes were about to take place," she told her collaborator.
"One of the first places [school authorities] took us was to the dormitories. I
have a vivid recollection of the long row of white cots on the sleeping porches
. . . they reminded me of the crowded hospital where my father died. I was
grief-stricken and frightened, and I can still visualize myself standing there,
feeling lost and alone." Initially she hated the school, and wondered in which
direction lay her home.[18]

III

Irish pupils were spared first-day baths, but the CNEI also insisted upon
high standards of "CLEANLINESS, NEATNESS, and DECENCY," as stated in
its "Twelve Practical Rules" for teachers. They were to set an example and to
satisfy themselves "by personal inspection every morning, that the Children
have their hands and faces washed, their hair combed, and clothes cleaned,
and, when necessary, mended." The schoolroom was to be swept and dusted
every evening and white-washed once a year.[19]

Even in remote areas, however, and even when they lacked shoes, Irish children
otherwise dressed more or less according to "civilized" norms. Indian children,
however, especially the boys, faced a near-total outward transformation: the appearance of "savagery" was washed off, cut off, and discarded, and the "citizen's
dress" of civilization was put on. As historians such as K. Tsianina Lomawaima
and Ruth Spack have pointedly noted, the disciplining of the body was a powerfully motivating drive for these nineteenth-century white Americans.[20]

"It made a marked change in the appearance of the children," wrote a teacher at the Kiowa and Comanche Boarding School in 1871, when his wife assumed the role of seamstress. Then "the children came to exchange their blankets, breech-cloths, [illegible], etc., for our style of dress; also they had their hair shingled, and [illegible] and various gaudy ornaments were willingly left off." A few years later the commissioner explicitly laid out the reasoning for such transformations of adults as well as children. "The blanket must give way," he wrote:

It is only tolerable in the rudest savage life. It is unfitted to be the garment of civilization and labor; and as the Indian is gradually brought to give up his nomadic life for one of labor and industry, the question of clothing becomes one of practical interest as bearing upon his advancement and civilization. . . . We should have a uniform material, made entirely of wool—like army cloth—for Indian clothing; and the garment should consist of coat and pantaloons. . . . The object should be to secure the comfort of the wearer and uniformity in style of clothing.[21]

While partly practical and economical, such ideas were also obviously ideological—the heavy emphasis on military-style clothing and uniformity was intentional and powerfully enforced at many schools. Whether "citizen's dress" was a uniform or merely acceptable white standards of clothing, many Indians recalled the shock—and sometimes the pleasure—of the new clothes. Perhaps nowhere was the change more pointedly conveyed than in the account by Francis La Flesche, the Omaha who attended a Presbyterian boarding school in Nebraska during the 1860s. When a new boy arrived, the young La Flesche and another pupil were directed to take him to the store to be outfitted in civilized clothes. Then, the clothes of savagery were tied up in a bundle to be returned to kinfolk—a powerful symbolic rejection of the past.[22]

Individual narrators remembered some of the problems caused by unfamiliar types of clothing. According to Luther Standing Bear (Lakota Sioux), when the boys put their new trousers on in the morning, some could not remember whether the fly buttons should be at the back or the front. Frank Mitchell (Navajo) was embarrassed to relate how those same buttons caused him and his fellow pupils so much trouble that they sometimes wet themselves before they figured out how to use them. Yet while one Apache claimed that boys of his tribe hated wearing trousers, another recalled how proud the Carlisle boys were in their new military-style uniforms.[23]

Indian girls also faced exterior transformation, and they too were provided with uniforms at some schools. Generally, however, they were allowed keep their long hair, although Zitkala-Ša faced a haircut, against which she struggled and screamed).[24] Long hair was obviously uncivilized for young male citizens, and Standing Bear told how some of the first contingent at Carlisle in 1879 attempted to resist the order that their hair be cut. One by one, however, the boys were taken from the room, only to return individually with shorn hair, and the incipient rebellion fizzled. Standing Bear noted the group dynamics: once most boys had short hair he too wanted his hair cut. Other Indians such as James McCarthy (Tohono O'Odham/Pomo), Albert Yava (Tewa-Hopi), and La Flesche also recalled the cultural importance of long hair to tribal boys and men, and thus their initial resistance to this deliberate assault on tribal and gender identity. But the resistance crumbled and the long hair tumbled.[25]

Along with the new clothes and new hairstyle went a new, civilized name. Many Indians described this process as less shattering than a haircut because in tribal societies individuals might be given a series of names throughout their lives. La Flesche's Omaha mates, for example, were permitted by their teacher to choose new names for themselves from a list that included George Washington and Philip Sheridan, a U.S. general. Over a decade later at Carlisle, Standing Bear received a similar privilege. He used the teacher's pointer—which he saw as a kind of stick for "counting coup"—to pick out the name "Luther" from the blackboard, before he could even read or pronounce English properly. Such apparent sensitivity to pupils' desires also implicated young Indians in the open rejection of their own cultures. Significantly, however, neither La Flesche nor Standing Bear indicated—even as reminiscing adults—that the children resented an assault on their very identity. Indeed, La Flesche recalled: "How proud I was to answer when the teacher called the roll!"[26]

Other Indians, such as Albert Yava, a Tewa-Hopi, and Daniel La France, a Mohawk, appeared initially more resentful about the change but continued to carry the new names into adulthood.[27] Significantly, as Thomas G. Andrews notes, Oglala day school children often reverted to tribal names in the evening. Thus white names served "as superficial markers of identity that most Oglala children left in the classroom at the end of each day." Name changing, then, not only expressed the power teachers possessed; more importantly, "it demonstrated how Oglala agency persistently circumscribed this power."[28]

Irish children appear to have suffered less than Indians in this situation. In the Irish narrator accounts, at any rate, school naming practices do not appear to have been an issue. Perhaps this was because many came to school with already Anglicized versions of Irish names, and because so many parents wanted their children to learn and use English.[29]

IV

"I didn't take long to cast my eyes all round the house," wrote Tomás O'Crohan of his first day at National School on the Blasket Islands about 1860. He noticed books and heaps of papers and a blackboard covered with strange marks:

I was beside myself with wonder what they meant until I saw a teacher calling up the oldest girls and point out the marks to them with the stick in her hand, and I heard her talking some kind of gibberish to them. . . . I asked [my friend] in a whisper what was the rigmarole the teacher was talking to the girls around the board.

Thus the monoglot Irish-speaker, like hundreds of thousands of his mates, confronted a school system that for most of the nineteenth century taught through English alone, even in predominantly Irish-speaking areas. The teacher knew no Irish, and only slowly would children like O'Crohan adjust. Even after six years as a pupil, he still had not mastered English.[30] Later I examine the place of English in the CNEI and BIA curricula; in this and the next section I focus on how pupils survived an environment in which the very language of instruction was often incomprehensible.

The master at the National School attended by Peig Sayers seems to have spoken Irish, but the "schoolmissus" spoke English only. A new teacher arrived who "hadn't one tittle of Irish in his beak." Lending credibility to her account is her memory of "the first time that Irish came into the school"—as she attended in the 1870s she probably refers to the 1879 decision by the CNEI to accept Irish as an extra subject for higher classes to be taught outside school hours.[31]

Similarly, Michael MacGowan from Donegal in the northwest "hadn't a single word of English no more than anyone else in my family and I couldn't answer the master when he asked me what was my name." He and his friends "might just as well have been . . . minding sheep," for all they learned. The teacher spent long periods teaching Latin to English-speakers and apparently ignored those without English. "Whatever learning I got on my tongue—and I tell you that wasn't much—I'd say that it was in spite of him and in spite of myself I learned it." A neighbor helped him outside school hours, so before long he knew the alphabet by heart, "and that's something we wouldn't have been able to do with the master himself teaching us for a year."[32]

Further, although we have only indirect evidence of it in the Irish autobiographical accounts, some teachers resorted to punishment to compel the abandonment of Irish. An older man told Maurice O'Sullivan how the teacher had pinned a board to his back with the warning: "If you speak a word of Irish you will be beaten on the back and flank." And Patrick Shea's father recalled how, at his school in Kerry, "the use of the Irish language was a punishable offense." As a result, the orally bilingual older man had never learned to read or write in Irish. Thus Shea's generation of the family grew up without the vernacular.[33]

Some teachers and parents may have resorted to the "tally stick," infamous in Irish folk memory. An informant recalled how his teacher placed a cord around the neck of a pupil and marked it each time a child spoke Irish, "and he would get a slap in the evening for each mark on the cord." The Irish Folklore Collection has gathered over seventy accounts of a tally stick in various parts of Ireland during the nineteenth century, but only a few are such first-person accounts. Other informants remembered having to wear a dunce's cap for speaking Irish.[34] None of the published autobiographies that I examined mentions the tally stick, however. Historian John Coolahan points to its use by parents even before the establishment of the CNEI in 1831, and Tony Crowley accepts the prevalence of the practice in the nineteenth century, whereas Victor Durkacz discounts the whole folk tradition.[35] Along with initial incomprehension and other indignities, it is nevertheless likely that some Irish-speaking children—like Indians—faced both humiliating and occasionally painful punishment for using the old language.

Due to the efforts of his English- and Irish-speaking mother, Peter O'Leary was bilingual by the time he began school at the age of thirteen around 1852. He mentions neither tally stick nor the punishment of those who persisted in speaking Irish, but he has left a memorable account of other difficulties facing monoglot Irish pupils, for whom the teachers had him translate. "They were never given the opportunity that had been given to me to get the knowledge of those English words," he wrote. "They would never hear a word at home but Gaelic or broken English. The English which they had to learn was the same to them as Greek." Even bigger boys gathered around, "so that they'd have me smothered, and I answered their questions, telling them the meanings of the words in the lesson." There were four national schools in an area where O'Leary later served as parish priest, and not one of the teachers spoke Irish. Yet they had to teach the whole CNEI curriculum to Irish-speaking children. "That was a terrible injustice to teachers and young folk alike," he wrote. "The teachers were killing themselves trying to teach through a language that was not understood, and the minds of those who were learning were being tormented, blinded and sent astray from trying to take in knowledge through the unknown tongue." The result was often a "horrible English," neither accurate nor natural sounding.[36]

Even more unjust, in O'Leary's view, was the attitude sometimes taken by CNEI inspectors who might mock both pupils and teachers for the inaccurate or Hibernicized English—all the time ignoring the pedagogical difficulties faced in Irish-speaking areas. One inspector asked a child why he had missed school the day before:

"I does be thinning turnops, sir," the child said.
"And what does your brother be doing?" the inspector said.
"He do be minding the cows, sir?" said the child.
"'I does be,' 'he do be.' That is nice teaching!" he said to the teacher.
"Well, Mr 'Do be,'" he said to the child, *"how are you today, Mr 'Do be'? And how is old Mr 'Do be'? And how is Mrs 'Do be'? And how are all the other little 'Do be's' and 'Does be's'"?*

It was a public insult to child, family, and teacher "before the entire school," fumed O'Leary.[37]

Not all CNEI inspectors were so insensitive. Although throughout most of its existence the CNEI tried to ignore the problems facing Irish-speaking children, a few official voices of protest arose. As early as the 1830s an inspector could comment on the fact that in a southern area Irish was the spoken language, and that some children knew no English. Almost twenty years later in 1850 another inspector noted similar problems. "They think in Irish," he wrote of southern and western children, "they pray in Irish, they traffic in Irish." And, he declared enthusiastically, "when able and obliged to use 'the *new* tongue,' the peculiar idioms and beautiful metaphors of the ancient Celtic, so foreign to the Saxon, are evident even in their rude and idle attempts to translate them into English" (emphasis in original).[38]

The oft-quoted words of then head inspector Patrick J. Keenan—who, as we saw earlier, noted people's desire that their children learn English—powerfully corroborated ex-pupil memories of childhood suffering resulting from the National Board's language policy. With an appreciation of bilingualism perhaps rare in his day, Keenan claimed that "The shrewdest people in the world are those who are bilingual; borderers have always been remarkable in this respect." Then he attacked the unwillingness of his employers to use Irish even for better teaching of English. "It is hard to conceive any more difficult school exercise," he wrote, "than to begin our *first* alphabet, and *first* syllabication, and *first* attempt at reading, in a language of which we know nothing, and all this without means of reference to, or comparison with, a word of our mother tongue" (emphasis in original). Yet this, noted Keenan, was "the ordeal Irish speaking children have to pass through." Primarily interested in the efficient learning of the new language, Keenan believed—as did O'Leary—"that the natural result is that the English that they learn is very imperfect." The correct policy was "to teach Irish grammatically and soundly to the Irish people, and then teach them English through the medium of their native language."[39]

In a memorable passage published in the annual *Report* two years later, Keenan returned to the policy's effect on pupils. "I was frequently engaged in the examination of classes of children who exhibited neither intelligence nor smartness, nor even ordinary animation whilst being questioned in English," he lamented. When he or the teacher resorted to Irish, however, and allowed the children to answer in their own language, the transformation was dramatic:

at once their eyes flashed with energy, their voices became loud and musical, and their intellectual faculties appeared to ripen up and to delight in being exercised. I never experienced a contrast more marked than the appearance of a class of Irish-speaking children, who were examined first in English and then in Irish, or who were required to repeat a lesson—even the simple multiplication table—first in one language and then in the other.[40]

Later in the century others echoed Keenan's criticisms of the system and his empathy with those children on the receiving end. In 1883, for example, the Rev. William Egan, parish priest and national school manager in Dingle, County Kerry, complained that to children of his parish English was "in truth a *modern or foreign* language," of which they heard not a word at home. It was like introducing an entirely English curriculum into the heart of France, "without any *graduated instruction*" (emphasis in original). We do not teach Greek and all other subjects only through Greek, he noted. "How absurd too to place the same programme before Irish-speaking children of the bogs, mountains & wilds of West Kerry as is required of the [English-speaking] children of Belfast, Dublin, or Cork whose homes and whose surroundings are a constant school."[41]

V

"When I first went to school," wrote Bertha Sheeply, a third-grade Indian school pupil, in an essay to her teacher, "everything was funny to me. I didn't know how to talk English very well. When the superintendent used to talk to me I would cry and make a sign toward home." Conveying a similar sense of disorientation and a sense of separateness even from fellow pupils fortunate enough to speak English, a fourth grader wrote: "The first day I went to school I knew nothing about the English. The boys line up and get ready to go in the schoolroom and I just stand by the wall. Some of the boys talk to me in English. I don't understand. I just keep standing by the wall." As in Ireland, the teacher gave him a book—which bigger boys took from him and threw near the teacher's desk. While he was looking for it the teacher returned, and as Beaver could not explain himself in English, "we get punish first day in school."[42]

Some American Protestant and Catholic missionaries used Indian languages in their schools and even translated and published religious materials in tribal vernaculars. Missionaries of the ABCFM, for example, believed like CNEI inspector Keenan, that the best way to teach tribal children English was through the study of their own language first. Even if such missionaries, as Ruth Spack notes, "fostered bilingualism to promote conversion rather than to honor and maintain the Dakotas' language and culture," they at least made the transition to school that much easier for Indian children.[43]

The BIA demonstrated far less awareness of its students' language problems. Moreover, just as the CNEI was reluctantly bowing to Irish revivalist groups and allowing limited use of the vernacular in its schools, the BIA was intensifying its rejection of all tribal languages. "There is not an Indian pupil whose tuition and maintenance is paid for by the United States Government," boasted Indian Commissioner J. D. C. Atkins in 1886, "who is permitted to study any other language than our own vernacular—the language of the greatest, most powerful, and enterprising nationalities beneath the sun." Like the CNEI, then, the BIA saw English as far more than a practical lingua franca; it was the language of progress and civilization. Or as Spack expresses it in the current discourse of postcolonialism, "language is a site of struggle over power, meaning, and representation."[44]

Not all Indian children were totally ignorant of English, of course. "When I first went to school," wrote Willie Blackbeard in an essay, "it was strange to hear them talk English and write." Like Peter O'Leary in Ireland, however, this Indian boy was relatively fortunate: "I know how to read and write some. My father and mother teach me ABC's and to read primer and chart. It wasn't very strange for me and it wasn't hard to me and I wasn't ever lonesome or homesick." Before he began school, he declared, "I was very anxious to come so I could learn."[45]

The vast majority of Indian children were far less prepared and motivated. When new students entered the Presbyterian boarding school in Nebraska during the 1860s, recalled La Flesche, they encountered the rule against speaking the Omaha language, "which rule was rigidly enforced with the hickory rod." Thus, the newcomer "was obliged to walk around like a little dummy until he had learned to express himself in English"—again the metaphor of the dummy, with its implications of both silence and stupidity. Expressing oneself in the new language was probably the least of the problems—as in the Irish schools, just understanding the teacher was the immediate necessity. "For me it was very hard," recalled Belle Highwalking (Northern Cheyenne). "No one spoke English and we couldn't understand the white people when they spoke to us."[46]

Yet when young Indians resorted to their own languages, they too sometimes faced punishments such as beatings ("the hickory rod"), having their mouths washed out with soap, or having to stand alone in corridors. At Rainy Mountain Boarding School students might be subjected to a bewildering number of punishments: soapy teeth brushings, extra drill duty, carrying step ladders on the shoulders for several hours, or restrictions on social events. One student recalled having to hold quinine tablets in her mouth for speaking Kiowa. Other forms of punishment were meant to humiliate: boys might have to wear dresses or carry a sign declaring "I like girls"; girls might have to stand facing a corner or take demerits that restricted school trips. Jim Whitewolf spent a day in the school chapel and worked for two days in the laundry with the girls.[47]

Lending weight to such recollections is Gertrude Golden's frank admission about her own actions as a teacher of Navajo children at the Fort Defiance Boarding School early in the twentieth century. "They were eager to learn," she wrote, "but their chief handicap was their ignorance of the English language." One of her "most disagreeable tasks" as school principal was the reporting and punishing of children for speaking Navajo instead of English: "It was only natural for the poor desert children to express themselves in the only language they understood." However, the rule against speaking Navajo had to be enforced. It had been made by the school superintendent, at the suggestion of visiting officials, "in order that the pupils might master English more readily."[48]

Perhaps Standing Bear most poignantly expressed the difficulties of learning English. Initially he hoped that merely by sleeping in a white man's house he might awake speaking it. But he soon realized that he "must learn one word at a time." Anna Moore Shaw progressed faster when taught by a fellow Pima through the Pima language (Irish inspector Keenan would not have been surprised). But when this Pima instructor left the school, Shaw again found it difficult to understand the words of a white American who taught through English. La France, a Mohawk, also recalled how inadequate teaching made things more difficult: in his school the teacher taught only pronunciation and memory work, so, initially at any rate, the pupils could pronounce the words in the famous McGuffey Readers but had no idea what they meant. An eloquent if melodramatic cry of retrospective anguish came from Dr. Charles Eastman, a Dakota (Sioux). "For a whole week we youthful warriors were held up and harassed with words of three letters," he recalled. "Like raspberry bushes in the path they tore, bled, and sweated us—those little words rat, cat, and so forth—until not a semblance of our native dignity and self-respect was left."[49]

Although BIA officials generally accepted this imposition of English, a lonely voice was occasionally raised in objection. Using words similar to those of CNEI inspector Keenan, the BIA superintendent of schools, William N. Hailmann, spoke out for a bilingual approach. Perhaps, as Spack suggests, Hailmann's own immigrant origins influenced him, for he argued against punishment of pupils who resorted to the vernacular. "The possession of one language, far from being a hindrance in the acquisition of another, rather facilitates it," he wrote. "The sympathy and respect which a teacher shows for the idiom of the child will be rewarded in a hundredfold by the sympathy, respect, and affection with which the child will apply himself to the acquisition of the teacher's idiom." Even if Hailmann and Keenan formulated their approaches from within what Spack calls "the context of the civilizing projects," they not only attempted to question the policies and practices of their employers. They also tried to empathize with pupils who confronted deeply insensitive and—even in terms of CNEI and BIA goals—deeply flawed pedagogical practices.[50]

In one way, however, Indian experiences were far more demanding. Thousands of them attended multitribal schools, where even their peers might speak many different languages, something less often faced by Irish children. (A lone Irish-speaker among English-speakers faced similar, though less extreme problems; as did Maurice O'Sullivan, a lone English-speaker among the Blasket Island children; Irish immigrants in multilingual American or English classrooms probably sometimes faced similar linguistic variety to that experienced by Indian pupils).[51] Such Indians had, of course, an extra incentive to learn English just to communicate with each other. Yet the first lingua franca was not always the language of civilization. At Carlisle some Apaches learned the famous sign language of the plains, which their own people had never used—an ironic result for educators determined to obliterate all forms of aboriginal culture. At the Wahpeton Boarding School in North Dakota, about twenty-seven tribal groups were represented. Sam Writer, an Ojibwe, found he had to learn Sioux to speak to his new girlfriend there. Essie Horne humorously recalled how students from different tribes could pick up some of each other's languages and learn about each other's cultures at the multitribal Haskell Institute in the early twentieth century. "We would also compare notes as to how students would say common items such as sugar, salt, or bread in their language," She wrote. Embarrassing situations could result. Creek students supposedly told their word for bread. "You might try to show off your new-found knowledge . . . only to have [them] laugh hilariously because the word you uttered . . . might just as easily be a body part or a bit of profanity." She was pleasantly surprised to find that Shoshone and Comanche were closely related languages—more knowledge of tribal culture gained in the schoolyard, contributing to a sense of what would later be called Pan-Indianism.[52]

There was nothing remotely funny about the experience of Elsie Allen, a Pomo from California who initially spoke no English. At the Covelo Boarding School she found that only one other pupil spoke her dialect of Pomo, and these two almost never met because of the nature of the school regime. So, for her first year—until she began to learn English—she could speak to no one at the school, neither fellow pupil nor staff member. Yet, she appears to have borne no grudge. A kind teacher at her next school helped her learn the new language, which she later insisted on speaking to her own children.[53]

VI

Irish and Indian children who suffered such initially bewildering policies give us only glimpses of how they survived them. Family attitudes toward English were no doubt highly motivational, as was the help of more fortunate English-speaking schoolmates. For those entering the school out of different cultural environments, when the very language of instruction is new, such assistance is especially crucial. Sayers recalled the cyclical nature of mediation: pupils appeared to begin school at all times of the year, so marginally older children would help a younger one, who might later perform the same role. Peig Sayers's little helper was only three weeks senior to her and had been "terrified out of [her] wits" at first. By the time Sayers arrived equally bemused, the slightly older girl claimed—perhaps overconfidently—that "it doesn't bother me at all." And she immediately agreed to help: "I'll be your friend," she said. "I have English and I'll tell you what the schoolmissus is saying."[54]

Sayers also suggests the importance of pupil self-help. Once literacy in Irish became a permissible extra subject after 1879, she compared languages: the textbook contained Irish and English vocabulary, and after school she noted how "white cow" was English for "bó bhán." She also enjoyed memorizing English poetry; even if she never fully understood the text, this probably improved her knowledge of English. And she thrilled at becoming literate in Irish, which for her and her parents had been an oral language. Such vernacular literacy no doubt helped her progress in English. Yet even if she grew to deeply like school, she claimed that by the time she left, she knew very little of the new language.[55] Like Sayers, a male folklore informant remembered how, when faced with a teacher who refused to speak Irish to pupils, he too exercised his own initiative. The boy took the English textbook home and, possibly with parental help, worked on vocabulary, some of which he still remembered almost 70 years later:

FROST: frozen water.
CATAPULT: a forked stick with elastic made to fire small stones.[56]

Late-nineteenth-century CNEI concessions could not save Irish as a spoken language of the majority of Irish Catholic people—this was never the intention. Nevertheless, the reforms meant that later generations of children from Irish-speaking areas might be spared the miseries inflicted in earlier decades on O'Crohan, Sayers, MacGowan, O'Leary, and countless other monoglot Irish children.

Indian narrators also offer glimpses as to how they similarly adjusted to the new language regime. Kin attitudes toward English and literacy also influenced them, as did the help of schoolmates. Learning from an older friend at the mission school, Francis La Flesche thrilled at his own progress in the language. "I felt proud of his praise and worked all the harder. We had gone through the alphabet swimmingly. . . . When I was able to read short sentences, I felt sure that I should soon take my place among the advanced pupils." In status-conscious tribes such as the Omaha, personal ambition could therefore be a powerful stimulus. A Pomo man felt a similar sense of achievement: "I became so proud of myself when walking home from school," he wrote, "you could see my little humming bird chest sticking out like a pigeon's breast." Other resourceful Indians plunged into self-learning, just like Peig Sayers in Ireland. Refugio Savala, a Yaqui, recalled: "I started writing and became a word hunter in English and Spanish. The dictionary was my hunting ground." When Irene Stewart moved to a school without a rule against speaking Indian languages, she voluntarily continued to use English with some like-minded mates. And in an essay another student told how she "had been trying hard to talk English." Apparently she convinced her teacher, who then let her home for vacation.[57]

For Jim Whitewolf, Kiowa-Apache, a combination of many influences were important: he too benefited from the help of an older student, specifically assigned to him by the school, and from the "object method" of teaching languages then prevalent in some of the schools, whereby a teacher pointed to known objects and provided their English names. His own enthusiastic application of the object method outside the classroom was no doubt vital. "When we went out to play," he recalled, "I would see real birds and call out 'bird.'"[58]

Thus Indian and Irish children struggled to some measure of understanding, often through the help of friends and through their own persistence—

and, it is only fair to add, through the efforts of generations of often harried, sometimes brutal, and sometimes kind and sensitive teachers. I examine the role of staff in chapter 6, but here we might meet one teacher who was crucially helpful to a young Apache. Asa Daklugie surrendered with Geronimo at the end of the last Indian war in 1886 and was sent by his chief to Carlisle Indian Industrial School. He deeply resented "white eyes" into his adult life—his is a bitter autobiography. Yet he remembered warmly the efforts of one teacher. She was "very patient and kind," he wrote, and "not bossy like most white ladies are. She seemed to know without being told that I desperately wanted to learn [English] and she helped me."[59]

My own experience is perhaps instructive here. I too was confronted with a two-language school situation in the 1950s and 1960s, as the government of Ireland persisted in attempting to revive the Irish language (then spoken as a vernacular by fewer than 5 percent of the population). A native speaker of English, I heard phrases of Irish from my mother and began to learn more at school from the age of five. At Irish-speaking schools (not all were) teachers just threw that language at us—prayers, expressions, texts. Gradually I picked up more and more until, by the age of sixteen, I was almost bilingual. I studied most of my subjects in Irish up to and through junior high school level—including Irish itself, history, geography, arithmetic, algebra, geometry, physics, and chemistry. My friends and I appear to have "just picked up" the second language. Of course, the home language—English—was also used in the classroom, so we were not as disadvantaged as Michael MacGowan, Charles Eastman, and their peers. But I suspect that they too, and hundreds of thousands of pupils like them in Ireland and America, slowly picked up English in a similar fashion.

The explicitly ideological language policies of the CNEI and BIA massively aggravated difficulties for large numbers of boys and girls. Many of those who fled Indian schools or resisted attendance at national schools probably did so in part because of the frustration of sitting in class "like little dummies," week after week or even for years. It is surprising, then, how many of the Indian and Irish narrators remained so relatively positive about the terrible adjustments demanded of them decades earlier. I found none who doubted the value of learning English, at least as a second language. In terms of language change, at least, the BIA and CNEI broadly succeeded in their assimilationist goals.

VII

Whether in local day schools or in large multitribal boarding schools, children were immediately and deliberately subjected to regimes of rigid discipline and control. In its 1845 "Twelve Practical Rules for Teachers" the CNEI admittedly instructed them to "cultivate kindly and affectionate feelings among their Pupils." However, the demand for order, discipline, and obedience rings out far more clearly than for the softer qualities. Teachers were "To observe themselves, and to impress upon the minds of their pupils, the great rule of regularity and order—A TIME AND A PLACE FOR EVERY THING, AND EVERY THING IN ITS PROPER TIME AND PLACE." They should pay "the strictest attention to the morals and general conduct of their pupils, and to omit no opportunity of inculcating the principles of TRUTH and HONESTY; the duties of respect to superiors, and obedience to all persons placed in authority over them." A few years later in 1849 the National Board presented typical sample timetables for boys and girls, class by class, that rigidly divided the day into 15- to 30-minute periods for each subject according to grade—a segmentation of time almost as new to many, especially rural, Irish children as to Indian children. Indeed, this syllabus, typical of those being presented to children in Western nations during the new age of mass education, reminds one of the famous claim by a French minister of education that, at 11:00 on any day of the week, he knew exactly what was being taught in any schoolroom in France. At 11:00 in Ireland in 1849, the second class of boys were doing arithmetic, which would end at precisely 11:15; then they would begin mental arithmetic, tables, and reading until 11:45. At 11:00 girls were beginning gallery lessons or sacred poetry.[60]

In 1909, close to the end of the life of the CNEI, inspector W. R. Connelly was using similar language of discipline and order. The teacher had "a more important function to fulfill than that of ordinary instruction." He should also be "a teacher of morals." The primary purpose of a school, he emphasized, was to cultivate good habits and to form character. "Information is soon forgotten, but the habits acquired, bad or good, remain. Chief among them are ready obedience, a sense of duty and honour, forethought, courage, effort, and—if only it could be fostered—dour obstinacy and perseverance in the face of disappointment."[61] Therefore the CNEI saw itself engaged in not merely the education of children in book learning but also in a campaign to promote discipline and character. The goal was to "uplift" the socially and even morally deficient children of the Irish poor.

Order, too, was a major BIA goal. Great improvements had occurred among the Omahas, wrote agent O. H. Irish in 1861, since the organization of a tribal police force or company of soldiers. Before this, he claimed, "there was no law in the tribe except brute force; but now they have a code of law consistent with the laws and policies of the United States." The goal of the schools, he believed, was "to inculcate precepts of the highest and best form of morality, the simple, earnest truths of our holy religion, subordination to lawful authority, and the pursuit of honest industry." Then the people could be redeemed from "the barbarism of ages, and made to take a favored place among the civilized people of the earth." The report from another agency claimed that the "most serious difficulty to the advancement of these Indians, lies in lack of power to control them."[62]

"Control," "power," "compelled": such language echoes through the documents. Agent Milroy of the Far Northwestern tribes asserted in 1876 that the superintendent "should have absolute control over the school-children, wholly independent of their parents, and, except in cases of sickness, [they] should be separated from and permitted to associate as little as possible with their parents and outside Indians, as is consistent with humanity." In 1881 General Samuel C. Armstrong, the celebrated principal of Hampton Institute in Virginia, conveyed a similar undisciplined image. Indian children "have, as a rule on their arrival, absolutely no idea of obedience. They yield to a command they feel is just and reasonable, but simple obedience to authority seems an idea quite foreign to their minds and is one of very slow growth."[63]

The school bell became a crucial instrument for teaching internalization of control. "At school we just went by the bell," recalled Frank Mitchell, a Navajo. "Every time the bell rang, it meant that we had to get in line, or go to bed, or get up and get ready for breakfast, or dinner or supper." An ex-student at the Chilocco Boarding School in Oklahoma powerfully conveyed how bell-marked time waited for no child: until he accommodated himself to its rhythm, he missed out on meals:

And they put the food on [the table] and then they blew a whistle or rang a bell or something. . . . Rang a bell, I guess that was it, they rang a bell, and you started, then you were supposed to eat. If you weren't fast . . . about the first three days I almost starved to death, because I'd sit there and they'd ring this bell and by the time I looked up, the food was all gone, [other students] would just reach out and grab it. (emphasis in original)

Eastman graphically conveyed the difficulty of adjusting to such segmentation of time into regular intervals—it was like trying to walk along a railway track, each step from tie to tie was too short. La Flesche also caught the essence of the bell. It was used "to call us to order." So effective did its use become that an Indian could even admit to missing its structuring regularity in later life: "It was very hard when I left there," one told an interviewer, "because there were no schedules, no bells ringing and no whistles blowing, I didn't know what to do."[64]

Leaving school for home each afternoon, Irish children could daily escape the regimentation of the school. R. B. Robson, an Ulster Presbyterian, actually attended boarding schools—a CNEI model school and later its Dublin teacher training college, where student teachers but not pupils boarded. At the latter students were given the duty of ringing a bell at certain times of the day. Robson had attended a number of elementary schools before boarding school, and as he spoke English and dressed "properly," his experiences at such schools were not as challenging as those of most Indian boarding school pupils.[65]

In 1855 CNEI inspector Keenan lamented the absence of the bell at national schools; his attitude was highly similar to that of the BIA: "I wish that there were a large bell on every National School, to ring for a quarter of an hour before school commences, and thus summon all within its hearing to prepare for the business of the day, and warn loiterers of the danger of being late." Often well informed about educational developments outside Ireland, he noted that many European school systems operated this way: "in such countries loitering or coming late to school is a thing quite unknown." Bell or not, the CNEI strove, like its American counterpart, to instill order in its own way, down to the smallest classroom detail. In 1880, for example, inspector P. Connellan complained about "a very injurious practice" in some national schools: "teachers have ceased to insist on any uniform method of holding the pen." There was one correct way to do things: "in writing, as in every other art, the use of instruments should be systematically taught."[66]

VIII

The more all-embracing order of the Indian boarding schools was dramatically evident in the military-style discipline enforced at many, though not all, of them—not at the Presbyterian boarding school attended by La Flesche, for example. BIA officials, and celebrated reformers such as Generals Pratt and Armstrong, powerfully espoused the idea that schools be run as much as possible like army posts. "The boys have been organized into companies as soldiers," wrote Pratt in 1880, just after the opening of Carlisle, "and the best material selected for sergeants and corporals. They have been uniformed and drilled in many of the movements of army tactics. This has taught them obedience and cleanliness, and given them a better carriage." The military organization, wrote Armstrong in 1890, "was the most potent factor in solving the problem of law and order which confront the [student] officers of the schools." Such an organization was "not only repressive, but directly and actively educative as well," he believed. "It enforces promptness, accuracy, and obedience, and goes further than any other influence could do to instill into the minds of the students what both Negro and Indian sadly lack, a knowledge of the value of time."[67]

Hardly surprising rhetoric, coming from old soldiers. However, at many boarding schools run by nonmilitary men and women, this form of quasi-military organization took hold. BIA teacher Golden strongly defended the military system of organizing the pupils into companies according to age and size and drilling them "in marching, setting-up exercises and simple military maneuvers." It was the officers' duties not only to march fellow students, but to inspect them for cleanliness and neatness before entering class. This training, she believed, was invaluable. "It helped the children overcome habits of procrastination and slovenliness, so inherent in their natures. They had the mañana trait, often attributed to Mexicans. Any time was time enough, punctuality meant nothing in their lives. They ate, slept, worked and played only when the spirit moved them." Yet later she told how, in the blazing heat of Southern California (110F–c.45C) military drills still took place outside. Pupils and teachers at the Fort Yuma Boarding School had already spent half the day in class, the other half working in the garden, the laundry, or the kitchen. As a result "they were literally dead on their feet and could hardly be dragged through the setting-up exercises and marching." Yet a rule was a rule, so they marched.[68]

With little rancor Essie Horne described the routine at Haskell Institute around the same period. Here the students had to drill in formation before breakfast. "This was certainly foreign to anything we had ever learned before," she noted with admirable understatement. "We rose at 6.00 a.m., combed our hair, brushed our teeth, and got dressed in our everyday [military-style] clothes. We had to be in formation by 6:15 a.m., five days a week." Students were divided into companies by grades and sex; and as elsewhere the male and female officers were students. Competition for various awards stimulated rivalry between the companies. "This was all a purely military thing, just like the armed forces," and she joked that had she not been a mother of two young children during the Second World War, she "would have been a natural for the WACS or WAVES," women's branches of the U.S. military. The regime had become "an integral part" of their lives," Horne believed. Indeed they had internalized it so well that on occasion formations could drill on their own without the need for commands.

By working her way through the ranks Horne became an officer, a position that demanded leadership skills, a superior academic record, and knowledge of military organization. Even as an old woman, heavily imbued with late-twentieth-century pride in Indian culture and identity, she also took pride in claiming that once an officer, she knew no favorites and was willing to discipline her friends. She admitted that sometimes student officers could become bullies, and that the military regime was designed to break down tribal values. However, she rationalized her earlier harshness toward fellow pupils partly by appealing to Indian community values: tribal peoples taught their young to be responsible human beings. Students might exploit the system, but obviously authorities partly succeeded in achieving internalization of an alien regime at this and at many other schools.[69]

With varying and sometimes ambivalent responses, other Indian women described the regimen at their schools. Lucille Winnie, also at Haskell, spoke bitterly about the military regime—for girls. And she left a disturbing picture of the bullying and mistreatment of pupils by Indian officers, including her own older sisters. Hopi Helen Sekaquaptewa also remembered marching to and fro to band music, along with the endless bells and the rigid adherence to schedule. She recalled the daily lineup of boys and girls in uniform, just like on a real parade ground, and how they held out their hands for inspection. The officers noted every flaw. With typical ambivalence, Sekaquaptewa could note that the regime, especially the corporal punishment, was "obnoxious to most students." Yet she simultaneously spoke well of the uniforms. Like Horne and Winnie, Sekaquaptewa also enjoyed her studies and felt that boarding school opened the world to her, military discipline or no.[70]

Indian boys also recollected the military regime with ambivalence. "We dressed, we ate, we drilled, we studied and recited our lessons with a precision that left not even one minute without its duties," recalled Shawnee Thomas Alford. Pupils needed a pass to leave the school campus and had to salute officers, teachers, and fellow students. Despite all this, "we liked it." The Shawnee also grounded acceptance in tribal education: "we had [earlier] been trained to respect authority, and that is the secret of a successful apprenticeship to military life." James McCarthy, a Papago, remembered with pride how the two rifle companies at his school gave performances on a Sunday, and local white people would come and watch.[71]

Although Irish national schools did not employ such military discipline, the CNEI also became convinced of the usefulness of outdoor drill, in military-like formations. Not only would such activities promote student health, but they also inculcated the desired goals of order, discipline, and obedience. Writing in 1890, and again calling upon the motto first espoused over half a century earlier—"A place for everything, and everything in its place"—inspector S. E. Strong lamented the lack of physical education. "Marching with head erect and shoulders squared is seldom seen" he complained, "while a lounging attitude in draft or one boy leaning against another is seen often enough, nor do I know a single school where pupils are made to sit with unbent back while writing exercises." Many of his colleagues in the inspectorate—whatever about local teachers responsible for instilling such discipline—would have agreed with Strong: "the cultivation of good habits, and the acquisition of a good address, as well as a certain manliness in deportment, are 'of the essence.'" Over a decade later Mr. Craig, inspecting the teacher-training model schools of the National Board, noted with almost classic directness that drill was "fairly well taught, and in some cases with really excellent results, as it has tended to promote habits of order and obedience, as well as improve the gait and carriage of the pupils." Old soldiers Pratt and Armstrong could not have expressed the rationale more effectively. Much had still to be done, Craig felt, because "the general discipline and the demeanour" fell far short "of what might have been expected from the precision with which the Drill exercises were executed."[72]

Indeed the next year (1904) the CNEI actually included "Physical Drill" in its detailed "Programme" or curriculum for its schools. The Report presented the various kinds of movements to be taught to each grade of students. The rationale for such activities is, again, explicit:

NOTE.—Suitable games should be encouraged by teachers during play time. Great attention should be paid to the manner and deportment of the pupils. They should be trained to habits of prompt obedience. Energy, gracefulness, and precision of movement in the various exercises should be particularly cultivated. (emphasis in original)[73]

Of course, establishing a program did not mean that it would be well taught, or even taught at all. Yet, although the full military regime was absent from CNEI national schools, the rationale behind such thinking was strong in Ireland too. Disciplining the body along with the mind was a major part of the drive to mass education and mass conformity. American scholars have more associated such "muscular Christianity" with Protestant churches. The CNEI, comprising mostly Catholic employees, obviously also subscribed to such a belief in the blending of morality, character building, physical drill, and exercise.[74]

IX

Ideally, incentives such as food or uniforms at boarding schools or books at day schools might encourage pupils to internalize the new value systems. Yet during the period under review most educators accepted the need for some forms of punishment, including corporal punishment. Educational authorities on both sides of the Atlantic strongly opposed excessive physical or other kinds of abuse of pupils. Thus missionary, BIA, or CNEI teachers found resorting to brutality might lose their jobs. According to narrator accounts in both areas, however, and to corroborating reports by teachers or inspectors, boys and girls could suffer terribly at the BIA and CNEI schools. Indeed, it must be admitted that for many pupils, Indian and Irish, fear was a major motivating factor for obedience.

In 1855 Patrick Keenan reported acceptable levels of discipline within the National Board schools, due "to the stand which the Board has taken against *severe* corporal punishment. No instance of severity came under my notice in any of the schools which I visited" (emphasis in original).[75] Keenan probably wrote in good faith, and he was quite willing to publicly criticize his own board for perceived failings. An inspector, however, even one who arrives without announcement, hardly witnessed punishment that transgressed the board's rules. Judging from autobiographical accounts, the slapping of Irish children and other forms of physical punishment were endemic, and outright brutality could sometimes occur. It is analytically difficult to distinguish the teacher from the pain he or she inflicted. In this chapter, however, my focus is on the children's experiences of punishment as regimentation.

A comment reported by Blasket Islander Micheál O'Guiheen suggests the nature of the situation: "and a good mistress she is," said one boy of a teacher, "for she beats us only seldom." Patrick Shea remembered being punished before the class until the teacher's cane "had stung half of my body into throbbing agony, sending me home crying bitter tears, humiliated and angry and full of despair." An assistant, a good teacher according to Shea, had a cruelly clinical approach: "he used the cane with chilling accuracy; he knew well that a sharp stroke delivered on the end finger joints sent a shudder of pain right to the victim's toes." Such caning would probably not have been considered excessive by the board; it was, after all, merely a slap on the hand using an acceptable instrument. That teacher's other form of punishment certainly would have been condemned by the authorities, so he hardly indulged in it during inspector visits. For some offences a boy might find himself suspended by a tuft of short neck hairs clamped between the man's thumb and forefingers.[76]

Frank O'Connor remembered one teacher who "combined the sanctimoniousness of a reformed pirate with the brutality of a half-witted drill sergeant. With him the cane was never a mere weapon; it was a real extension of his personality. . . . He was a real artist with it and with his fat, soft, sexual fingers he caressed your hand into the exact position at which a cut could cause the most excruciating pain." If his cane broke while beating a slow child on the bare legs, he calmly found another. In a humorous but pointed passage O'Connor recalled his thinking about such cruelty. On days when visiting the doctor or dentist—hardly pleasant relief—he passed the school and heard the shouts of the masters and cries of the boys. He had often wondered about Catholic doctrine: how could the saved souls enjoy the pleasures of heaven, knowing that the damned were suffering in hell? On such mornings, he believed, he had found an answer, one that did not speak well for human nature: the experience enabled him "to contemplate the sufferings of the damned with no diminution of my own ecstasy."[77]

Sean O'Faolain was horrified to secretly observe from another room how "Sloppy Dan" beat two older boys who had "mitched" (played truant). The teacher, a member of the Presentation Order of Brothers, held one boy by the left arm and "was lashing with his leather strap at his naked thighs and bottom. Even through the closed door I could hear [the boy] screaming, probably not so much from pain as from fright and shame." To make matters worse, six or eight other boys sat on each side of the room at long desks. "Their heads were bent low in, I now guess, pity and embarrassment . . . I gave no more than one glance at the, to me, bestial scene . . . turned and fled out to the evil-smelling jakes [toilet] and hid there shivering, until the school was over."[78]

O'Faolain conceded the difficulty of controlling some of his schoolmates, who might themselves assault a teacher. Indeed at times he almost rhapsodized about the school experience. Because, he writes, "in spite of the cold, the dirt, the smells, the poverty and the vermin, we managed to create inside this crumbling old building a lovely, happy, faery world. And when I say 'we' I mean the [Presentation] brothers and ourselves, because those brothers were brothers to us and I think we sincerely loved them." Indeed the teachers sprang from the same poor conditions as the boys. Piling ambivalence upon ambivalence, however, O'Faolain wondered whether he would send a child of his own to such a school. Despite the good sides that he so magnanimously portrayed, his answer was a reluctant "no." Life had been harsher in those days, and children might anywhere encounter cruelty: "But still, not in school!"[79]

The regimen could be equally harsh at Indian schools. We have seen the varied physical or psychological punishments inflicted for the speaking of tribal languages. For other offenses, or even for none at all, punishment might also be swift. In *The Middle Five* (1900) Francis La Flesche has left a sometimes critical but also warmly appreciative account of life at his Presbyterian boarding school. Discipline was strict, and the rod was constantly used. Yet nothing prepared La Flesche and his schoolmates for the brutal assault by one missionary teacher on a new arrival. Joe, a big, dim-witted, but harmless boy got caught up in a sod-throwing game and accidentally hit this teacher. "Gray-beard" fetched a piece of board, but when he attempted to slap Joe's outstretched hand, the boy withdrew it, and the teacher hit himself. Then the man exploded: he "dealt blow after blow on the [boy's] visibly swelling hand. The man seemed to lose all self-control, gritting his teeth and breathing heavily, while the child writhed with pain, turned blue, and lost his breath." La Flesche himself had got a "violent shaking" because of his part in the incident, "but the vengeful way in which [Gray-beard] fell upon that innocent boy created in my heart a hatred that was hard to conquer." It was, wrote La Flesche in a passage very similar to the one penned by O'Faolain, "a horrible sight." Actually, there was no hatred in La Flesche's discriminating account. Further, he immediately noted how, when the stunned boys told the principal about the incident, the man reprimanded Gray-beard and apologized to the students; Gray-beard also apologized.[80]

Other Indians wrote of similar assaults. Zitkala-Ša, a Nakota, remembered how one girl "shrieked at the top of her voice" while being beaten by a female teacher—who also realized that brutality did not solve problems and immediately tried to console the girl. Don Talayesva faced similar treatment—from Indian disciplinarians at the Sherman Institute in Riverside, California, at the beginning of the twentieth century. The young Hopi refused to participate in a debating society in front of a large crowd. (Hopi culture strongly disapproved of open self-promotion, but no doubt many American boys of the same age would have felt awed by the situation). Talayesva was taken to the school basement, and the two boys disciplining him let down his trousers. "After about fifteen blows with a rawhide strap in a heavy hand, I broke down and cried. I slept very little that night and was sore for several days afterwards but was never again asked to debate in the auditorium."[81]

Can we believe such accounts? Like La Flesche and Irish narrators, Talayesva gave a very mixed and sometimes positive account of his schooling; his autobiography is no anti-school polemic. Further, recall how this Hopi left a shocking picture of an equally severe earlier beating by the Kachinas. In both accounts Talayesva gives unflattering images of his own responses. BIA teacher Golden told that when some older pupils came back to school intoxicated, the disciplinarian "applied what might be called 'cruel and unusual punishment.'" He put them on a bread-and-water diet, sentenced them to solitary confinement, "and, with some of the worst offenders (it was rumored), hung them up by the wrists for hours."[82]

Hopi women, such as Sekaquaptewa and Qoyawayma, both of whom became extremely positive about their schooling, also recalled sporadic, sometimes nasty punishments. The former remembered the regular use of the whip at the Phoenix Indian School and the humiliating treatment of student runaways. Girls might be made to clean the yard and cut the grass with a scissors, while wearing a card that declared, "I ran away." Boys were put in the school jail or made to wear dresses. Fellow Hopi Qoyawayma remembered how at her day school the girls gave little trouble, but the sometimes unruly boys did. "Retaliation was prompt. A few of them were booted, others were slapped in the face"—both these forms of punishment would have been against BIA rules. Qoyawayma "remembered vividly" the deeply humiliating treatment of a too-talkative Hopi girl at another school. The teacher made her sit on a unheated stove at the front of the class and shoved an eraser into her mouth. "She sat there stiff with fright, head bent in shame and saliva dripping, until the teacher's sadistic appetite had been satisfied."[83]

At some Indian schools teachers systematically implicated other pupils in the beating of their mates. Paul Blatchford, a Navajo, remembered how those who committed the heinous offense of being late for dinner were forced to run the gauntlet of fellow students: "All those who could swing with their right arms swung belts at the person." Horne openly admitted that as a student officer at Haskell she had spanked a disobedient young Indian girl. For the serious offense of running away the gauntlet also awaited: "A company would be lined up in two long lines facing each other. The students would remove their belts and strap clothed offenders on the rear as they dashed through the line." The rest of the description is somewhat apologetic: fast runners might avoid much of the punishment, and many of the students whipped only hard enough to impress the student officer in command. Yet the use of belts and the group dynamics, with student officers "whipping on" the lower ranks—all suggest that the experience was anything but pleasant for the recaptured escapee.[84]

Chapters could be filled with further instances of small, casual acts of violence—a blow, a tugging of the hair, the constant and sanctioned use of the cane or strap—and with occasional acts of great brutality. Further, these narrator accounts are almost all by Irish and Indian ex-students generally positive about their school experiences, and in some cases highly positive. We can believe that life sometimes became very difficult for pupils in BIA/missionary and Irish national schools.

X

"Every time my mother used come to see me I would cry to go home with her in the wagon," wrote Indian pupil Lottie Parton in an essay. "Then the Septertendement came and taked me back to school."[85] Yet she, like many pupils in both America and Ireland, seems to have gotten used to the new institution with its relentless and sometimes harsh regimentation. This sense of gradual acceptance—if not always for reasons hoped for by school authorities—resonates in pupil memories of both systems and in accounts by many historians. Local day schools challenged Indian and Irish children—especially those from remote areas—in broadly similar ways. For Indians removed to distant boarding schools—even for those who enrolled voluntarily—the demands were obviously far greater. Yet so could be the rewards. At least some Indian ex-pupils indicated that this "total institution" could actually become what the authorities hoped: "I felt quite at home and independent," wrote La Flesche of his experience. After leaving school Betzinez awaited a visit of their principal to the reservation: "we were anxious to see General Pratt as if he were our own father."[86]

Following the death of her father and the resulting family difficulties, Horne believed that "boarding school provided a safe environment for me . . . I had security there. . . . I think too that the sense of community at Haskell was very strong. Among Indian people this is very important. We had a pride in our school and in our [sports] teams, and we had such a strong school spirit." Critics might validly attack the schools for their assimilationist policies, she admitted, yet "the students and teachers at Haskell will forever be an integral part of who I am as an American Indian."[87]

Such a powerful identification with the school, even if not with all of its program, rarely occurs in Irish accounts. Yet O'Faolain warmly recollected the Presentation Brothers' school, despite the squalor and occasional brutality. Other Irish narrators such as Peig Sayers also enjoyed school, although she never picked up enough English to fully participate.

Vast numbers of Irish and Indian children suffered, adjusted, endured; some enjoyed the schooling experience; some tribal children even enjoyed the military regimentation of boarding school life. A major theme of this book, then, is the *resilience of pupils*, the impressive capacity many of them showed for coping with new kinds of discipline, regimentation, and punishment—often imposed through an unknown language.

In the midst of their initial and persisting bewilderment, moreover, pupils in each area also confronted a curriculum designed to alienate them from their own communities and cultures. It is to the curricula imposed by the BIA and the CNEI that we now turn.

5. Curriculum

The Navajos believe all kinds of things, but we schoolchildren don't believe.
Cecelia Bryan, Navajo pupil,
early twentieth century

"Missionary education was doing more than to purvey knowledge or teach skills," writes A. J. Ashley. "It was an important part of the missionary effort to effect a transfer of pupils from one universe to the other."[1] Whereas in a "normal" school the teachers attempt to indoctrinate pupils more deeply into their own cultural universe (or an approved version of it), in an assimilative situation the goal is radically different. Missionaries—and the teachers of the BIA and the CNEI were cultural missionaries, whatever their attitudes toward religion—often accept a far more ambitious task: to discredit or simply ignore the universe in which the child has been reared and to transport him or her into a new universe of meaning and value.

The regimented school environment forcefully and sometimes brutally transported the child to the different universe. In the mass school systems throughout the Western world, writes Vincent, "a new sense of clock time was dramatized by the official curriculum." Earlier educational practices had often produced "shapeless lessons in which the children spent a few minutes at the teacher's desk and the rest of their day working at their own speed." This was "replaced by blocks of time, beginning and ending at a specific moment, within which pupils collectively undertook a specific task without pause or interruption." This segmentation of time ignored "the existing rhythms of the household and the local economy." Pupils were punished not only for failing to learn the content of the new curriculum, but for failing to do so on time.[2]

And what of curricular content itself? Broadly generalizing across "the Imperial curriculum" of many colonial regimes, J. A. Mangan validly claims that "school knowledge is a political assertion. It attempts to establish the parameters of acceptable knowledge, impose ideological boundaries, determine the range of permissible interpretations, point the way to action, and, both overtly and covertly, create images of self-belief *and* self-doubt" (emphasis in original).³ All forms of education establish regimes of knowledge. The imperial curriculum established new forms of knowledge that legitimized not the child's home culture but an (initially) alien culture.

Although every subject taught in Indian and national schools aimed to transform cultures, not all subjects were taught in every school; nor were all subjects taught in the same school throughout the period under review. Indeed, there was far greater variety from school to school *within* the BIA and CNEI systems than between those systems. Circumstances, teacher availability, and money decreed the mix of subjects. Neither in Ireland, however, nor in Native America did authorities make many concessions to local cultural circumstances. The assimilationist BIA curriculum in some form was presented to Lakotas and Navajos and Hopis, the CNEI curriculum to urban English-speakers and rural Irish-speakers. Fashions did change. Child- and community-centered progressive educational ideas began to influence educational authorities later in the period under review, for example. Yet the assimilatory drive was powerfully maintained throughout, both in what was presented and in what was erased by the curriculum.

I

The BIA and CNEI espoused variants of the "half and half" curriculum: a mix of literary or academic subjects with vocational and manual labor subjects and practices. As general moral uplift and Christian religious instruction were central to both systems, we might more accurately refer to the "three thirds" curriculum. On both continents the ideal persisted of training both mind and body and of preparing the vast majority of children for modest roles in society, supposedly appropriate to their gender.

The literary or academic element was central. Indeed, it is highly likely that on both continents most parents enrolled their children so they might learn the English language and reading and writing, along with academic subjects of supposedly higher status than those relating to mere manual labor or vocation. What immediately becomes apparent is the similarity between the academic curriculum in America and Ireland, indeed across the Western world. "Performance in reading and writing, and also arithmetic," writes Vincent, "became the basic unit of exchange between the school and the state, the teacher and the family, and the education system and the labour market." The length of sentences a child could read and spell accurately "became the means by which governments could measure the efficiency of their expenditure of tax-payers' money, by which the parents could determine that their children were making some kind of progress . . . and by which employers could discriminate between applicants who could now sign their names on a piece of paper."⁴ Also characteristic of CNEI and BIA systems for most of the century was the fact that English, along with being a curricular subject to be taught at increasingly difficult levels from grade to grade, was the language of almost all interaction with teachers, irrespective of the home language of the child—a policy that produced the massive difficulties of adjustment and learning we examined in the previous chapter.

Small local day schools, generally coeducational in the BIA system, provided a very basic academic offering to Indian children. The Nez Perce school was meant for about sixty Indian pupils, but there were seventy-five boys and girls crowded into it, according to the superintendent in 1889, and many of the recent arrivals were "totally ignorant of the English language or civilized customs." The progress of the older boys who understood some English had been satisfactory: "Our more advanced pupils work in fractions, read in the Fourth Reader, have a fair knowledge of the geography of North America, letter-writing, and simple English composition. All our Indian pupils show great aptness in penmanship, drawing, and music."⁵ One of Gertrude Golden's students at a different school wrote to tell how she had learned much from her teacher, but "I just don't know what is the matter with me. I just could not get the fractions but I hope I would learn more arithmetic." At the Fort Defiance Boarding School in Arizona, according to Navajo Frank Mitchell, "they taught us the ABCs and 1, 2, 3 and all that"—the three R's. "As soon as you got up to ten you knew you were educated," he continued. "We never had tests or grades. We never knew who was top of anyone else."⁶

Had Mitchell gone beyond the first few grades, he would have been privileged with a far more varied and demanding academic curriculum. He should have progressed from grade to grade and from reader to reader, often the famous McGuffey Readers used in white schools, with their challenging and multisyllabic vocabulary.⁷ For, as was happening throughout the Western world, the new school systems were moving to the examining and grading of pupils, and their categorization into a hierarchy of classes according to age and ability. Even in small schools the idea of hierarchy appears to have caught on quickly. Francis La Flesche reveled in besting his Omaha friends at the Presbyterian mission school in the 1860s: "don't mind those boys," he told Brush, his older pupil mentor, "what do they know? They're all way back in the Second reader, and you are in the Fifth, and I am in the third."⁸

The three R's, then, along with some combination of geography, history, algebra, geometry, and music, were the fare presented at smaller Indian day and boarding schools. A very similar curriculum faced Irish children—with the exception of history, which only made the CNEI curriculum in 1908. If Irish pupils thus lacked a historical perspective on their own peoples, so, ironically, did Indians: the history taught in BIA was Euro-American history, not local tribal or even Pan-Indian history. Recall the 1889 words of Commissioner Morgan, that Indians should not be reminded of "their own sad histories," only of their glowing future as U.S. citizens. And in 1891 another commissioner hammered home the same message. "Special attention is paid in the Government schools to the inculcation of patriotism," he declared:

The Indian pupils are taught that they are Americans, that the Government is their friend, that the flag is their flag, that the one great duty resting on them is loyalty to the government, and thus the foundation is laid for perpetual peace between the Indian tribes in this country and the white people. Over every Government school floats the American flag, and in every Government school there are appropriate exercises celebrating Washington's birthday, the Fourth of July, and other national holidays.[9]

II

At Carlisle and other large boarding schools, as at larger Irish schools, the academic curriculum was far more ambitious. In 1883, for example, the principal of Carlisle's education department reviewed "the work of the school-rooms," which then catered to young Indians boys and girls from about twenty different tribal groups. Noting first the difficulty of "maintaining a good system of grading" with the newcomers, the writer went on to detail, year by year, the academic curriculum.[10]

In the first session first-year pupils, mostly ignorant of English, learned the objective study of the language—through giving names to objects—writing words, phrases, and sentences on slates, blackboards, and notebooks. They also used objects to learn addition and subtraction orally and to count, write, and read numbers. In the second session similar work continued, but they began to learn Roman characters, using special charts and lessons. That first year they also began subjects such as drawing, singing, gymnastics, modeling in clay, and "phonic drill" for enunciation.

In the second year similar work continued, but pupils began the First Reader. Pictures were to be used in class, along with charts to help understanding. In English studies pupils went on to sentence making, letter writing, and descriptions of pictures or objects, and they produced oral and written stories. Arithmetic included addition, subtractions, multiplication, and division. Drawing, music, and gymnastics were also included. In the third year pupils moved to the Second Reader, began to write diaries, continued arithmetic with the "simplest tables of reductions and fractions by using kindergarten blocks and other objects." Geography began with the molding board.

By the fourth year, teenagers of both sexes began with the Third Reader, supplemented by simple lessons in natural science, history, and geography from various texts. In English language they moved into areas such as abstracts of lessons, diaries, letters, descriptions, and compositions. Geography included the learning of natural divisions of land and water, names and features of continents and the United States. Arithmetic continued with fractions, tables of time and measure, and weight; and with practical issues such as finding the cost of supplies of food, fuel, and clothing. In the fifth year these approaches continued. There were some very advanced students at Carlisle, a few of whom had almost completed seventh grade grammar school studies; they were at the level of many white students, in other words. As sometimes happened in the Irish system, two of these young people had been groomed as teachers and had taught their fellows, under supervision. In addition, all students had to write a "written review" that would not be graded, thus removing examination jitters.

It was an ambitious and highly systematic program, drawing on the kinds of readers and other texts used at white schools. This academic side of the curriculum was broadly shared by both sexes; gender differentiation would become clearer in the vocational/manual labor side. The teacher was modest in his claims for results, noting that progress in textbook work, especially through the readers, had been slower than in previous years. He validly pointed to the fact that many of Carlisle's students began at a later age than white children, "after the best years for memorizing have passed away." Even younger beginners were overwhelmed by "the multiplicity of objects and events which come under their notice"—a nineteenth-century way of expressing "information overload," perhaps, made especially difficult in that the pupils came from entirely different cultures and generally lacked English.

In 1890, reflecting then-current progressive education emphasis on the need for schooling to be more student centered and relevant to the local community, a new "Course of Study" was promulgated by the BIA.[11] The first four years constituted a "primary grade"; the next four an "advanced grade"—making for an eight-year course of studies. In English, through the use of "objects," pictures, and conversations, the second-year pupil (primary grade) was to learn "to describe in English what he sees and hears, and makes a beginning at letter writing." Further, "pupils should not only acquire the habit of expressing themselves in complete sentences, but also of making some variety and discrimination in the choice of words. The thought must proceed expression." As part of the cultural mission, "Every exercise should be [an English] language lesson."

By the end of the fourth year (advanced grade—actually eighth year), pupils faced a wide range of subjects: reading (Fifth Reader), orthography, arithmetic, including percentages and "practical application of principles"; penmanship (business letters, notes, receipts, etc.); drawing ("individual advancement to be encouraged"); language (English); geography ("of North and South America, with instructions in general upon the races, the countries, the climates, and the commerce of the world."); United States history; physiology and hygiene; civil government ("Simple oral lessons . . . meaning of terms town, village, county, State, etc.; elections, citizenship, etc."); observation lessons (plants and animals); general exercises, such as music, calisthenics, morals, and manners—which involved "treating pupils as young ladies and gentlemen."

This varied, eight-year program might not yet lift tribal children to quite the same academic level as similar-aged white children. Yet, as the commissioner explicitly concluded, it was about equal to that obtained in six years at public school among the whites, and it fitted the pupil "either to make his own way alongside white citizens or to take the advanced course offered in some Indian industrial training school."

A possibly racist downgrading of goals for Indians did occur around 1900, as we have seen; the new Course of Studies gave greater emphasis to the manual labor component. Throughout the period under review, however, some version of this impressive academic curriculum was presented to Indian children at the most advantaged schools, for at least some part of the day. Girls as well as boys took most of the "literary" subjects; republican gender ideals demanded that "civilized" homemakers should be adequately educated to raise Christian, patriotic, informed children.

III

Irish national school pupils faced a very similar literary and academic curriculum, although about half of them, by 1900, did so in a single-sex environment: boys taught by men, girls and young children of both sexes taught by women.[12] Instruction was also entirely through English for most of the period under review. Here too the content varied from school to school, but the CNEI was equally insistent upon a system and over the decades carefully laid out its educational goals. Like the academic side of the BIA curriculum, the academic side of the Irish curriculum was intended for both boys and girls; yet even this exhibited some gender differentiation, coming to include subjects such as needlework, for girls, in the regular curriculum. The CNEI also saw itself as educating the sexes to different roles in life. Speaking specifically of readers prepared for girls, Antonia McManus notes how these books provided them "with a thorough preparation for their future lives as domestic servants, housewives and mothers, and took every precaution to ensure that they would carry out their duties with efficiency and integrity." Janet Nolan also points to the increasing attention to "housewifery" as the decades wore on, with lessons added specifically for girls in such skills as sewing, cooking, and laundering.[13]

In 1873, shortly after the beginning of the "payment by results" regime, the National Board presented a detailed "Programme of Instruction and Examination for National Schools, and Scales of Results Fees."[14] The first class used the First Book (Reader) and learned English spelling and writing. They also learned arithmetic, at least the addition tables. The second class continued in a similar vein, using the Second Reader. They should now be able "(a) To read correctly, and with due attention to pauses, the lessons in the Second Book. (b) To answer simple questions on the meaning of words, the subject matter of lessons, and to point out on the map place therein referred to." At this level needlework was added (later explicitly for girls). In the third class the pupils were introduced to geography and moved on to the Third Book. By the fourth class, grammar entered the curriculum, and—explicitly for boys—agriculture, but apparently more as memory work than a practical subject. They must "answer intelligently on the subject matter of the lessons in Part III (Crops) of the Agricultural Class Book." Girls (now explicitly) were "to exhibit proficiency in hemming, stitching, and top-sewing, and in plain knitting."

The fifth class was broken into two stages; in each the subject mix was similar, but different levels were demanded. The reading requirement was the same for both levels: "(a.) To read with fluency, correctness, and intelligence the first 200 pages of the Fifth Book of Lessons. (b.) To answer intelligently on the subject matter read. (c.) To speak correctly six of the poetical pieces in the prescribed portion of the Fifth Book." The arithmetic demands of the second stage included new subject matter, such as working in "Compound Proportion, Practice, and easy questions in Vulgar Fractions and Decimals." And grammar at this stage required knowledge of Latin roots and prefixes. By the sixth class the Sixth Book was in use. Although boys and girls studied arithmetic, one area—"Involution and Evolution"—was reserved for boys only. Further, students might study and teachers achieve points (and additional salary) in a wide and impressive list of extra subjects such as vocal music and drawing, classics and French, geometry, algebra, "or other approved branches of science" (which might include plane trigonometry, navigation, mechanics, hydrostatics and pneumatics, light and sound, magnetism, and electricity). Obviously the goal was to provide a growing academic curriculum for those schools blessed with suitably competent teachers. The details differ, but an Indian child would have been equally at home—or equally at sea—facing this CNEI curriculum.

By the early twentieth century the National Board's academic offerings had developed somewhat, also partly in response to progressive ideas. The Revised Programme of 1900 was "in many respects radically different" from that used in the recently ended "payment by results" era, according to the CNEI. The "essentials of education" were "a knowledge of Reading, Writing, and Arithmetic on rational principles" and also included manual instruction, drawing, school discipline and physical drill, and vocal music.[15] The new program was far more ambitious than its predecessor. Indeed, in the 1904 *Report* the revised curriculum ran to *thirty pages*.[16] Like that of the BIA, the Irish National Board's revised curriculum was "promulgated provisionally and tentatively." Recognizing the poor state of things in some localities, especially "the lack of expert teachers in the higher branches of manual instruction," the program was drawn up in two forms, one for single-teacher schools, the other for two-teacher schools. In most areas, the board conceded, teaching might not go beyond the second standard; in some areas to the fourth and fifth; and a few pupils might go further (this was sometimes mentioned for Indians too), as teaching might be available through the new Department of Agricultural and Technical Instruction.

The program was also linked to graded readers, and it went through seven "standards" within each subject. At standard five of English, for example, a Literary Fifth Reader was used, which pupils should be able "to read with correctness and intelligence, and to recite from." A "suitable Historical Reader" should also be used—a new development—and a standard work of popular fiction introduced. Proficiency in spelling should be acquired through reading, dictation, and composition. Writing itself was a separate subject, also spanning seven standards. Then came grammar—level six demanded analysis, etymology, syntax, correction of errors, common roots, prefixes and affixes. Geography included some knowledge of Ireland and a basic knowledge of the globe. Then came arithmetic: by the seventh level pupils should have a knowledge of reasons for processes, decimals, averages, percentages, stocks, square roots, compound proportion, along with easy mensuration of rectilineal figures and the circle. Singing involved a highly detailed list of requirements up to the seventh standard. Drawing at least appeared less technical and less demanding: by seventh standard pupils should be able to draw simple natural objects such as flowers. Needlework, "(girls)," was followed by physical drill and, if possible, musical drill. Manual instruction (including placing bricks in plan and elevation) only encompassed two levels. Object lessons and elementary experimental science followed, including the "Principle of Archimedes extended to other liquids, than water."

The program then presented a young children's curriculum for large schools, and other variants for smaller schools, and—the result of nationalist agitation—the bilingual program in both Irish and English. It also included the requirement for "extra subjects" such as Irish, French, Latin, and mathematics (algebra, geometry, and mensuration), and concluded with the curricular requirements for monitors.

A version of science for girls *was* included—but with a more domestic emphasis: "Household temperature of rooms, of hot bath; temperature of the body in health and sickness, the clinical thermometer." Despite the inclusion of practical experiment, the boys' scientific material appears more theoretical and thus more prestigious. Cookery was specifically for girls.[17]

The recommended CNEI curricula were also highly systematic and carefully planned, the product of seventy years' experience of teaching Irish children. As in the American system, individual ex-pupils could recall their internalization of the hierarchical agenda. Patrick Gallagher was a national school student in Donegal in the 1870s and at age ten was using the second CNEI book (reader): "until I passed into the third book," he wrote, "I would not be looked on as a scholar." Reflecting a more relaxed view, but also suggesting how readers on both sides of the Atlantic could stimulate the young ego, Sean O'Faolain believed that it depended on each student "how much interest in literature he got out of our English Readers—I know that I loved to recite poetry from them and became vain in my power to do it readily and well."[18]

By the early 1900s a major difference in the academic side of the Irish curriculum from that of the BIA was the gradual inclusion, first as extra subject, then more fully, of the local vernacular. Of course, even had the BIA wanted to encourage Indian languages, it would have been extremely difficult to do so in large, multilingual schools such as Carlisle. It was more possible at small single-tribe schools, as missionaries sometimes showed. Few BIA teachers appear to have studied Indian languages, however; and even for the minority in both areas who had gone through forms of teacher education, there was little training in approaches we today call TOEFL (teaching of English as a foreign language) or ESL (English as a second language).[19] This pedagogical lack also applied in the Irish system.

IV

The second "half" of the curriculum on both continents, was the "manual labor" element. Pupils in BIA schools would spend part of each day learning about and even gaining practical experience in certain kinds of labor supposedly appropriate to their class and gender. Internalizing the Protestant work ethic was, of course, more than a matter of preparation for a job; it was part of the moral training of the Indian child for economic self-reliance in accord with American values, preparing him or her for civilized citizenship in the United States. "The Indian has a natural aversion to manual labor of whatever kind," claimed superintendent P. F. Burke of the Albuquerque Indian Industrial School in 1887. "This aversion is hereditary. . . . idleness suits him much better than work. To overcome this natural tendency to laziness is the first and most important step to take."[20]

Indian men were thus to forsake their supposedly lazy, nomadic hunting and warring ways and mostly settle as farmers. Their women should also cease wandering to gather berries or, in farming tribes, working outside the home in their fields—this was man's work—and become model housewives taking care of their farm cabins on their separate plots of land. Actually, like nineteenth-century white American and Irish societies, Indian peoples also reserved distinct, complementary roles for men and women; thus there were deep compatibles between educators and those to be educated. Yet many whites perceived the tribal woman as "the squaw drudge"—exploited by males and therefore awaiting her deliverance into Victorian ideals of civilized womanhood. "In the past days the Indian woman was expected to do most of the work that was to be done," declared a Yankton Sioux pupil of Hampton Institute at its commencement day in 1885, showing how an Indian girl could internalize such a stereotype. "The man did very little work; he used to hunt most. When he was at home, he was invited to feast with his friends." A decade later the Indian commissioner sympathized with tribal women "in their groping attempts to acquire the arts of complicated civilized housekeeping."[21] Ironically, this "uplifting" into "true womanhood" would deliver Indian women—and indeed their Irish sisters—from one set of limited choices to another, just as limited.[22]

Superintendent A. T. C. Pierson described a typical BIA small-school approach to manual labor teaching in the early 1850s. The Winnebago boys spent two hours in class learning spelling, reading, and writing; "the balance of the time is spent in labor in the field or cutting wood for the school." Potatoes and other products cultivated by the boys were divided between the children in winter. When the school had built a "shop," the agent had no doubt that the boys "would make good mechanics." Significantly, the girls devoted only *one hour* a day to books; the balance of their time was "devoted to cutting, sewing, and knitting garments, for themselves and boys, of materials furnished for that purpose." As long as the system of manual-labor schools was "fully, carefully, and kindly sustained," concluded the agent, "so long the best results may be expected in the improvement of the Winnebego, both socially and morally." Over two decades later Peter Ronan, agent to the Flathead people of the Montana Territory, similarly described a Catholic school, run by nuns in a generally successful way, at least for the girls. Industry was "the great civilizer," wrote the agent, "and it is only by leading the rising generation into habits of industry, as well as education, that they will be brought to the understanding of the advantage and elevation of labor and industrial pursuits."[23]

Late in the century Captain Pratt of Carlisle developed the "outing system"—sending pupils out to work for white employers—which soon spread to many other Indian schools. This approach, according to the commissioner in 1887, was "an important auxiliary in educating Indian youth and preparing them for self-support." Noting how the system allowed young Indians to live as members of a white family, he felt that "such a training on a farm is the best possible way of fitting them for the ownership and cultivation of the lands which are being allotted to them by the Government." Thus manual labor training, in conjunction with the academic curriculum, "places them beyond all reasonable doubt upon a footing of self-support"[24]

The new Course of Studies introduced by the BIA in 1900 did not radically change the academic contents of the curriculum or methods of teaching. However, the BIA now placed far greater emphasis on the vocational side of the Indian school curriculum. The goal, according to Estelle Reel, superintendent of Indian schools in 1903, was still "to give the Indian child a knowledge of the English language, and to equip him with the means of earning a livelihood." Perhaps the boy would become a farmer, the girl a housekeeper. They were "the children of a child race," who should be trained in "relevant" vocational pursuits, rather than supposedly irrelevant academic knowledge. Attention had been given to "the industrial features of the course," including various approaches to agriculture—most likely the occupation of the majority of Indians in the future.[25]

Historians have been critical of such downgrading of academic subjects. The schools, as Frederick E. Hoxie expressed it, would now teach Indians "to follow the direction of their 'civilized' neighbors and [later] labor patiently on the fringes of 'civilization.'" And K. Tsianina Lomawaima claims that the core goal of education of girls at Chilocco School was "the development of subservience among Indian women rather than realistic training for employment."[26] Indeed, in 1898 the superintendent of the Albuquerque Indian School implied what such historians have since claimed. "In most instances," he wrote, "the educational value of the shops and the farm has been lost sight of, and the true function of these departments has been degraded to merely turning out a certain amount of work, and the instructors are consequently only foremen." He recommended more careful thought and planning, and the realization "of the vital connection between mind and hand training."[27]

Other BIA officials admitted that some Indian peoples objected to manual labor for their children. In 1906, for example, William B. Dew, superintendent to the Fort Lapwai School, Idaho, claimed that "as in the case of all ignorant races, education is supposed to consist entirely of literary training, and anything else is considered servitude." The superintendent for schools in the Indian Territory (Oklahoma) pointedly declared in 1907 that to these Indian parents "manual labor was fit only for the negroes and white renters."[28]

Whether one sees the manual labor requirement as leading to "proletarianization," or as increasingly racist, or as a realistic attempt to help Indians adapt, the whole approach was part of the assimilatory process. Its goal was not the improvement of tribal approaches to work or of traditional economic patterns, but the total substitution of each tribal work ethic by the white one—or by two, gender-based white work ethics. The Hopi farmer was "the dry-farming expert of the world," conceded Theo G. Lemon, superintendent of the Moqui (Hopi) School in 1906. "The lands of his nativity furnishes ideal conditions for the production of certain crops by 'dry farming,' and the ages have taught him what crops and where to find the conditions." Despite such apparent expertise, Hopi customs lacked "practical common sense" and were "the height of folly." Whereas "under reasonable laws and customs [the Hopi] might live here in peace . . . but his laws and customs are not natural or reasonable." Therefore, as with so much else, the people and their laws and customs had to change.[29]

Indian ex-pupils remembered the working side of school life, often with deep resentment. By the sixth grade Irene Stewart, a Navajo, had become a "well-trained worker." She had never forgotten "how the steam in the laundry made me sick; how standing and ironing for hours made my legs ache late into the night. By evening I was too tired to play and I just fell asleep wherever I sat down. I think this was why the boys and girls ran away from school; why some became ill; why it was so hard to learn. We were too tired to study." Kay Bennett, another Navajo, claimed that while girls accepted the tidying of their rooms, they objected to having to clean the washrooms, showers, and toilets. All received some such duty periodically, but work could also be used a punishment for rule breaking.[30]

Some pupils could express ambivalence, however, or even positive attitudes—in their own societies they would have faced similar responsibilities. The study of agriculture was "especially important to the Indian boy and girl for this reason," wrote a Haskell student on an examination answer in 1915. "When they have grown up and gone to their homes they can show their people how to farm." Reminiscing adult Indians also spoke appreciatively of such demands. Luther Standing Bear actually enjoyed his "outing" period, working at the Wanamaker Store in Philadelphia, along with his spell as a recruiter for the school among his own people. He resented having to work at tinsmithing, however: he felt that this skill would be useless when he returned to the reservation, and he strongly believed that obligatory manual labor was inhibiting him in his academic studies. Similarly, Apache Jason Betzinez came to resent the three summers spent "outing" for an admittedly warm-hearted Quaker family. He too felt that his education as well as his efforts to learn English "were being retarded by being absent so long from the school." Although Daniel La France, a Mohawk, appreciated the variety of vocational skills to be learned at his school and actually enjoyed his "outing," he too felt he might have graduated faster had he been able to concentrate on the academic curriculum.[31]

Payment for work not only communicated the capitalist ethic but also elicited positive responses from Indians. Even if Helen Sekaquaptewa felt that manual training had prevented her from graduating after many years at white schools, she enjoyed both the sense of responsibility and the money involved. She took charge of the school laundry one summer, around 1912, at a salary of $15 per month. "What I earned then," she recalled happily, "was the only money I ever had," although most of it quickly went into a school bank for later use. She established a number of profitable "outing" arrangements while still a pupil at the Phoenix Indian School and sold her embroidery and crochet work. "I never bought candy or pop but bought thread to make things so I could earn more." This must have thrilled her teachers, hardly aware that the Hopi people have an equally demanding work ethic.[32]

Don Talayesva, a Hopi, was similarly stimulated by money. He used his earnings to buy a second-hand pistol, for he believed "that a man with a gun in his holster looked important." A payment of $2 per day made "outing" work in the Colorado beet fields more bearable for James McCarthy, a Papago. Lucille Winnie, an Iroquois, worked Sunday mornings for one of her teachers. "The dollar she paid me was a small fortune," she recalled, "and I could make it stretch to at least four trips to The Shack [an off-campus eating place]."[33]

V

"We hope thus to assist in spreading improved notions of husbandry amongst the young and the old," declared the CNEI of its proposed manual labor curriculum in 1840. This would be done both inside and outside the classroom through "agricultural departments" attached to national schools. Thus the National Board also saw itself as a force not just in political and educational transformation but also in Irish economic modernization. This ambition was still evident at the other end of the century. In 1890 inspector Alexander

Hamilton lamented with obvious modernizing disdain that "the Irish peasant is intensely and unreasonably conservative. His knowledge is very limited; his distrust of everything new is all but invincible. In some degree he is
a fatalist. Poor crops, like bad seasons, come he knows not why and he knows
not whence." Mr. Newell, head inspector, complained in 1893 about the tendency of pupils to spend money thoughtlessly or to avoid saving it at interest.
He continued: "coupled with the natural generosity of the Irish character,
[these habits] tend to counteract successful inculcation of those lessons of
forethought, and the formation of those commercial habits which it is so
desirable that children should acquire."[34]

In 1842 the board noted the need to encourage local initiatives by having
teachers "taught the principles and practice of improved agriculture during
their training course, and by receiving agricultural students at our Model
Training Farm at Glasnevin [in Dublin]." By 1845 the CNEI had established
five model agricultural schools, with five more planned. In addition, there
were seven ordinary national schools that had land attached and offered agricultural instruction. Scholarships had been established in two of these. The
devastation of the 1840s Great Famine—"the present alarming and calami-
tous state of Ireland"—intensified the need "to teach our people modes of
cultivating better crops, and even in the less afflicted districts . . . this requires
more skill and knowledge than the average Irish peasant yet possesses."[35] By
1870 the board was administering a scheme of nineteen model agricultural
schools and recognizing eighteen more under local management. Further,
like some Indian schools, eighty-three schools had farms attached.[36]

Later in the century, due to failed expectations and to Treasury stringency,
a practical approach to manual labor began to fade. The Royal Commission of
Inquiry into Primary Education of 1868–70 (the Powis Commission) opposed
the continuation of the agricultural model schools but allowed agriculture
as a "payment by results" subject—as rote memorizing rather than hands-on
learning. The CNEI disposed of these schools, keeping the one at Glasnevin
and the Munster Institute in Cork. Just as the BIA was intensifying its crusade
to bring the American work ethic to the Indians, the CNEI, for mixed financial and other reasons, was quietly backpedaling initially ambitious efforts in
this area. Many of the regular school subjects, such as needlework, were, of
course, vocational in nature; as we have seen, there was increasing emphasis
on such subjects for girls later in the century.[37]

It is likely that a further reason for the CNEI's failure was the widely shared
attitude of Irish people that academic learning was socially superior to work
with the hand or even to advanced technical skills—a prejudice also shared
by some Indians and indeed further afield.[38] In 1884 inspector Downing pro-

claimed that "Repugnance to physical labor of all kinds is growing apace. Education is sought for by the masses only as a means of 'getting a situation'; not at all with a view to the improvement of the productiveness of agriculture, the manufacturing industries, and the trade of the country." Yet, he lamented, the bulk of the people would have to accept manual labor: in later life they would not need "intellectual power to grapple with abstruse studies; but sound moral principles, good habits, good address, and as much useful knowledge and mechanical skills or handiness as can be imparted to them. . . . No aspirations should be aroused likely to end in disappointment." Five years later in 1889, Miss Prendergast, one of the few female inspectors (for girls' subjects) made a similar judgment. "There unfortunately exists, in some parts of this country," she claimed, "a strong distaste for manual occupations. This is largely due, I believe, to a mistaken sense of what is 'proper pride'—an outcome of the lively Celtic imagination—which represents such work as socially lowering to the worker." Therefore a girl who might struggle to learn a rule in arithmetic, something she would have no practical use for later, "brings dull mind and idle hands to the lesson in needlework, which she considers beneath her notice"—although such learning would be highly useful in later life.[39]

A fragmentary yet suggestive corroboration of such views comes from a folklore informant. He remembered how boys in his school rebelled even against the textbook on agriculture. "Shortly after us getting this book," he told an interviewer, "two of the lads in the class put their heads together and said to one another that they had no business of this book on farming as they wouldn't ever be on that profession." There followed a class conspiracy: "we all refused to study the lessons about tillage and grass and crops and for a few days we were slapped but after that third day the master got enraged and dashed the book to the ground. We had no more classes out of that book." Whether such a glorious revolution occurred is open to question, but the informant hardly pulled the idea out of the air. Further, like inspector Prendergast, he too believed that the knowledge he and his mates rejected long ago would have been useful in later life: most of the boys were farmers' sons "and badly needed what was in that book but the two who didn't want it organized them into resistance and it worked."[40]

Compared to the continual references in the Indian sources to various forms of manual labor at boarding schools, there are only a few other comments by less exploited Irish ex-pupils. Eamon Kelly's school had a garden attached, in which the boys actually enjoyed growing fruit of all kinds. A female folklore informant remembered work duties at her school: some pupils arrived before the teacher in the morning to dust the room and light the fire. R. B. Robson, who later became a principal at a CNEI school in Ulster, spent six weeks at Glasnevin Agricultural Model School, a boarding school, but he regarded it as a holiday and told little on the nature of the program or teaching. He did remember being reprimanded for holding a tool incorrectly, and the superintendent once called his group "the worst pack of slackers he had ever met."[41]

With a more willing treasury and stronger public support for manual labor, the CNEI too would probably have persisted in what the commissioners saw as a vital project in modernization of the lower classes. The BIA treasury *was* willing, and Indian peoples were less strong in their resistance than the Irish, so the Indian manual labor program intensified rather than faded away, as the century wore on.

VI

Not just the missionary societies but the supposedly secular, or at least non-denominational, BIA and CNEI authorities believed they were doing far more than filling the children with facts or training them in vocations and gender roles. It was a deeply Christian universe, whether Catholic or Protestant in its emphasis, into which the teachers and other staff were to lead their charges.

For American authorities and teachers, the mission was to spread the "Christian civilization," of which the United States was the foremost exemplar. This was part of a broader American and indeed Western view: educational reformers believed in the need to, as Peter N. Stearns expresses it, "provide children with an embracing moral context. . . . Schools, in this view, had a pivotal role to play in surrounding children with guidance and restraint."[42] Yet the U.S. Constitution enshrined the principle of church-state separation, so the BIA strove not to favor any Christian group. Although the Indian Service appeared to work equally well with Catholic missionaries, it is likely that, at least until the early twentieth century, most officials and "Friends of the Indian" assumed a Protestant destiny for the tribes.

BIA officials were quite forthright on their moral goals. "Although sectarian teaching is forbidden in the schools," declared the Indian commissioner characteristically in 1899, "they are not godless institutions. The broad principles of the Bible, of religion, and morality are taught, and, as far as it is possible, only strong religious characters are placed in charge of the children" Another commissioner was brutally explicit when in 1903 he declared, "The moral condition of the schools is of supreme importance." Whenever "a supervisor or other conscientious inspecting official has reported that the moral tone of an Indian school was not good the superintendent or some employees, or both, have been relieved." Such occasions were few, he claimed, compared with the total numbers of schools and employees. Perhaps the most powerful and ambitious expression of the need to blend academic, moral, civic, and character training came from the commissioner in 1890:

The highest efficiency of a school is tested by its results in moral character, and thence the highest duty is effective moral teaching. These facts are recognized in the present course of study, which makes provision for instruction in morals and manners to supplement the mental training furnished by the regular instruction and discipline of the schools. The course should include lessons on cleanliness and neatness, gentleness, politeness, kindness to others, kindness to animals, love for parents, benefactors, etc., respect and reverence, gratitude, obedience, truthfulness, purity, honesty, courage, honor, reputation, self-control, self-denial, confession of wrong, forgiveness, [rejection of] evil-speaking, profanity, good habits, industry, temperance, frugality; also civil duties including love of country, obedience to law, respect for civil rulers, fidelity to official trusts, nature and obligations of oath, the ballot and other duties involved in good citizenship.[43]

Rather than explicitly attacking "heathenism," BIA teachers appear to have simply ignored tribal beliefs and promoted Christian ones. Ex-pupil Luther Standing Bear, a Lakota, nicely caught the character of the campaign. All Carlisle students were free to choose any Christian denomination, he recalled without irony; most of the pupils then selected the Episcopalian Church. His memory is confirmed by Captain Pratt, who in his 1882 report noted: "All our students attend Sabbath School, the girls in their own chapel, the boys at the different churches in Carlisle [town]." Such religious influences, concluded Pratt, "have produced gratifying results." At Hampton Institute in the next decade, however, tensions between already Christianized Indians apparently resulted in "bitter strife and sectarian feelings." Principal H. B. Frissel believed, nevertheless, that the training provided could give such pupils a broader vision. The different denominations were represented among teachers, other staff, and students, "but we all work under the same banner of Him whose name is above every name—Jesus Christ, our Lord and Savior."[44]

Thus BIA officials struggled to reconcile varied Protestant and Catholic approaches to Indian schooling—as did the CNEI in Ireland. Yet the vast majority of Indian pupils were non-Christian "heathens"—a situation not faced in Ireland—and at no point did the BIA or missionaries seriously contemplate the possible validity of Indian tribal religions. In 1892, for example, agent David L. Shipley strongly advocated schooling for the Moqui (Hopis). "A great deal may thus be accomplished," he wrote, "towards breaking up and destroying their crude forms of worship, superstition, etc., and thus gradually supplant them with a knowledge of true Christian principles." And in 1896 acting agent Capt. W. H. Beck wrote that the Omaha people "claim they have a right to their religious observances." However, these were "in fact the bar-barous customs of their progenitors." If some way could be found to prevent them indulging in old ways of feasting and "counseling," he wrote, "a great advance in civilization would be made. Persuasion is not very efficacious."[45]

As might be expected, Indian children responded in diverse ways. Zitkala-Ša, a Nakota, claimed that even while a pupil she rejected Christianity, perhaps partly as a result of her general unhappiness at the boarding school, along with a sense of guilt over having left her mother. Helen Sekaquaptewa, a Hopi, resented the mandatory attendance at Sunday school early in the twentieth century. "I couldn't understand a thing [the preacher] talked about," she de-clared, "but I had to sit and listen to a long sermon. I hated them and felt like crying. If I nodded my head kept going to sleep, a teacher would poke me and tell me to be good." Every time the preacher seemed about to finish he would start all over again. Corroborating the Hampton report on religious rivalries, Sekaquaptewa noted dismissively that the "different sects were always urging us and bribing us with little presents to join their church. It didn't appeal to me and I didn't join any of them." Her bitter comments are so out of character with the rest of her serene autobiography that she must have been especially disturbed by these experiences.[46]

Others, such as Frank Mitchell, also complained about sermons, especially when preached in English. One missionary used the Navajo language, but he mispronounced words: while he thought he was addressing them as "my dear children," he was in fact calling them "abalone shells." Don Talayesva actu-ally joined the YMCA, gave at least one sermon at a meeting, and even won a prize for learning the names of the books of the Bible; he appeared to have ac-cepted a form of Christianity. Yet a deeply frightening dream-vision, brought on when he talked badly about a Hopi "two-heart" (a witch), pulled him back to traditional beliefs.[47]

Some narrators indicated how young Indians attempted to incorporate the new knowledge into their own worldviews. Francis la Flesche also resented boring sermons, but he enjoyed Bible stories, especially when read out to him by his friend, who made them sound like traditional narratives. Sanapia, a Comanche woman, "really did enjoy" the mission school she briefly attended in Oklahoma. Yet even with such a positive attitude, she and her mates had difficulty accepting such Christian truths as the virgin birth of Christ. "Did you see the baby?" they asked their teacher, more out of disbelief than mock-ery. Mary Inkanish, a Cheyenne, had never seen lions, so she found the story of Daniel hard to understand. She thought, however, that Judith, who cut off a man's head, "was a real mean woman . . . as mean as a Sioux."[48]

Individual Indians did open themselves to the new religion, although we can never be sure about motivation. Brush, an older boy at the Omaha school and mentor to Francis La Flesche, lectured his friends on the importance of Christianity. Yet in La Flesche's account Brush at least initially appeared more interested in the Western clothing of the missionary. Jason Betzinez, a young Apache adult when sent against his will to Carlisle after the Geronimo War of 1886, became a willing convert to Christianity. He felt no resentment at having to attend church, and he too joined the YMCA. Unlike Talayesva, he seems to have held to Christianity into later adulthood. "This influence became stronger and stronger as I came to understand English better," he wrote. "It changed my whole life"—almost a classic expression of an evangelical rebirth experience. When Howard Whitewolf, a Comanche, returned from school he first discarded white clothes and went "wild." Yet later he too experienced a life-transforming conversion. He became an interpreter in the Reformed Church in Oklahoma and strongly advocated schooling for Indian children in order to achieve self-reliance.[49]

Thomas Alford, a Shawnee, went into some detail about his long and agonizing conversion experiences: "In the end the voice [of Jesus] won, and I was happy in the love of God." However, the elders of his tribe had earlier instructed him to learn all the knowledge of the whites except their religion, so he also felt deeply ambivalent and feared that he could never become a leader of his people. While the historian has no right to doubt the depth and sincerity of Alford's conversion experience, his attitudes suggest a lingering traditional belief that the object of spiritual help is success in this rather than the next life. Once the conversion had taken place, he wrote, "I was [now] able to concentrate on my studies." Despite the BIA and missionary goal of complete replacement of one universe for another, Alford, like many of his peers, appeared to be simultaneously living in two universes.[50]

These fragmentary glimpses into student experiences corroborate what scholars have been saying for decades about Indian responses to various forms of Christianity. While they do not deny the wholehearted acceptance by individuals of Christian spiritual beliefs, historians have also noted the often pragmatic or instrumental reasons for conversion. Indians did not generally think of religious ideas in terms of "true" and "false," but in terms of usefulness.[51] Further, although most forms of Christianity are exclusive, following in the First Commandment ("Thou shalt not have false Gods before me"), tribal spiritual beliefs were generally inclusive. Any spiritual force might be helpful to the individual. Therefore conversion to Christianity did not necessarily imply apostasy or desertion of the true (although Alford's Shawnee elders may have thought so), but rather the supplementing of traditional spiritual forces. White Americans were powerful; therefore their god was to be appropriated for individual and community use.[52]

Each individual pupil had his or her own mix of personal and ethnic reasons for accepting, rejecting, or going along with Christian ideas. Some were influenced by Christianized kin; some were impressed by the supposed prestige or even power of the preacher; some saw easy compatibles between, for example, "seeing the light" and the Indian idea of a vision; many syncretized their own and Christian ideas.[53] Edward Goodbird, a Hidatsa, presented a whole swathe of reasons for accepting Christianity: respect for his teacher, enjoyment of Bible stories, and even pure habit: "As I grew older," he recalled, "I thought of myself as a Christian, but more because I went to the mission school, than because I thought of Jesus as my savior."[54]

Even the most anxiously progressive and Christian pupils and ex-pupils retained some of their older cultural ideas, however, becoming what Malcolm McFee has called "150% men/women"—living partly in their traditional worlds, yet enriched, in their own views, by the new knowledge.[55] For others, the Christian elements in the curriculum were to be selected from, brushed off, ignored, or even bitterly rejected. And some individuals went through chains of such responses over time.

As with the academic and vocational sides of the curriculum, in religious terms too the Indian was to be transported from a false to a true universe. Perceptive teachers and missionaries often realized the difficulty of such total transformation, having to accept that Indian pupils thus lived in more than one universe, or even in simultaneously overlapping universes at the school, although to put it this way is to perpetuate an essentially Judeo-Christian understanding of spirituality. Young Indians no doubt saw one universe only, throbbing with all kinds of spirit forces, any of which—including Christianity in some form—could help or hinder the individual.

VII

Anxious to avoid all forms of religious controversy with the jealous major churches, CNEI authorities also strove for denominational neutrality. Yet the final goal was similar. In its "Twelve Practical Rules" for teachers the National Board admonished them "to pay strict attention to the morals and general conduct of their pupils, and to omit no opportunity of inculcating the principles of truth and honesty." The CNEI, like the BIA, assumed that all pupils would receive some Christian instruction. The objective, as the National Board insisted from the beginning, was to bring all the children of Ireland together "as subjects of the same King, and fellows in the same redemption."[56]

During the 1840s the CNEI insisted that a nondenominational "Lesson" be hung up in every school. This admonished pupils to "live peaceably with all men," even with those of a different religious persuasion. They should "show

ourselves followers of Christ, who, 'when he was reviled, reviled not again,'"
and they should do this by behaving gently and kindly to everyone. Three-
quarters of a century later in 1915, in its "General Rules of the System" the
CNEI was still insisting that a similar lesson be hung in each school.[57]

Irish Catholic children who had earlier entered schools run by Protestant
missionary societies often did share an experience similar to that of many
Indians. By 1831, however, the government had settled on a school system that
would respect the religious rights of children and parents, be they Catholic,
Anglican, Presbyterian, or other. This is surely a case of "empowerment" of
a dependent people, due to the particular demographic circumstances in
the country. Had Catholics been a small minority of the Irish people, or had
the majority of Irish people practiced non-Christian "heathen" beliefs, it is
highly likely that the British government would have continued its attempts
to impose a different religion upon them—to treat them like the BIA was then
treating Indians, in other words.

Thus close to a century after the CNEI's establishment, despite changes in
details, the great principle of denominational neutrality persisted. In a 1900
retrospective the National Board still quoted from Lord Stanley's 1831 letter
and thus still saw as its task to provide "a system of combined literary and
separate religious education, capable of being so far adapted to the views of
the different religious establishments in Ireland 'as to render it in truth a system of National Education for the poorer classes of the community.'" In 1915,
setting out its "Fundamental Principles of the System of National Education,"
the board noted that it was "the earnest wish of His Majesty's Government"
that clergy and laity from all denominations should cooperate in this venture.
No school could be conducted in a place of worship, nor even connected to
one by any direct internal communication. No inscription tying a school to a
particular denomination could be accepted, nor could symbols of a denomination be displayed during the hours "of united instruction." There followed
more details of just how religious instruction was to take place, with the
fundamental stipulation that "opportunities must be afforded to all pupils
of all schools for receiving religious instruction as their parents or guardians approve." Therefore the times for such instruction should be fixed—so
there could be no accidental proselytizing of children—and "so that no child
shall be thereby, in effect, excluded, directly or indirectly, from the other advantages which the school affords." Teachers should clearly announce the
beginning of religious instruction and even exhibit "tablets" (large notices)
specifying whether religious or secular instruction was in progress; significantly, the two tablets "must not be exhibited at the same time." Patrons and
managers could decide which versions of the scriptures were to be read during the religious period.

These rules cover close to six pages and suggest the extreme anxiety of the board to avoid any hint of favoring one religious group or any accusation that a Catholic child might have been exposed to even a moment of Protestant instruction, or vice versa for a Protestant child. To an outsider it all might seem the most pointless bureaucratic pedantry, but the CNEI had learned well the lessons of Irish history. As we have seen, the BIA faced similar problems in working with Christian denominations in its schools too.[58]

There is little reference to religion in Irish ex-pupil accounts. This indicates that in general the teachers did keep academic and religious instruction apart. Controversy sometimes raged outside the schools on this issue. Inside the Irish classroom, however, there was little religious conflict, especially because, as the century wore on, more and more pupils were being educated with co-religionists. Except for the Presbyterian Robson, and Robert Briscoe, a Jew, all the narrators whose accounts I studied appear to have been of a Catholic background and thus attended schools under the authority of Catholic patrons and managers.[59]

Apart from noting the significant fact that—in accordance with CNEI rules—he provided his religion affiliation the first day of registration, Robson also ignores the subject, indicating that there was little religious controversy within his Presbyterian national school. A folklore informant recalled how Protestant and Catholic children attended his school; the Catholics actually envied the other group, who could leave class during the period of religious instruction. He claimed that they all "got on famously together and never a word about religion mentioned amongst us." Yet he simultaneously hinted at tensions between the groups: sometimes, he admitted "the bigger lads might say something about Orangism [Protestantism] but it never went any further." One wonders. He believed that the removal of Protestant pupils from his school to one of their own actually worsened community relations. Such fragmentary evidence suggests that even in the midst of Ireland's chronic ethnic-religious divisions, children of different denominations might occasionally get along together in class.[60]

When Frank O'Connor moved from a CNEI school to one run by the Christian Brothers, he noticed a statue of the Blessed Virgin and recalled in passing that "religious images were not allowed in the national schools." And Patrick Shea vividly conveyed how one of the board's rules was faithfully obeyed in his Athlone national school. On the wall behind the teacher, he remembered, "hung a large rectangular display card"—a CNEI "tablet"—"with, on the one side, in heavy black letters, the words 'SECULAR INSTRUCTION' and on the other 'RELIGIOUS INSTRUCTION.' The finger-worn stains on the bottom corners of the card bore witness to [the teacher's] punctiliousness in

ensuring that, as required by the rules of the Commissioners of national education, the exposed side conveyed what was truly going on in the school."⁶¹

Although the CNEI approach of respecting the child's home religion appears quite different from that of the BIA, to some extent pupil experiences in
both systems were similar. Indian schools were also to respect the Christian
beliefs of pupils. Further, religious instruction appears to have been segmented in each curriculum, assigned by the CNEI to special periods and by
the BIA to Sunday Schools and such services. Despite exhortations to infuse a
Christian ethos throughout the schools, BIA teachers hardly did so continu-
ously, nor do inspectors, superintendents, agents, ex-pupils, or ex-teachers
refer often to religious teaching. The major difference between BIA and CNEI
systems, of course, was what happened during the time set aside for religious
instruction: in Ireland the pupils were further indoctrinated into, rather than
out of, the faith of their kinfolk.

VIII

The BIA saw itself as replicating for Indians what the common schools were
doing for white Americans of all kinds, and especially for the millions of new
immigrants flooding the United States: transforming members of deviant
cultures into loyal American citizens.⁶² Reports by Indian commissioners, superintendents, and teachers, along with published curricular materials—all
reveal a near-total absence of any teaching content relating to tribal cultural
traditions. Adult Indian reminiscences sadly corroborate this erasure.

There were occasional exceptions to my generalization. By early in the
twentieth century, for example, some schools might allow students to perform plays on Pocahontas and other supposedly traditional Indian stories.⁶³
Carlisle actually employed a Winnebago woman, Angel DeCora, to teach
Indian arts and crafts at the school. Hopi artist Fred Kabotie recalled how in
the second decade of the twentieth century a principal at the Santa Fe Indian
School became interested in the Hopi character and themes of the young
Indian's paintings. This principal was soon transferred because, Kabotie
believed, "he was reviving Indian culture rather than eliminating it, as the
schools had been ordered to do." Essie Horne felt privileged to have been
taught by a number of Indian women who gave students an appreciation of
both Shakespeare and Indian cultural traditions. Later, as a teacher, Horne
also tried to blend traditions, though she too felt that she was risking her
job while doing so. Thomas G. Andrews has recounted the ways in which a
teacher from the local community could influence developments at a Lakota
day school. Clarence Three-Stars walked a tightrope, also risking his job, to

develop "a uniquely Lakota approach, employing bilingual, bicultural techniques that contrasted radically with those of his non-Lakota colleagues."[64]
The vast majority of teachers, white and Indian, followed the assimilationist line. Significantly, even as adults, ex-pupils rarely objected to the almost totally ethnocentric nature of the academic curriculum. A Hopi child who went
to live in a Navajo community would not expect to be taught Hopi traditions;
neither should he or she expect that at a white school. When Don Talayesva
became homesick to the point of tears at the Keams Canyon Boarding School
in Arizona, an older student simply but accurately explained the rationale
for attendance: "to learn the white people's way of life."[65] In one of his accounts of Carlisle schooling Luther Standing Bear depicted himself as a typical struggling beginner who rapidly "got used to it" and indeed came to enjoy
and benefit from much of his education there. In a later publication, however,
he wondered why the schooling had to be completely one-sided: "So, while
the white people had much to teach us," he conceded, "we had much to teach
them. . . . However, this was not the attitude of the day, though the teachers
were sympathetic and kind . . . in the main, Indian qualities were undivined
and Indian virtues not conceded." Never once, he also wrote sadly, were white
educators "intelligent enough to concede that they learned something from
us." As a student, however, neither he nor his schoolmates appear to have questioned this policy.[66]

The apparent acceptance of the one-way, assimilationist curriculum emerges from a batch of examination questions and answers given by Haskell students in 1915.[67] The questions were meant for senior boys and girls, generally
sixth to eighth grade, and the subjects ranged across the curriculum. Apart
from references to American history and life, the questions could easily have
been produced by the CNEI. There is no hint that they were meant for Native
American pupils. History questions ask, for example, about the discovery of
America, education in the colonies (obviously white education); those in civics ask about the duties and rights of citizenship and the nature of American
political institutions. Those in English ask highly detailed questions on parts
of speech; students were also to write an essay on "What must I do to be cour-
teous." Points to be considered were "subject matter, neatness, paragraphing,
agreement of subject and predicate in number, spelling and originality of
thought."

In about seventy pages, eleven boys but only one girl poured out their
responses. As we shall see, Indian pupils were capable of using the English
language and writing skills to question white cultural authority. But not in
these exams. The responses read like typical, book-learned answers, the
kind every high school or even university teacher knows too well. "No man

or woman can be a gentleman or a lady if courtesy is lacking," wrote one boy
in an obviously learned response, "because courtesy is the root of a good
character." The history answers appear to hand back the book or class teaching, with no reference to tribal culture or perspective. In an English essay
one pupil mentions a night horse ride and hearing coyotes calling—but he
does not appear to mean the trickster Coyote of many tribal mythologies.
There are few mentions of Indian peoples at all, apart from references to the
French and Indian War of 1756–63 (the Seven Years' War). One lonely history
question, instructing pupils to compare eastern and western Indians, elicited responses hardly learned in the Sioux tipi or Navajo hogan. Although the
eastern Indians "made their living planting corn and other vegetables . . . and
lived in long bark houses," wrote a boy, they "were not as wild as those in the
west, because they were rovers and made their living by hunting and were all
the time looking for war." Another boy noted how southern Indians "were
civilized" compared to those living on the eastern coast. A number of pupils
unwittingly (or perhaps to satisfy the civics examiner) noted how all those
born in the United States were citizens—some Indians were citizens in 1915,
but not until 1924 were all Indians allowed this privilege.[68] Perhaps these answers were selected to demonstrate the assimilatory success of the mission;
or perhaps the pupils were just "giving the teacher what he wants." Taken in
the context of stated BIA policies and practices, they depressingly suggest the
extent to which Indian pupils were supposed to erase their tribal heritages.

   Although broadly assimilationist in its own orientation, the Meriam Report
of 1928 was highly critical of such radical BIA ethnocentrism, its lack of respect for any areas of tribal cultures.[69] Yet it was only with "The Indian New
Deal" that a serious attempt was made by the BIA to question its policies. That
was in the 1930s and is beyond the scope of the present book.

Except for religious teaching, the situation was very similar in Ireland for
most of the period under review. The refusal to accept Irish in the syllabus
until 1879, and then only as an extra subject, let alone to allow a bilingual
curriculum in Irish-speaking areas until the early twentieth century—these
were the most obvious examples of Anglicizing bias.[70] The CNEI, nevertheless, reluctantly and slowly gave ground to the demands of nationalist groups
for more Irish cultural content in the Irish national schools. In 1897, for example, the Sixth Reading Book could even include Thomas Moore's "Shall the
Harp, Then, be Silent"—written on the death of Henry Grattan, leader of the
movement for Irish legislative independence before the Union. Apart from
more references to the geography of Ireland, to the land, its culture, and history in curriculum and sanctioned texts after midcentury, the impressive

and systematic program I have outlined above could just as easily have been for English children, or indeed for American Indian children. Of course, as Lorcan Walsh ironically notes, the Irish being British, material about Britain was, in effect, also about Ireland.[71]

Two other areas of neglect or deliberate erasure, beyond the Irish language, also drew criticism: the failure to adequately present Irish geography and history. Irish geographical features do come up for mention in the board's curriculum and sometimes on sample examinations. In a 1904 reference to the revised curriculum of 1900, "General knowledge of the map of Ireland" is required of fourth standard pupils. For schools with fewer than two teachers, junior pupils also studied the map of Ireland, but the geography requirements for fifth and higher standards might have been for any group of English-speaking children: "A knowledge of the maps of Europe and Great Britain [no doubt including Ireland] and a general knowledge of the map of the World, with special reference to the British possessions; also a general knowledge of the elements of mathematical and physical geography."[72]

As on the issue of teaching through English only, even the CNEI's own inspectors publicly complained about such near-erasure. In 1888 Henry Worsley insisted that "an acquaintance with the resources and capacities of the different parts of Ireland is clearly a first condition to the starting of technical instruction in this country." Lessons on commercial geography, especially as related to Ireland, needed to be added to the books, he believed. "The lessons on the industrial resources of Ireland in the Fifth book"—an advanced book—"do not adequately meet modern requirements." A year later inspector Beatty was even more scathing: a child in third class "is launched into the wide world before he knows anything about his parish, his county, or his country." In many schools, "I find children who can show Borneo or Madagascar, and yet cannot point out Ireland or tell the name of the county they live in." Such an "anomaly" might be averted, Beatty believed, by focusing on Ireland first, then the world. In 1893 inspector Worsley repeated his "strong conviction that the industrial resources of Ireland should form part of the curriculum for the advanced students." A knowledge of the interchange of goods between Ireland and Britain, and between the United Kingdom (including Ireland) and other countries, would also be useful. Despite such suggestions from its inspectors, the revised CNEI curriculum gave only limited coverage to the pupils' own country.[73]

For BIA officials, Indian peoples did not have a history (or histories) worth teaching. For the CNEI, Ireland had too much and too contentious a history. Acting on the premise that nonpartisan history was unfeasible, writes David Fitzpatrick, the CNEI "simply eliminated all systematic teaching of history from the curriculum"—including systematic teaching of British and Imperial history. Large numbers of CNEI employees appear to have accepted this reasoning. As the decades wore on, Irish nationalists, individual CNEI inspectors, and some teachers became ever more critical of the near-erasure of Irish history, indeed of almost all history. Only in 1898 were teachers permitted to use approved works in Irish or British history in class, in combination with other general readers; in 1905 a more specific historical element was added for fourth and higher standards. In 1908 history finally became "a definite course of instruction," supported by a broadening range of approved textbooks on British and Irish history for advanced pupils. The fourth standard, for example, would study a general outline of Irish history, including knowledge of the life of a "representative man in each period."[74] Perusal of some of these sanctioned texts shows that the Irish history generally stopped well short of the current period.[75] According to CNEI Minutes, the board was ever-vigilant in banning works it felt were in any way seditious, especially after the 1916 Rising, when it strove to defend itself from accusations that its schools had bred Irish nationalism and disloyalty to Britain.[76]

The board's own inspectors also publicly wondered about the wisdom of depriving children of any systematic knowledge of their country's past. Noting in 1885 that history might be more associated with Irish geography, inspector E. MacCreanor continued: "Every race, and every country has its history, and the National schools of a country cannot fairly ignore the National history of that country any more than its geographical position on the map of the world." A decade later inspector James McAllister implicitly acknowledged the religious and political divisions that could make history teaching difficult, yet he opined that "there are, I presume, some facts in history which all creeds and parties recognize as indisputable; these might be included, for it cannot but be regarded as a blot on our system, that in all Europe it is with us alone that for the vast majority the history of their native country is a blank."[77]

The same year inspector Worsley, who had also appealed for greater emphasis on Ireland in geography teaching, added his voice to the controversy. He pointedly noted that in the English Code, under the heading of Reading, one book should relate to English history for each standard above the second. History was also a special optional subject for English children. He too believed that there now existed enough texts "of sufficiently impartial character" on Ireland, and he also argued for optionality. "The book of history," he wrote, "with the lessons to be derived from it, is at least as important a branch of study as the book of nature." He insisted that "the study of the evolution of the country of their birth is an integral and essential part of any adequate scheme for the education of the different orders of the community"—as English authorities recognized for their own children, but not for Irish children.[78]

Perhaps the most famous and biting criticism of whole ethnocentric thrust of the CNEI's policy toward Irish history and culture came from one its most important members, resident commissioner D. W. J. M. Starkie. In 1900, just as history was creeping into the curriculum, he declared:

I fancy few practical educationalists will deny that the National Board were guilty of a disastrous blunder in thrusting upon a Gaelic-speaking race a system of education produced on a foreign model, and utterly alien to their sympathies and antecedents. Such an attempt was unsound both philosophically and practically. . . . And I think there can be little doubt that the Board were guilty of narrow pedantry in neglecting as worthless the whole previous spiritual life of the pupil and the multitude of associations, imaginations, and sentiments that formed the content of his consciousness.

Change but a few words, and the passage might have come from the Meriam Report on Indian education. Ironically, Starkie himself would later worry that the inclusion of Irish history had helped nationalize the people: children read to their parents from the texts, "with the result that their vague beliefs about English misrule are made definite: they generally know little about Cromwell, the Penal Laws . . . but now they know these facts from our miserable textbooks." Perhaps this did sometimes happen. However the National Board and the vast majority of its employees did far more to anglicize than to nationalize Irish students.[79] Starkie and the board were certainly right in one sense: history was intensely controversial in Ireland. Thus, until forced to do so by empowering Irish organizations and its own inspectors, the CNEI included little of it, indeed little of anything specifically Irish, in the academic side of the curriculum.

The main difference for the Indian schools was that controversy never arose on the issue until the 1920s. Despite the growth in the early twentieth century of Indian-led lobbying groups such as the Society of American Indians, there were no sufficiently influential national organizations to speak for more inclusion of Indian histories or cultures in the BIA curriculum. Those politically influential groups of mostly white "Friends of the Indian," such as the Indian Rights Association, staunchly supported a policy of near-total assimilation.[80] Even when changes did come in the 1930s, it was generally because *white Americans* insisted; Indians had a relatively small say in the so-called Indian New Deal. On the curricular issue, then, Irish people slowly found a voice late in the period under review. Far less powerful demographically and politically, Indians did not yet.[81]

IX

How did teachers actually teach these ambitious curricula? In this section I focus on sanctioned and unsanctioned pedagogies—rather than on teacher personality or ability, or general lack of professional training (which I examine in the following chapter). The CNEI, BIA, and many missionary societies used age-graded classes, under the constant control of one teacher (sometimes aided by monitors or advanced pupils)—far more like the twentieth than the eighteenth century. Embarked as they were on a mission of cultural assimilation, both authorities desired the full internalization of their message. Both admonished teachers to *interest* pupils in their studies, to get them beyond parrot-like learning to a real understanding and appreciation of content. "Rote learning is [to be] scrupulously avoided," wrote CNEI inspector Keenan in 1856. A "high tone of power and accuracy" was to be given to memory, he conceded, but "judgment is not to remain untutored or quiescent." In a sensitive note of concern, Merial A. Dorchester, special agent in the Indian School Service, warned teachers against the humiliation of pupils. Because of "the natural timidity of these children, especially of the girls," he wrote in 1889, "it shall be a dismissable offense for any teacher or employé to laugh at or in any other way make fun of the work of any child."[82]

CNEI inspectors could acknowledge good pedagogy. "The teachers in my experience," wrote James McAllister in 1895, "are, as a rule, fairly conscientious and industrious. A few of unusual ability, and enamoured of their work conduct their schools with remarkable success."[83] However, inspectors were far more likely to criticize what they saw as poor methodology. Dr. Patten complained in 1865 that the "The usual method adopted is to permit each child of the advanced division of the first class to read over by rote [from a printed card], without meaning, three or four sentences each." If the inspector turned the card upside down and asked the children to repeat the sentence "An elm has bark," they could not do so. When Patten asked the class "What is an elm?" nobody knew. One child "with more quickness than the rest" chanced it: "A dog, sir." Until the teachers

adopt the intellectual method of teaching the junior classes, instead of the mechanical, which I now find in operation in most schools not previously visited by me, little improvement can be expected in reading. Let a lesson be understood, and it will be read by the majority of the class in a natural and pleasing tone of voice, frequently with ease and freedom, and often with expression.[84] *(emphasis in the original)*

Rather than decreasing over time, such rote learning was massively encouraged by the "payment by results" system in Ireland. Writing about senior pupils a dozen years later, inspector MacCreanor noted that poetry, "which they have with much labour committed badly to memory . . . amounts to a jumble of nonsense in their attempts to recite at some schools." The want of explanation "produces ludicrous effects when the sixth class pupils are called on to write a short letter on the matter of some familiar lesson of a book they have passed over." In 1890 inspector W. J. Brown also noted that poetry "was committed to memory, often without the slightest glimmering of meaning." Even worse, in some schools "missing the proscribed task in poetry entails corporal punishment, or keeping in, or both"—hardly an ideal method of stimulating interest in the beauties of the genre. "The pupils are naturally disheartened and disgusted, and a strong and lasting distaste for poetry is the result."[85]

Ex-pupils of the national schools generally corroborate such accounts. Recall Peter O'Leary's first-day shock at the mindless memorization of the older pupils. Similarly, when Frank O'Connor passed his school on the way to the dentist one morning, he "heard the chant of the other victims roaring out the multiplication tables on the first three notes of the scale, as though at any moment they might burst into 'Yankee Doodle.'" Sean O'Faolain felt that he had memorized the catechism so well that decades later as an adult he could "still rattle off all the answers, often to questions whose nature I did not yet understand [as a child]." And a folklore informant remembered being asked his catechism every day by the teacher, "and he'd slap you if you missed."[86]

As twelve-year-old Patrick Kelly prepared for Catholic confirmation around 1920, "reams of the catechism had to be got off by heart," and the children had to get their tongues around "big rocks of words" like "consanguinity." He practiced at home with his mother, memorizing passages such as:

Q: What else is forbidden by the sixth commandment?
A: All lascivious looks and touches, idleness and bad company; all excesses of eating and drinking and whatever may tend to inflame the passions.

"God help us!" he wrote, "All we ever saw in flames was a furze bush." If his mother lost her temper, at least she didn't slap him for missing catechism, as the teacher did. What was worse—and here he echoes many of the criticisms of rote learning expressed by CNEI inspectors—"there was no explanation from the master or my mother as to what the words we didn't understand meant. I only had to guess at what was implied by, 'Thou shalt not covet thy neighbor's wife.'"[87]

O'Connor recalled the more imaginative approach employed by an elderly woman brought in to prepare pupils for their First Holy Communion. She lit a candle and offered money to a pupil who would put his hand in the flame. When none volunteered she delivered her sermon: "And yet you'll risk an eternity in hell when you won't even put your finger in a candle flame for five minutes to earn a half crown!"[88] O'Connor's account is powerfully credible for this historian. One of my own most literally vivid memories of Irish national school (about 1952) was when the nun pointed to the fire and told us to look at the red, long-burning coal embers: that is how your body will burn forever in hell, she told us, should you end up there.

Irish narrators give few indications that, as children, they objected to the ever-prevalent rote learning. However unfashionable it may be in the contemporary Western pedagogical world—and even back in the nineteenth century—many of these pupils came from predominantly oral cultures, where memorization was a crucial mode of learning. Peig Sayers claimed that she began school in the Blasket Islands with verses of poetry "on the tip of my tongue . . . because I was always listening to parents reciting. I was pert too and they had a habit of making me recite for entertainment."[89]

As the examination answers quoted above suggest, it is highly likely that the generally untrained teachers of the BIA and missionary societies fell into similar patterns of teaching (or failing to teach, in the real sense of the term). One agent closed a Jesuit school when the priest admitted that, outside of a specific exercise, pupils would not have been able to answer questions on material learned. Reflecting current progressive education ideals, William N. Hailmann, BIA superintendent of Indian schools, in 1897 delivered a tirade against the whole mechanical system of both organizing and teaching the curriculum. Admitting that in some places the course of study had been adapted to local needs, he still criticized "the tendency of schools to fall into routines." The "pernicious character" of such an approach was almost self-evident, he believed:

The children are rushed daily through a series of subjects of instruction. The interest of "getting through" is so intense that it overshadows all natural interests in the work in hand . . . and in [the pupil's] consequent bewilderment he becomes indifferent to all but the merest routine features of the work. There is no time for instruction, for the clearing up of doubt, for relating new points with the child's experience, for applying them to the many practical concerns of life, for connecting them with what may have gone before or with other related subjects.

There was only time, he lamented, "for hasty 'hearing of recitations'" and hasty assigning of the 'next lesson.'" The lessons remained isolated in the child's memory, and facts learned through recitation and memory work were "to be forgotten as soon as the recitation is over." He appealed for greater attention to the needs of the pupil and to fostering "spontaneous interest" in those being taught.[90]

Indian autobiographical narrators at times corroborate such views. Francis La Flesche gave an ex-pupil perspective on the patriotic content and parrot-like learning of history teaching at the Presbyterian mission. When visiting dignitaries entered the classroom the questions asked of the pupils were such as "Who discovered America?" At night in the dormitory the conversation revolved around classic American episodes like the Boston Tea Party. Without apparent irony one Omaha boy told how colonists "painted up like wild Indians" and threw tea into the harbor. Then, according to another pupil, the English king "was hopping mad . . . he said to his soldiers, you go and fight those 'Mericans. And they did fight, and they had the Rev'lution. That war lasted eight years, and the kings soldiers got licked. Then the 'Mericans made George Washington their President because he couldn't tell a lie." The language sounds contrived and the humor strained, perhaps. But elsewhere La Flesche claimed that he carefully attempted to reproduce the kinds of language (English and Omaha in English translation) spoken by the children at the school. Further, the simplistic, clichéd, memorized account of the American Revolution is hardly much different from what white pupils of the same age would have given.[91]

La Flesche also conveyed the boredom in mission school class while one girl recited "in a tone that made it difficult to resist the drowsiness that attacked everyone in the room." When she failed to spell a difficult word the teacher, "who was sitting with eyes shut, pronounced it for her with a suppressed yawn." And when Luther Standing Bear returned from Carlisle, he boasted that he tried to teach Lakota children to understand and not merely repeat English words—unlike teachers who had taught as though pupils were "a bunch of parrots."[92] Yet, as with Irish children from oral cultural backgrounds, while at school few Indians objected to such a pedagogy. Memorization was also a crucial method of passing on knowledge in such cultures. Anna Moore Shaw, a Pima, claimed that at school she enjoyed memory work, especially when it related to religion.[93]

Thus in both systems for much of the period under review, rote memorization and other forms of regimented and uninspiring techniques seem to have been the dominant classroom style for teaching both the academic and religious elements in the curriculum. We learn little about how the manual labor elements were taught. In BIA schools most likely the children were thrown into work in the kitchens or on the farm and generally learned on the job—whatever about the elevated ideas of work as a moral exercise. In Ireland, apart perhaps from "hands on" subjects such as needlework, vocational education became merely another form of memory activity, to be learned by heart for the "payment by results" examinations and even after this approach was discontinued.

In the later nineteenth century, however, both the CNEI and BIA were influenced by the more pupil-centered and pupil-activating approaches of the progressive education movement. Drawing especially on the ideas of Swiss educator Johann Heinrich Pestalozzi, the "Object Method" was designed to help pupils learn new languages and also other forms of knowledge. Utilized in Indian and Irish schools, such an approach advocated that teachers employ all kinds of available "objects," such as local plants or tools, the English names of which students would immediately learn. This would help link the classroom to the local, familiar environment.[94]

In 1903 Estelle Reel, superintendent of Indian schools, gave a powerful explanation of this approach. She blended racial condescension, a practical sense of classroom problems involved in teaching such "special" children, and at least a superficial knowledge of Siouan language terms. Indian teachers "were beginning to see that the methods of teaching used in public schools must be modified and adopted to meet the needs of the children of a child race." Therefore the BIA teacher

must deal with conditions similar to those that confront the teacher of the blind and the deaf. She must exercise infinite patience in all her teaching, which at first must be done objectively. She must present objects familiar to the children, giving them the English names, and constant repetition is necessary; then lead them gradually to representations of their surroundings and things that they are acquainted with in their neighborhood.

For instance, she continued, the Sioux boy knew the sky above him as "mahpi-yah" and the stars as "wi-can-hpi"; when he had learned the English words "sky" and "stars" he would progress to others. "Give him only the first words that he will have everyday use for. After he has learned to speak a word, the written form can follow.[95]

In a recent major study Ruth Spack has shown how, both at Indian missionary outposts and especially in a major boarding school such as the Hampton Institute, Virginia, individual teachers improvised creatively and used the object method to get beyond rote memorization. The instruction at Hampton was theoretically monolingual, but teachers were willing to use interpreters when necessary; they also employed African American students at the school as intermediaries and sent Indians on "outing" trips. They dropped more conventional textbooks and grammar-centered ways of teaching language, at least initially. They brought watches into class to teach both new words and new attitudes toward time, and they had a globe, along with pictures of life in areas such as Alaska, South America, and elsewhere. They also brought in live animals and related geography to the students' natural environment. "Given the special linguistic circumstances of the Hampton classroom," writes

Spack, "the Pestlozzian [object] method proved invaluable, insomuch as it called for dealing first with observation and direct participation rather than definition and abstract [grammatical] rules." These teachers also used forms of role-playing and organized evening singing events and debating societies. Recognizing the shyness of many students, the teachers encouraged them to speak English. When they judged published texts to be inappropriate, they produced their own leaflets. They encouraged letter writing and just about anything else, including the reading of children's magazines, that would help their students learn.

I suspect that few BIA or missionary teachers were as creative. Through it all, as Spack notes, these teachers participated "in cultural oppression in their efforts to persuade students to replace the Native way of life with Euro-American Christian culture." Yet pedagogically it was a most impressive performance, as they struggled to adapt to a classroom environment that was almost as new to themselves as to the pupils.[96]

For Irish educators too, this object method offered hope. In 1884 inspector Downing advocated that "language teaching must always be based upon object teaching." He was shocked by the linguistic poverty of his students, many of whom lacked either English or Irish words even for local wild birds or plants—evidence of how teaching Irish-speakers through English could result in very poor language learning all round, as inspector Keenan feared. Some pupils, perhaps from the barren islands off the west coast, had never even seen a tree! Still, Downing believed, the best hope was for a kind of object teaching, using both pictures and objects—including seashells, unusual plants, or even forms of seaweed, as some innovative teachers were doing at schools he had visited. Thus they "aim primarily at imparting a knowledge of objects and facts; and, concurrently with this knowledge, will grow up in the most natural manner, easily and quickly, the language necessary to denote the facts." Trying to teach reading otherwise was but "'a tinkling cymbal.'" Yet two decades later in 1903 CNEI inspector Craig could still lament that although "Object Lessons, even of an elementary kind [could help] to cultivate habits of minute observation," they were seldom used effectively in the schools. "Frequently they are mere conversational lessons, drawing from pupils' prepared answers, and failing entirely to develop the curiosity or the innate enquiring qualities of the youthful mind."[97]

Early in the twentieth century, however, Éamon Kelly told how his teacher effectively used "object" approaches to teach geography. He began by getting pupils to draw a map of their local area, showing houses and fields they knew, and to further subdivide the fields according to uses such as potato garden or cabbage patch. Then they added local roads and streams and later nearby hills and other landmarks. From their little homemade maps the teacher moved to one of County Kerry, then of Ireland, and later of the globe. We can surely believe Kelly's remark that "having started at home and learned about our own surroundings gave us a better understanding of the wider world."[98]

X

Of both American and Irish campaigns we must still ask: to what extent were *pupils* affected by the curriculum and its assimilationist but usually unimaginative presentation? Considering how much most of us have forgotten from elementary school, and considering the numbing boredom of most class time, how much did Irish and Indian pupils—often ignorant of English—purposefully digest? Fitzpatrick notes how the vast majority of inspector reports on the teaching of history in Ireland in the early twentieth century were critical, pointing to problems such as treating the subject as a mere reading lesson, the ignorance of the teachers, inadequate textbooks, lack of context for facts, lack of linkage to geography, and—of course—rote memorization. Admittedly, many—perhaps most—of those Irish and Indian pupils who attended regularly learned enough English and other skills to survive at lower socioeconomic levels in a changing world. Much assimilative and modernizing education did occur, in other words, and the remainder of the present book concerns itself with these issues. Yet scholars such as Fitzpatrick, Vincent, and Stearns have warned us against accepting educational curricula or the claims of teachers and authorities, for what actually went on in classrooms across the Western world. Ex-pupil accounts reinforce this view. "Shockingly low standards of instruction and classroom boredom saved most pupils from effective manipulation within school hours," writes Fitzpatrick with a nice sense of irony. "The would-be manipulators of the Irish school-child's mind left a hasty scrawl rather than an indelible imprint on that *tabula rasa*."[99]

Nevertheless in both systems individual Irish and Indian pupils, no doubt a tiny minority, not only learned their lessons but also recalled moments of "indelible imprint," even of inspiration within generally uninspiring environments. If escaping one universe could be difficult, entering another could be earthshaking. In almost a literal sense, as Indians were sometimes shocked to learn of the Copernican theory. "The tall brave is frank to confess," claimed a teacher at Hampton, "that to his mind it is by no means proved that the earth is round." This indeed was to understate the case. Initially awestruck, Edward Goodbird admitted that new knowledge gave him a sense of superiority over his supposedly more benighted Hidatsa kin: "I came home daily with new proof that the world was round." Similarly, when Charles Eastman heard "that our world was [round] like that . . . I felt that my foothold was deserting me. All my savage training and philosophy was in the air, if such things were true." After three years of schooling, he was "deep into a strange life from which I could not retreat." Despite the difficulties, he recovered his balance. "I absorbed knowledge through every pore," he wrote in an affirmation to delight the heart of any teacher. "The more I got, the larger my capacity grew, and my appetite increased in proportion." His later intellectual journey all the way to Boston University and an MD degree prove that these were no empty words.[100]

Other ex-pupils convey a similar sense of shock, turning to real intellectual excitement as they mastered English and began to learn about the new world: this is also true of Francis La Flesche who later, as an ethnologist, would embark on a quest for greater understanding of his own Omaha and related peoples. It was also true of Hopi Helen Sekaquaptewa, who conveys a deep appreciation of school learning, even when the issue divided her family. Thomas Wildcat Alfords believed that after four years he had mastered "the first four rules of arithmetic" to his teachers' satisfaction, and had a smattering knowledge of geography, physiology, grammar, and had taken a peep into the fascinating study of natural philosophy and other branches of higher learning and science." Even more significantly, "I had glimpsed the wonders of education. I had only tasted the joy of knowing things, and had a consuming thirst for new knowledge." Perhaps the most joyous discovery of a new universe—a new way of perceiving the world—was made by Asa Daklugie, the bitterly anti-white Apache. He called Carlisle "a vicious and hostile world" that he and his wife-to-be hated and feared. However, the sensitive teacher who had helped him learn English later introduced him to an atlas and pointed to Arizona:

for the first time in my life I saw a map. I was fascinated. When she showed me mountains and rivers I could tell their names in my language. I knew the Spanish for some of them and a few in English. She let me take that geography book to the dormitory and [my friend] and I almost wore it out.[101]

Many scholars have validly noted the hegemonic implications of the map, "a technology of empire," according to John Willinsky. It "provided a running record of imperialism's reach. . . . Through this projection of discovery and conquest, the world was gradually outlined, filled in, and renamed in imperialism's image."[102] By the time of Daklugie's "map experience" Apache lands were mostly lost to his people; they had been mapped into and indeed under the United States. Yet knowing this did not prevent him from wondrously entering a new way of looking at the world, one that had suddenly been opened up before, or perhaps we should say below, him. In a powerful sense he had, as advocates of the object method hoped, connected a picture (map) with something intimately known outside the classroom—his Apache homelands.

Irish ex-pupils also recalled highly positive learning experiences. Peig Sayers deeply regretted being taken from school early; whatever the difficulties with language and curriculum and discipline. "I was attending school every day and getting on well," she recalled. "I missed my lessons very rarely because we were at them hard and fast when we came together at night [to do homework]." There is no hint of parental pressure here, more of enthusiastic group cooperation. Apart from O'Sullivan, who began to feel "disgusted with school," others of the Blasket narrators seem to have enjoyed their time there; O'Guiheen "was doing fine" and, like his Mother Peig Sayers, met friends at night for study sessions.[103] Patrick Shea positively remembered the learning of physics. With the aid of a basin, a few test tubes, a tiny spirit heater, some pieces of glass tubing, a zinc bucket, and some water, the teacher demonstrated such mysterious phenomena as atmospheric pressure, the distillation of water, and the workings of the thermometer. "It was," wrote Shea, "an hour of magical interest."[104]

O'Faolain similarly memorialized the work of the Presentation Brothers in Cork, who, for all their faults and occasional outbursts of brutality, were determined to give the poor young city boys a better chance in life. "Do not. . . begin to imagine," he wrote, "that we learned nothing useful in our old tumbledown [school]." And almost in a summary of the early-twentieth-century CNEI curriculum he continued:

[The Brothers] ground the three "r's" into us unforgettably. . . . They gave us a solid basis for whatever we might later wish to build . . . we had learned fractions, proportion, compound interest, the nature of stocks and shares, of bills of exchange, of discount. We were introduced to the rudiments of physics and chemistry . . . the nature of oxygen, why a teapot handle has an inset of nonconducting material, what metal expands when heated, the lever, the law of Archimedes, and so on. Above all we got (even if it was by Sloppy Dan with a black strap) a thorough knowledge of parsing, grammar and analysis.[105]

Further, as Janet Nolan ironically notes, a curriculum designed to teach the poorer classes not to look above their station could actually stimulate the desire for social mobility—especially in girls and women, but obviously in boys too.[106]

Thus, apart from the absence of history in the CNEI curriculum until late in the period and changing emphases on manual education, the curricula taught in Indian and Irish national schools were strikingly similar. Indeed, there were greater differences within each system, especially between small and large schools, than between the two systems. Even in terms of the manual labor element, both systems started out with similar goals, if they later drifted apart in practice. Both eschewed sectarian preferences, yet both saw all elements of the curriculum suffused with Christian and moral significance; the BIA and CNEI were equally solicitous of the Christian denominational loyalty of their pupils. The difference here, of course, was that the BIA, unlike the CNEI, nevertheless attempted to erase the spiritual beliefs of the vast majority of Indian pupils—mere "heathenism." Both provided a degree of common education to boys and girls, while soon bifurcating the curriculum (especially its vocational side) according to prevailing concepts of appropriate gender roles: boys to become farmers, artisans, some perhaps teachers or principals; girls to become homemakers, domestics, or also teachers (and less often, principals). These strategies were typical of the mass systems being provided in many other industrializing nations during the nineteenth century.

In another way, however, the Indian and Irish assimilationist systems were quite different from what France, Germany, and England were doing for their own peoples. Of course, even in such consciously unified nations, élite ideologies came to dominate elementary education.[107] Yet generally these nations reinforced the universes of those being educated. Both BIA and CNEI curricula presented alien universes to their charges. Even the CNEI's acceptance of Irish religious circumstances and, late in the day, of the Irish language and some elements of Irish culture, were tactical retreats from the assimilationist ideal, designed to win the majority population to the Union. For much of the period under review, then, Irish national school pupils learned very little about Ireland; Indian children learned even less about their tribal cultures or histories.

6. School Staff

"It may be set down as an aphorism generally true," declared CNEI head in-spector W. H. Newell in 1857, "that the teacher is the life or death of a school." Recent improvements in one Dublin model school, he believed, were in part the result of his board appointing "zealous and effective teachers in the room of careless and inefficient ones."[1] Those at the top of the CNEI and BIA bu-reaucracies certainly believed that their own roles as commissioners, inspec-tors, or other officials were central to the smooth running of the educational machines. However, all accepted the "aphorism" that for a school to live or die, local staff, especially teachers, were crucial.

Over half a century later another CNEI inspector waxed even more eloquent on the potential influence of a good teacher. Among the lessons to be learned from biographies of the world's celebrities, wrote J. P. Dalton in 1913, there was "none more striking than the frequency with which associations with a man of scholarly tastes and cultivated ideals has acted on the young as a sum-mons to a career." The well-educated teacher was "diffusing round himself an invisible force that will insensibly, and without conscious cooperation on his part, lift the best of his scholars from time to time to higher levels of pur-pose and endeavor."[2]

While examining school regimentation and curriculum we have already met individual teachers and seen something of their methods of discipline and pedagogy. The goal of the present chapter is to comparatively analyze the crucial role of school staff in the CNEI and BIA/missionary assimilation-ist crusades. The work of commissioners, inspectors, or U.S. agents as links between school and educational authority is touched upon. The major focus, however, is on those staff running the schools. In Ireland this meant prin-cipals, teachers, and trainee teachers, along with monitors and other pupils placed in control of classes. In America it meant superintendents, teachers, trainees, and "officers" chosen from among the pupils themselves; at board-ing schools it also meant matrons, school blacksmiths, cooks, farmers, and others employed around the school. All such employees, permanent or tempo-rary, bore responsibility for advancing the cultural missions of Anglicization and Americanization.[3]

I

If both the disciplinary and curricular requirements bore heavily upon pupils, the demands on staff were also onerous. The position of national school teacher in Ireland, as John Coolahan has noted, was peculiar. On the one hand he—especially the male—benefited from the older hedge school tradition. There is thus some truth to Oliver Goldsmith's famous lines about the villagers' awe of the local master: "They gazed and gazed and still the wonder grew / That one small head could carry all he knew." Illiterate local people might therefore respect him as a man of learning and indeed power. To the CNEI authorities, however, the teacher was a very lowly and carefully supervised cog in the great machine. His (or her) main function, writes Coolahan, "was seen as cultivating approved moral qualities . . . and inculcating necessary levels of literacy and numeracy."[4]

The situation was similar for teachers of white Americans in "the little red school" on the home front, although such men and women were answerable to local and state, rather than federal or national authorities. To an extent teachers at Indian schools carried the prestige of learning, especially to peoples for whom reading and writing initially appeared as strange and magical skills. In addition, once the awesome political and military power of the United States became obvious to tribespeople, white teachers were seen as possessors of some of this power. Yet they too were lowly cogs in a huge machine. "The compensation is so small," wrote U.S. agent George W. Frost in 1877—acting as an inspector of schools in his jurisdiction—"that but few teachers of ability and who are adapted to the work can be secured." The job, he noted, "requires peculiar tact, patience, and energy of character to be successful; and when it is known that the cost of living [on the Montana frontier] is double what it is in the States, the pay is small indeed."[5]

Whatever the reward, the challenge was great. "The class-room work of an Indian school requires and demands teachers of ability," wrote George W. Scott, superintendent of the Fort Stevenson School in South Dakota in 1888. "*The idea that any one who has the necessary patience can teach Indians is a fallacy*" (emphasis added). The tribal child possessed "peculiarities of nature not met with in other nationalities subject to the common school system of this country"; he or she was reared in a "blind superstitious, semi-religious ardor [that was] antagonistic to real aspirations for civilization." For such children rote-learned "machine education" that produced "parrot-like products" was not enough. The task required skilled, dedicated, and trained teachers. "The Indian," Scott believed, "is capable of something better." The best teacher was she (perhaps reflecting the increasing numbers of women entering BIA school service, Scott used the female pronoun) who could grasp the best method as the occasion presents itself. "There is no royal road leading to the tree of knowledge where an Indian can pluck the fruits of civilization and bask in eternal laziness. He can not be successfully instructed by teachers whose ability is below the average." It was a job that required "a superior tact and skill. She has a field of work not surveyed by educational writers. History furnishes no example of a government undertaking such a task. The teacher can draw from no source, but must follow the true principles of her science." She had to be able to interest her pupils, who were strangers to every aspect of the knowledge she carried to them, all in an unknown language.[6]

Confronting such demands, new teachers—especially those assigned to boarding schools in remote and even dangerous frontier areas—faced difficulties beyond those experienced by teachers on the home front or in Ireland. The BIA described one boarding school as "a fairly desirable location" to a job applicant. Once on the job, he later wrote to a friend: "I am in hell." Recalling her first day as an Indian teacher, Minnie Braithwaite Jenkins believed that her pupils "must have felt they were on the verge of some strange and startling experience." Actually, she admitted, "I was as afraid as they were."[7]

Gertrude Golden told how teachers at the Fort Yuma Boarding School in Arizona had to teach from 8:30 in the morning until 4:00 (with one hour off for lunch), and then in the evening they had study hour duty. They also supervised all the janitorial work in the school building each day, and on Saturday they would "see that a thorough scrubbing, dusting and window-wash took place." Neither was Sunday a day of rest: they had to conduct pupils to church and back and see that their behavior there was befitting the occasion. Adding to the misery at that school was the stifling heat.[8]

Of course, all this could be seen as special pleading. A decade or so later, nevertheless, the Meriam Report corroborated such claims. Referring to the problem of getting and retaining qualified teachers, the 1928 study accepted that "it would be difficult to find an educational work where the hours are as confining, the amount of free time as nearly nil, the conditions of housing as poor." In the boarding schools teachers and other staff were "almost literally on a twenty-four hour service basis, seven days of the week." Living conditions represented "a survival of primitive rural conditions of forty years ago."[9] In a study of the autobiographies of a number of female white teachers—including Golden—at BIA schools late in the period under review, Patricia A. Carter reinforces this picture. Isolation, loneliness, demanding responsibilities far beyond mere classroom teaching, lack of training in cross-cultural education and of adequate teaching materials, clashes with other teachers and with superiors—all reinforce the picture of the difficult life faced by BIA teachers, which led to constant turnover of staff. "The adventure," writes Carter, "no matter how beguiling [from a distance], eventually dissipated into years of marginally rewarding labor with no guarantee of future economic security or hope of changing the system." She admits that some women managed to find a degree of fulfillment, but this was "despite the petty tyranny and mercurial rhythms of the BIA."[10] Although male teachers might be beneficiaries rather than victims of pervasive gender inequality, they suffered all of the other trials of BIA school life.

II

It has perhaps already emerged, and will in later chapters, why individual Indians moved into positions of responsibility such as officer, disciplinarian, and even teacher (Essie Horne, for example): the pay helped, as did the sense of responsibility; for some young Indians the sense of power over their peers also may have been a motivating factor, as was the influence of special teachers. Furthermore, in their own societies tribal boys and girls would also have expected to bear increasing burdens of responsibility as they grew older.

But why did white men and women volunteer to teach Indian children? BIA teacher motivations were complicated and personal: a sense of adventure, the need to travel, boredom with small-town life, the desire to escape family domination, the need for a job, the desire to test oneself on an always mysterious and sometimes dangerous frontier, a fascination with Indian life—all contributed in different ways and degrees. Further, some BIA teachers were probably imbued with the desire to spread American civilization to the tribes. We have little evidence of a distinctly Christian missionary imperative among BIA teachers. As Carter, especially, shows, all such motivations were complicated by issues of gender, especially the desire of females to transcend the limiting roles allowed them by nineteenth-century America. "Women are not really members of the human race, but merely appendages to it, to be wagged by men," wrote teacher Estelle Audrey Brown, indicating one the reasons why she took up Indian schooling.[11]

Gertrude Golden well conveyed the mixed emotions that propelled her, and no doubt many like her, to the Indian field. "I was tired of it all," she wrote at the beginning of her autobiography, *Red Moon Called Me*. "Although I was not longing for adventure especially, I did crave a change of scenery." Teaching in the schools of Monroe, Michigan, "was all right as far as it went, but it was too limiting, too monotonous a life. This, added to low pay and hard work, had created a situation from which I wanted to escape." So, when the opportunity came she took the civil service examination, passed, and headed off to eastern Oregon. Life in the Indian service would be far more demanding than she imagined, but her initial response to the job offer was anything but ambivalent. "I was elated," she wrote. "Here was everything: a salary twice what I was getting, with the promise of an increase; a chance to study human types in which I had always been interested; an opportunity to travel and see something of the country."[12]

Missionaries might share many of these personal and idealistic motivations. In addition to the patriotic desire to spread American civilization, the men and women of the Board of Foreign Missions (BFM) of the Presbyterian Church in the U.S.A., for example, were powerfully moved by the need to save "the heathen," who appeared to be vanishing physically and rushing to damnation without the gospel. The historian must of course be skeptical of missionary (and secular) rhetoric, but it is difficult not to be impressed by the deep sense of evangelical impetus behind their vocation. In addition, of course, missionaries were caught up in rivalries with other denominations—to win their heathen to "our church" as distinct from another intensified missionary motivation.[13]

Little has been written on Irish teacher motivation at this time, nor have many CNEI teachers, men or women, left narratives. R. B. Robson devoted a full book to his days as pupil and teacher with the National Board but tells us little about why he followed this vocation. A prankster, expelled a number of times, he always gravitated back to school, then to model school, and to teacher training college in Dublin. He took pride in winning prizes and was deeply impressed by his first CNEI teacher, all of which probably affected his attitude. After bad seasickness, he decided "to take the necessary steps with a view to re-entering the teaching profession, which after all was my true vocation in life"—a strong expression of commitment, but not offering any explanation as to why.[14] Less than the BIA teachers, at least some of whom looked to adventure on the frontier, and far less than the evangelically driven missionaries, I suspect that for most Irish aspirants, teaching in the CNEI machine offered the chance of relatively secure employment—far more secure than that enjoyed by the hedge schoolmasters. Further, despite their lowly place in the hierarchy, they might still enjoy a degree of prestige and even power in the local community, once securely ensconced in their jobs. For Irishwomen too, teaching became an increasingly respectable profession. Although paid less than males, writes John Logan, for many women "teaching had become an attractive occupation that provided, at the very least, a degree of financial independence," with a possible principalship some time in the future.[15]

III

Despite the severe demands facing its employees in the field and its radical goals of near-total cultural transformation, the BIA was far more negligent than the CNEI in organizing a program of systematic teacher training. Individual schools such as Carlisle and Haskell did set up "normal" departments to train young Indians as future teachers of their peoples. For the period under review, however, there appears to have been no serious attempt to establish a full teacher-training program for the Indian Service. White teachers had little professional competence to work with tribal children who initially spoke no English; nor do many appear to have studied individual Indian cultures before entering the field. Of course, by their very membership of American society, they were to some extent experts in its values and knowledge, yet they remained a highly unprofessional group during the period under review.[16]

The U.S. government was not totally negligent on this issue, however, and from early in the nineteenth century intensified its efforts to control Indian schooling. In 1819 school administrators, including missionaries, were required to send in reports to the government, and by 1837 Indian agents had to make at least a yearly check on schools in their jurisdiction.[17] By 1890, as Commissioner Morgan strove to build a more orderly school system, the duties of agents were more extensive. According to the detailed BIA "Rules for Indian Schools," the agent had "general supervision of all school work under his charge. He must visit all schools whether Government, mission, or contract, at least four times each year, keep himself thoroughly informed as to their condition and efficiency, and make quarterly reports concerning the same to the Indian Office." To fill the schools he had power to withhold annuities or rations owed to Indians.[18]

Such supervision did not compensate for professional training, but it did place pressures on school staff; these pressures increased when in 1873 Congress authorized the appointment of five inspectors of BIA field services, including education; in 1882 an inspector, later a superintendent of Indian schools, was appointed. By 1890, according to the commissioner, "the present energetic, conscientious, and faithful Superintendent of Indian Schools" had inspected and reported upon about eighty boarding and training schools, about half of those wholly or partly supported by the government.[19]

The same year a detailed "Application for appointment in the U.S. Indian School Service" required answers to thirty-six questions relating to the applicant's citizenship, marital status, health, use/nonuse of alcohol and drugs, education, household training and child care (for women), and mechanical, agricultural, and other trade experiences (for men). There were questions on whether the applicant regularly read an agricultural or educational paper, and on how he or she got along with other people. A series of questions, beginning ominously with "Have you ever taught school?" related to aspects of the applicant's suitability as a teacher and inquired whether he or she possessed a teaching certificate or musical abilities. Applicants who had some teaching experience were required to provide references for information "regarding your moral character, and your proficiency in your studies, and your success as a teacher." Applicants also had to write a separate letter briefly outlining the qualifications and training that fitted them for the position sought.[20]

During the 1890s more and more educational personnel came under the merit system and civil service protection and also faced examinations to enter the Indian Service. Still no full-scale teacher-training schools specifically for the obviously different Indian field were established—indeed, the examinations had little relevance to Indian cultural conditions.[21] In addition, at this time the BIA began to encourage its teachers and other school staff, white and Indian, to attend summer "institutes" of lectures and discussions to upgrade their skills. The commissioner reported in 1897 that a number of institutes for superintendents, teachers, and others in the service had recently been held: "Good attendance, excellent programs, and lively interest insured their being of great value to the service." Papers presented at the Omaha meeting by teachers and other experts included "Education for True Manhood and Womanhood"; "The Relation of Returned Students to Reservation Schools and Reservation Life"; "The Reservation Schools and the Indian Home"; "Indian School Employees in the Indian Schools"; and "The Organic Connection between Industrial and Academic Training in Indian Schools." In line with the superintendent's conviction that the employment of Native people was "evidently destined to prove successful," one Indian, Clara M. Folsom, presented a paper on an always controversial subject, "Returned Students of Hampton." Apparently city authorities in Omaha and elsewhere extended cordial hospitality—such events were important not just in improving staff training and morale, but also in building bridges to the larger American society.

As a result of suggestions made at summer institutes, the commissioner claimed, perhaps wishfully, that numbers of teachers had voluntarily begun to "take an interest in the study of the Indians upon their reservations," by visiting families and even learning something of the languages of their pupils. Such activities might teach BIA employees to realize that "the lower civilization of the Indian is merely a different civilization," and that in no fundamental way were Indians different from white people. Hopefully such an interest would "enable the teachers to connect intelligently and fruitfully with the previous experience of the children the new knowledge and skill which it is their business to impart to them."[22]

The goal of all such activities was to deepen both the motivations and skills of BIA personnel—including Indians—and in some ways to professionalize them. The purpose, wrote the commissioner a decade later in 1906, was "to bring the system of Indian education to a higher standard of efficiency." At general and local institutes experienced teachers gave demonstration classes; for example, staff from the Hampton Institute showed how they had combined both literary and industrial teaching. In addition, specimens of classroom work from many areas were displayed. There were different kinds of Indian people in America, concluded the commissioner, "and by comparison of methods and interchange of ideas each teacher present and each school represented receives the benefit of the others."[23]

Such activities were voluntary, and Essie Horne recalled how in 1931 she enrolled for courses in the Valley City State Teachers College, North Dakota. She sensed some racial antipathy from teachers and students, yet she appeared to have enjoyed and benefited from the course in state history, among other things. She later attended summer school courses in anthropology at the University of New Mexico, including one that promoted progressive methods of integrative teaching, an approach that she found theoretically interesting but hard to use with students. She believed, nevertheless, that it developed her professional skills and morale.[24]

To encourage teachers toward greater professionalism, "reading circles" were started at many schools early in the twentieth century, and the BIA encouraged teachers to prepare "theses" on relevant subjects, which would be placed in their files and given ratings. Those with a record of "excellent" would receive promotions and salary increases. To induce more teachers into this demanding service, employees would be allowed, in addition to regular holidays, fifteen days of paid "educational leave" each year to attend summer schools or institutes. Because it was particularly difficult to retain the services of matrons, industrial teachers, and disciplinarians, who were often on call at all hours at boarding schools, such staff were permitted extra time off each week.[25]

Despite these constructive developments, Indian teachers as a group had not become fully professionalized, in the sense of having undergone systematic preservice training or of having established professional autonomy and their own standards and organizations.[26] Indeed, as late as 1928 the Meriam Report decried the "disastrous effect of lack of training standards" in the BIA's educational division. This could be problematic enough on the home front, where teachers generally were familiar with the culture of their own people. "Too frequently a teacher is deposited at an Indian school with no previous knowledge whatsoever of Indian life, of the part of the country where the work is located, or of the special conditions that prevail." The training of teachers and principals should be raised, declared the report, "to the level of at least the better public school systems."[27]

IV

Theoretically, the situation in Ireland was far better. From its establishment in 1831 the CNEI immediately moved to set teacher training on a systematic, permanent, and professional basis. In its Report of 1835 the National Board noted that should finances be adequate, "a new class of schoolmasters may be trained, whose conduct and influence must be highly beneficial in promoting morality, harmony, and good order in the country parts of Ireland." Such teachers would live in friendly relations with the local people, "not greatly elevated above them," but paid enough "to maintain a respectable station." They would be "trained to good habits; identified in the interests of the State, and therefore anxious to promote a spirit of lawful authority." They would thus become "a body of the utmost value and importance in promoting civilization and peace."[28]

Year after year in its annual report the CNEI listed the duties such teachers were expected to perform. "Twelve Practical Rules for the Teachers of National Schools" admonished them especially to abide by the founding ideals of the board and to keep religious and academic instruction apart. They were to avoid fairs, markets, meetings, and religious controversy, "but above all political meetings, of every kind." They were to teach according "to the approved method," using sanctioned books, and, of course, to impress upon the minds of the children that great rule that there was a time and a place for everything, and everything should be in its proper place. By teaching and example they should also demonstrate the virtues of cleanliness, neatness, and decency, and make daily inspections of the children in these respects. They should inculcate truth and honesty, respect for superiors and for "all persons placed in authority over them." They should look out for the welfare of their pupils, treat them firmly but kindly, "and aim at governing them by their affections and reason, rather than by harshness and severity." Other duties related to financial and administrative matters. The actual appointment of teachers, the report clarified, rested with local patrons and school committees, but "the Commissioners are to be satisfied with the fitness of each, both as to character and general qualification." A teacher thus should be

A person of Christian sentiment, of calm temper and discretion; he should be imbued with a spirit of peace, obedience to the law, and of loyalty to the sovereign; he should not only possess the art of communicating knowledge, but be capable of moulding the mind of youth, and of giving to the power which education confers a useful direction.[29]

Such demands, onerous though they might be, were typical of what authorities in many countries were insisting upon from often poorly paid teachers in this "age of the school."[30]

To achieve its pedagogical goals, the CNEI immediately began formal teacher education. It established a model school and teacher training college at Marlboro Street, Dublin. In 1835 it proposed the creation of five professorships there: one responsible for training aspirant teachers in the art of teaching and conducting schools; one for composition, English literature, history, geography, and political economy; one for natural history in all its branches; one for mathematics and mathematical science; and one for the elements of logic and rhetoric. No student would be admitted to the training college without having passed an entrance examination. Money became available only in the 1840s, but awareness of the need for systematic teacher training was apparent from the beginning of the board's life.[31]

At the same time the board proposed the establishment of thirty-two model schools, one for each county. By the 1860s twenty-five of these schools, often impressive buildings, had been built. These were the first schools in the United Kingdom to be established and fully financed by the state. In each, a number of candidate teachers should be boarded at the CNEI's expense after their selection from the best monitors at ordinary national schools. (Monitors, in turn, were selected from promising classroom pupils). After a number of years teaching and training, and after passing the entrance examination, they might then progress to the national training school in Dublin for a two-year course.[32]

Despite all this effort, by 1870 only about one-third of national school teachers had any formal training. (Many Catholic female teachers had received some training as monitors in convent superior—secondary level— schools, however; far fewer Catholic boys possessed such "training.") This lack was partly due to religious rivalries. In the spirit of the CNEI, the new model schools and teacher training school were to be nondenominational; therefore, the major churches objected to the whole scheme. Indeed, the Catholic Church, determined that elementary teachers for its children should be trained in a thoroughly Catholic ethos, banned attendance at either the model schools or Marlboro Street. Although individual Catholics may have defied this ban, in effect it meant that teachers for the vast majority of the Irish population during most of the century were cut off from formal teacher training. The Royal Commission of Inquiry into Primary Education of 1868–70 (the Powis Commission) recommended that state aid be given to denominational training institutions, and that the model schools be discontinued. In 1875 the bishop of Dublin supported the establishment of a school for Catholic male trainees under the Vincentian Fathers, and one for women under the Sisters of Mercy. Only in 1883, however, did the government relent and concede the principle, and by 1900 seven such institutions had been established: the original central training establishment at Marlboro Street, a Church of Ireland college, and five Roman Catholic colleges.[33]

By 1901, of the CNEI's 11,897 teachers, 6,309 had been "fully trained"; by 1903 some 57 percent were trained—a figure far higher than in England or Wales, claimed the CNEI. By 1919 the board noted that about 80 percent of its principal and assistant teachers were "Trained Teachers."[34] Early in the twentieth century, due to nationalist pressures, the CNEI recognized a number of summer colleges established by the Gaelic League at which teachers could improve their knowledge of the Irish language—a move reminiscent of the BIA's summer institutes, except that the American version did not train for the teaching of tribal languages. For each teacher who passed the Irish examination at the end of the course, the CNEI paid £5 to the respective college.[35]

R. B. Robson went through the whole national school system from 1865. He recalled the five professors at Marlboro Street in the 1880s, and how, after one of them had publicly humiliated him in front of an amused class, "the kindly old man at once coloured up, and made such an ample apology, that I immediately stepped up to the board and finished my work." On another occasion a professor called upon the students to critique Robson's performance as a nervous teacher trainee. This man too showed a sensitive and encouraging side: in "his nice, gentle, polished style" he "impressed upon them that it was much better [for a teacher] to be a trifle nervous, than to be too confident." Robson claimed that although student teachers at the college came from both the (Protestant) North, like himself, and the (Catholic) South, there was little friction between them. "It might have been well for Ireland," he reflected, "had it continued in later years to be the only training college for teachers." Sitting in class "shoulder to shoulder with students of different faiths," he somewhat wishfully claimed, "tends to rub off the sharp corners, and to minimize the likelihood of those bitter animosities which have so often disgraced our country."[36]

In terms of actual teachers formally trained, then, there was not a great difference between the CNEI and BIA until late in the nineteenth century. We can speculate, nevertheless, as to why policy was so different in Ireland and America. Despite rhetoric to the contrary, perhaps at some level the Americans did succumb to the assumption that "anyone can teach Indians." After all, BIA teachers had spent their lives until then immersed in American life; they knew civilization, they knew Christianity—special training was not necessary for them to lift "savage" children to their own cultural level. In this case perhaps action—or inaction—speaks louder than words. Further, in the American federal system the individual states were responsible for primary and other forms of education. Therefore, although the BIA's very existence reflected official acceptance that Indian affairs was a federal responsibility, perhaps the habit of federal passivity in educational matters lingered. Therefore for a variety of reasons, only toward the end of the period under review, through the use of civil service examinations, summer institutes, and other such measures, did the BIA move in the direction of systematic training for its teachers. It is somewhat ironic, of course, that for all the CNEI's enterprise, the majority of its teachers also lacked formal training for most of the period under review. Therefore, children in both jurisdictions were too often placed in the charge of men and women woefully unprepared for the arduous job in hand—no doubt a major cause of the often poor, rote-reliant teaching methods we examined in the previous chapter.

V

It is perhaps surprising, nevertheless, to discover how well suited at least some of the men and women turned out to be. We would expect inspectors, agents, and principals to be critical of those whom they supervised, and they often were: "Archimedes could not lift these teachers a jot," wrote one CNEI inspector, quoting a frustrated principal.[37] Ex-pupils, who, unlike inspectors, spent long periods in class with teachers, left a highly varied picture, however. Were their accounts of teachers predominantly negative we might suspect a lingering prejudice; were they predominantly positive we might justifiably suspect romanticization. The powerfully mixed picture that emerges lends a sense of credible human diversity to school staff in both America and Ireland.

We have already seen just how harsh or even brutal individual teachers could be: men like "Sloppy Dan" in the Cork Presentation Brothers school and "Gray-beard" at the Omaha mission. Harshness from a self-professed man of God was especially shocking. An Irish folklore informant also remembered "a very religious man" who often beat children for misbehaving while on their knees praying: "and off he'd go with the cane between his teeth and whack [a boy] on his bare legs." In Ireland the local schoolteacher could on occasion inspire such awe that he might punish children in class for misdeeds outside the classroom, or enter the homes of suspected wrongdoers and give their fathers a lecture in the bargain. A folklore informant claimed that even after finishing their schooling, boys would hide their pipes if they saw this teacher approaching on the road.[38]

Instances of pupil mistreatment far beyond then-accepted levels of corporal punishment could be multiplied; on occasion school staff and officials broadly corroborated later autobiographical accounts by pupils. An Indian agent, for example, reported in 1895 how a teacher at a school under his jurisdiction "in a fit of passion slapped a boy in the face"—only to receive in return a blow on the forehead from a slate thrown by the boy. The two incidents, according to the understanding writer, "were about equally censurable under all circumstances." Esther Horne, generally so positive about most aspects of boarding school life, recounted how when she was a teacher in the early 1930s the principal of the Wahpeton Boarding School in North Dakota exceeded all reasonable and legal boundaries. Sent to chase down some runaways, he drove back to the school with the three young women tied to a heavy rope, "trotting" behind the car. They were not actually being dragged along the ground, but the man's behavior led to instant dismissal. "While this kind of disregard for student welfare might have been tolerated in the early days of the boarding schools," claimed Horne, "it was not an acceptable disciplinary measure at this time." The man had been a strict disciplinarian, and the children were afraid of him: "We were all shocked at his insensitivity and were glad to see him go."[39]

In Ireland too, even at an earlier date, authorities could discipline teachers. When in 1900 parents of an allegedly abused pupil complained, the CNEI inaugurated a full-scale investigation, collecting teacher, parental, and pupil statements. One boy claimed that a teacher had kicked him about twelve times and added: "He never punished us for anything but scripture lesson." Gilbert Peel, nine years old, claimed that for missing his arithmetic tables, the teacher hit him on the wrist with a ruler "that was heavier than the usual school ruler. The slap cut me and the cut bled." The boy complained of being hit at other times, and that the teacher pulled his hair. "I was also kicked by Mr. Palmer," he claimed, but admitted that "I was not pained very much by the kick." The teacher admitted that he intended only to strike the boy with the flat side of the ruler, but the pupil had moved, getting a more painful blow—something the boy himself also confirmed. Comments added to the report, apparently by a CNEI official, accepted that the teacher had punished two boys "in a very improper manner," for which he faced reprimand.[40]

Occasionally, narrators such as Helen Sekaquaptewa recalled sexual harassment of Indian pupils at schools, and historian John Bloom has alerted us to the degree to which young girls and indeed boys were vulnerable to staff. One ex-student interviewed by Bloom remarked that although the male student supervisor at his school was strict in preventing student boys and girls from mixing, this man was "sneaking out with the girls." As we now know from later revelations in Canada, for example, and in Irish industrial schools, reform schools, and other such institutions, the placing of adults in positions of near-absolute power over large numbers of children could result in shocking instances of abuse, sexual and otherwise. Perhaps because sexual matters were less freely discussed during the period under review, we hear relatively little of this side of staff abuse of pupils in CNEI and BIA schools.[41] Historians such as Carter and David Wallace Adams have suggested that not only pupils but female teachers too were vulnerable to abuse by male staff—to everything from discriminatory treatment to unfair dismissal to unwanted sexual advances.[42]

At the other end of the spectrum were teachers who, by personality and perhaps pedagogical expertise, positively influenced and occasionally inspired young boys and girls. Charles Eastman has left a deeply affectionate portrait of his early mentor, Rev. Alfred L. Riggs, founder of the Santee Normal Training School in Minnesota. "The Doctor's own personality impressed us deeply, and his words of counsel and daily prayers, strange to us at first, in time found root in our minds," wrote Eastman. "Next to my own father, this man did more than perhaps any other to make it possible for me to grasp the principles of civilization." The Lakota implied that Riggs had the wisdom to work with, rather than smash against, traditional upbringing. For he "also strengthened and developed in me that native strong ambition to win out, by sticking to whatever I might undertake." Francis La Flesche left a similar account of the principal of the Omaha school, probably the Rev. R. J. Burtt of the Presbyterian Church, who took a special interest in La Flesche's friend, loaned him books, and discussed them with the boy.[43]

Esther Horne remembered a Miss Stella Robbins who, although not averse to the use of corporal punishment, "broadened my horizons for a lifetime." She gave Horne an appreciation of not only great music but also of the backgrounds of the composers. She was also a compassionate woman: when Horne froze with stage fright at a school performance, Robbins covered for her by moving the program along. In one of the greatest compliments a pupil can pay to a teacher, Horne recalled how she later attempted to be equally compassionate to her own pupils.[44]

Similarly, the principal of the national school attended by Robson in Northern Ireland during the 1860s was "a man who inspired, in his pupils, respect and confidence by his gentleness, forbearance, and strict impartiality." Frank O'Connor, himself destined for fame as a writer, grew to idolize a teacher would also become a writer—Daniel Corkery. The boy "enjoyed having a hero among the hereditary enemies—the schoolmasters." O'Connor was so impressed that even in later life he could use the word "love" to describe his affection for the older man, and he has left a wonderful account of boyhood adulation:

I hung on Corkery's coat-tails at lunch . . . I borrowed Irish books from him that I could not understand . . . and sometimes I waited for him after school to accompany him home as he butted his way manfully up the cruel hill, sighing. . . . I imitated the old-fashioned grace with which he lifted his hat and bowed slightly to any woman he recognized: I imitated his extraordinary articulation so carefully that to this day I can render it with what seems to me complete fidelity, and for a time I even imitated his limp.

O'Connor claimed that because of Corkery's influence, "any intellectual faculty I possessed was now developing like mad." An Irish-speaking folklore informant has left a briefer, yet highly complimentary remark about one of his teachers: "*An rud a dfhoghluim siad, níor ciall siad riamh é*" (Whatever they learned, they never lost it).[45]

Some informants in both areas explicitly contrasted the good and the bad. Jim Whitewolf remembered that when the principal of his Indian school ordered an employee to whip runaway boys, the man refused. He felt that the pupils, who had already been assigned extra physical labor, had been punished enough. The principal actually struck the man, and an ugly fight ensued, but the staff member stood his ground and protected the boys. Similarly Fred Kabotie, a Hopi, told of a teacher, "a wonderful guy," who played rough games and ensured that pupils ate well. Another man at the same school, however, "was the meanest teacher we ever had," and that was when the young Kabotie began running away from school.[46] In Ireland, Patrick Shea could regard his headmaster as a mercurial bundle of contradictions. "In the midst of an outburst his anger would subside and the face of the clown would appear." His stories were wonderful, and he was a gifted mimic of everyone from parents to inspectors to the parish priest. He was, concluded Shea in breathless ambivalence, "a comedian and a scholar and a holy terror and he was the best teacher I have ever known."[47]

Most of the teachers and other staff described by Irish and Indian narrators were neither terrible nor great. Many were barely memorable, others pathetic. Some historians have suggested that an unusual proportion of BIA teachers were physically disabled or incompetent misfits, implying that the Indian Service was a place for those unable to secure employment elsewhere. Some perhaps were, but I have not found much evidence to confirm this.[48] The ill-educated, sickly, but inoffensive man who came to teach in the Great Blasket Island school of southwestern Ireland in the early 1860s might also fit such a description, and he was obviously neither hero nor villain. Tomás O'Crohan remembered how the pupils were disturbed by his pock-marked face and his "three-legged wife," dependent on a crutch. In all, he was "a decent man, and we weren't as frightened of him as we would have been of an evil-tempered man." Like other national school teachers, he brought sweets (candy) to pupils and even called at homes to coax absentees back to the classroom: he had "such a kind way about him that few of the children missed a day." The man left the school for health reasons and died soon after. Although not well-educated himself, his gentle human qualities allowed him some success as a teacher: "There was little learning in him that we hadn't picked up before he went," concluded O'Crohan sadly. An Irish folklore informant believed that there were not many outstanding teachers in her area, and thus few remarkable pupils. But a particular woman was "only remembered because she was such a bad teacher," old and delicate, with no control over the children.[49]

Even narrators critical of schools could remember good teachers, and those generally positive could depict individual teachers or staff members—including monitors or Indian "officers" who rose from the ranks—as harsh. The accounts are almost interchangeable: if names or places were omitted it would be difficult to tell whether they were written about staff in CNEI or BIA schools.

VI

Yet in at least one major way, the Irish and the American teachers were different. A Dublin man or woman who began teaching in remote parts of the country might experience culture shock—if somewhat less extreme than that of an American teacher arriving at an Indian school. Yet all Irish teachers were of the same "race" and color as those whom they taught. By the early twentieth century a large percentage of BIA teachers, disciplinarians, and school employees were Indian (about 45 percent). Yet the vast majority of the staff during the full period under review, including teachers and superintendents, agents, and others, were not only of a different culture and speakers of a different language than the children—but they were also a different color, "white." This difference in skin color was less significant to Apaches than another physical difference. Thus the term used by Asa Daklugie: "white eyes."[50]

Even if we accept twenty-first-century understandings of "race" as a culturally constructed rather than essential quality, we might still ask whether Indian pupils drew any significance from the different physical appearance of the white staff. The short answer is no. From over one hundred autobiographical accounts it appears that such issues rarely bothered Indian pupils. Even as adults, those who recalled the many shocks of entry to school neglected to mention color and focused on traumas such as hair-cutting, language disorientation, and other such trials. Apart from Daklugie's reference to "white eyes" and Polingaysi Qoyawayma's reference to a red-faced, whiskered teacher with hairy hands at the Hopi school, skin color or race occasioned hardly a mention. Of course, some of these narrators had seen white people—missionaries, traders, soldiers, settlers, perhaps—before entering school. Many had not, and they seem to have ignored or been uninterested in physical appearance or race. What counted for pupils was teacher behavior.

This is hardly surprising, for "race" is generally seen to be a Western concept, and indeed a relatively recent one at that.[51] Full theories of biological racism—that nonwhite peoples are inherently inferior—began to blossom only in the nineteenth century. Therefore we should not expect children from cultures who did not think in such terms to react as Western children, brought up in racially conscious societies, might.[52]

If such differences in appearance were irrelevant to young Indians, what about the reverse? Did white staff draw racial implications from Indian "color"? Again, the short answer is no. Undoubtedly there was an intensification of racial thinking in the United States, indeed across the Western world, around the beginning of the twentieth century. More and more Westerners began to see Africans, Indians, and other nonwhite people as permanently stunted by their racial and biological origins, or capable of change only over eons of evolutionary time, thus needing predominantly vocational training.[53] In autobiographies written decades later, we might expect narrators to have become more aware of racial prejudice than would a culture-shocked child. Yet there is little evidence that teachers and others at the schools became significantly more racist toward their charges, perceiving them as biologically incapable of matching white people in educational level. As I have argued, the BIA goal was assimilation of Indians into citizenship; compare this whole crusade to the federal disinterest in the educational fate of African Americans during the period under review.[54]

A few racially charged incidents were recalled by ex-pupils. Mary McDaniel (Lakota Sioux) told her interviewer that during the 1930s the matron at her boarding school punished "full bloods" more severely than "mixed bloods," and their English teacher called them "idiots." When Luther Standing Bear first experienced racial prejudice, it was as a worker in Philadelphia; he failed to find lodging because of his race, he believed.[55] The most explicit experiences of racism I uncovered were recalled by Indians who attended state public schools or other schools with white children—reinforcing an impression that for all their faults, the Indian schools protected young tribal boys and girls from the worst failings of white society.[56]

How each teacher treated them—this was the issue for young Indians. Continuity rather than change thus marked the performance of the teachers. Whether at Irish schools, where teacher and pupils were members of the same nation or "race," or at Indian schools, where, despite increasing Indianization of staff, the situation was quite different, pupils responded to teachers as teachers responded to them.

VII

If race did not significantly complicate the Irish and Indian pupil-teacher relationship, did class? Even the most ambitious and egalitarian BIA official or missionary hardly expected the mass of Indian people to enter the higher levels of American society. Yet, as in the case of Dr. Charles Eastman, for example, a few might rise in class, and in 1900 Commissioner Francis E. Leupp left the whole subject open. "It is not considered the province of the Government to provide either its wards or its citizens with what is known as 'higher education.' That is the proper function of the individual himself." The Indian boy or girl who had progressed through the literary training of the schools had laid "the groundwork for future education, and can fit himself or herself for the bar, the pulpit, or the magazine pages." Five years later Leupp wrote that "I would give the young Indian all the chance for intellectual training that the young Caucasian enjoys."[57] To the extent that Indians might be disadvantaged socially, BIA officials thought more in cultural—or sometimes racial—terms of their charges, most of whom would remain at a lowly level in American society.

As the CNEI explicitly sought to provide a basic education for the ordinary, predominantly poorer people of Ireland, class loomed larger in the Irish system. CNEI authorities and inspectors clearly perceived the mass of Irish people as backward and deficient in civility. However, many of the CNEI teachers were sons and daughters of ordinary people themselves; the majority were untrained. Therefore we do not come across much evidence of them looking down their noses at the local people, the way those higher in the organization often did. City-versus-country prejudices or local-versus-outsider prejudices may have arisen, although there is little evidence of them in my sources. Hints of a sense of cultural or class superiority among ordinary teachers do occasionally emerge. Back in the days of the hedge schools, observers sometimes commented upon the erudite pretensions of individual teachers. Patrick Bradley, writing about the early twentieth century and thus of national school teachers, asked "whether it has been generally recorded that practically all schoolmasters at that time were noted for the flowery language? Pompous and polysyllabic words and rounded phrases seem to have been a necessary badge of the profession." One teacher, for example, noting sarcastically that a young student was likely headed for the gallows, said: "Paddy Murphy, I am very much afraid that owing to the inscrutable degree of Providence, you were born to encourage the growth of hemp, and that you will die supporting its manufacture." Whether or not Bradley exaggerated, he obviously felt that many teachers in the old days put on such airs.[58] Yet, just as Indian narrators recall little overt racism in their teachers, we do not find Irish narrators complaining much about the class pretensions of their teachers, lowly servants in the CNEI machine, many of whom were fairly close to themselves and their families in social standing.

VIII

And what of gender? As the nineteenth century progressed, increasingly large numbers of Irish and American Indian teachers were female. By 1900 the BIA reported that of 347 teachers it employed, 286 were women. By the same year, the CNEI employed 11,938 principal teachers and assistants. Not surprisingly, male principal teachers outnumbered females by 4,697 to 3,547, but females outnumbered male assistants by 2,606 to 1,078. Therefore, of this CNEI total, over half were women: 6,153 to 5,775, although males dominated the higher ranks within the school, and from there on up in the CNEI (and BIA) hierarchy.[59] Women were supposed to embody the traditional female qualities of nurturing and suitability to teach small children. S. C. Armstrong of the Hampton Institute, for instance, talked of "the refining and elevating influence of a woman's presence . . . to soften and civilize the sons of the savage"— not to speak of the daughters. Obviously their proper place was in the home, or, by extension, in the classroom. And as Adams writes, women were also cheaper to employ. In its 1904 Report, the CNEI referred to the importance of having female teachers for all younger children, boys included; and it noted "the general opinion as to the advantages to be gained by having boys in their earlier years under the training and instruction of women."[60]

At BIA and Irish schools, boys and girls shared certain elements in the academic side of the curriculum, and there might be overlap in teacher duties: women or men might teach religion or English or history, for example. Yet, especially in America, the vocational side became increasingly bifurcated into learning supposedly appropriate for the sexes. In such circumstances female teachers, matrons, and cooks instructed the young and not-so-young girls in the forms of female duties, vocational education, hygiene, and health, and men taught the boys in artisan skills and on the school farm. In Ireland too female teachers taught sewing and other girls' subjects. Obviously, then, in both systems, there was some gender demarcation for teaching.

Did Indian and Irish pupils see much difference between male and female teachers and staff, however, in terms of skill, sensitivity, or even brutality? Or—of specific significance for this study—in terms of dedication to the goals of assimilation? Here again, the answer appears to be no, not much. Actually, I found no difference whatsoever between male and female teachers when it came to spreading the cultural values of the United States, Christianity, "proper" gender roles, or the anglicized message of the CNEI. Few teachers of either sex subverted the assimilatory ideals and attempted to inculcate local culture. On this core issue of assimilationist teaching, then, gender had little or no bearing.

The more violently brutal teachers tended to be men, but women too could be harsh to children, as Maurice O'Sullivan discovered when his teacher beat boys severely and then tied them to a post. Intriguingly, the brutal attack on a dull boy by "Gray-beard," described earlier, may actually have been the work of a woman (La Flesche may have balked at presenting a brutal female teacher). If not, then there were two teachers at the Omaha school liable to fits of explosive temper. In 1862, around the time La Flesche attended, Presbyterian missionary Isaac Black reported how one of his colleagues, a Miss Smith, had become "an object of terror" at the school. "Possessing as she does an ungovernable temper her actions were frequently such as were unsuitable for one in her position." A number of times "her passions have been let loose in an inhuman manner against some offending little girl." Black himself had seen this teacher "beat a little girl on the *head, shoulders,* and *ears* in a way that was perfectly shocking" (emphasis in original). And in Sabbath School she "pulled a boy out of her class and beat him cruelly on the head before the school." Teacher rivalries may have been in play in Black's report, but he would hardly have reported such activity, shameful to the whole enterprise, unless it had occurred. Indeed, it is one of the worst accounts of teacher brutality that I encountered, and it concerns a woman.[61]

Far less dramatic, but also relevant, was Lucille Winnie's recall of how female "officers" at Haskell—including her own sister—could be abrupt and officious with newcomers. Indeed, this Iroquois's account reads like any description of army officers and NCOs pushing around new recruits. Essie Horne appears to confirm this—she admitted that as an "officer" at Haskell she was sometimes severe with ordinary students, and she even resorted to corporal punishment. A female superintendent could make life miserable for teachers too. Gertrude Golden complained bitterly about the autocratic woman who had been placed in charge of her school, whom she referred to as "her august majesty" and "the reigning sovereign of the first absolute monarchy under which I ever had the misfortune to live."[62] Thus, in America as in Ireland, women staff emerge as diverse as the men; a little less harsh, perhaps, but not especially sensitive, soft, or nurturing; certainly not more culturally tolerant.

IX

Despite the vast cultural gulf between white Americans and Indians, in one sense BIA staff had an easier task than their Irish counterparts. As Americans, they were carrying variants of their own culture to the Indian field and into the schools. We have no indication that many white teachers agonized then—as some might today—over the universal validity of the American Christian civilization. Neither did they agonize much about the worth of the Indian cultures being destroyed "to save the man" or woman supposedly trapped within. The difficulty was in transmitting the obviously superior American way to reluctant or even benighted Indian children and, through them, to tribal adults.

CNEI personnel were themselves Irish. Admittedly, a substantial number of teachers in Ulster, especially, saw themselves as not just Protestant and Irish, but as British too. The vast majority, however, sprang from the Catholic community; some spoke the Irish language. As the nineteenth century wore on, they must have been aware of the increasingly influential Repeal and Home Rule movements against the Union with Britain, or of the more militant nationalist organizations such as the Fenians, or of the Gaelic League or other revivalist groups.

To what extent, then, did CNEI teachers loyally carry out their assimilatory tasks? In 1866 the CNEI admitted that thirty-seven national school teachers had been arrested "for alleged complicity with 'Fenianism,'" but it claimed that "as a body, the National Teachers of Ireland are loyal men." After the 1916 Easter Rising, too, the CNEI was equally at pain to protest the loyalty of its teachers.[63] Whatever the validity of such claims for loyalty, their very existence proves that CNEI employees lived at times of conflicting cultural and political demands, especially later in the period under review. Even from the autobiographical accounts of ex-students, however, many written after most of Ireland had attained independence from Britain, there is little evidence that teachers attempted to inculcate nationalist ideas into the children.

The 1899 letter of an anonymous national teacher, extracted in *An Claidheamh Soluis* ("The Sword of Light," published by the Gaelic League) in 1899, suggests some of the reasons why this may have been so. The writer first sarcastically noted that recently sanctioned readers for the national schools "never once refer from cover to cover to the language, the literature, the history of this land of ours." Would this occur in any part of the civilized world? he or she asked—obviously unaware that American Indian children, then living in the "civilized" United States, suffered a very similar fate. The writer thus wondered why there was "any spark of nationality" alive in the national schools. A teacher's "whole surroundings, from the day he is first apprenticed to his craft is West British [Anglicized Irish]." Trained two years in a Catholic training college, "during all that time we never got a single lecture on the language, literature, or history of the land to whose young generation

1. Rev. William Hamilton, a superintendent of the boarding school established among the Omahas by the Presbyterian Church in the United States, with members of that tribe and some other white Americans. In the early 1860s Francis La Flesche attended this school; his book *The Middle Five: Indian Schoolboys of the Omaha Tribe* (1900) is a classic reminiscence of Indian boarding school life. Courtesy of the Nebraska State Historical Society, neg. no. P928–15.

2. A group of pupils and teachers posed outside the school at White Earth, Minnesota, ca. 1873–74. Photograph by Hoard and Tenney, courtesy of the Minnesota Historical Society, neg. no. 33012.

3. Student battalion and band in parade formation at Carlisle Indian School in Pennsylvania, 1880. Founded by Capt. Richard H. Pratt in 1879, Carlisle was the first of the large off-reservation Bureau of Indian Affairs boarding schools. Luther Standing Bear described the initial difficulties Indian students faced when encountering Western musical instruments—and the pride he later took in marching in and leading the band. Courtesy of the Cumberland County Historical Society, Carlisle, Pennsylvania, neg. no. PA-CH3-01.

4. Chiricahua Apache students as they arrived at the Carlisle Indian School from Fort Marion, Florida, November 4, 1886. "Before/after" photographs were used by educators to show the effects of "civilization" on former "savages" (See also photo 5). Although these boys and girls wore items of American clothing, they appeared unkempt and "uncivilized." The boys' long hair was especially deplorable to white educators. Courtesy of the Cumberland County Historical Society, Carlisle, Pennsylvania, neg. no. 12-24-1.

5. The same group of students shown in photo 4 photographed four months later to show the effects of schooling on the appearance of each boy and girl. Both sexes wore military-style uniforms, an expression of the explicitly military regimentation at Carlisle and many similar Indian schools. The uniforms were liked by some Indian pupils and disliked by others. Courtesy of the Cumberland County Historical Society, Carlisle, Pennsylvania, neg. no. 12-25-1.

6. Matron Mary R. Hyde and some pupils at the Carlisle Indian School, ca. 1890. Boarding school matrons often acted as surrogate mothers for Indian children, especially girls, caring for, disciplining, and training them in "proper" health, hygiene, and gender roles. Courtesy of the Minnesota Historical Society, neg. no. 52383.

7. The Carlisle Indian School track team with their famous but controversial coach, Glenn S. "Pop" Warner (*back, in suit*), in 1909. Jim Thorpe (*front, fourth from left*) and Lewis Tewanina (*front, third from right*) won medals at the 1912 Olympic Games in Stockholm, Sweden. During the late nineteenth and early twentieth centuries, sports (including track and field, baseball, and basketball, and especially American football) became a major form of extracurricular activity at Indian schools big and small. Few organized sports existed at Irish national schools at the same time. Courtesy of the Cumberland County Historical Society, Carlisle, Pennsylvania, neg. no. 15A-2-3.

8. The baseball team at Flandreau Indian Boarding School, South Dakota, ca. 1900. Courtesy of the South Dakota State Historical Society.

9. Interior view of the Indian government school on the reservation near Morton, Minnesota, ca. 1901. The large photographs of President William McKinley and Vice President Theodore Roosevelt are obvious expressions of the BIA's drive to Americanize young Indians. The print of the famous Jean-Francois Millet painting *The Angelus* (on the wall below the "Government Indian School" banner to the left), perhaps reflects the simultaneous drive to Christianize "the heathen." Courtesy of the Minnesota Historical Society, neg. no. 7193.

10. Phoenix Indian School, Arizona, ca. 1900. Another of the major government-run off-reservation boarding schools. The photograph gives a sense of the size—and thus the ambition—of the school. Courtesy of the National Archives and Records Administration, neg. no. 075-PA-I-2.

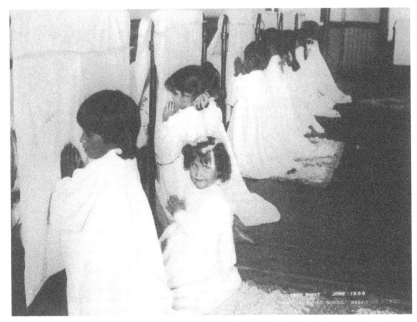

11. Evening prayers in the girls' dormitory at the Phoenix Indian School, ca. 1900. Courtesy of the National Archives and Records Administration, neg. no. 075-EXP-2B.

12. A domestic science dinner at the Phoenix Indian School, 1900. Young Indian men and women learned "civilized" manners and cooking methods at such affairs, which built on the vocational training, supposedly appropriate to gender, learned at the schools. Courtesy of the National Archives and Records Administration, neg. no. 075-EXP-2F.

13. Girls in the gymnasium of Haskell Indian School in Lawrence, Kansas, ca. 1900. Educators in both America and Ireland believed that physical exercise and drills not only improved pupil health but also taught proper deportment, military-style discipline, and prompt obedience. Courtesy of the National Archives and Records Administration, neg. no. 075-EXH-IC.

14. Girls performing a drill in gym class at the Ursuline Convent School, Waterford (Munster), 1908. A number of Ursuline schools operated within the national school system. In the early twentieth century the national school authorities also instituted such forms of exercise. Courtesy of the National Library of Ireland, neg. no. POOLE. W.P.1796.

15. Schoolboys and teacher at Derrycreagh National School, County Cork (Munster), May 1899. Such photos corroborate reports by inspectors that some Irish pupils did come to school barefoot and poorly clothed (compare the clothes of the teacher). The taller boy in the center may have been perhaps a monitor or an older pupil who had returned to school during the farming off-season. Courtesy of the National Library of Ireland, neg. no. R.22395.

16. Children at Ballidian National School, County Monaghan (Ulster), ca. 1903. The tall girl on the left may have been a monitor. The boys in the background appear to be performing drills. Courtesy of the National Library of Ireland, neg. no. R.23168.

17. Micheál O'Guiheen and his mother, Peig Sayers, two famous Blasket Island autobiographical narrators whose reminiscences of Irish national schooling are featured in the present book. Courtesy of the NCD Delargy Centre for Irish Folklore and the National Folklore Collection, University College, Dublin, neg. no. MO10.06.00005.

18. Miss Crowe and Mr. Gildea, along with pupils of the Kilglass National School, Ahascragh, County Galway (Connacht), ca. 1902. Some of the youngest boys wore pinafore dresses like the girls. Courtesy of the National Library of Ireland, neg. no. R.23.360.

19. Members of the Royal Irish Constabulary (RIC) watching the cleanup of the village of Ahascragh, County Galway, after a "fair day" (a market day during which animals were brought into town), ca. 1902. Patrick Shea recalled how he and his brothers were attacked by schoolmates because their father was a member of the RIC, which was seen by many nationalists as the eyes and ears of the British Crown in Ireland. Courtesy of the National Library of Ireland, neg. no. CLON.485.

20. Pupils at Ballingeary Irish College, County Cork (Munster), ca. 1905. Over time the National Board allowed more of the Irish language into its curriculum; by around 1900 it had recognized a number of colleges set up by the Gaelic League to help train teachers in Irish. The blackboard illustration of a teapot reflects some then-fashionable progressive education ideas: in the "object method" the teacher showed familiar objects to students, who learned their names and characteristics in the target language—Irish in this case. Of further interest: the illustration above the blackboard shows a classic image of American Plains Indians. Courtesy of the UCD Delargy Centre for Irish Folklore and the National Folklore Collection, University College, Dublin, neg. no. DO81.20.00007.

21. Boys outside Clash National School, County Limerick (Munster), ca. 1905. Again, the lack of shoes is striking. Courtesy of the UCD Delargy Centre for Irish Folklore and the National Folklore Collection, University College, Dublin, neg. no. DO81.21.00007.

22. Two older schoolboys from Clash National School, County Limerick (Munster), ca. 1905. The relative sophistication of their clothing, compared to the shoeless boys at the same school (previous photograph), is also striking. Courtesy of the UCD Delargy Centre for Irish Folklore and the National Folklore Collection, University College, Dublin, neg. no. DO81.21.00010.

23. A rather self-consciously tough-looking group of young boys, along with their teachers, at the Dromintee National School, County Armagh (Ulster), 1911. Courtesy of the UCD Delargy Centre for Irish Folklore and the National Folklore Collection, University College, Dublin, neg. no. DO81.25.00004.

24. Pupils, teachers, and—apparently—monitors at the Mullabawn National School, County Armagh (Ulster), 1920. Courtesy of the UCD Delargy Centre for Irish Folklore and the National Folklore Collection, University College, Dublin, DO81.25.00002.

25. Boys and girls at a national school in Glenfarne, County Leitrim (Connacht), ca. 1920. The older girl on the right, Elizabeth "Libby" Gilgunn, may be a monitor. She was the mother of the present author's sister-in-law. Photographer unknown. Courtesy Anne Coughlan.

26. The remains of a small, probably one-teacher national school (corrugated iron roof added later), photographed in the 1980s. The sign between the two windows reads: Fintra National School, 1841. Fintra is in County Donegal (Ulster). Photographer Diarmuid Ó'Gráda, photo courtesy of Diarmuid Ó'Gráda.

we were afterwards supposed to act as guides." Even worse, "the supreme penalty—dismissal—is meted out to any member who merely stands within hearing distance of a politician who may preach the nationalization of the land to the assembled Gaels."[64]

The writer perhaps exaggerated, and indeed the CNEI was accepting more Irish material by then. And we do get occasional glimpses of subtle or overtly nationalistic behavior from Irish teachers. Frank O'Connor's beloved mentor, Daniel Corkery, unobtrusively attempted to subvert the official line. He wrote a motto on the board in Irish and explained it to the curious English-speaking pupil: "Waken up your courage, Ireland." He too, believed O'Connor, had to be careful, because neither the CNEI nor the Catholic Church "would have stood for much of that nonsense." Corkery lent the boy Irish books, and he taught the famous words of Walter Scott: "Breathes there a man with soul so dead / Who never to himself has said / 'This is my own, my native land?'" Only later did O'Connor realize that Corkery "was using the standard English texts to promote disaffection in the young, right under the nose of the old policeman-schoolteacher." Sean O'Faolain remembered how "His Majesty's Commissioners of Education had taken every precaution to keep from us the bitter, ancient memories of our race." Yet he recalled too the effect on young pupils of "a phrase, a word from a teacher, or no more than an inflection in his voice," or of a phrase from a history book about the bravery of Irish soldiers in earlier centuries." Gradually, "drop by drop," his patriotism grew.[65]

There was little subtlety in the actions of Patrick Shea's teacher. "He was a visionary and his vision was of a free Ireland cleansed of everything that had come from England, including its language." From him they heard that taxes paid in Ireland kept the English in luxury, that in a free, independent Ireland there would be little or no need for taxation. And Dan Breen, later a guerrilla leader in the War of Independence (1919–21), similarly remembered how a substitute teacher in his Tipperary school in 1902, a member of the Gaelic League, gave the pupils "the naked facts about the English conquest of Ireland and the manner in which our country was held in bondage." When the children emerged from the classroom, they were "no longer content to grow up 'the happy English children,' as envisaged by the Board of Education."[66]

Such scattered passages imply that a few individual teachers were willing to risk their livelihoods. Some used subtlety, some resorted to a rabble-rousing explicitness. And at least in the case of particular students, they appear to have had a successful effect. Further, by late in the period under review, when teachers could legally teach Irish and something of the country's history, they were in effect preaching a kind of sanctioned cultural nationalism, even if

CNEI policy still prohibited its teachers engaging in any kind of political activity, inside or even outside the classroom.

Indications are that almost all white BIA teachers also followed the assimilationist party line without question during the century under review. There was little competition from an alternative political or cultural ideology; Indian "savagery" did not rate as a viable lifestyle in a fast-expanding America. Occasionally we do come upon a published dissenting white view. In his 1868 report on educational developments among the Omaha people of Nebraska, U.S. agent W. P. Callon (also responsible for education) pleaded for better understanding of "the Indian character." Perhaps implying racial limitations, Fallon still claimed that "the Indian" could never become assimilated with the white race. Nevertheless, he went on to extol Native virtues. "Of his individuality and of his race he is proud, and though unlearned in our wisdom, boasts many accomplishments of which we must confess ourselves ignorant." His own traditions and national history were "all preserved in signs and symbols, and handed down from one generation to another." Many other nations were as tenacious about their traits, Fallon claimed, and then compared Indians to the ancient Saxons, who resisted Norman domination in late medieval England. In a ringing plea quite out of character with BIA and missionary goals the agent asked: "Why may we not then respect what we cannot destroy—his nationality—educate and improve him in his own language, and ultimately create for him a literature of his own, adding English merely as an accomplishment?"[67]

In her study of the reminiscences of six female BIA teachers during the early twentieth century, Patricia Carter sees these white women to some extent engaging in subversion of BIA cultural goals. One teacher questioned whether by "teaching the children to like and want the things we liked and wanted, we were heading in the right direction." Another disagreed with the prohibition on the use of tribal languages in the classroom and employed an interpreter from among the pupils; she also objected to the military discipline. Others of this group attended traditional ceremonies or formed relationships with local people—"took on the role of amateur anthropologists," in Carter's words. The historian does not claim that such women systematically subverted the cultural goals of the BIA, merely that in different ways and for personal reasons they combined both reproduction (of the official message) with resistance.[68]

Apart from such rare white defenders of tribal life, "subversives" were most likely Indians themselves. By 1900 there were 2,175 men and women employed by the BIA in its educational enterprises: almost one-third of these were

Indians, 695 compared to 1,480. Of teachers, 59 out of 418 were Indians. Over the next few years these figures decreased, but Indians were heavily employed throughout the period under review.[69] From all accounts, including those written by Indian ex-students, few even of these Indian staff ever attempted to rock the assimilation boat—we should remember that some, at the larger schools, sprang from different tribal cultures than many of their pupils.

Yet Angel DeCora, a Winnebego who taught at the multitribal Carlisle, worked to enrich students' understanding of different kinds of Indian art, both tribal and pan-Indian.[70] When Essie Horne picked Ella Deloria (Lakota) and Ruth Muskrat Bronson (Cherokee) as two other Haskell teachers who deeply influenced her life, it was partly because they demonstrated qualities intrinsic to good teaching: "They listened to us. They were interested in what we thought . . . and in our lives. They taught us that we could accomplish anything that we set our minds to. Their positive attitudes and pleasant dispositions convinced us that they must be right; but they also taught us not to believe that everything we learned was the truth." Further, they also encouraged pupils to be proud of their tribal heritages. These Native Americans could teach Shakespeare and Longfellow in an inspiring way—meaningfully incorporating Indian material in the latter case—yet they also "taught us about Indian values, and kept them alive in us." At a time when the government was still spreading the capitalist ethic of accumulation, they "taught us about generosity and about sharing—what goes around comes around." Tribal peoples had been criticized for such communal generosity, "but there is so much joy and satisfaction in giving," Horne wrote.[71]

Horne too attempted to teach both the new and the old. Through the meeting of various tribal groups at Haskell, "we learned each other's culture, and we developed a healthy respect for each other's vision." She certainly saw her work as at least partly subversive: "Had I been caught engaging in this 'heathen' activity, I quite certainly would have been fired." She was not in sympathy with BIA assimilationist goals and taught her Creek students "to have pride in themselves as individuals and a respect for their heritage. I tried to follow the example of Ruth and Ella, my Indian mentors at Haskell." She admitted hiding materials on Indian cultures prepared by her students, when BIA supervisors came. She also thanked her father, who, although white, had encouraged her to appreciate both her Shoshone and American heritages. "All my life," she wrote, "I have tried to teach my children and my students to have a deep appreciation of their own heritage, as well as that of others."[72]

From such limited evidence in both the Irish and American cases, we can draw certain tentative conclusions. More Irish teachers than white American teachers probably attempted to subvert the official assimilatory goals of their own organizations. I suspect that it hardly entered the minds of white BIA employees to teach respect for tribal cultures; apparently few Indian employees did so. Considering the somewhat different situations in each case, we might have expected even more evidence of Irish resistance. For reasons that combined fear of dismissal, loyalty to their CNEI employers, bureaucratic inertia, and in some cases genuine loyalty to the Union between Great Britain and Ireland, relatively few Irish teachers appear to have explicitly braved the National Board and openly questioned the Union. The gathering separatist and nationalist tendencies of the later-nineteenth-century Ireland mostly gathered outside the national school classrooms.

X

Historians, myself included, have built a portrait of BIA and missionary schools as often harsh institutions. Yet, influenced by New Social History and postmodernist emphases on coping strategies and counter-manipulations, scholars have also striven to demonstrate that Native peoples can sometimes acquire a degree of empowerment, even in deeply unequal power situations. K. Tsianina Lomawaima, for example, argues that by creating "relatively free spaces" to resist authority, and by building their own subcultures, pupils at the Chilocco Indian Boarding School in Oklahoma "made [the school] their own." And, in an extreme expression of the empowerment argument, this Native American historian claims that the Chilocco culture "was created and sustained by students much more than by teachers or staff."[73]

Having thus rightly moved beyond viewing Native peoples as passive victims, however, we now risk "over-empowering them"—indeed we risk erasing the all-important issue of power itself. During the nineteenth century the awesome demographic, economic, political, and military power of the United States continually increased; inevitably, Indians did far more adjusting to white Americans than vice-versa. Yet the men, women, and children of the tribes retained some freedom of action in many local situations, leading to complex and shifting symbiotic relationships—relationships of interdependence—between them, the teachers, and educational authorities. Symbiosis also developed in the Irish educational arena. In the latter case Irish people began to gain increased leverage at both the national and local levels, far more so than in the case of Indian peoples.

Thus a "symbiotic embrace" characterized the relationship between the BIA staff and Indians.[74] As boarding schools spread, staff came to rely more and more on the labor of Indian children. For every dollar spent by the government on a student, boasted the principal of Carlisle in 1910, the student produced nearly a dollar in return—whether working on the farm or in the kitchen or elsewhere.[75] Large numbers of absentees or even a sudden epidemic of runaways could seriously threaten the efficient running of a school and might call down the wrath of BIA superintendents or agents or (later) inspectors.

Further, for all their apparent power in the classroom and schoolyard, BIA teachers and other school staff found themselves more and more caught up in the interrelated dynamics of bureaucratization and professionalization. BIA assimilative goals implied, as Commissioner Leupp wrote in 1908, that the Indian Office should work itself out of existence "at no very distant date."[76] The bureaucracy, however, just grew and grew. In 1824 the educational superintendent had the service of two clerks; his responsibility included administration of the civilization fund, tribal annuities, and other funds; deciding on land claims; and handling Indian correspondence. In 1837 an education division was added to the BIA, and by 1888 the school service alone employed 757 white and 137 Indian men and women in almost 60 distinct job categories and subcategories, including superintendents, teachers, matrons, clerks, and laborers. In the early twentieth century 132 headquarters employees were processing 77,000 letters annually; by 1911 the number of letters had almost trebled to around 200,000, with less than a doubling of the headquarters staff. By 1937, instead of fading away as Indians merged into American society, the BIA had become one of the largest of the federal bureaucracies; one that, as historian Francis Paul Prucha notes, "dominated every aspect of the Indians' lives."[77]

It also dominated the lives of its employees. The commissioner was responsible to the secretary of the interior, and members of the BIA educational division struggled to justify expenditure. Once agents were obliged to send in reports on schools in their jurisdiction, and once Congress in 1870 authorized appointment of inspectors, pressures on teachers intensified. Civil service protection increased their sense of security, but individual teachers were at the mercy of school superintendents—themselves liable to agents' and other BIA inspections. The Omaha agent, for example, noted in 1861 how he had visited the Presbyterian mission school at least twice a week and had examined the progress of individual scholars.[78]

The teacher's sense of professional security or insecurity depended heavily upon Indian adults and children, who might cooperate with the school or act in ways that brought disrepute upon it and its staff. In 1864 U.S. agent Charles Hutchins sent in a deeply critical report of a school in Montana run by the Jesuits. Intended by treaty to teach both manual labor trades and academic learning, only the latter, according to the agent, was being done. Then he noted how so few Indian children regularly attended; when their kin were close by, perhaps forty did; when the kin moved around on hunting expeditions, only a fraction of this number turned up. The agent asked if he suddenly dropped in on the Indian camp—away from the schoolroom, in other words—and asked the children about "their letters," would they answer correctly? The crestfallen but honest priest admitted that they probably could not. "I therefore regard the school as a failure," reported the agent, "and to continue it would be a purposeless and futile waste of public money, and have accordingly ordered the discontinuance of the school and a stoppage of all expenses on account of it." A few years later in 1870 Nathan Tinson resigned as principal of the Kaw Manual Labor School because he could not persuade enough Indians to send their children.[79]

Gertrude Golden told how both teachers and superintendents felt the pressures. In 1901 she passed the civil service examination yet still faced a year's probation before appointment as a BIA teacher. She was thus at the mercy of the school principal. "Our being retained or promoted depended entirely upon the reports he sent to the Indian Office," she wrote. "These reports dealt with our efficiency, obedience to established rules and our general fitness for the position." At another school, according to Golden, the superintendent was equally insecure. Because of visits from BIA inspectors and local whites, she "placed great stress on having attractive-looking work on the blackboards and walls of the classrooms . . . [she] kept pupils copying and recopying papers, sometimes for a week at a time or until they were practically perfect and fit to be placed on the wall for inspection." Pupils who excelled at drawing and painting might even be excused other instruction, so important was it to impress visitors.[80]

In a memorable expression of such anxiety, George W. Scott of the Chilocco School further conveyed just how a superintendent, especially, could find himself caught between the bureaucracy, Congress, and Indian people. "The present plan requires all the energy of a man throughout the year," he complained in 1889, "subjecting him to liability under his bond if he fails to keep up his average attendance. Even one less than the appropriate attendance robs the school of its share of the appropriation made by Congress. Summing it all up, *it depends on the caprice of the Indians whether the children are secured*" (emphasis added). Ironically, therefore, Scott found himself at the mercy of those whom the United States supposedly controlled: "The superintendent must visit reservations, council [sic], plead and coax a lot of untutored Indians for children." It is an almost pathetic image of Indian empowerment and white frustration, reminiscent of passages quoted earlier in which outraged teachers remarked that some tribal people deemed it a favor to send their children to school.[81]

Even the compulsory legislation of the 1890s, along with the employment of agency police and others to round up children, never permanently solved the problem of absenteeism during these decades. When children did attend, they presented problems far greater than those faced by English or German teachers educating children of their own nations. The widespread punishment of pupils for speaking vernaculars at school was only partly the expression an ethnocentric desire to stamp out the languages of "savagery." It also reflected the frustration of teachers who were thrown against a language barrier, yet continually judged on the effectiveness of their teaching.

Simultaneously, pragmatic and adaptive Indian peoples became increasingly dependent upon the white teachers to bring the new knowledge to their children, the vast majority of whom attended some school by 1930. Although the runaway has perhaps attracted more attention in the history of Indian schooling than the enthusiastic student or even the quiet and obedient plodder, many Indian children came to accept or even enjoy aspects of schooling. For them too, the teacher—white or sometimes Indian—attained special importance. "We were ready to do anything for Miss Burgess," wrote Luther Standing Bear of one of his Carlisle teachers.[82] In different forms, then, with different degrees of intensity, a symbiotic embrace characterized the relationship between school staffs, educational and national authorities, and Indian peoples, leading to a situation that white Americans of necessity dominated, but that no group completely controlled.

We can also employ the concept of symbiosis in the Irish context.[83] Even a teacher who lorded it over his pupils deferred to the CNEI inspector. He (almost all inspectors were male until the addition of a few women to examine in domestic science and other "female" subjects) in his turn reported to National Board headquarters. The commissioners were responsible to Parliament and had to struggle continually with the British Treasury for adequate funds. In such a web of interdependence the lowly CNEI teacher was, like the BIA counterpart, at the mercy of both superiors—and of clients. As inspector John E. Sheridan expressed the obvious truth in 1861, "teachers cannot work successfully without the active and willing cooperation of parents."[84] The latter, in their turn, often desperately needed the teachers to instruct their children in the English languages and other tools of survival, whether they remained in Ireland or emigrated.

Appointed by the local manager (often a parish priest or Protestant clergyman), teachers were subject to regular oversight by inspectors. In 1832 four inspectors were selected, but by 1858 the number had grown to sixty-six. They were organized into head inspectors and district inspectors, with two chief inspectors having overall authority under the commissioners. Each district inspector was responsible for about a hundred schools. The inspector became the linkman between the board and the expanding school network.[85]

In its 1836 "Instruction to Inspectors" the CNEI noted that they were at all times to strive for good relations with the patrons, managers, and teachers. Although some inspection days were set in advance, and pupils and teachers might sometimes learn of an unannounced visit, inspectors generally were to arrive when not expected—this element of surprise was one of the most unnerving aspects of the whole system, from the teacher's point of view. Once in the school the inspector was to "immediately examine whether the fundamental regulations of the Board are complied with, and point out privately to the teacher whatever may be deficient." The inspector would then "observe the mode of teaching . . . and suggest to [the teacher] such improvements as may occur to him." At all times the inspector was to treat the teacher "with the most perfect kindness and respect, appraising him privately of what he may see as defective . . . but by no means addressing them authoritatively, or animadverting upon their conduct in the hearing of their scholars." He would then examine pupils in the various subjects. He should also observe their general appearance, whether the school was clean and orderly, and assure—yet again—that there was "A place for everything and every thing in its place," and "a time for every thing and every thing in its time."[86]

After the 1872 inauguration of "payment by results," it became the inspector's responsibility to tabulate each pupil's answers and award the individual teacher (rather than the school, as in England) stipulated increases accordingly.[87] In 1871 head inspector M. Fitzgerald pointedly suggested just how the new system, which was to last three decades, would greatly increase the already heavy responsibility of inspectors—and of teachers. "Henceforth," he noted, "the Inspector will have to measure exactly the work done in each school, with the consciousness that upon every act of judgment he forms in respect of it, a portion of the teacher's income will depend." In fact, "by every decision adverse to the teacher, [the inspector] inflicts, on the spot, a pecuniary fine—small, no doubt, in individual amount, but rising in the aggregate, possibly to a considerable sum."[88]

Ex-teacher Robson believed that he had been visited by about twenty-four inspectors, and with the exception of three or four, he found "these men most anxious to do what was fair and right by the teachers, and to give credit where it was due." If the teacher convinced the inspector that he made an honest attempt, he "had nothing to fear." During the November Results Examination, on which so much depended, one inspector ranged around Robson's class, listening to the each boy's singing ability, or lack thereof, and command of musical theory. The girls were examined in a similar fashion the next day. Overall, Robson seemed to give credence to the claims of the CNEI, expressed in its instructions, that inspectors should at all times treat teachers with consideration and respect.[89]

Perhaps some did. Nevertheless the inspector has gone into Irish folk memory as one who could instantly terrify the most terrifying of teachers. Often without warning he would appear in the school yard, or at the door, and the tyrant of the classroom was suddenly reduced to a cringing sycophant.[90] "If the pupils held the teacher in awe," recalled a folklore informant, "the teacher in his turn was in no less fear and trembling in the presence of the inspector." Strangely enough, she reported, pupils and teachers could sometimes enter into a conspiratorial truce at the suspected approach of the inspector—warned, perhaps, by a strange carriage on the road. All worked hard at their lessons, and pupils and teachers dressed for the occasion. This informant claimed that some teachers were too nervous and deferential to even offer the inspector a cup of tea.[91]

Unused to spectacles in the 1860s, pupils on the remote Blasket Islands burst into laughter at the sight of a "four-eyed" inspector. The teacher "nearly fainted with shame," according to O'Crohan, and "suffered a good talking to." On a later occasion a different teacher—"you would have thought it wasn't the same man at all [when] the inspector came"—had to ask O'Crohan's help with some figures on a slate, so flustered was he. Another folklore informant remembered how his unfortunate teacher, "already very nervous and excited," went to a cabinet—and out flew a bird the pupils had earlier left there, knocking the man to the ground in shock. The pupils laughed, and later, looking back on the event, so did the teacher. At the time he must have felt that his whole livelihood, or at least the hoped-for extra payments, were in jeopardy. The same narrator recalled the stern and humorless response of an inspector when a local fiddler struck up outside the window just as a student began to recite poetry. Of course "we all tittered," he wrote, "but [the inspector] gave us such a look that we all dried up at once."[92]

Things became especially difficult for Irish teachers when older boys, unemployed during the winter months, temporarily re-entered school, causing all sorts of disciplinary problems. "The master would be in mortal terror of the inspector in those days," wrote a folklore informant, "and indeed it was no wonder too that they should be. The inspectors in my young days used be very harsh and tough with the teachers, and the teachers used be in a troubled mind when the inspector would be expected."[93]

The common denominator of all educational reforms in the nineteenth century, writes David Vincent, was the notion of system.[94] Especially after the introduction of the new "payment by results" approach, the CNEI became more and more statistically orientated. Every attending pupil had to be marked on the rolls as present or absent. In 1865 inspector Patten complained that attendance at many schools was highly irregular, "particular as regards the punctual arrival of children in the morning." To gain full rewards from schooling, children needed to "be present after the hour specified on the 'Time Table' for commencing the business of the day." He clearly assigned the blame for such pupil failings: "The teachers themselves, I am sorry to say, often exhibit to their scholars a bad example by themselves being late."[95] Aware of the growing statistical accountability, some teachers may have resorted to falsifying attendance figures and other accounts—a further reason for them to fear inspectors, some of whom publicly made such accusations.[96]

Thus, as in the American situation, if ambitious parents and even pupils needed the teachers to provide a modern education, teachers needed pupil and parental cooperation to satisfy the inspector, the local manager, and, indirectly, the school patron and the board—the bureaucracy. The inspector too was at the mercy of the CNEI, just as the CNEI was dependent upon Parliament and the Treasury—but these aspects of the power nexus were generally beyond the ken of the children or even adult ex-pupil narrators. Their almost paradoxical recall of teacher power or insecurity thus credibly presents the relationship of symbiotic interdependence that also developed in Ireland. Michel Foucault's insight is applicable to both systems: power "is a machine in which everyone is caught, those who exercise power just as much as those over whom it is exercised. . . . it becomes a machinery that no one owns."[97]

From this analysis of the roles of school staff, especially teachers, we can see that in Ireland and the United States these men and women appear highly similar: humanly varied in personality and performance, and generally untrained for most of the period under review. A few Irish and American (including Indian) teachers were effective and even inspiring educators; a few were brutal well beyond the generally accepted standards of the time. Although white American teachers were of a different color than their charges, Indian children—and adults in retrospect—were far more conscious of behavior than race. The same was true of gender: somewhat less prone to brutality, women were no more sensitive to traditional cultures than the men.

The deeply symbiotic nature of the educational situation also becomes apparent. As the bureaucracies developed, as teachers and their employers strove toward greater professionalization, as Congress and Parliament strove to bring order and wholeness to their respective polities, as Native American and Irish peoples became more acutely aware of the need for modern education to survive in the modern world—all groups became increasingly entangled in a complex and changing "symbiotic embrace."

Power was not equally distributed in such relationships: with the U.S. population expanding to nearly one hundred million, compared to less than one half million Indians, the latter had far less capacity to influence developments. Yet, especially at the local level, Indian adults and children could influence things; even whether a particular school lived or died. In Ireland the situation changed toward the end of the period as nationalist groups more and more came to dominate the political scene. Yet at a local level, throughout the period under review, Irish teachers and school staff were in a very similar position to their BIA counterparts—endlessly caught between authorities and clients.

Therefore through fear of dismissal or at least reduction in salary, through passivity, dependence on local educational aspirations, and perhaps through conviction, teachers in both systems generally became willing conduits of the assimilationist messages of their employers. Whatever their personal and pedagogical failings, teachers and other school staff partly succeeded in their Anglicizing and Americanizing missions. By the 1920s the vast majority of Indians were learning English and attending schools. Most of Ireland was by then independent of Britain, but it was a predominantly school-going, English-speaking nation.

7. Peers and Mediation

"I remember the first day I went to school," wrote Maurice O'Sullivan of his experience in the Blasket Islands around 1908. "Peg de Róiste brought me, holding me by the hand, and it was with great plámás [persuasive talk] she coaxed me to go." Later in class Peg sat beside O'Sullivan, explaining the strange doings of the teacher. When offered sweets, he had "a drowning man's grip of Peg for fear of the mistress," as she accompanied him to the top of the class.[1] Essie Horne not only encouraged her Shoshone mother to send a younger brother and sister to Haskell Boarding School. Having been away for so long, Horne hardly knew her siblings. But she knew the ropes. She returned home, accompanied them by train, and kept a special watch over her five-year-old brother. Both new arrivals were initially lonely but "seemed to adjust quickly . . . to the school routines"—partly because of pampering by personnel, but in good part, no doubt, because of the kindness of an older student, their sister.[2]

As he approached school for the first time, the young Charles Eastman experienced both kindness and bullying. Two older Indian pupils took him aside and explained many of the strange ways of the whites, especially their obsession with dividing the days into amazingly small pieces, and how they had "everything in books." There were no more buffalo to chase, they warned him; "your pony will have to pull the plough like the rest." Later that same day, however, Eastman temporarily fled the school, was called a baby by other older boys, and was jeered at as a "long hair" by more acculturated pupils, who had internalized too well the assimilatory goals of the school.[3]

In these characteristic vignettes ex-pupils conveyed the importance of peers to adjustment at the schools. Pupils sometimes helped, sometimes jeered and bullied each other. Sometimes they became "cultural brokers," mediating between school, pupils, home, and the larger world. Especially in big, multi-tribal boarding schools, they formed into officially sanctioned extracurricular cultures, or into secret subcultures. All such arrangements intensified or problematized peer relationships; they also worked to reinforce or obstruct the assimilatory goals of the school. Many, though not all, of these processes were highly similar from Ireland to America in the period under review.

I

Fellow pupils did not always make things easier for each other. Indeed, although teachers could be draconic and even brutal, much of the everyday misery suffered by pupils at CNEI, BIA, and missionary schools was imposed by peers. An Irish informant admitted that many of the games he and his mates played in their schoolyard "were pretty rough and sometimes a boy would get a knock that would put him out of action for some days." When the parish priest visited the school he counted eighty-four falls by pupils, any one of which was sufficient to break a boy's bones.[4] The violence at Patrick Shea's school was more than over-enthusiastic horseplay. "I was first made aware of political conflict," he wrote, when he and his two brothers "were suddenly attacked by a howling crowd of boys who knocked us down and beat and kicked us, calling us 'traitors' and 'English spies.'" The brothers did not see themselves as anti-nationalist. Admittedly their father was a member of the RIC (Royal Irish Constabulary, the regular Irish police force until independence in 1922, seen by many nationalist Irish people as the eyes and ears of British administration in Ireland). But he was actually a supporter of Home Rule, to be achieved by peaceful means. Later Shea learned more about the reasons for the assault—RIC men had raided a number of local houses in search of weapons "or other evidence of rebellious intent" hidden by revolutionary advocates of Irish independence. Whatever the reasons, children beat children.[5]

Another folklore informant told how pupils from different villages in the 1880s engaged in fights "with stones and sods flying" between them. The unfortunate child who got a name for telling tales at school was "picked at" publicly, and "if he hadn't sods pelted at him he'd have his ears deafened with everyone shouting around him and calling him a tell-tale." Although the informant did not remember any "tell-tale rhymes" from her own period, her interviewer did: "Tell-tale, tell-tale hang to the cow's tale." This might be repeated for a mile along the road "at the top of the children's voices till their throats became too hoarse to shout any more." Some then resorted to other versions of the rhyme: "Tell-tale-tit, your tongue should be split, and all the birds in the world should get a bit." Nor could the offender expect much sympathy at home, as parents usually took it for granted that even their own offspring got what they deserved.[6]

R. B. Robson also recalled "tell tales." A new student arrived at the Dublin teacher-training college in the 1870s who seemed to take without complaint all sorts of "harmless tricks" played upon him by the other students. Then the boys found out why. The newcomer had been keeping a secret diary, detailing by name every violator of the rules. The guilty boys were called before an investigator; some were fined, but Robson faced expulsion, a punishment that

almost ended his chosen career as teacher. Ultimately he succeeded in pursu-
ing his vocation and took grim pleasure in finding that the tell-tale himself
"never adorned the profession."[7]

The misery Indian pupils caused each other is vividly conveyed in Francis La
Flesche's account—continual confinement in boarding school obviously offered great scope for peer abuse. The boy who could not fight "found it difficult
to maintain the respect of his mates, and to get a place among the different 'gangs' or groups of associates the boys had established among themselves." La Flesche could fight, and he gained admission to the "Middle Five"
gang, after which his autobiography is named. However, a dull and childish
boy "became the butt of every trick a schoolboy could devise, and there was
no one who would do battle for him." Perhaps by the time La Flesche wrote
(about 1900), he had imbibed elements of a popularized social Darwinism;
even in retrospect he does not claim to have protected the boy, which would
have made La Flesche appear soft and thus jeopardized his own standing in
the gang. Sadly, this was the same boy beaten savagely by Gray-beard, so La
Flesche implicated pupils as well as teachers in his suffering. Although occasionally a teacher might lose control, however, much of the daily round of
misery was imposed by pupil upon pupil, with the fortunate, the brave, and
the popular picking on those less fortunate.[8]

Other Indians too recalled bullying and fighting, sometimes in graphic
language. Clinton Rickard, an Iroquois, held on desperately to the head of a
bully, while he "kept gnawing at my wrist and every time he did so the blood
spurted out." Rickard knew that if he let go the other boy would give him a
beating. Similarly John Rogers, an Ojibwe, had to fight a bully at his school or
else endure the taunt of "coward."[9] Such fighting and bullying was not confined to boys. Kay Bennett was physically attacked by a female bully at her
school, who grabbed the Navajo girl by the hair, jerked her head back, and
slapped her hard. Bennett gave as good as she got, and the two girls rolled
to the ground, wrestling and hitting each other, only to be separated by a
teacher.[10]

At the Keams Canyon Boarding School the (generally bigger) Navajo boys
and girls got more food than the small Hopi girls. But even Hopi girls, mirror-
ing adult Hostile/Friendly factionalism, could abuse each other. The Friendly
"tormentors" (Helen Sekaquaptewa's term) mocked the Hostile girls by donning and dancing around in traditional clothes. Bigger Hopi girls extorted
Sekaquaptewa's food and physically mistreated her, reducing her to tears.
That she was studious made her the special butt of jealousy and of ostracism,
a form of group control well known to Hopi children. Another Hopi girl, ac-

cused of being a witch—a deadly serious accusation—was beaten so badly that she went screaming to the matron. Like La Flesche, Sekaquaptewa refrained from actually helping a particularly vulnerable victim, but by refusing to participate in the attack she condemned herself to even greater isolation from the group.[11]

Any sort of deviation from a peer norm might bring trouble. A Kiowa woman of a later generation compared Indian children to crabs in a bucket. When one tried to get out, the others pulled it back. This reflected, the woman believed, the begrudging attitude of less studious tribal children to the more successful students, especially those "making it into the White system." Another ex-student, a light-skinned and fair-haired Cherokee of mixed-heritage, recalled being badly treated and ostracized by full-blood Indians, who deliberately spoke their different tribal language in her presence. She begged to be put in another, more crowded but also more congenial room with mixed-blood children.[12]

Ironically, a far more negative image of pupils emerges from the autobiographical accounts written by ex-pupils than from government or missionary accounts. Officials obviously saw little, or at least reported little, of this side of school life.[13]

II

Yet children also reached out to each other, helping younger pupils adjust to the strange new regimen. Cultural brokers or mediators between Indian and Euro-American cultures have in recent decades been the subject of many scholarly studies. Most of this work focuses on adult brokers who exploited mediatory roles between their own peoples and the encroaching white civilization—usually for complex blendings of personal and communal motivations. Although, as Margaret Connell Szasz has written, "the greatest inroads upon native [Indian] culture were made through their youth," little attention has been paid by historians to the crucial roles of children, especially school-children, as cultural brokers.[14] They, after all, spent far more time than most tribal adults in contact with the messengers of the new order. Further, little has been written from this brokering perspective on Irish educational history. Therefore, drawing on my own and others' work in Native American studies, I first sketch the brokering role of Indian children and then use this perspective to help throw light on similar activities at CNEI schools.

Often Indian boys and girls acted on their own initiative, helping others adjust to school: this I have labeled "unofficial" brokering or mediation. At other times pupils allowed themselves to be used by the school authorities:

they acted as translators, mentors, disciplinarians, "officers," or even truant hunters. Sometimes they became translators for teachers visiting the home community or represented the school on trips into white society. All these school-imposed duties I have labeled "official" brokering or mediation.

Examples of "unofficial" brokering abound in the accounts by Indian ex-pupils. Mildred Stinson, a Lakota Sioux, remembered how two aunts (in the tribal kinship system not necessarily much older) helped her survive boarding school. They "were lonesome too, and I was lonesome—we were all lonesome." Similarly James McCarthy was relieved to find that an older Papago relative was to accompany him and younger children to boarding school. Don Talayesva's older cousin showed the sad young Hopi child how to ride on exotic new animals (pigs), lifting the boy's spirits. Later Talayesva used the same methods to help an even younger cousin.[15] Thus, as BIA authorities hoped, one "generation" of pupils on its own initiative sought out and helped a less experienced one—perpetuating tribal values of responsibility but also helping each other negotiate the assimilatory school demands.

Not all mediators were close kin. Asa Daklugie was moved by the tears of another Apache boy, at that time the youngest child at Carlisle (who ultimately would not adjust and left the school). Although it was against the rules, Daklugie managed to get more syrup for him. Daklugie was later officially appointed to look after the younger boy, but his initial solicitude was definitely an example of "unofficial" brokering. A slightly older Pima girl volunteered to help Anna Moore Shaw on the trip to school. Wisely realizing the worth of such encouragement, school authorities assigned both girls to the same room.[16]

Mediation in many forms dominates La Flesche's Middle Five. If young Omahas persecuted some of their peers, they could also help each other, and especially newcomers. La Flesche's wrenching first day was rendered bearable by an older boy who reminded him that he could go home each Saturday. Members of the Middle Five gang actually enticed a curious young Omaha into school, helped the teacher choose an American name for him, and bathed and dressed him in "citizen's clothes." Brush, La Flesche's best friend and mentor, took the younger boy under his wing: "Frank, you're learning fast," Brush told him early in his school days. "I'm glad; I want you to catch up with me so we can be in the same classes." Such brokering had a dramatic effect: "I felt proud of his praise and worked all the harder." Brush appeared to make the learning interesting: "he always managed to teach me something of the English language, and I was a willing student because he taught me in a way that made the work a pleasure." A chain of learning thus grew: a sensitive teacher had earlier encouraged Brush, who in turn befriended a bright younger pupil, who continued the influence upon yet younger pupils. It might appear that the chain had been broken by the tragic death of Brush from tuberculosis. Yet even on his death bed the young Omaha persisted in his brokering role. He exhorted La Flesche to "tell the boys I want them to learn; I know you will, but the other boys don't care. I want them to learn, and to think. You'll tell them, won't you?"[17]

When we apply the brokering concept to the less voluminous Irish autobiographical narratives, we can glean similar processes. If an older girl helped Maurice O'Sullivan through his first day, he later continued the cycle, helping a new boy, "a sturdy little lump of a fellow," with his arithmetic. This pupil then returned the favor, in a somewhat ironic way. An English-speaker, O'Sullivan initially found himself disadvantaged among totally Irish-speaking children, but his new friend helped him. "Thomás and I were together every day now," he wrote, "going and coming from school. I was picking up Irish rapidly, getting to know the boys and girls and becoming a fine talker dependent on no one but as good as another at the language." Although potentially subversive of the anglicizing goals of the CNEI, such brokering activities simultaneously made the new experience more bearable for the child and thus helped him learn.[18]

Tomás O'Crohan, another Blasket Islander, noted how in the evenings "there were four of us getting on very well, helping each other to learn." And Micheál O'Guiheen, the son of Peig Sayers, remembered how frightened he was on beginning school, as all the other boys were staring at him. Then one of them whispered: "I'll be your butty [buddy]. I'm used to school and I'll help you." O'Guiheen's response was similar to that of La Flesche on being befriended by Brush: "It was a great ease to me when I heard him saying that much."[19] A folklore informant "wasn't a bit afraid goin' to school, the first day," however, as "me sisters had learned me a good bit before I went to school at all; so I was all right." It was a common thing, he believed, for the older children to thus prepare the younger ones. Another informant indicated why such a process often worked well. The schoolbooks "were the same year in year out. This was a great thing for different members of a family for the one leaving the fourth book passed on his book to the one coming into fourth and so on. In this way the elder one knew the lesson quite well and could instruct the younger ones."[20]

At other times close relationships could have negative effects for schooling. O'Crohan remembered one good friend "whom the hammers of a smelting mill couldn't drive from my side." Yet this boy "kept me from going ahead, for he was always glancing restlessly this way and that. That's the chief fault

I had to find with him, for he was always distracting me just when I was beginning to make some progress."[21] It is likely, however, that friendships generally helped rather than hindered adjustment in both Ireland and America.
They were thus a major element in forwarding the assimilatory goals of the
school systems.

The CNEI, BIA, and missionary authorities wisely employed and sometimes shamelessly exploited pupils to help run the schools: what I term "official" brokering or mediation. We have already seen how pupils worked on
school farms and in laundries. Here I focus on how authorities used boys and
girls as mediators, deputy teachers, monitors, and mentors for each other.
All such activities, of course, tended to further official goals, but they also
helped assuage the suffering and loneliness of pupils, especially those beginning school. Official mediation could further involve using pupils as brokers
between the school and the local community, and even between the school
and the larger society.

The Pima girl who even on the train introduced Shaw to the mysteries of the
school was supplemented (not replaced) by an official monitor once the children arrived at the Tucson Boarding School. This second girl taught the newcomers proper manners, how to sit at the table, and—most important—how
to say "Grace" in unison. A student officer at Haskell, who just happened to
be Lucille Winnie's sister, washed the younger girl's face and briefed her on
school protocol. La Flesche's small school used apparently willing pupils in all
kinds of roles, thus implicating them in the destruction of their own culture,
ranging from helping to name and clothe newcomers to instructing them in
the rudiments of Christian prayer. "At supper I showed [the new arrival] how
to bow his head when the blessing was asked," wrote La Flesche, "and how to
turn his plate. He silently followed my whispered instructions."[22]

Jim Whitewolf's responses to boarding school in Oklahoma were typically
ambivalent, yet his ultimate acceptance of the regime was probably facilitated
when the school provided the young Kiowa Apache with his very own mentor. Logan, a distant relative, instructed the younger boy in every aspect of
school life, especially on the importance of the bell and how it ordered the
day. Logan sat behind him in class, showing him how to play with bricks until he learned more English; Logan actually told Whitewolf how to learn the
new language, by first repeating the strange words himself as a model for the
younger boy. Even heavier burdens were placed upon Logan: he was sent out
to hunt down truants or runaways. He and another older boy actually came
after Whitewolf, who had fled the school: they "were afraid we might freeze
somewhere or maybe die. They were responsible for us and had to find us."[23]

Students of many ages and abilities attended Haskell, some who spoke much English, some who spoke little English. As a teacher, Essie Horne "had to be creative in discovering a solution to help all these and all of my students out." The solution she hit on was characteristic. "I initiated the practice of peer tutoring," she writes, "children helping children." Bilingual pupils in Creek and English came to the aid of those with no English. "They translated the children's needs to me and encouraged them to become more proficient in the English language." Such a cooperative venture was a success, she believed, but required sensitive approaches all down the chain: "I had constantly to monitor and praise the efforts of the teacher-learner team, so as to avoid overbearing or bullying behavior, which was rare but did occur."[24]

It certainly did. Lucille Winnie complained bitterly of the insensitive or even rough treatment by student "officers" at Haskell, some of whom were her own kin. Narcissa Owen, a Creek who attended a small missionary boarding school in the 1840s remembered how student officers might administer physical punishment, with the result that ordinary pupils were always looking out for ways to get revenge upon them. Similarly, the disciplinarians who beat Don Talayesva because he refused to speak in a debate before a large crowd were most likely Indians. Hoke Denetsosie, a Navajo who attended the Tuba City Boarding School in Arizona during the early twentieth century, left an especially vivid and bitter account of the enjoyment of power by Indian "captains." They insisted on getting extra shares of dessert, so the younger pupils carried cake in their pockets for them. This happened so often "that our coat pockets would be so stiff and messy that they would hardly bend and we would have a hard time keeping our hands warm on cold days." Pupils who disobeyed "usually got a kick in the behind or some other form of punishment, but those things were never reported for fear of reprisals."[25]

Irish schools, even small local schools, also made extensive use of "children helping children"—and hunting children: "official" brokering. Shea told how his teacher would "bring out a dozen of the bigger boys and deploy them at strategic points" around the wood where he suspected the "mitchers" (truants) were hiding. "At a word of command the search party would begin and when the maverick had been run to earth the search party would be gathered around him for the march back to the school." Although the atmosphere appears jovial, Shea remarked that no mitchers ever seemed to escape detection, and their fate "planted in my mind at an early age the belief that life is hard for those who don't conform."[26] O'Faolain conveyed well the joy of release from school that such duties presented, and with some honesty he acknowledged the ugly sense of power he enjoyed. "It was a delight to be sent out into the street just before the roll call to hasten the laggards," he wrote, "and to tell the shivering wretches that Sloppy Dan would KILL them when he got them inside."[27]

Other services performed by Irish children were less dramatic but equally useful to the school. Peter O'Leary not only helped Irish-speakers with English. As his mother's preschool teaching had also provided him with more book knowledge than possessed by many of his mates, the teacher put him "teaching for a while and then learning." A kind of conspiracy seems to have emerged between him and the master. Bigger boys clustered around O'Leary, anxious for his knowledge. The teacher "used see us, but he would not let on that he saw. He knew that good was being done, and he was satisfied."[28]

At CNEI and BIA schools such deliberate exploitation of children became part of the whole system, epitomized in the training and employment of monitors, officers, and disciplinarians, all risen from the ranks. In 1892, for example, the annual report from the Hampton Institute in Virginia claimed that the military discipline would above all help the pupils internalize ideas of obedience and command (over other students). Further, this system, along with the student court that tried cases and taught students to give and weigh evidence—all involved "the control of the students by those of their own number."[29] Although the generally smaller Irish national schools never evolved such ambitious systems of military training and discipline, they too saw the wisdom of utilizing pupils in supervisory positions. In 1881 CNEI inspector J. W. Rodgers noted the potential of schoolchildren as examples to as yet unschooled peers. "Every school-going boy and girl," he wrote, "is a missionary inviting laggards and truants to come and be taught."[30]

III

Indeed, the mediatory tasks of pupils, both unofficial and official, could extend far beyond the school, into the local community (influencing other children along with adults), or even beyond that, out into the broader national community. BIA officials and Christian missionaries were agreed that, as the Hampton report of 1892 phrased it, students were "to be teachers and leaders of their people." Or as Omaha agent T. T. Gillingham wrote in 1875, with no hint of awareness that his view clashed brutally against tribal respect for age, "the child is educator of the parent." Superintendent Barclay White powerfully expressed the same conviction in 1877. "It is only from the minds of the young and rising generation," he claimed, "that we can hope to eradicate the plants of superstition and ignorance which now so darkly shadow the intellect, and to plant there instead the seeds of virtue, knowledge, and truth." A report from the Hampton Institute in 1889 told how some returned stu-

dents—married couples—had settled close together as "little colonies" on
the reservations. These became "little centers of intelligence," and their influence, "socially and religiously, [would be] strongly for good."[31]

Even before completing school, pupils could begin the betterment of their
people. George Webb remembered his childhood awe upon seeing visiting
Carlisle students in his Pima village, resplendent in their "dark blue uniform
with yellow stripes on the arms and down the side of their pants!" His desire
to attend the distant school stemmed from such recruitment tactics, employing apparently willing students as recruiters and almost as missionaries, to
entice other young people to enroll. Luther Standing Bear was recruited by
students and later became a willing recruiter for Carlisle. At first he had difficulty persuading his Lakota people to send their children, as many had already died at the school. He prevailed and enjoyed the sense of responsibility
involved—the word "proud" appears regularly in his account of the episode,
written decades later. Even in recollection, the anomaly of a youth lecturing
older men does not appear to have disturbed him.[32]

La Flesche too conveys the importance of students as links between school
and tribal community: Brush sometimes interpreted for the superintendent
at the Omaha village. Jim Whitewolf told how his brother also served as interpreter between his school and the Kiowa-Apache people. More than that:
the boy told his kin about what he had learned at the school and indeed per-
suaded his parents to convert to Presbyterianism.[33]

Further, the whole BIA and indeed missionary campaign depended upon
support from the home front—from taxpayers and church members in
American society. Educators were thus acutely aware of the need to adver-
tise the supposed success of their schools in civilizing and Christianizing
Indians. Thus the publication of carefully posed "before/after" photographs,
dramatically juxtaposing "savage," blanketed, or half-naked Indian children
with later shots of similar or even the same children resplendent with hair cut
or trimmed, in the clothes of civilization.[34] School authorities sometimes sent
young Indian pupils on publicity trips to the East or into white communities.
Thomas Alford actually visited Washington DC to attend the inauguration
of President Garfield. "I was flag sergeant at the time," wrote the Shawnee
with pride similar to that of Standing Bear, "and had the honor of tipping the
flag to the President." The object of one such tour, he wrote frankly, "was to
interest the people in the education of the Indians and in helping Hampton
Institute in a financial way." The trip also exposed the students to some of
the wonders of American urban life: "it enlarged my vision." Hopefully the
Shawnee would bring this enlarged vision back to his peers at the school, and
to his people, young and old.[35]

Luther Standing Bear, a Lakota, deeply respected Captain Pratt yet was as clear-sighted as Alford in depicting how the schools could exploit pupils for publicity. The Carlisle superintendent "was always very proud to 'show us off' and let white people see how we were progressing," wrote Standing Bear. "Sometimes we were drilled for days before starting out on an invitation for dinner, so that our deportment would be all correct and proper." Pratt himself unapologetically corroborated Standing Bear's claims, noting in his autobiography how the school contributed over three hundred boys and girls to a New York parade in 1892. Some of the boys carried a large silk banner on which was emblazoned in large letters "United States Indian Industrial School, Carlisle, Pennsylvania," and conspicuously under that "Into Civilization and Citizenship." Pratt went on to quote "some of the many encomiums in the great newspapers" about the Indian capacity for citizenship.[36]

Neither Standing Bear nor Alford appeared to resent such exploitation. Daniel La France, however, bitterly recalled how the authorities at the Lincoln Institute of Philadelphia paraded as second-year students those who had been at the school for eight years, and displayed goods bought in Philadelphia as samples of student work. La France became a prime exhibit: an Indian who could sing and play an instrument, who could write good essays in English, and who supposedly came to school without a word of the language. La France was no opponent of schooling; indeed, his frustration developed as publicity-conscious school authorities hindered him from continuing his education at Carlisle.[37]

IV

We have less sense in the Irish sources of such pupil mediation between school and the home, or between school and the broader Irish society. Stray comments in the literature, however, along with awareness provided by Indian examples, alert us to similarities in the two situations. The folklore informant who noted how books would be passed on from child to child also pointed out the effect of some of these books on adults. "I remember well," he wrote, "the wonder the old people made of the 'sum book' as they called it," a new arithmetic book first used about 1865. Similarly, another informant told how, according to an older man, Irish-speaking adults made great effort to pick up words of English from the children. In 1908 an inspector noted how children at one school took turns bringing home the single copy of a book on Irish mythology, and each one "read it for the household."[38]

Ironically, in terms of the Anglicizing mission of the CNEI and its gradual and reluctant acceptance of Irish as a curriculum subject, teaching the old language could help revive it in places where it was dying, and could pull school and family together. In some Irish-speaking areas, wrote inspector

D. Mangan in 1909, "the reading of Irish stories with a local flavour affords a good deal of pleasure to young and old, and never fails to interest the parents in the school and the work their children are doing there." The systematic teaching of Irish, then, exercised "a humanizing influence and tends to link up the home and school in a way that all would desire to see more general and more marked."[39] Again, the children were the link, the brokers between school and home community.

Too effective a link, according to resident commissioner Starkie, who, as we have seen, claimed that by carrying recently sanctioned Irish history books home, children were actually corrupting their parents with nationalism. Narrators offer little evidence to sustain this claim, however, and the brokering was generally one-way. Irish children, like Indians, mostly brought the assimilationist message into the home.

V

Much of the above account of brokering is based on ex-pupil reminiscences. We are fortunate in having occasional access to the words of Indian children as pupils. For example, students of Gertrude Golden told in compositions how they too attempted to convey their new knowledge to kin. "I always tell my folks they must be clean with their dishes and yards," wrote Helen Price, a sixth grader. "I always show my little sister and mother how to keep the things clean." Another student, unnamed, tried to take care of her home-bound sister, apparently sick with tuberculosis. "I thought of my school," she wrote, "what we had learned about the health of anybody so I did the best I knew how, and my mother was pleased with it." When this student returned home she forbade her sister "to spit things" and actually made little paper spittoons, which she wisely burned under a tree. Because of schooling, she wrote, "I know what causes germs."[40]

A group of Cherokee children clearly conveyed their own roles as brokers between the people, missionaries, and American society. These eleven Cherokee girls, ranging in age from nine to fifteen years, wrote letters from the ABCFM Brainerd Mission School in the late 1820s, as their people faced the threat of forced removal from Georgia to the distant Indian Territory of Oklahoma. The letters all appear to be written in the same hand. Yet with their different levels of English and different personal tones they are undoubtedly copies of the children's own work, transcribed by Miss Ames, their white teacher. As such they allow us a further contemporaneous glimpse into the minds of Indian cultural brokers, proud of their capacity to learn the new way, yet also proud of their Nation and fearful for its future.[41]

One girl told how she was now "writing fine hand." Luckily for her, an older student helped: "Betsy Taylor wrote it for me and begun it for me." Nancy

Reece interpreted for Miss Ames, but her mediation went further. The oldest
of the girls taught Sunday school at the mission: "I ask those children who do
not talk English if they understood the sermon that was read . . . I try to tell
them how to spend the Sabbath day and tell them where they will go when
they die if they are not good."[42]

Sometimes the children addressed siblings, attempting to imbue them
with enthusiasm for Christianity and indeed for the whole cultural message
of the missionaries. Polly Wilson, a twelve-year-old, wrote her brother John,
apparently a pupil at another school:

*I cannot say much but I will speak a few words to you. Love your God and pray to him
and you must not play on the Sabbath; think about God, and you must mind your teachers and love your school mates. You must not quarrel with them. . . . You must not be
idle at school. I hope that you are learning fast. You must study diligently, speak up loud
when you read. . . . Aunt Peggy McCoy's little boy is bur[n]t to death by catching fire to
his clothes. This is another call for us to repent of our sins. I hope you will think of this.
From your affectionate Sister Polly Wilson.*[43]

Like Standing Bear, Nancy Reece and others proudly told how Cherokee
children dared to instruct their elders. Pupils, wrote Reece, could "take care
of their houses and their brothers and sisters and perhaps can learn their parents something they do not understand." They also directly advised parents
by letter: "Mother and Father," wrote another, "you must talk to my brothers
about God, who lives in heaven, [and] tell George that he must pray to God."[44]
However radical the idea of being admonished by children, those Cherokee
parents, often the most acculturated members of one of the Five Civilized
Tribes, must have been impressed by the pupils' facility in the new language
and especially by their literacy in English.

The girls also wrote directly to white Americans, apparently at the behest
of their teacher. Showing how well she had internalized the teachings of
the ABCFM missionaries, Elizabeth Taylor, daughter of a prominent member of the Cherokee elite, did not want to talk of the old ways. Perhaps such
reluctance was a product of shame at her people's "backwardness" or even
expressed a vestigial sense of taboo. Ultimately she agreed, "because I think
when Christians know how much we need the means of knowledge; they will
feel the importance of sending missionaries." She followed with a denuncia-
tion of traditional Cherokee practices: "The unenlightened part of this nation assemble for dances around a fire. . . . And keep up their amusements
all night. . . . When they wish it to rain they send a conjuror who will throw
a black cat into the water, hang up a serpent, etc." Using "they" to distance
herself from the "unenlightened part" of the people, Parker also wrote that

there were other Cherokees, such as herself and her kin, who were becoming enlightened: "Many about this station are more civilized. . . . I have learned that the white people were once as degraded as this people; and that encouraged me to think that this nation will soon become enlighted."[45]

Yet it is clear from their letters (and from the work of modern historians) that neither the girls nor the acculturating part of the people wished to forsake all Cherokee identity. Although they showed great curiosity about the outside world and begged American benefactors to visit Brainerd School, they still identified with their Nation, and were relieved by Miss Ames's insistence that Cherokees were not racially inferior to white people. "My teacher says that I can write as well as the scholars in the North if I try," wrote one. "When Miss Ames first came into school," wrote another, "she said that 'can't' was a phrase which must not be used in the school. In a short time I did not wish to use the word."[46]

These girls and their families manifested what William G. McLoughlin has characterized as an evolving, adaptive, modern tribal nationalism, which accepted much of the new way—including, unsurprisingly considering their southern location, the enslavement of African Americans. Such adaptive policies provoked divisions within the tribe. Even highly acculturated members insisted on Cherokee rights, however, which they would now defend through American courts and by exploiting missionary schooling and their own school systems.[47]

And sometimes they defended their rights by directly addressing powerful Americans. When young Christiana McPherson wrote to President Andrew Jackson, she did not directly mention the removal issue, but no doubt she and the missionaries (generally against forcing the people off their lands) hoped that her words would soften the heart of the great man:

To the President of the United States
Brainerd Cherokee Mission
Sir,

We heard that the Cherokees were going to send you a mink skin and a pipe. We thought that it would make you laugh; and the scholars asked our teacher if we might make you a present and she told us that she did not know as there was anything suitable in the whole establishment. Then she looked among the articles of the girls society and told me that I might make you a pocket book. Will you please accept it from a little Cherokee girl aged nine years.

Christiana McPherson[48]

Alas for the Brainerd girls' efforts, within a few years most of the tribe was forced upon the infamous Trail of Tears to Oklahoma. Yet in writing to local and distant Americans, to white Americans of national importance, and to kin young and old about the mission, and in helping each other at school, the Brainerd girls were accepting their ongoing role as mediators between their own culture and the dominant civilization bearing down upon them. The youngest were no doubt merely following the teacher's orders. However, fifteen-year-old Nancy Reece was obviously combining both "official" and "unofficial" brokering roles as she thrilled to the knowledge of the new way, interpreted the mission to her mates, yet simultaneously tried to garner support for her people from white Americans.

Massively exploited by the school systems, many Irish and Indian pupils were doubly exploited—by kin too, who often sent them to missionary, BIA, or CNEI schools so they would learn to read and write and be useful to the family or community. Such a double burden must have been hard to bear, but there was obviously reward for individual children. To an extent they too exploited the system, sometimes coming to enjoy the new knowledge and to see its usefulness in later life, sometimes flaunting it to supposedly less-enlightened kin at home. Respect for individual teachers motivated individuals. Irish and Indian pupils could also enjoy the sense of power as they rounded up mitchers and runaways. Ultimately, by reaching out to their peers, Indian and Irish children gained in many different ways, simultaneously perpetuating local or tribal patterns of responsibility for those younger than themselves.

VI

At CNEI, BIA, and missionary schools various kinds of extracurricular activities further bound children to each other and to the schools. By such term I mean regular and *sanctioned* student activities. Even if particular extracurricular activities originated in the minds of the educators and to some extent promoted the goals of the schools, others appear to have been initiated by pupils; all served to influence pupils' attitudes to each other.[49]

In smaller Indian establishments such as that attended by La Flesche there appear to have been few organized extracurricular activities—unless one includes Saturday visits to the nearby village. A trip to a circus in Gallup was "the greatest experiences of their lives" for Kay Bennett and her Navajo friends.[50] Despite careful segregation of the sexes outside class, schools sometimes arranged dances and other supervised activities that boys and girls could attend together.[51] In 1897 the superintendent of Indian Schools claimed that in the great majority of reservation boarding schools (which he distinguished from the larger boarding schools), the evening hour that had earlier been devoted to "perfunctory and spiritless study" was more and more turned over to all sorts of enjoyable and "stimulating intellectual entertainments": the singing of songs, telling of stories, reading and recitations, magic lantern shows, conversation, games, "fancy work and a variety of other art work." This conspired to make this hour one of the most fruitful hours of the day. It gave pupils "opportunities for kindly social intercourse with each other," as well as with teachers, along with fueling ambitions for all sorts of worthy activities.[52]

At small BIA schools students sometimes participated in organized sports. For example, in 1901 the Mescalero Boarding School in New Mexico claimed an attendance of all the school-age children of the reservation: a total of only 128 boys and girls. Yet the school had a baseball team. According to the U.S. agent it "won some very nice games at the agency with other teams and had some very nice trips to Alamogordo and other places to play local teams." The activity "did the boys a great deal of good." The writer conveys an atmosphere of enjoyment, rather than the kind of fierce competitive ethic that developed at the large schools.[53]

At the generally small Irish national schools during this period there appear to have been few systematically organized extracurricular activities. Individual pupils got together for schoolyard football or hurling (the national field game, played with sticks and a ball), or for fights, rather than in teams to play against other schools. O'Faolain remembered boys "howling outside in the yard," taking part in "the Roof Game." They threw a homemade ball onto the school roof, "and then there would be a mad rush and a mad tangle struggling under the gutters to catch the ball when it fell"—sometimes it went straight through a roof window, scattering glass on those inside.[54] By comparison, the Mescalero Apache boys' baseball team was almost Prussian in its level of organization.

An Irish folklore informant also remembered how the boys played football and hurling for most of the year. They too had to make their own hurley sticks out of furze roots and the balls out of rags and paper, "tied and sewed securely together." On Maurice O'Sullivan's first day at school he was knocked unconscious by a football. "As I fell I heard Peg crying that I was dead, and I remember no more till I awoke inside the school to see the boys and girls all round and the tears falling from Peg." Although in 1907, as sports organizations proliferated in Ireland, Jeremiah Murphy and his mates knew the names of the great Kerry Gaelic football players, at school they played only a little football: "the schools were poorly situated, having few playing fields," he wrote. Thus "the children were forced to play on the roads or in some neighbouring field." This did not promote good relations with local farmers, though it probably did strengthen—or shatter—many peer relationships.[55]

Sometimes Irish teachers provided the entertainment. Deerpark National School "was not all violence and anger," wrote Shea. The most ferocious teacher could bring a traveling juggler, musician, or man with performing animals into the school. Pupils each provided a penny toward the entertainer's fee. Then for a whole afternoon the desks were pushed aside, "and we were treated to professional entertainment which the master presided over like a proud ringmaster." At other times this teacher would gather the children around and tell them stories about boxers and horse racing—hardly acceptable fare for the commissioners.[56] A teacher at another school also invited in traveling entertainers; there was a man who put his body through a number of rings and walked on his hands. The regular visits of a doctor, who cured warts by rubbing them with a heated black stone—which turned out to be volcanic lava—also broke the monotony of the day. When the children carried this story home, the adults found it difficult to believe that water and fire could come out of a mountain. Another medical visit that turned into a kind of show, if not quite entertainment, was the occasional visit of a dentist; the informant reported without significant comment that the man was black, hardly a common occurrence in rural Ireland then.[57]

A few other forms of occasional or more regular activities emerge in Irish accounts. Eamon Kelly remembered how the boys looked forward to working one hour every week in the school garden, perhaps because—in contrast to regular work at Indian schools—it was a break in normal routine. They learned the useful arts of growing and harvesting vegetables, berries, and apple trees, which led to "much celebration among the boys the spring we planted the four apple trees, when these [bore] fruit." This brought them "more satisfaction than we got from reading, writing, and arithmetic," he concluded. Later in the period, members of the Gaelic League could come into schools to promote Irish, and pupils might then attend outside *feiseanna* (festivals) that included plays, singing, dancing, and other activities. Kelly noted how he enjoyed seeing school plays performed by pupils of his own age, especially those who were native speakers of Irish.[58]

VII

At large Indian boarding schools in the late nineteenth century, authorities and pupils came together to initiate far more ambitious and systematic activities than were dreamed of in Shea's school, or even in the Mescalero School with its baseball team. Actually it is not clear from either official or pupil sources whether the many ventures were the result of pupil activities blossoming into regular fixtures, or whether they were a product of deliberate school policy. Musical performances, debating societies, and theater groups sprang up. School newspapers were published, obviously with staff assistance and even control, but with heavy student input, such as the Red Man and the Carlisle Arrow.[59] A Navajo boarding school at Fort Defiance organized a literary society in 1901, attended by staff and senior students, which met biweekly most of the year. By 1918, claimed the commissioner, at larger BIA schools there were literary societies, religious organizations, brass bands, orchestras, choirs, athletic clubs, physical culture classes, art classes, "and various other student organizations and enterprises for promoting cultural training."[60]

Lending credence to such official claims are the recollections of ex-students such as Hopi artist Fred Kabotie. At the Santa Fe Indian School during World War I, Kaboti joined an art club, helped organize a school orchestra, and also acted in a school play. When a band was begun, Kabotie hoped to get "the big round one with tubes inside" (a French horn) but ended up with the much smaller clarinet, which he nevertheless enjoyed learning to play. Polingaysi Qoyawayma also felt that music helped her survive the Sherman Institute in California. "Hopi reticence" at first held her back from public performances, but later she "began to receive pleasure from giving pleasure." Luther Standing Bear told how much earlier the Carlisle School set up a student band. Most of the children had never seen brass instruments before, and some spat into them or blew into the wrong ends, almost reducing the poor music teacher to tears. Finally the band learned to play and to march. Standing Bear mastered the bugle but took even greater pride from being chosen as band leader, performing in great cities like Philadelphia and New York.[61]

Essie Horne especially remembered the Halloween and Christmas activities at another large school, Haskell, which claimed an average attendance of more than seven hundred pupils in 1920. On both occasions the students went to great efforts to decorate the school and individual rooms. At Halloween they even got to stay up late, and at Christmas there was competition between the students. The boys got to judge the decorations in the girls' dormitories (no doubt under teacher chaperoning), and the girls judged the boys' dormitories. "Christmas was a joyous time of anticipation for us," wrote Horne warmly. "Haskell was our home away from home, and everybody stayed on the campus during the holidays. There were [Indian] kids from all over the United States, including Alaska." Irene Stewart, a Navajo, gradually began to like the same school, at least in part because she could join a glee club and participate in basketball.[62]

Historians such as David Wallace Adams and John Bloom have shown that educational authorities began to see some extracurricular activities, especially American football, as conveying important moral and ideological messages such as virility, competitiveness, or even the ideals of fair play and Christian values. Bloom also believes that sports "ended up becoming institutionalized into the very fabric of daily life at boarding schools, and became part of the culture *that students created for themselves at these institutions*" (emphasis added). Indian boys especially, but girls as well, could deeply enjoy participation, and as Bloom notes: "Through their athletic contests, boarding school students, and Native Americans generally, celebrated a popular nationalism that showed 'what an Indian can do.'" All such activities were polysemic, capable of being interpreted in many different—and sometimes conflicting—ways by those who promoted and those who participated in them.[63]

Shortly after Carlisle's founding in 1879, its annual report contained a proud but prescient prediction: "Regular physical instruction is given," wrote Captain Pratt, "and from all that now can be seen we may eventually rival Cornell, Amherst, or Columbia in athletic prowess." It almost did not happen, however. Shocked by the roughness of American football, Pratt decided to ban competition against other schools. But *students* came to his office to protest his decision. "While they stood around my desk, their black eyes intently watching me," he wrote in a frank account of the affair, "the orator gave practically all the arguments in favor of our contending in outside football." Pratt relented, on the understanding that the boys would always play hard but fair with opponents—thus not allowing themselves to be depicted as "savages"—and would develop so they could "whip the biggest football team in the country."[64]

By any measure, writes Adams, "the gridiron record of Carlisle was remarkable." Between 1899 and 1914, mostly under controversial coach Glen "Pop" Warner, Carlisle took on and defeated such college giants as Harvard, Princeton, the University of Pennsylvania, and Cornell (just as Pratt predicted). Such victories obviously gave special pleasure to Indian students. "The thing that pulled me through," wrote the bitter Apache Asa Daklugie, "was the athletic training at Carlisle." He did not play football himself, but he enjoyed watching the games, the festive activity, and the performance of Indian dances to celebrate victories. He took special pride in the fact that his school "had the world beat. Our football players were fast and husky. They could outrun, outdodge, and outsmart the players of the big Eastern universities." For a player in one of these epic games, the joy was even greater. "As long as I live," wrote Jim Thorpe, later to became one of the great athletes of the twentieth century, "I will never forget that moment. There I stood in the center of the field, the biggest crowd I had ever seen watching us, with the score tied and the game depending on the accuracy of my kick." He was tired, his muscles ached, but, he commented:

I had confidence, and I wasn't worried. The ball came back true and square, and I swung my leg with all the power and force that I had, and knew, as it left my toe, that it was headed straight for the crossbar and was sure to go over. . . . When the gun was fired and we knew we had beated Harvard, the Champion of the East, a feeling of pride that none of us had ever lost came over all of us, from [coach] Warner to the water boy.

Years later when ex-students met, wrote Thorpe, "the remembrance of that Harvard victory comes back and we smile again as we did that day."[65]

Even when the victories were local, pupils got great satisfaction from their achievements. Frank McCarthy, a Papago, was proud that they had organized the baseball team at the Santa Fe school, and he enjoyed his status as a hero of the smaller boys, who asked to carry his mask and catcher's glove. When Santa Fe beat the Albuquerque Indian School it was somewhat less cosmic than the Harvard-Carlisle game—they had not even beaten a white school. Yet it remained one of McCarthy's great memories: "A big crowd was on hand to watch the game between the two Indian schools," he wrote. "That afternoon we beat the champions 5–0."[66]

Girls were far less directly involved in such competitive sports. Some, like Bennett, enjoyed basketball and participated in athletic events. Yet as Bloom notes, whereas competition came to dominate male sports at many large schools, exercise and general health became the rationale for female sports. "The boy is the rough, restless element, full of tireless energy, seeking opportunities for a display of bold, spirited deeds," wrote a superintendent in 1900. "The girl represents home, quiet, rest, and content. She it is who touches our moral nature and makes us gentler, kinder, more manly." Even when organized competitively, girls teams such as the Pipestone Indian School's basketball team, from Minnesota, played under rules revised to emphasize traits like nurturing, teamwork, and selflessness.[67]

Yet looking back, older women too expressed pride in the athletic prowess of Indian students. Lucille Winnie enjoyed the achievements of the Haskell boys' teams on the athletic track and football field, although she claimed that one of her brothers died from over-exertion on the track. During Horne's tenure at Haskell, girls did not participate in athletics outside of physical education class, and she noted how in general at the school they had less freedom than the boys. However, she told how girls sometimes volunteered to help male athletes with their schoolwork: "It was a combination of hero worship, supporting the team, and resistance to the noncooperative boarding school system." She too took pride in the sports achievements of the boys, noting that not only did Haskell excel in football, but the track team also did well and "competed against some formidable universities." Haskell was "a winning team and we were enthusiastic supporters of the team's efforts," She wrote, neglecting to distinguish between male and female students when it came to team support.[68]

By the early twentieth century criticism of an overemphasis on sports began to mount, especially in the case of large Indian schools, which seemed even then to be moving toward a kind of professionalism and ignoring the athletic needs of less skilled boys and girls. "The larger Indian boarding schools have developed sports extensively," concluded the Meriam Report in 1928, "but it is almost wholly athletics of the specialist type, in which only the 'star' athletes, or those approaching stardom sufficiently to make the first teams, have any chance of participation." Such high-profile sports were soon discontinued.[69]

Of course, Indian pupils implicated themselves in this perversion of the sports ethic. Often coming from tribes that vaunted especially male competitiveness, many threw themselves wholeheartedly into sports, as players or spectators. They also enjoyed the personal perks and adulation. As Bloom notes, they used sports to help negotiate their own changing identity in white American society—as Lakotas, or Sioux, or Papagos. Also, as Indians taking on white Americans in the stadium—and in 1926 Haskell had actually built a stadium capable of holding 10,000 spectators. Sports, then—especially football—had both compensations and temptations. "For Native Americans and other marginalized groups," writes Bloom, "interaction with dominant society involves complex negotiations and can be extremely dangerous."[70]

Participation thus facilitated assimilation while simultaneously allowing Indians to take on and symbolically defeat white Americans at their own games. Neither school authorities nor Indian narrators mention attempts to seek out tribal games such as lacrosse or any local activities that might be counted as "sports." Hopi runner Lewis Tewanina, however, carried his tribal heritage of distance running to Carlisle and actually went on to win silver medals in the 5,000- and 10,000-meter races at the 1912 Olympics in Stockholm, Sweden. According to Kabotie, Western athletic training weakened Tewanina in comparison with other Hopi and Zuni runners who defeated him later in local races, perhaps because they still employed Native rituals.[71]

Some of the CNEI model schools did take in boarders (aspirant teachers, not pupils), as did the Marlboro Street teacher-training college. Ex-student Robson gives no indication of ambitious extracurricular activities or organized sports even there, however. Student teachers did get "an occasional day off," which they might spend exploring the city or the countryside around Dublin. Some of them arranged a visit to the famous Guinness Brewery and enjoyed the free sample given afterward—hardly a board-approved extracurricular activity.

They also enjoyed occasional "entertainment nights," involving singing and (Irish) dancing. Toward the end of the course a full "social" or get-together was arranged—whether by staff or students or both is unclear—for young Presbyterian men and women. Some of these occasions brought Northern (Protestant) and Southern (Catholic) student teachers together socially and had, according to Robson, a very salutary effect: "the best of good feelings prevailed." However much they may have lightened the atmosphere of study and even—the Guinness excepted—contributed to the CNEI's goals of character-formation and denominational cooperation, these activities pale before the massive Carlisle and Haskell sports ventures.[72] Although by then larger Irish secondary (high school) boarding schools did engage in team sports, neither larger nor smaller CNEI schools appear to have competed much—as with better facilities they might have—in rugby or soccer, or in Irish games such as hurling or Gaelic football, against even other national schools.

Why this difference between Ireland and America? Size was probably the most significant factor. Small Indian schools also had small or non-existent extracurricular programs. The nature of the boarding experience also explains much. About the same number of children (a thousand) attended Carlisle and the Marlboro Street College in 1900. However, pupils at the CNEI institution went home in the evening; only the teacher trainees boarded. The very long periods spent by some—though not all—Indian children at schools, with few holidays at home, forced both students and school authorities to seek out all methods of making the school a home, as the BIA intended. Also, the growing American passion for team sports, along with growing professionalization, may help explain the differences. Indeed, the Meriam Report specifically linked the growth of "star" sports systems at Indian schools with similar developments—requiring similar "clean-up"—at white private and public colleges.[73]

VIII

Sometimes overlapping with, but often independent of such sanctioned extracurricular activities, Indian and Irish pupils developed subcultures or countercultures (I will use the more neutral term "subculture" here). Such subcultural activities were often unknown to staff. In his classic 1977 study Paul E. Willis examined an English working-class school counterculture. He saw its activities—resistance, subversion of school authority, informal penetration of the weaknesses and fallibilities of the formal, and an independent ability to create diversion and enjoyment—as primarily antagonistic to school order and discipline. Celia Haig-Brown in her study of Indian children at Kamloops Residential School in Canada, and K. Tsianina Lomawaima in

her examination of such activities at Chilocco Boarding School see such subcultures or countercultures as coping strategies initiated by pupils, methods
of accommodation as much as resistance. Haig-Brown characterizes a school
counterculture or subculture (she uses both terms) as "groups of children
who defined roles, projects, and ways of daily life for and with one another
. . . without the sanction, and in some cases without the knowledge of those
who officially held the power of administration." Subcultural actions might
span a continuum from cooperation with the regime to secret but harmless
activities, across into resistance or even rejection of the school. In the present
chapter, however, I comparatively examine the development of subcultures
at Indian and Irish schools in terms of peer relationships, showing how they
brought students together, and how they helped boys and girls accommodate
to and negotiate the school experience.[74]

There is little in the Indian or Irish autobiographies that corresponds to
Willis's picture of English working-class boys waging "continual guerrilla
warfare" against the school and book learning. Or to the picture Rosalie Wax
gives of the Pine Ridge Reservation during the mid-twentieth century when,
especially with inexperienced teachers, "the peer group may become so powerful that children literally take over the school." Even Lomawaima's claim
that the children created the Chilocco School culture may be somewhat extreme.[75] All such accounts suggest the further importance to pupils of other
pupils, nevertheless, and their ability to surreptitiously flaunt regulations
and create their own subcultures, with their own rules and rituals. Ironically,
such developments often worked to the advantage of authorities, especially
at the large boarding schools, in helping pupils adapt, thus furthering assimilationist goals.

     When they continued to speak their own language, whether by desire or
because they had not yet mastered English, pupils were to some extent living
in a subculture, enjoying a measure of privacy from the prying ears of the
teacher. Such pupils were also dependent upon other members of their tribal
group for companionship. Recall the relief of O'Sullivan as, ironically, he began to pick up *Irish* at school, thus becoming more a member of the group.

     Equally ironic, *English* could become the expression of a pupil subculture.
At Haskell, according to Lucille Winnie, "kale" was money, "your aunt" was
a girlfriend, "your uncle" was a boyfriend, and "a bad case" was a serious
romance. Only from the opposite sex could one get "a pleasant"—a smile.
"One thing that boarding school life *did* provide me with," writes Horne in
corroboration, "was a larger vocabulary." There was "a slanguage" (her word)
common to Haskell, "*the usage of which made us feel like we were a bonded part of*

the group" (emphasis added). Horne remembered "kale" and other words that Winnie mentioned, adding examples such as "chape" for "shape" ("What a great chape"). Obviously a whole etiquette of inclusion and exclusion developed; if you misused words you tried to take the peer ribbing with grace. "If you didn't your life could become unbearable, but if you did, you were in."[76]

Such subcultures were thus exclusionary as well as inclusive. So we should not think of a boarding school as having a single student subculture, but as having a number of them. Rituals developed around fighting, for example; go-betweens might carry taunts to and from reluctant or aggressive combatants. Indeed, we might see bullying and peer victimization as a form of subcultural process at all the schools under review, Indian and Irish. In one of the most ritualized accounts of such events, a Choctaw described how, in the early twentieth century, he was brought before a secret student kangaroo court at Armstrong Academy, Oklahoma. A "judge or chairman, and members already in session" tried him. Before being accepted into the student group he had to fight a number of boys—although fighting was strictly against school rules. Meeting secretly, the "court" insisted on speaking English, thus upholding a different school rule. These rituals, then, were obviously examples of both resistance and acceptance, or at least accommodation, and must be distinguished from the officially sanctioned student courts established with some fanfare at schools such as Hampton and Carlisle.[77] The very fact that pupils were imitating a white model, even if secretly, shows the degree to which they had become acculturated; it also shows how they could manipulate the new forms to their own ends.

Perhaps because he later became a professional ethnologist, La Flesche was especially alive to such patterns at his small mission school. All pupils used cake as a form of currency, and life would become hard for those who failed to pay their debts. Older pupils might seek out the younger as potential members for the many gangs. Once pupils were thrown together away from their people, the hierarchy of Omaha life, in which each boy and girl knew his or her place in clan and status groups, began to break down, and students had to work out new arrangements based on ability to fight or otherwise win friends.[78]

Although much was new at the Omaha school, older tribal patterns persisted too. As with "warrior societies" within the tribe, the boys' gangs were often age graded, had their own rules and rituals, and possessed different privileges and secrets. Little or nothing of this was known to the school authorities. James Allen, a Pomo Indian, also told of such gangs at the Sherman Institute in California early in the twentieth century. Irene Stewart, a Navajo, told how at Haskell in the 1920s an interest in fashion cut across tribal dif-

ferences among the girls; this also suggests that although certain individuals were "in fashion," others were not.[79] Although gangs plotted flight from
schools on occasion, there is little to imply that such subcultural groupings
rejected school life. Why go through the ritual, the fights, the humiliations,
unless a long period at school was foreseen?

To the extent that bullying was a regular pupil activity at Irish schools, often practiced without teacher knowledge and designed to separate the "ins"
from the "outs," it would qualify as a subcultural activity. Gangs must have
existed, but Irish ex-pupils tell us little of them. The after-school gatherings
to study together recalled by Blasket Islanders might also qualify. All such
activities intensified pupil-to-pupil relationships and, as in the Indian case,
made school life easier for some, harder for the "outs." Ultimately Indian
boarding schools, even small ones like that attended by La Flesche, offered
more potential for the development of elaborate pupil subcultures than local
Irish national schools that pupils left every afternoon. Thus Irish pupil school
subcultures appear less formal, more haphazard, and individualistic. Some
Irish children no doubt responded creatively to their schooling with many
kinds of secret and mutually binding experiences. Yet it is likely that they had
less need than the Indian boarding school children for such subcultural creativity—or perhaps they just have not left enough records for the historian to
be more precise on the issue.

IX

In this consideration of peer relationships we must finally ask the extent to
which pupils began to see themselves as more than members of local communities or tribal groups—as members of larger communities or even nations. Children of up to ninety tribes attended Carlisle together. Did this lead
any of the children to begin to think of themselves in "Pan-Indian" terms, as
not merely Hopis or Navajos but as American Indians, members of a conti-
nent-wide "people" wronged and discriminated against by white Americans?

A number of writers, both ex-pupils and modern historians, believe that at
least at large, multitribal schools a Pan-Indian sentiment did develop. Bloom
and Adams, for example, justifiably see football successes as heightening a
sense of Indian pride. When Asa Daklugie boasted about the great Carlisle
footballers beating the white schools, he did not single out Apache members
of the team. He, and Indians such as Jim Thorpe, knew that Indians had beat-
en whites from elite universities. Jon Reyhner and Jeanne Eder also see the
boarding schools as furthering Pan-Indian identification; being coeducational, these establishments helped encourage cross-tribal marriages. Writing of

the Chilocco School, Lomawaima believes that "a pan-tribal 'Indian' identity ... evolved in opposition to school authority."[80]

It is likely that some sense of themselves as being Indians as well as—not instead of—being tribal members grew more at large boarding schools. Even with the hindsight of an ethnologist, La Flesche does not claim such a broadening of perspective at the Omaha mission. Indeed, he recounts that when Ponca pupils entered the school, they stimulated intertribal rivalry, although they were culturally related to the Omahas. McCarthy the Papago and such Hopis as Talayesva and Sekaquaptewa emphasize more the bitter encounters with pupils of other tribes.[81] At Haskell, according to Horne, there was less friction. "Indian kids came ... from all over the United States and represented a myriad of tribes," she wrote. "I don't remember any intertribal hostilities." Not only did pupils get along, she claims, but "we were curious about one another's tribal culture and language. We'd discuss the kinds of dances or ceremonies that each tribe had and learn about each others traditions." This suggests a double process: a growing awareness of tribal variety, intertwined with an increasing sense of being "Indians."[82] For some beginners, the awareness of different "Indians" could come as a shock: Daniel La France claimed that before attending a white school he did not know that other Indians existed.[83]

Narrators besides Horne give a strong impression that pupils from different tribal groups learned to get along together. Charles Eastman told how he befriended "one of our traditional enemies," a Mandan. Standing Bear met a Pawnee at Carlisle and suddenly remembered that he had seen the same boy earlier as a prisoner of his own Lakota people. He did not claim the two became friends, but neither did they resume tribal hostilities (unlike the Hopis and Navajos, and even here no pattern of serious intertribal violence persisted at school).[84]

Navajos, Hopis, Lakotas, Pawnees—all had similar problems of adjustment. White teachers were deeply ignorant of tribal differences and treated pupils alike. Although that may have been ethnically insensitive and even pedagogically unsound, it was also crudely functional from the point of view of pupil adjustment. If tribe did not matter to teachers, many pupils must gradually have come to think that, at least at school, it should not matter quite so much to themselves either.

More than clan members, they were Santee Sioux; more than Sioux, they were Indians; and more than Indians, they were Americans—large numbers of Indian men fought for the United States in both world wars. Individuals such as Charles Eastman clearly moved toward Pan-Indian identification: he began to see himself as a spokesman for "The Indian" and helped found the Society of American Indians in 1911. But the broadening of identity went further: "I am an

Indian" (not, be it noted, a Santee Sioux)—he declared at the end of *From Deep Wood to Civilization*. "Nevertheless, so long as I live, I am an American."[85]

Others such as the Hopi Talayesva and the Navajo Frank Mitchell were far less changed. Indeed, we should not exaggerate the effect of the schools in this respect. Large numbers of pupils remained focused on their own tribal society, to which they returned after school. Actually the Indian sources that I read gave little indication that Pan-Indianism, as distinct from toleration of other tribal groups, had taken hold to any extent *within* the schools. In 1891 Indian commissioner Morgan optimistically claimed success at "blending together of many tribes," especially in the multitribal schools, with the further implication that pupils were assimilating into American life. "The children learn to respect and love each other," he continued, "and there is thus broken down those tribal animosities and jealousies which have been in the past productive of so much harm and a fruitful source of so much trouble to the Indians and the nation." Twenty years later superintendent Friedman of Carlisle claimed that the members of the ninety tribes represented at the school were "given a wider horizon and a broader conception of life. They form lasting friendships." However he, like Morgan, overestimated the assimilatory effect of boarding schools when he claimed that this achieved "the nationalizing" of Indians, in the sense of detribalizing them.[86] No full-fledged Pan-Indianism emerged at the schools, and Indian tribal identifications powerfully persist into the twenty-first century. Yet by pulling together so many children from so many tribes, the big schools, especially, were a major breeding ground of such a broadening of views. Counterfactually we might argue that had Indians never been brought into multitribal schools, a broader sense of Pan-Indian identity (complementing rather than replacing tribal identity), would have been far slower to develop.

The children in CNEI schools were Irish and Christian (about one-quarter were Protestant in 1900). In addition, the vast majority attended national day schools in their own communities with children from a similar socioeconomic background. At times they might sit with members of a different denomination, but this decreased during the period under review and had little effect in blurring denominational identities or prejudices. The questions for Irish children might be the following: Did the relationships *between pupils* (the subject of this chapter) contribute toward or against the assimilatory goals of the National Board? Did these relationships weaken the sense of local community and accelerate a sense of British subjecthood? Or did pupils—speaking Irish together, or even speaking English—develop a "Pan-Irish" identity, a sense of Irish nationhood beyond local identification?

We would expect Protestant pupils from Ulster to have more deeply devel-oped their sense of being Protestant and British in CNEI schools. Further, for most of the period under review Catholic pupils also learned more about being British than Irish. Their CNEI schoolbooks no doubt broadened their perspectives on the world but until about 1900 did little to promote any Irish identity. Yet despite the board's best efforts, it seems unlikely that bringing together generations of Irish boys and girls ever fully convinced most of them to identify with Britain and the Union. In terms of pupil-to-pupil influence, then, mass education in Ireland did not have the same deeply transformative, mind-expanding effects as had Indian schooling, either in producing strong "outside" (British) subjecthood or strong Irish nationalism. Pupils certainly helped each other adapt as they began to speak English to each other and sometimes to parents, thus accelerating the assimilatory effects of the na-tional schools. However, it was probably from the curriculum, regimentation, and influence of dutiful teachers that a degree of loyalty to Britain developed, rather than from each other. Again, it was probably from the odd teacher willing to subvert the British message, or from events outside the classroom, rather than from each other, that a trans-local sense of Irishness or even na-tionalism developed.

Irish children did have their minds and cultural horizons expanded at the schools. But few faced the kind of cognitive shock experienced by a young Lakota thrown into a school full of boys and girls from dozens of different tribal cultures, speaking perhaps as many languages.

Some of the effects of peer relationship were negative: bullying, abuse, hu-miliation. Some were positive, in that children mediated for each other, help-ing each other survive the alien regime. Ironically, by directly promoting adjustment, peer mediation also promoted the assimilatory goals of the BIA and CNEI schools. The processes in both areas were broadly similar, and as an Americanist I have tried to bring perspectives gained in Indian history to bear on Irish history. I also highlight differences, often explained by the size and multitribal nature of the Indian boarding schools. Ultimately, whether at a tiny local BIA school or a CNEI national school, or at a large Indian board-ing school, almost nothing was as important to pupils as other pupils.

8. Resistance and Rejection

Irish national school students devised crafty ways to fool their teacher and get time off from the classroom. One group brought a stray donkey into the schoolyard before the master arrived. He then asked for volunteers to return the animal to its owner—and the culprits, according to a folklore informant, would "spend most of the day on this mission." Others connived with a local farmer to cart turf to the school, and the teacher called on volunteers to shift the load into a shed. Even lunch-hour football became a problem: the master often had difficulty getting the boys back to class as "they were inclined to roam during the play-hour." More devious and indeed dangerous, a group decided to fake a near-drowning. When "they had no excuse one way or the other for any diversion," they threw one boy in the river. Four of his mates jumped in and pulled him out. They then carried him to school, having also sent a messenger to his home and to the master "and made a terrible story of it." Between the noise they kicked up and the "rí-rá" (shouting) of the teacher, "the rest of the day went without any class." Adding greater spice to the whole affair: the parents rewarded the supposed lifesavers with gifts of money, and the teacher ensured that they got certificates.[1]

Many other Irish and Indian narrators recalled such harmless or potentially dangerous forms of resistance. The incidents are often interchangeable; without identifying names or locations, it would be difficult to tell whether they occurred at CNEI or BIA schools. Or further afield: Peter N. Stearns has claimed that there was "a battleground quality" to student-teacher relations in America during much of the nineteenth century, especially at academies and colleges, and at some French boarding schools, in which pupils played all sorts of pranks on their teachers.[2]

"There were times when the pupils became very tired of their books," wrote Francis La Flesche in language like that used by the Irish informant, "and longed to take a run over the prairies or through the woods." Then they "sought for ways and means by which to have the school closed, and secure a holiday." On one occasion the mission school pupils loosened the joints of a chimney pipe and later deliberately tramped into the room, causing the weakened pipe to collapse. They also allowed some pigs to escape from the school farm. Gray-beard immediately called for volunteers among the boys to catch them. The unfortunate girls had to remain in class, intensifying the enjoyment of the plotters—who were later publicly thanked by the superintendent for their sterling work in capturing the pigs.[3]

I would like to distinguish such pupil *resistance* from *rejection*. Obviously they are two ends of a continuum. By *resistance* I mean pupil violations of school rules, pranks against teachers or other staff, and temporary truancy. Such activities—sometimes blending with the secret subcultural activities examined in the previous chapter—were forms of accommodation, of "negotiation." In the incidents cited above, Irish and Indian children merely sought for ways to get an afternoon off. Pupils who struggled to escape permanently were engaged in *rejection*. We cannot always categorize a pupil as either resister or rejecter; a boy or girl might play truant, voluntarily return to the school, and later flee permanently or be expelled.[4] The present chapter, then, focuses first on forms of pupil resistance and then on rejection.

I

"This is a story of Indian students," writes K. Tsianina Lomawaima on the Chilocco Indian School, "loyal to each other, linked as a family, and subversive in their resistance." Of major recent historians of Indian schooling, she above all argues for the resilience of students, who created "relatively free spaces" in the school through their resistant and subversive activities. Other scholars, myself included, have also been deeply influenced by New Social History admonitions, and to some extent by postmodernist and postcolonial concepts of empowerment. We seek to understand the perspectives and actions of the "outs" of history, those until recently ignored by historians, and to show how they were more than merely passive victims. Although not all historians of Indian education would fully accept Lomawaima's vision of student empowerment, most would concur that resistance was pervasive. One thing is abundantly clear, writes David Wallace Adams. Even at the supposedly total institution that was the Indian boarding school, "students, often in collaboration with their parents, frequently went to great lengths to resist."[5]

Sometimes resistance could be merely mocking, such as laughing at a teacher's mispronunciation of Indian names or employing nicknames for unpopular staff. "Gray-beard" was not necessarily pejorative, but hardly what a missionary wanted to be called. Frank Mitchell and his mates used all kinds of descriptive Navajo words: one "mean" teacher became "Miss Chipmunk"; another became "Miss Red Corn" because of her complexion; another, a member of the kitchen staff, was "an awful looking thing"; and another became "the woman who makes you scream." Girls at the Phoenix Indian School used the name of a Pima witch, "Ho'ok," for a teacher who liked to use the strap, and at night they mimicked her voice and characteristics.[6]

Conspiring to get the better of teachers obviously constituted an important form of resistance. Two stories about underwear illustrate this well. In the interests of modesty girls at Chilocco were supposed to wear long bloomers under their dresses when going to carefully regulated school dances with boys. Resisting such disciplining of the body, the girls merely wore bloomer legs that they removed before the dance and put back on again before inspection by the matron. Luther Standing Bear recalled a similar incident among boys at the Carlisle school. He and his friend so hated the regulation itchy red flannel long johns that they secretly bought themselves more comfortable underwear. They had to quickly change into the red flannels for inspection each Sunday morning and then back into their own underwear.[7] A Creek Indian—actually Curtis Lomawaima, the Chilocco historian's father, who attended the school from 1927 to 1935—caught much of the motivation for such resistance. "There's no other way you could survive in that kind of environment," he told his daughter. "We used to *deliberately* do things . . . just to show 'em that we could do it and get away with it. It wasn't *malicious*, we did it for the fun of it, just to let them know that, that we could outwit them" (emphasis in original).[8]

Indian boarding schools contained large numbers of teenage boys and girls and sometimes even post-teen students. At Hampton Institute provision had to be made for married couples.[9] Schools thus arranged supervised dances and other social occasions, and pupils of both sexes strove to escape the chaperoning.[10] The fact that individuals were often caught and severely punished means that the authorities knew, in a general way, of such evasions; but they were kept in the dark about the many strategies employed.

La Flesche claimed that even at the Presbyterian mission school, "little romances were going on right under [the teachers'] eyes." Lilah Lindsey, also a pupil at a Presbyterian school in the post–Civil War decades, noted how sexual segregation only stimulated curiosity, and how students attempted to peek into each others' rooms and to communicate through secretly passed notes. Six decades later the Christian Pima and dedicated scholar Anna Moore Shaw described similar evasions at the Phoenix Indian School. Indeed, she met her future husband, Ross, there and clearly conveys the parallel nature of mixed-gender activities: sanctioned dances and get-togethers, coexisting with surreptitious meetings. Moore and her future husband "wrote notes because the matron was very strict and only let us see each other at social functions. But sometimes Ross would sneak over to the girl's side of the campus, where we could play croquet until the matron discovered us and shooed Ross back where he belonged. Soon we were going together. We were childhood sweet-hearts." Essie Horne recalled similar rules at Haskell, and how other students attempted to evade them. She declined to do so, "not so much because I didn't want to but because I didn't have the nerve. The punishments were pretty harsh." She also reported how one student became pregnant and had to be sent home. Naturally the authorities kept such episodes quiet, "but we kids knew most of the secrets."[11]

At the Keams Canyon Boarding School in Arizona there was a veritable migration of boys to the girls' dormitory. The assistant disciplinarian had climbed in the window "to sleep with his sweetheart," according to Don Talayesva. Another similarly inclined Hopi was caught and spilled the beans, giving a long list of offenders. They were more than "shooed back" to where they belonged. Boys and girls received a whipping, and the boys were then locked up for days and given only bread and water. The culprits of both sexes must have known the risks, yet they had obviously persisted for some time in their serious violation of school rules.[12]

Such forms of mass resistance were supposed to be secret. On other oc-casions Indian pupils openly resisted school authorities. Pupils at the same school blatantly engaged in what has later, in different circumstances in Ireland, come to be called a "dirty protest." Locked into the dormitory at night to prevent them escaping, the boys found themselves without any toilet facili-ties. They had to urinate though the window or through holes in the walls. Unwilling to abstain from supper, they decided, in the words of Edmund Nequatewa, "they will just crap all over the floor, which they did." Yet next morning the dirty protesters openly admitted their actions to the furious disciplinarian and explained the reasons why. Although the locks remained, buckets were supplied the following night.[13]

If Carlisle boys could openly protest Captain Pratt's ban on interschool football, a later group engaged in an equally brave display of student pow-er. Coach "Pop" Warner had a reputation for tough treatment of his players. When he verbally abused and publicly swore at them, however, several of the stars threatened to quit football. In an amazingly frank passage he recalled:

many of the best players turned in their suits and announced that they were not coming out for practice any more. . . . I took some time to get at the trouble, but finally learned that "they didn't like to be cussed at." I apologized profoundly and sincerely, and should have thanked them too, too, for the rebuke made me do some hard and helpful thinking, and from that day to this I have never gone in for "rough stuff."

Quietly yet powerfully, these Carlisle students had also won their point.[14]

Equally open but far less restrained was resistance at Haskell in 1919, where, according to Brenda J. Child, "a full scale rebellion had to be put down." Students rioted, smashed light fixtures, looted food, and—symbolically blasphemous—took possession of and rang the school bell. Later five girls and four boys were expelled. "Most rebellions were small, personal, and far more subtle," concludes Child, "but rebellion was a permanent feature of boarding school life."[15]

Other students, especially unwilling newcomers, used open violence against staff. When Mourning Dove was delivered by her Salishan parents to a convent school, the young girl screamed and fought and actually kicked the nun—who unceremoniously dumped her in a dark closet to quiet down. Similarly, Zitkala-Ša bitterly and physically protested the cutting of her hair. A seven-year-old boy, brought in by his father to the Uintah Boarding School in Utah, in turn attacked, scraped, and cut a number of teachers. And in a shocking act, but one with a certain poetic resonance, considering how Indian boys generally had their hair cut at school, he pulled out most of the hair of a female teacher who attempted to outfit him in white clothes. Yet these violent resisters, girls and boys, later came to accept school.[16]

More seasoned students could also physically assault a teacher, as in the case of a big Yuma girl who grabbed the punishment strap and chased a matron and disciplinarian around the room. At a Presbyterian boarding school in the Creek Nation an Indian girl broke two ribs and wrenched the wrist of a female teacher. In an extraordinary case, Asa Daklugie, an Apache, claimed that when Captain Pratt was about to punish him, he actually took the whip away from the teacher. Pratt then grabbed Daklugie by the collar, who in turn took hold of the older man's collar. Daklugie then jerked the famed superintendent of Carlisle, a seasoned Indian fighter, off his feet "and held him at arms length, and shook him a few times, and dropped him to the floor." He told Pratt that nobody had ever, or would ever, whip him. Hard to believe, except that in Daklugie's account Pratt then laughed, asked the boy to sit down, and discussed the whole issue with him—a description consistent with other accounts of Pratt as a man of strong convictions along with a surprisingly tolerant sense of humor. In his own memoirs Pratt described how a Carlisle girl slapped a matron in the face; just as Pratt had done in Daklugie's account, the matron in Pratt's account diffused the situation by a calm and nonviolent response.[17]

II

Unfortunately there has been little scholarly study of pupil responses to Irish national schooling during the period under review. Therefore by bringing "bottom-up" perspectives to bear on the national schools I intend to encourage the historian to seek beyond official accounts to the voices of those on the receiving end of policy.[18] Accounts by Irish folklore informants and autobiographers, like those of Indians, are rich in memories of such generally—but not always—harmless forms of resistance. In Ireland too such behavior both subverted the assimilationist goals of the schools, yet similarly helped pupils accommodate to their demands.

Some such resistance also completely escaped the notice of teachers, as when Blasket Islander O'Sullivan switched slates for a friend, giving him a completed sum and finishing the boy's unfinished task too. Again, even in retrospect the old narrator enjoyed the element of deception involved, especially as the teacher believed in corporal punishment. Equally deceptive and equally unbeknownst to the victim, pupils at one informant's school learned how to manipulate a male teacher's interest in a female colleague. Once the pupils realized "his soft spot," they encouraged him to talk about her: "he would smile to himself and pull his whisker." And "he'd get so engrossed with this that he's forget the lesson and oftimes it would be time to go home before he'd wake from his reverie." And "needless to mention . . . [we] spun many a yarn to the master in order to evade our lessons."[19]

Sometimes Irish pupils did temporarily control the school. As we have seen, "winter boys," some up to twenty years old, unemployed during the farming off-season, often reentered the classroom. They especially could embarrass teachers when inspectors visited and were generally disruptive. The teacher "used to be ragin' with them," recalled a folklore informant, "and slap them and they'd put up their hands high and he couldn't reach them, they were that big and he so small." Another teacher "was afraid to say anything to them no matter what pranks they played in the school, with the result that they got out of hand entirely." One particular older boy especially impressed the narrator, and no doubt the teacher too. Fear "was one thing [this boy] never knew," and therefore the master "dreaded his coming to school at all because he ruled the school and all the small boys looked up to him as a hero."[20] Not every younger boy admired the big ones, however. Michael MacGowan recalled how they threw things at each other and wrestled. Being "so big and hefty . . . the master was afraid to interfere with them." As a result this ex-pupil felt that he learned little in class.[21]

Less violent forms of resistance could also be devastating. "He wasn't nice to the rabble of scholars," recalled Tomás O'Crohan of a new teacher at the Blasket Islands school around 1880. The pupils were not nice to him either. Both the boys and the girls began to laugh at him and jeer him, and he lasted only three months. Hard to believe, perhaps. Yet many of us will remember teachers who, no matter how tough they tried to be, were "not cut out for the job." As we saw, pupils could force a teacher to cease using a book on agriculture; they might also refuse other books. English parsing, according to an informant, was the most hated of subjects at her school—until algebra and Euclid (geometry) were introduced. "A boy became so moithered [upset] one day that he brought his Algebra and Euclid books up to the rostrum up to the teacher, and told him to keep them there." Arithmetic was not too popular either, apparently, and the informant recalled a pupil rhyme from the period, suggesting an oral literature of resistance:

> "<u>Freight and tare</u> (?) makes me swear"
> Fractions sets me mad.
> The rule of three puzzles me,
> And practices is bad.[22]

R. B. Robson, the Ulster Presbyterian, also faced down a teacher. Later a principal and no doubt a pillar of his community, he hardly wished to highlight rebellion unless it took place. He and others at a CNEI model school for teacher trainees resisted what they saw as unjust punishment. They had not intended "anything more drastic than refusing our hands" to the cane. Reminiscent of Pratt's response to Daklugie, the angry teacher threatened them with further punishment if they misbehaved again but allowed them their victory of passive resistance on that occasion. In an initially powerful symbolic act of resistance, Patrick Withers burned his teacher's cane: "For ages I had wanted to do that. . . . I had destroyed my worst enemy!" The teacher calmly fetched another cane and rendered the symbolism void.[23]

"Mitching" or playing truant was another form of pupil resistance—one that could easily shade into full rejection of the school should the pupil decide not return. Priests (local school managers) and teachers had a hard time, according to an informant, not only in persuading parents to send children to school, but in "keeping check on the children so that they didn't mitch too often, or stay away altogether from school before they were at least twelve years of age." Later historians agree with this informant. "Disappearing or mitching," write A. Norman Jeffares and Anthony Kamm, "was the resort of many pupils in Irish school, a safety valve, an occasional opting out from what could be outrageously severe regimes."[24]

Even when regimes were not so especially severe, pupils lit out for the fields. "We often went on a mooch [mitch] too," recalled an informant. "One evening and we were going from school and we made a plan that we'd go on strike next day." They spent the stolen hours fishing, pulling turnips from a farmer's field, and even milked a neighbor's cow. "Next day we had to render an account of ourselves to the old master," he admitted. "We paid for our day." But they were "mooching" again before too long."[25] Another informant remembered the excitement when a fox hunt began at the school, complete with hounds and a colonel dressed in velvet coat and cap and mounted on a gray horse. When the bugle sounded, "it was our signal to be off too. Away we went following the hounds all day until night closed in." Then the mitchers returned "hungry and footsore to await the anger of our parents . . . and a sure beating from Mr. Lang." He used a heavy hazel rod "which he laid on our back in no uncertain manner and believe me one would not forget it in a hurry." Nevertheless, the next time the hunt began the boys were off again.[26]

Some forms of resistance could result in physical pain or at least danger to the teacher. A few of the boys at one school mixed julep into the man's milk and stirred it up well. "I often thank God since that no bad results followed," said the informant. Patrick Withers claimed that in a football match he tripped his teacher, who fell on his face and began to bleed: "inwardly I smiled to myself. I had paid him back all right." Then the man turned white, and Withers too was greatly relieved that no lasting damage had been done. Future principal Robson calmly recounted an even more malicious trick he played. After wiping off their writing slates with a wet rag, national school pupils placed them in front of the fire to dry. Holding a still-hot slate in a handkerchief the young Robson then handed it to his unsuspecting teacher—against whom he had no apparent grudge. "Needless to say," wrote Robson unctuously, "the slate was soon in pieces on the floor, and judging from the contortions of his face, I concluded that he was not in a very amiable mood." Robson had acted impetuously and with no intention of ending his schooling, yet he wisely fled the classroom and was later expelled from that school, or removed by his parents.[27]

Robson also described a fight between the teacher and one of the bigger pupils, who hung onto the man's beard. Perhaps the most violent assault on a teacher, however, was admitted by Patrick O'Malley, later a Member of Parliament at Westminster! When this teacher hit a younger boy with a pointer, O'Malley himself intervened: "I was so shocked and indignant that I walked straight up to the master and struck him fair in the face! It was an impulse of the moment, but I never regretted it." A prominent member of the community would hardly have invented such an act of rebellious violence. "The master was very respectful to me after that," he claimed.[28]

We need not romanticize pranks, mitching, and other such activities—or the nastiness of Robson's trick—as heroic acts of Native empowerment against an oppressive colonial system. Indeed, the Ulster unionist Robson was in sympathy with the Anglicizing goals of the national schools. Further, it is difficult to tell just which of such acts, in Ireland or America, actually took place. Susan Douglas Franzosa claims that adults reminiscing about school life "attempt implicitly (but more often explicitly) to contest the school's power of characterization and reclaim the authority to create their own identities. Their educational autobiographies represent an attempt to displace the school to become the 'true' author of the educated self." Such memories may then be retrospective symbolic victories over the school system that as children the narrators accepted but as adults they imagined they resisted.[29] Yet when we cross-check pupil memories, corroborate them with each other and with contemporaneous official accounts, we may accept the broad credibility of such accounts. In addition, many of us will recall similar "small victories" over those who supposedly meant us well but often made our young lives miserable.[30]

There is little sense of resistance to assimilation as such, in the above accounts. Other activities, however, could be read as cultural or nationalist reactions to the Americanizing and Anglicizing programs of the schools.

III

As the BIA and CNEI sought massive, almost total cultural transformation, all types of syncretic blendings of traditional or local culture with the official curriculum could be seen as examples of cultural resistance. Therefore, when boys and girls spoke Irish or a tribal language to each other, they were not only participating in a subculture; they were also resisting the program of assimilation, even if individually some longed to become proficient in the language of the school.

Such resistance clearly emerges in reminiscences, but more obviously so in the Indian case. At the Toadlena Boarding School in New Mexico after the summer holidays authorities imposed penalties to force students into a resumption of speaking English. From their perspective the authorities were right: periods at home did weaken the assimilatory effect of the curriculum. Yet, according to Kay Bennett, the children kept away from the teachers as much as possible, covered their mouths with their hands, and whispered to each other in Navajo. Similarly, Frank Mitchell claimed that at his school pupils spoke that language to each other. And La Flesche recalled how, to impress younger students with a sense of gang ritual, the leader of the Big Seven (as distinct from La Flesche's gang, the Middle Five) spoke to the younger boys in Omaha, "thus fearlessly breaking one of the rules of the school."[31]

At the Rainy Mountain Boarding School, by far the most common rule violation was speaking Kiowa. Ex-pupils there also recalled the many whispered conversations in their own language, which did not, of course, imply that they failed to learn English. Further, the Kiowa students quickly lapsed into their own language when parents visited the school and, of course, on visits home. "The survival of the Kiowa language," concludes historian Clyde Ellis, "meant that an important barrier to assimilation remained in place. The full meaning of this resistance was later to become clear." Ex-students, writes Ellis, became "a galvanizing force" in the continuation of a changed but adaptive Kiowa culture in the middle of the twentieth century.[32]

If students could develop their own subcultural English "slanguage," they also utilized the new tongue to more explicitly oppose full assimilation. Amy Goodburn has shown how, in the early twentieth century, pupils at the Genoa Industrial School (Nebraska) developed sophisticated "rhetorical strategies" of resistance. She has analyzed the books they read, the English essays they wrote for the school newspaper, and the letters they wrote home and to white officials. The boys and girls exploited their new linguistic competence "to question and resist school policies." They argued publicly for and against the persistence of Indian languages and openly criticized white mistreatment of their peoples. "I think the Indians should always be able to spea[k] their own language whatever comes," wrote one student. "They should also learn the English, as most of them do." Others went over the head of the superintendent and wrote directly to the Indian commissioner for permission to return home or to complain about the staff: "We are seeking for a new superintendent and a disciplinarian," wrote two students. "We would like to have an Indian disciplinarian." Goodburn thus sees such English as "a complex and contested zone of literacy, one in which students found spaces to assert their voices and to claim ownership in their education." Most did not reject the school; their attitudes were more ambivalent than that, and they used English to express these attitudes. Language, be it a traditional language or English, was thus a two-edged sword.[33]

Ruth Spack has also impressively demonstrated how the "language of civilization" could facilitate assimilation or subversion, both while children were still at school and later in life. "Because language can be used to justify or resist oppression," she writes, "it is a site of struggle over power, meaning, and representation." Thus students such as La Flesche, Standing Bear, Zitkala-Ša, and others—whose use of English Spack examines in telling detail—became simultaneously "owners, performers, and negotiators of language." In sometimes similar and sometimes contrasting ways they used English both to reinforce and to resist the assimilatory message of missionaries and the BIA. Significantly, by the early twentieth century many Irish nationalists also used the English language to advocate separation from England. Thus in Ireland too, English could be, to employ Spack's formulation, "a disruptive and destructive instrument of linguistic and cultural control . . . [and] also a generative tool for expressing diverse ways of seeing, saying, and believing."[34]

Pupils at Indian schools devised many other ways of culturally resisting, without fully rejecting, the policies of their educators. Narrators such as La Flesche (Omaha), Chris (Mecalero Apache), and Irene Stewart (Navajo) recall at night in the dormitories, when groups of pupils told stories from tribal mythology or sneaked from the school to hear the old men tell such tales. Chris claimed that students had spiritual visions in the dormitories. At night after "lights out," and after Gray-beard had retired to his room, according to La Flesche, students recounted Omaha stories: "Way long time ago," went one, "four brothers lived on earth. Good hunters, they shoot straight, kill deer, buffalo, elk, and all kinds of animals. They got plenty of meat and skins." Suddenly Gray-beard descended upon them with his cane. But once he had returned to his room, the pupil continued with his story of how putting a splinter into some buffalo hair would produce a baby. These pupils knew they were repeatedly violating school rules. They appear to have enjoyed the very act of defiance. Whether they were consciously resisting the assimilatory message is less clear; perhaps they were just enjoying a good story with familiar cultural elements. Yet by defiantly telling such "savage" stories, especially in their own language, they were in fact resisting the total cultural message of the school.[35]

Stealing need not be romanticized as anti-hegemonic resistance, but it too could have cultural implications, as when Jim Whitewolf and friends stole food from butchering places at the school. "I think the reason . . . was that we wanted to cook [the food] our own way, roasted in ashes." Further, they tried to send some of the stolen goods back home, an example of traditional sharing practices so criticized by white Americans who preached a severely individualistic version of the Protestant work ethic. Ex-student Curtis Lomawaima noted how at Chilocco in the late 1920s students sometimes engaged in traditional all-night stomp dances and distributed, in tribal fashion, parched corn. K. Tsianina Lomawaima, the historian, notes how Creeks, Cherokees, and other southeastern tribes participated in such obviously traditional activities, which were frowned upon even late in the period under review, but not forbidden. "Stomp dances held the boys together in a shared cultural complex," she writes, "and the very sociable pastime of parching corn united all tribes . . . [it] symbolized group belonging and solidarity." The activity also "delineated their separation from the school's control." One ex-pupil of Chilocco recalled peyote meetings in student rooms, dominated by Ponca girls. This woman did not as a pupil enjoy the taste of the sacred cactus, but she remembered how the Poncas just laughed at her and chatted away unintelligibly in their own language.[36]

At Haskell, students from different tribes could tease each other, but they also taught varied tribal beliefs and practices to each other—the stirrings of Pan-Indian identification might also be seen as a form of perhaps unintentional resistance. Horne remembered how one Ponca girl gave her an eagle feather: "Always carry it with you. It will protect you." Even as an older woman she kept the gift, which she saw as a manifestation of the Great Spirit. "Traditional values, such as sharing and cooperation, helped us to survive culturally," writes Horne, "even though the schools were designed to erase our Indian culture, values, and identities."[37]

To flee the school was another way of resisting its control. For Indian children "going runaway" to the home village often had greater cultural implications than "mitching" had for Irish pupils. Indeed, Lomawaima sees the flight of Indian children as "the final rebellion."[38] We should distinguish, however, between those who fled the school temporarily and those determined never to return. Large numbers of Indian students fled with every intention of returning; yet even for them, running away was often an explicitly cultural action, to renew contact with family and with the old life. In a particularly evocative case, one that recalls the Irish informant's account of mitching to follow the local fox hunt, La Flesche told how a deep sadness descended upon the whole school when the rest of the Omaha people left the nearby village on their annual buffalo hunt. Once he and a few friends actually fled to follow them. They did not wish to end their education then but merely wanted to be with their people on such an exciting occasion. They were caught and returned by La Flesche's uncle. Boys at the Mescalero School made a similar escape, but this time to hear the stories of the old men. Even when one of them warned the boys against returning before a storm broke, they left: "I had to get back," wrote Chris, "I was late for school, and I got into trouble, for I was not supposed to go away like that."[39]

Similarly, Edward Goodbird "played hookey" to attend a Hidatsa scalp dance—could any act of resistance have been more "savage"? The scalp, he reported, "was raised aloft on a pole, and the women danced about it, screaming and singing glad songs. Warriors painted their faces with charcoal, and danced, sang, yelled and boasted of their deeds. Everybody feasted and was merry." Yet Goodbird returned voluntarily the next day and even enjoyed a sense of power over his missionary teacher. She told him how naughty he was, "but she never punished me, for she knew if she did I would leave the school." At moments like this the symbiotic nature of the educator/educated relationship also clearly emerges; indeed, it is difficult to tell just who was controlling and who was adjusting to the other.[40]

Such autobiographical claims for the persisting pull of tribal culture, even upon students supposedly quarantined in boarding schools, are further corroborated by T. W. Conway, superintendent of the Pawnee School, in 1892. During the previous year, he claimed, there had been "many outside influences at work that have had a general tendency to retard the progress of the school." The most pernicious of these was "the ghost dance craze, which vicious doctrine has not only permeated the older members of the tribe, but has greatly influenced the children in school." This revitalization movement rapidly spread across the plains in the later 1890s, which led to the Wounded Knee Massacre of hundreds of Sioux men, women, and children in 1890. During the winter months when "the craze was at its height," lamented the superintendent, "children were greatly excited, and it took the closest vigilance of every employé to keep them in school, as well as to keep them from coming under the influence of this peculiar belief, which has done more to revive the old barbarous customs of the Pawnee Indians than any other practice in the past quarter century."[41]

Probably the most pervasive type of resistance is the most difficult to document—passive resistance. Scholars have noted its various subtle forms: refusal to learn, going slowly, or just a general lack of interest. Such apparent passivity could drive teachers to despair. One was so frustrated by "mute, graven images"—did she stop to think of how well these children understood English?—that she left the Crow Creek School after a few months. Adams believes that "the students, not the teachers, often determined the pace of classroom work."[42]

Frank Mitchell, a Navajo, gave little indication of having taken much interest in studies; he did not greatly resent school, nor did he enthuse about it. On other occasions the passivity became a pointed cultural weapon. Perhaps La Flesche romanticized the Indian warrior ethic of stoic passivity in the face of pain, but his account of a classmate's endurance is striking. After leading a series of nightly visits to the Omaha village—and voluntarily returning each time—an older pupil was publicly thrashed by Gray-beard. The boy, however, "gave no sign of pain . . . he stood unmoved, every muscle relaxed, even his hands were open, showing no emotion whatsoever." Finally the stick broke, and the beating was over. The boy "put on his coat, then, with head uplifted and unfaltering steps, went back to his desk, took his pen, and completed the unfinished motto [he had been writing]."[43]

IV

We see less obvious evidence of explicitly cultural resistance from pupils in the Irish sources. Whenever they spoke Irish, they too were resisting Anglicization and helping perpetuate the old ways. Informants remembered doing so on the way home from school or otherwise out of earshot of the teachers, who might beat them, they believed, if they heard the recourse to the old language.[44] Rural students generally lived in oral cultures that honored the storyteller and populated the world with fairies and such spirit beings. But ex-pupils have left little evidence of recounting these stories within the school. The Indian boarding school dormitory—at night and in the dark— was a more likely venue for such cultural narration than a daytime classroom or schoolyard.

Occasionally, as we saw, individual Irish teachers attempted to subvert the Anglicizing message of the CNEI by subtly or even openly presenting nationalist ideas in class. However, there is little indication that pupils subverted the CNEI's mission at school. Irish boys and girls were at least as mischievous as their Indian counterparts. Yet they, like the majority of Indians and, indeed, of most schoolchildren, seem to have broadly gone along with what was taught. Daniel Corkery, who had attempted to instill nationalistic ideas into Frank O'Connor and other students, was perhaps too subtle at least for immediate effect. O'Connor powerfully conveys his own conversion from a highly Anglicized boy to an Irish nationalist, but this occurred after he left national school and after the 1916 Rising. He gives little indication that Corkery's words inspired him or his mates to forms of cultural resistance while still at school.[45]

Hints of such tendencies occasionally emerge. As early as 1844, for example, a CNEI inspector complained that pupils were wearing "Repeal" badges in class—indicating support of Daniel O'Connell's movement for the repeal of the 1801 Union. All forms of political symbolism were, of course, forbidden, and the inspector noted that such behavior "will be prevented." Had pupils been wearing symbols of unionism these too would have been criticized.[46] Somewhat later in the nineteenth century, after Fenians (revolutionary nationalists) were released from prison, boys in one informant's district built a big bonfire on Amnesty Night. Later they stood around the fire "singing songs from the *Nation*," the newspaper founded by Thomas Davis that supported a new kind of secular Irish republicanism. At the beginning of the twentieth century pupils turned a snowball fight into a mock Boer War between England and Afrikaners: "How we cheered when we had the English at our mercy securely surrounding Ladysmith or Pretoria," recalled the same informant. Providing further insight into local attitudes even after almost a century of CNEI education, he noted: "We were all Boers at that time except for a few Protestant families whose children attended our school for the sake of the good education."[47] Patrick Shea's account of how fellow pupils attacked him and his brothers because of their father's RIC membership also suggests some national politicization of pupils, despite the best efforts of the CNEI.

In Ireland and America, then, pupils developed myriad kinds of resistance to the new schools, some of it similar to the activities of students everywhere, some of it implying cultural, national, or ideological resistance to schooling and to its mission of assimilation—and much of it a blending of both kinds. More cultural resistance was in evidence at Indian schools, especially boarding schools. At such "total institutions" there was more time for, and perhaps more need for, forms of resistance that tenuously maintained links with home culture and kin.

All forms of resistance dealt with so far were compatible with continued attendance at school; indeed, allowing vent to pupil needs and frustrations may have *increased* adaptability. Such acts of resistance in thousands of Irish national and Indian schools, then, were forms of accommodation or of negotiation with an often harsh system that the student and the parents generally accepted. Sometimes, however, negotiation broke down, or never really began, and pupils, for highly varied personal and cultural reasons, rejected schooling.

V

Focusing on those who at least began school—as distinct from those who rejected it by never attending—one thing becomes immediately obvious in the American case: large numbers of Indian children sickened and died at the schools. Many recent historians—and long before them the 1928 Meriam Report, which noted "the deplorable health conditions"—have shown that, whatever their attitudes, the bodies of many Indian children often could not take the living conditions at the schools. Some, like La Flesche's great friend Brush, were deeply appreciative of the new knowledge, yet Brush died at school from tuberculosis. Death, then, was a physical rejection of the school.[48] Throughout the decade under review, Indian agents, teachers, and other staff continually lamented the loss of their pupils through sickness.

It is unclear whether more or fewer tribal children would have survived at home.[49] However, boys and girls with little resistance to Euro-American diseases were brought together in crowded buildings with poor food, inadequate toilet facilities, and the sharing of towels and sometimes musical instruments—all this makes it likely that during the period under review more died within this institution of "civilization" than outside it.

Many deaths occurred in schools remote from modern medical centers, and there is no indication that white teachers attempted to avail themselves of tribal curing practices.⁵⁰ Even at Eastern schools such as Carlisle and Hampton, pupils died. "The death rate here has been very serious this year among pupils from the Lower Brulé [Lakota] and Crow Creek Agencies," admitted the report from the latter school in 1885. The teacher in charge of the laundry reported that there was "a great deal of sickness among the girls [working there] this term." When Standing Bear tried to recruit new pupils to Carlisle, older Sioux complained to him about children who never returned from such faraway places: "so many had died there that the parents of the boys and girls did not want them to go." To make matters worse, he claimed, some parents had not been notified of the deaths of the children until after they had been buried.⁵¹

Jim Whitewolf was infected with measles by a returning runaway in 1893, who also infected other pupils; Whitewolf survived, but his brother died. Chris's half-brother died at Albuquerque Indian School. Irene Stewart contacted double pneumonia at the Fort Defiance School, which, she believed, almost killed her.⁵² "Non-reservation boarding schools," writes Jean A. Keller in a recent major study, "earned a deserved reputation for being unhealthy environments for Indian children." She also shows how, through increased federal concern, along with concerted action by school authorities, marked improvements occurred at the Sherman Institute in California late in the period under review. She thus corroborates accounts by Indian narrators both on the physical dangers of schooling and on the dedication of individual staff at times of health emergencies at the schools.⁵³

Some Irish schools were also situated in very remote areas. Modern medicine was probably more readily available as the overall distances were so small compared to the vastness of the United States. Nevertheless, the conditions in many national schools would have equally shocked those who wrote the Meriam Report. To their credit, CNEI inspectors continually lamented the squalor. These schools too were a breeding ground for epidemics, and their poor construction in "the weeping climate" of Ireland made them likely places in which children might pick up all kinds of chest and other infections. Their bodies might reject the school irrespective of attitudes.

After giving a long and stomach-turning description of toilet facilities— "the privies are often sickening"—inspector Bateman in 1884 noted "the sicknesses prevalent in the schools" and also the presence of epidemics in his area and the necessity for quarantining pupils. "This is a great danger to the community," he wrote, "and valuable lives may be lost." Inspector Skeffington claimed that many schools in his area, rural and urban, had in 1899 suffered from epidemics: measles in the city of Waterford, for example, as well as

scarletina. This latter "was considered so dangerous that the sanitary officers wished the schools closed to prevent the spread of infection." The law
excluding children from infected homes had been rigidly enforced, he noted
approvingly, although it clashed with the Compulsory Education Act.[54]

However, compared to the Indian schools, far fewer lives appear to have
been lost. Certainly, the death of pupils is not a constant refrain in the Irish
reports. Nor do ex-pupils recall sickness and death to the same extent as
Indian narrators do. The major reasons for this greater prevalence of disease
and death in BIA schools have already emerged: Indian lack of resistance to
Euro-American diseases, the even greater remoteness from full Western medical services (along with total neglect of Indian medicine), and the boarding
school environment, which kept infected students together day and night.

Suicide was perhaps the most tragic expression of rejection—intellectual,
psychological, and physical—a pupil could make. I found no evidence of this
in the Irish sources, hardly surprising in a predominantly Roman Catholic
country with a powerful ethical perception of suicide as despairing of God's
help. Nor is there much more evidence in the American case. Hampton
Institute in 1885 reported an Indian boy who was uncaring about his health.
When asked why, he remarked: "Because the white man is afraid to die, but
the Indian is not."[55] Some wintertime runaways, as we shall see, were so reck-
less as to appear suicidal.

Another radical form of rejection was to seriously damage the school.
We have little evidence of such violence in the Irish sources, but marginally
more in the American accounts. The dramatic Haskell riot of 1919 was actually far less dangerous than the lone actions of students who burned down
schools. In 1899 Commissioner Jones reported "the most disastrous fire of
years" at one boarding school. An Indian girl had confessed that she placed
oiled rags in one of the upper rooms and set fire to them, and consequently
she had been sent to a reformatory institution. In 1905 the commissioner reported that fires at two schools had been caused by pupils. Such perpetrators, he believed, should be treated like white criminals: "incendiarism in the
schools has become too frequent in the last few years to be passed over indulgently"
(emphasis added), and young Indians had to learn respect for the law.[56] BIA
teacher Gertrude Golden characteristically attempted to explain the motivation of such children at her school: to escape a tyrannical head matron. The
"desperate little group" of pupils piled clothing in the middle of a dormitory
room and set fire to it. Luckily the blaze was discovered before much damage
was done.[57]

Only rarely does an ex-pupil tell of such a drastic expression of rejection;
autobiography is hardly the best place to look for evidence of criminal ac-

tion. In later life, however, Narcissa Owens met an ex-schoolmate, by then in a mental health facility, who confessed to the Cherokee that he had burned down a school. Elsie Allen also claimed that a fire had been started "by some older girls who hated the school."[58] Note how girls were also involved in such violent and dangerous acts of rejection.

If pupils could use English to contest and negotiate with authority, they could also employ the language of the school to reject the school. One Musquakie boy wrote in English begging his mother to take him home. The school authorities badgered him about not making his bed and about how he dressed: "Handkerchief around my neck. Poor jacket and all that. How dirty my clothes was. . . . So I don't like what they told me. I almost cry too. so please send for me. . . . I want to get out of here soon. I also don't like it up here. Do your best mother! Please!" The boy did not get home that year and appeared to be adjusting better to school. Yet some time later he did leave, and these words were his last to the school: "I am sorry to say that I am not coming back, because I am in the same fix as last year, not enough clothes and everything else." In 1894 another young Indian, burdened by some teacher with the name Rip Van Winkle, addressed letters in English to a higher authority, in this case the reservation agent. "I am going to write you this morning I don't want to stay here," began the boy's poignant plea. "I want to go home. I have stayed here over four years and half pretty nearly five years. I want [you] to write the commissioner for me so I can go home." Amazingly, the agent did help the boy, who was later released from school.[59]

Passivity could also shift from a form of resistance into total rejection. Kanseah was one of the youngest Apache prisoners taken to Carlisle after the Geronimo War of 1886; according to another tribal member, he "was unhappy and not interested in school." So he was sent home. When Standing Bear's father visited Carlisle, the superintendent asked him to bring another boy back to the reservation. This boy "did not learn anything, nor seem to want to," recalled Standing Bear. Again we see how even the most dedicated of educators could be undone by the quietest, least demonstrative, and least violent kind of rejection. Essie Horne felt that although one of her sisters stuck at Haskell for a couple of years, "she couldn't adjust to school." The younger girl was "so homesick that she was physically ill most of the time," and like Kanseah, she too was finally sent home.[60]

White officials also reported cases of either passivity or inability to adjust. In 1880, around the year of the incident reported by Standing Bear, Captain Pratt, the Carlisle founder, told of having to send fifteen pupils home "because of imperfect physical and mental condition." The agent for the Pimas and Maricopa Indians reported in 1882 how he had to expel a boy who adamantly refused to have his hair cut. In 1914 the commissioner accepted the recommendation of the superintendent of the Wittenberg Indian School that an uncooperative pupil be expelled.[61]

We have less indication of deliberate use of passivity by Irish pupils to reject the national schools. Bigger pupils who wandered in and out of the schools at different times of the year and as their fancy took them were surely unco-operative and certainly rejected the basic assumption of the CNEI (and of the BIA and all modern systems of mass education) that for schooling to have real value, pupils must pursue it systematically and cumulatively. A folklore infor-mant recalled how in his area some pupils attended only "now and again," or perhaps a few days a week.[62]

    In 1878, partly corroborating such accounts, CNEI inspector McMillan claimed that there were many causes, including poor teaching, but the end result was the same: pupils who so totally lost interest that they dropped out. "In some schools these straggling pupils, finding their up-hill work disagree-able, and . . . their presence not desired by the teachers, voluntarily withdrew from the school sooner than they would have done." McMillan also referred to a problem peculiar to older boys and girls: "It is said that grown up persons are ashamed to stand in classes [of younger children] in which they would be placed." Indians too complained of this particular form of humiliation. Further, having passed in a fourth or fifth class, the Irish pupils and their parents "consider their education finished . . . they, especially the girls, dis-like the hard work of the upper classes, and the people now put their children earlier to work." Many such students, the inspector concluded, "depending only on the three Rs, will enter life without either intellectual training or equipments."[63]

    Two decades later in 1899 CNEI inspector J. B. Skeffington admitted that immediately after enactment of the 1892 Compulsory Education Act, many heretofore "groups of idle children" had begun to attend schools. Yet partly be-cause of epidemics, and partly because they (and their parents) soon realized that the act had little teeth, idleness was again on the increase. Skeffington ended with an implicit admission that large numbers of Irish children, or their parents, were still partly or fully rejecting the national schools. It ap-peared that over one-fourth of the pupils left school without passing even in the fourth class, and many did not attend at all. "For the sake of the children, as well as of society," he wrote, "some means of getting them to acquire the elements of knowledge seems urgently needed."[64]

    Indifference, humiliation, unwillingness or inability to learn, parental and social pressures—all certainly imply rejection of the national school by many older rural boys and girls. This inspector gives no indication that such students violently resisted or caused disciplinary problems; instead he conveys a sense of disinterested passivity on their part, and indeed on their parents' part.

VI

For some Indian "runaways," flight was more than a prank or a temporary visit home. It became a desperate and sometimes deadly dangerous attempt to escape the school forever. Navajo Max Henley recalled that at certain times of year running away was tantamount to suicide; some pupils were frostbitten; "others froze to death." Tribal young were trained to seek and endure physical hardship, however, so every case of runaway death from exposure should not be seen as suicidal. Nevertheless, to have faced the continental winter alone, a runaway must have been desperate to escape. In 1908 the superintendent of Wittenberg Indian School, in Wisconsin, reported one such runaway. Even the boy's parents had begged the official to put him in the school jail because they too feared that he would freeze to death. He was placed in the jail and chained for a week. As soon as the chains were removed, he was off again.[65]

Such chronic truancy was a major headache for BIA and missionary educators; historians have chronicled its occurrence at school after school. Naturally the authorities were upset by all runaways, who were stigmatized as "deserters" around the time of the First World War. To secure funds the authorities had to maintain full enrollments. Further, the teaching of English and advanced subjects required constant and regular attention. Also, flight was a symbolic rejection of the Christian civilization and American citizenship. The sheer extent of the problem can be gleaned from figures compiled by Lomawaima: from January 1 to April 21, 1927, eighteen girls and one hundred boys went AWOL (absent without leave; Lomawaima uses the American military term) from Chilocco School, whose population was around eight hundred at the time. There is no reason to assume that the school was in any way unusual in this respect. The huge discrepancy between boys and girls probably resulted from the more careful supervision of girls. Some of those students, though hardly all, probably intended to return.[66]

After attendance at a number of schools, punctuated by periods with his Navajo family, Frank Mitchell finally fled the Fort Defiance School with a mate to get a job on the railroad "and never did go back to school again." Jim Whitewolf also fled a number of times. On the first occasion he voluntarily returned, but two other runaways did not. On the second occasion Whitewolf intended staying away for good. Logan, his school mentor, came after the boys, who might have frozen to death. "I didn't want to go back," recalled Whitewolf, "but I had to." The third time he and a group escaped, they were brought back by agency police; it is unclear whether they would have otherwise returned.[67]

Obviously peers could be of great importance for runaways. Helen Sekaquaptewa told how often "a boy and a girl would have it planned, and go at the same time." Four Navajo boys and girls, probably couples, fled the Toadlena Boarding School together. More closely supervised, the girls were missed sooner. Upon recapture their hair was cut off, a deep humiliation. The punishment boomeranged, however; the parents found out what happened and took their daughters home.[68] Sometimes even larger numbers fled together. When Hopi superintendent James Gallagher opened the Keams Canyon Boarding School in 1887, word got around that he was about to kidnap the children and send them to Washington: "After about two weeks, there was a general stampede for the mesa." He quelled the rumor, and the school began again, but decades later Navajo policemen still had to drag some Hopi children to school. In 1905 John H. Wilson similarly lamented the problems on his Omaha reservation. "It seemed to do little good to send the police after these runaways," he complained, "as they generally fail to find the boys." In most cases, but not all, their parents returned them to the school after one to ten days. Peer influence, he believed, was the problem: older boys came on campus, smoking and playing football, and enticing younger boys from the school. "The constant example of so many boys who were idle and who were not subject to any restraint could not fail to have a bad effect on our boys," wrote the agent.[69]

The latter episode also shows how it is often difficult to tell whether final rejection of school was a pupil or kin action, or a blending of both factors. These many incidents also show just how broadly frustrating was the issue of runaways: for the BIA officials, who needed to impress Congress; for the teachers, who needed to impress the BIA inspectors; and for some Indian families, who wanted their children to learn and, moreover, who feared for their safety if they fled.

Of course, the issue was important to the pupils too. The intensity of the need to escape was most powerfully illustrated in an account by a BIA teacher. Minnie Jenkins claimed that during her year at Fort Mohave the pupils "ran away in droves, the worst offenders being the wee kindergartners." The problem became so acute that the school authorities actually locked some of them in the school jail. Then one morning at breakfast a sound of loud blows was heard. Using a large log as a battering ram, these children had broken through the jail door and fled—kindergartners in a violent jailbreak! "At the sturdy jail there lay the sturdy door," recalled Jenkins, "broken from its hinges. There lay the log, a big one, and the many pieces of rope. We were amazed."[70]

Ultimately it is impossible to distinguish every case of temporary truant from final runaway and rejecter; many pupils themselves probably could not have told at the moment of flight whether or not they would voluntarily return. And there were narrators who in retrospect claimed that they would have flown, but for parental disapproval. G. W. Grayson feared a beating from his Creek father if he fled like other pupils. When Annie Lowry, a Paiute, fled a local day school in Nevada, her father did whip her, so she realized that running away was useless. A Navajo father used a more subtle yet perhaps more effective threat: "Do not forget," he told his son, "if you run away, I will have to go to jail." Asa Daklugie remembered Geronimo's orders to learn; he was also held at Carlisle by the presence of his wife-to-be.[71]

Irregular attendance plagued the CNEI authorities too, right up to 1922. Yet there is nothing like the problem caused by "the runaway" at the Irish schools, and narrators recall only a few cases of what I have called rejection through flight—pupils actually breaking out of the school, never to return. "Strange boys used to come to school sometimes," recalled a folklore informant of a boy from London who turned up in the class. Although the rest of the pupils spoke English, they could not understand the newcomer's accent, or he understand theirs. One day the master "chastised him" for some offense, and the boy "made a leap to go out the window." His classmates held him back, but then "he tried to climb up the bare wall"—a stark image of desperate action by one who must have felt as isolated as an Indian child among pupils of another tribe. Even the master was horrified and never attempted to check the boy again. Soon afterward he left for good—whether by his own wish or that of his parents remained unclear. His urban English background no doubt influenced his inability to adjust. Yet the informant emphasized that a boy from Liverpool, whose parents admittedly were Irish, got on well with his new peers: "he was the leading light in all our devilment."[72] Cultural factors no doubt influenced pupils, but adjustment or rejection was always a highly personal matter.

One folklore informant actually claimed that in every Irish parish he visited he heard stories of a pupil who "gave the master a slate between the two eyes" and then fled "never to darken the [school] door again." This suggests a rural mythology of violent resistance, but one possibly based on actual individual cases. Indeed, the informant who reported the story claimed to have seen a similar kind of incident. A boy at his school was hoisted onto the back of another pupil for a thrashing, but when the teacher approached with the cane, the boy kicked out backward with both feet, catching the man in the chest and knocking him over. Then the culprit "made one plunge for the door & was never seen at the school again."[73]

To some extent any pupil who left a national school or a BIA or missionary school before completing a full course of studies was rejecting the assimilatory message of the school. Of Irish pupils who actually mitched, many intended to return. After all, attending the school down the road, they had far less need than Indian children for flight to reestablish contact with the home culture. And they had less chance of being successful in their escape—those Irish parents who wanted their children to learn had little sympathy with permanent dropouts. Non-attendance, irregular attendance, seasonal attendance: these were the bane of the CNEI. They generally expressed a haphazard attitude to school, or even a positive attitude frustrated by poverty or other such circumstances. Thus in the Irish case, as in the Indian, it is unclear the extent to which such attitudes were those of the individual student alone, or a combination of student-parental-social influences.

VII

To get a greater sense of why even motivated pupils decided to leave school before their education was complete, we need to examine personal narratives. The formal education of James McCarthy, a Papago, and many of his mates ended suddenly in 1917 when the United States entered the First World War, and they volunteered for the army. Other Indians such as Rosalio Moisés and Refugio Savala, both Yaquis, quit to begin work, apparently without objection from school authorities. For Myrtle Begay, a Navajo, there was no agonizing dilemma: "I dropped out of Fort Apache before I finished high school," she reported. "I don't know why I never went back. I just stayed around home and worked for some families at Chinle." She bore little resentment toward the school; indeed, she later worked for the principal. Traditional and Anglo education were "the same in many ways," she believed—hardly the message authorities hoped to communicate. Helen Sekaquaptewa volunteered to continue from one institution to another. However, although not yet graduated from the Phoenix Indian School, and although the principal invited her to stay on, "something" told her to return to Hopi life after thirteen years away. Fellow Hopi Don Talayesva appeared so successfully acculturated that he wished for some magic that could "change my skin into that of a white man." Then he experienced a frightening dream-vision while sick at school. He remained a further year and a half at Sherman Institute, but the vision apparently influenced his permanent return to his village.[74]

Although highly pleased with their schooling, Luther Standing Bear and Christian convert Jason Betzinez decided to finally leave. Both asked Captain Pratt for permission, but although Betzinez was by then thirty years old, the Carlisle principal refused their request. Standing Bear claimed that he did not want to flee, but "to go in the right way." Seeing their determination, Pratt finally relented, and both left, Standing Bear after five years at Carlisle, Betzinez after ten. Pratt actually gave Standing Bear permission on the condition that he would return. The student, however, declared only that he would do so if he wanted to, which he never did.[75]

Irishman Maurice O'Sullivan told how he just gradually "let school drop." He no longer had homework or such things to bother him: "I was free from the master's control."[76] The lack of many such Irish accounts reflecting pupil choice is probably because families would have retained the right to decide on such an important issue, at least for younger children. Perhaps there was some truth, after all, in the stereotype that Indians often allowed their children a greater measure of freedom than did Euro-Americans. Also, despite their growing familiarity with the institution, ultimately the school was more alien to Indians. For a tribal child to reject it and return to traditional tribal life was not quite so radical a rebellion against adult authority as when an Irish child did so.

Thus there were striking similarities in how Indian and Irish pupils deceived teachers, played pranks, mitched, and fled the schools temporarily or permanently. To a lesser extent there were similarities in the specifically "cultural resistance" they displayed. There were differences too: the higher death rate at Indian schools and the more deeply frustrating runaway phenomenon, for example, both related especially to the boarding school regime. Clearly, though, in America and in Ireland, in all kinds of schools, children worked hard and played hard to limit the total control sought by educators and to manipulate the school to their own advantage.

We must not overdo the idea of pupil agency or "negotiation," however, or imply an equal battle of wills. Generally teachers called the shots locally, and those who employed them called the shots nationally. Yet large numbers of school-age boys and girls in Ireland and America failed even to enter school during the period under review, and large numbers attended so irregularly as to dilute the influence of assimilation. Even pupils who came to accept or enjoy schooling rarely internalized the full assimilatory message and could use the new learning against school authorities. Indians did not totally lose their tribal identity; nor did Irish children become totally Anglicized.

Obviously, then, the responses of Indians and Irish pupils were far more complicated, and the results of the campaigns far more unpredictable than educators could have initially expected. It is to these results that we finally turn.

9. Results

"It was of course the case," writes David Vincent of nineteenth-century efforts to use mass education to achieve mass literacy, "that parents and pupils everywhere subverted the intentions of the official curriculum" and made use of it in ways that "confirmed many of [the educators'] worst fears."[1] The present study strongly reinforces recent work by historians of education who emphasize the resilience and manipulative coping strategies employed by poor and dependent peoples to limit the control exercised over them by imperialists, colonialists, and other dominant groups.

Yet we must also ask who, in terms of real power, dominated the schools in Ireland and the United States? We need to see beyond a tendency to romanticize the oppressed and to latch onto their every action as evidence of resistance to hegemonic systems of domination. Successful teaching and some degree of assimilation coexisted in the schools along with manipulation and resistance by Irish and Indian peoples. The objective of this chapter is to broadly assess the results of CNEI and BIA/missionary campaigns in terms of the major goal of assimilation. I ask the following questions: To what extent did CNEI national schools achieve the assimilation of Irish people, Catholic and Protestant, into the Union with Britain? To what extent did the American campaigns detribalize Indians and win them to loyal citizenship of the United States? What can we learn by comparison of such outcomes? I first broadly generalize about the effects of government-sponsored mass education on these peoples as groups, and then I seek individual perspectives. Examining the campaigns in terms of assimilation does not produce simple answers; for groups and for individuals the results were complex and unpredictable.

I

Despite achieving domination of the Irish educational scene; despite a curriculum that generally ignored or downplayed local Irish culture and history; despite support by the Parliament of one of the richest, most powerful nations on earth; and despite strong support by the Irish people themselves, the CNEI failed in its central goal. By 1922 most of the predominantly Catholic areas of Ireland had achieved independence from Britain. In that same year the government of the Irish Free State abolished the National Board.

The goal of the Union, according to Philip Bull, "was of a fully integrated nation," and "the thrust of policy was strongly towards the elimination of differences between the various components of the United Kingdom." Yet by 1900 widespread rejection had produced an Irish "proto-state." Similarly, David Hempton accepts that late-nineteenth-century Irish nationalism was based on a powerful combination of a dispossessed people sharing a common faith and "a common feeling that the Union, as it had operated in the nineteenth century, was not the best arrangement for governing a Catholic nation."[2] Even a minority of Protestant men and women outside Ulster had come to share this sense of rejection. "If I contemplate Irish history in the *longue durée*," writes Adrian Hastings, "I can see no even moderately plausible alternative to what one may fairly call a nationalist interpretation."[3]

Despite its resources and its growing acceptance in Ireland, the CNEI could not alone have won the hearts and minds of the people to the Union.[4] Too many complicating forces were at work. Had the Great Famine not occurred, for example, had British policies on land and other issues been more far-sighted, had new forms of nationalism not been flourishing at the time in many other European countries, then the majority of the people might have accepted the Union, as indeed even many Catholics did, well into the twentieth century. Yet at the end of it all, the Union was sundered—even Ulster Protestants sought its preservation, rather than the establishment of a new substate of Northern Ireland within the United Kingdom. On the key issue of identity, most Irish people probably felt more Irish (rather than merely members of local communities) in 1900 than in 1831.

Ironically, despite its heavily Anglo curriculum, the CNEI may actually have stimulated Irish nationalism. Such modern ideologies work through literacy. Irish nationalists of various stripes more and more turned to English and used newspapers and other such publications to reach the increasingly English-literate Irish population. Vincent speaks of "the varied strategies of appropriation [of literacy], related but not reducible to complex inequalities in economic, social and political relations." At every point, he believes, "there were dialogues of meanings. What the newly literate thought they were doing as they took up a book or pen was neither controlled by nor independent of the purposes designated by authors and editors."[5] If it resisted providing the content for nationalism, in other words, the CNEI helped provide the skills for its dissemination. John Willinsky's appraisal of the colonial school also applies to those of the CNEI, and indeed of the BIA. "Colonized students learn more than the teacher seeks to teach. The master's tools, it may be fair to suggest, can take down the master's house."[6]

In Ireland the national schools also failed to produce a real mixing of Catholic and Protestant children, as was the initial intention of those who established the board in 1831. True, such learning in the same classroom did take place in many areas. Yet within a few decades of its origin, the CNEI had actually split into blocks of Catholic, Anglican, and Presbyterian schools, each catering predominantly to children of their own denominations. Considering the overwhelmingly Catholic population, the local nature of individual school management, and the fact that the vast majority of Protestant people lived in relatively small areas of Ulster, it is difficult to surmise how things could have been much different.

Further, CNEI religious goals were closely tied to its major assimilationist goal: only by "pouring oil on the troubled waters of Ireland," and by "bringing children of all denominations together . . . in feelings of charity and goodwill," could loyalty to the Union be established. The objective was not to blend all denominations into one Christian faith—even the most sanguine politician could never have hoped for that—but perhaps to remove religion as a divisive issue from education and from national identity. Again, this was a heavy burden to lay at the feet of educators and teachers. Protestantism remained central to English identity throughout much of the period under review, so the CNEI marked a brave—and highly pragmatic—turn in British political approaches to Ireland.[7] Ultimately, the CNEI's failure to pull the denominations together through the education of their children in the same classrooms further weakened the Union, especially as Catholicism increasingly came to be associated with Irish nationalism.

II

"The Indian is DEAD in you," declared the Rev. J. A. Lippincott at a Carlisle commencement ceremony in 1898. "Let all that is Indian with you die! . . . You cannot become truly American Citizens, industrious, intelligent, cultured, civilized until the INDIAN within you is DEAD."[8]

Yet by 1930 the INDIAN within tribal people was not dead. Even white reformers such as the Meriam group were beginning to criticize such an absolute and ethnocentric approach. With the inauguration of the Indian New Deal under Commissioner John Collier, the BIA moved to protect group identity, and many Indian peoples organized tribal governments under the 1934 Indian Reorganization Act (IRA). Ironically, children who had been through boarding schools and other white schools retained a tribal identity and also began to gain a complementary Pan-Indian identity. "Aside from what I know about my own tribe," wrote Essie Horne, "I learned at Haskell." By being thrown together the pupils "discussed our beliefs, our homes, our food, our arts and crafts . . . our lives!" Boarding school, she wrote in a telling phrase, was "a kind of cultural and historical feast," and she "was tremendously enriched by my association with people from other tribes."[9] This was not what the BIA and missionary societies intended, not at all.

Thus if the rupturing of the Union with Britain demonstrates the failure of the CNEI in its core task, so the survival of Indian tribalism—and tribes—and a growing sense of Pan-Indian identity demonstrate the failure of a core goal of U.S. educators. Almost a century later in 2006 Indian people are American citizens—a successful outcome of schooling, from the perspective of BIA and missionary educators—yet still strongly identify with tribal groups and subgroups.[10] Although scholars are pessimistic about the survival of tribal languages, many are still spoken. In BIA schools today (often run under contract by Indian tribes), the old languages are sometimes still taught.[11]

Unlike the CNEI which adopted a rigid "hands-off" approach to the religion of its pupils, the BIA and missionary societies—while they respected the beliefs of Christian Indian pupils—aimed for total obliteration of tribal "heathenisms." To investigate the success of in this crusade would take a series of studies, focused on different tribes and even subgroups within tribes, and, of course, on myriad individual tribal men and women. However, at the risk of gross generalization, we can say that although many Indian pupils converted to Christianity—including a number of autobiographical narrators—we have no way of knowing whether the conversion was total or syncretic. If syncretic, it was not successful by the standards of the educators. Certainly, Indian peoples did not en masse forsake the old ways. Indeed, many then and now experience no difficulty in blending elements of traditional and Christian spirituality. The total Christianization of Indians, holding to "no false Gods," had not happened by 1930. Nor has it by 2006.[12]

None of this is to imply that Indians have not changed. Throughout the nineteenth century they resisted, cooperated with, traded with, and adjusted to waves of white settlers; and many tribal people began to see the adaptive value of schooling. Individually, Indian boys and girls changed deeply at boarding and other white schools. Yet many core values persisted through the school years, to be reinforced again upon return to the people. "Judged by the ambitious scope of their assimilationist vision," writes David Wallace Adams, white educators "clearly failed to achieve their objective." Underlying the drive "was the presupposition that the acculturation process *was a relatively simple matter of exchanging one's cultural skin for another*" (emphasis added). Beyond comprehension was the possibility "that the acculturation process itself would involve various forms of selective incorporation, syncretization, and compartmentalization."[13]

Such complex results were equally beyond the comprehension of many employees in the Irish national school system. Lacking modern anthropological understandings of cultures as complex, deeply internalized webs of significance and meaning, CNEI, BIA, and missionary educators really did believe in total cultural transformation. They realized, of course, that the task was a massive one, demanding national commitment and financial resources, and also demanding great personal sacrifice from generations of male and female teachers. It would also demand much sacrifice of the pupils and of the communities that—mostly voluntarily by the end of the period—sent them to school. Yet at least in theory the job was simple: complete erasure of deficient traditions, complete assimilation into the superior civilization. Setting their sights so absolutely high, CNEI and BIA educators were destined, by their own absolutist criteria, to fail.

III

If we step away from such absolutist goals, however, we can acknowledge that CNEI and BIA educators actually achieved much, even by their own criteria. Assuming that two crucial measures for any organization are survival and growth, then the CNEI had much to be satisfied with by the early 1900s. Against competition from hedge schools and Catholic organizations such as the Irish Christian Brothers and various orders of priests and nuns, and against the schools of some Protestant groups, the national schools became the major elementary system. Compromises were extracted from the board, but a tenacious adaptability allowed survival and growth. Writing at the beginning of the twentieth century, Graham Balfour claimed that, compared to about 82 percent attendance for school-age children in the English system, the CNEI could claim only 64 percent.[14] Yet we can hardly compare the relatively peaceful and prosperous English society then with nineteenth-century Ireland. Significantly, Irish people voted for the national schools with the feet of their children, generation after generation. Considering the difficulties, survival and growth were no mean achievements.

In one region of Ireland we can perhaps claim that the CNEI did actually achieve an even higher degree of success. Although Protestants were prominent in all major Irish nationalist movements during the period, in general Anglicans, Presbyterians, and other Protestants agreed with the goals of the board: preserve the Union, respect the different denominational traditions, and provide financial support for the schooling of Protestant children. If the Union of all Ireland with Britain was not preserved, at least northern Protestants maintained their link with Britain, rather than being marooned in an independent Ireland. Thus once issues of Presbyterian and Anglican educational rights were resolved, Protestants were much more receptive to the board's Anglicizing mission than the majority population. So, especially in the Protestant areas of Ulster, the CNEI did succeed in its goals of Anglicization; or, it might be more accurate to say that the board worked effectively with a receptive population.

Moreover, the failure of the CNEI to win absolute allegiance of the rest of the (predominantly Catholic) Irish to the Crown does not mean that it failed totally. Anglicization, allied to modernization, characterized many areas of Irish society outside Protestant Ulster by 1900: in education, obviously; and in law, the civil service, and the military, for example. Indeed, the major Irish nationalist drive until after the bloody Easter Rising of 1916 was for a form of constitutional autonomy within the United Kingdom. When the First World War broke out in 1914, the Irish Parliamentary Party, wedded to Home Rule, encouraged Irish men to flock to the colors. Perhaps 200,000, about half of them Catholics, joined the British Army. Not all of them thought in terms of king and empire, of course. Yet the fact that such numbers joined voluntarily (there has never been conscription in Ireland, north or south) does suggest the extent to which many Irish people had been Anglicized, or at least had come to assume that the British Army was "our army." Similarly, for decades tens of thousands of Irish men had been serving in the RIC, despite its negative reputation among nationalists.[15]

Of course, all this might have happened without the national schools. Although proving item-by-item correlation would be impossible, it is highly likely that the CNEI played a major part in anglicizing the boys and girls, and through them many of the men and women of Ireland. To survive in the system, pupils, monitors, teachers, and others had at least to appear obedient. From ex-pupil accounts we get a strong impression that most of them went along most of the time. As Vincent and others suggest, we can never know precisely how a carefully planned and culturally loaded curriculum is digested by pupils.[16] However, much of the modernizing and Anglicizing knowledge had obviously been absorbed and taken as the natural order of things by Irish boys and girls.

It is highly significant that by 1900 the vast majority of the people had voluntarily ceased to speak the Irish language. With some validity, considering the slow and grudging acceptance of Irish into the CNEI curriculum, publications such as the Gaelic League's *Claidheamh Soluis* (Sword of Light) laid much of the blame for this collapse of the vernacular at the door of the national schools. The CNEI was not alone responsible, however. Even before its establishment, as we saw, parents willingly sent their children to hedge schools where instruction was through English. Had Irish people en masse resisted CNEI language policies, these might have been changed sooner—the board, after all, recognized Irish religious realities and accepted the rights of Catholics. Further, the Catholic Church's actions were also important. For many reasons, including the desire of a previously persecuted institution to prove its loyalty to the dominant power, the Catholic Church had begun the shift toward the use of English early in the nineteenth century. Thus a major sustaining institution, the recipient of increasing loyalty at local and national levels during the century, had decisively tilted in favor of the new language.[17] Through death and emigration, the Great Famine devastated Irish-speaking areas most heavily; the disaster further undermined faith in the old ways, which had failed so terribly.

An argument might be made that vernaculars inevitably die in the face of imperial power. However, not all do, and a brief comparative foray can help us realize that particular circumstances, actions, and intentions are vital to such changes. By 1800 Finland was still part of the Swedish crown, and about 15 percent of Finns spoke Swedish. As in Ireland, the "foreign" language was also the language of higher culture, of civil service employment, and of social advance generally. The writing was on the wall for the Fenno-Ugrian language spoken by the majority of the peasants. However, sharing Lutheranism with Sweden, and thus never having been persecuted (unlike the Catholic Church in Ireland), the Finnish Lutheran Church felt less need to demonstrate its loyalty to the Swedish crown and continued to use Finnish among Finnish-speakers. In 1809 Finland was transferred to the Russian Empire, and St. Petersburg initially favored Finnish, to weaken the link to Sweden. As in Ireland, romantic nationalism began to valorize the Finnish past and language. By 1900, Finnish had recovered, and today it is the first language of over 90 percent of the population. The situation around 1800 was perhaps marginally more hopeful for Finnish than for Irish, but the vernacular in each case was beginning its "inevitable" decline. Because of different circumstances on the ground, then, Finland and Ireland are today almost reverse images in terms of language loss/survival.[18]

Thus loss of the vernacular is not inevitable. And although there were many factors in nineteenth-century Ireland contributing to the demise of Irish, the CNEI can surely claim a major share of the credit—if that is the appropriate word—for the decline of the Irish language and for the linguistic Anglicization of the Irish people.

The CNEI also made a major contribution to the rising literacy—generally but not totally in English—of the Irish people. Literacy can be seen as yet another assault on traditional and oral Irish culture. Tomás O'Crohan perceptively commented on how the very act of reading could undermine faith in the old stories. "Very soon I had a book or two," he wrote, "and people . . . were coming to listen to me reading the old tales to them." The people knew a lot of the stories, but "they lost their taste in telling them to one another when they compared them to the styles the books put on them" (emphasis added). As J. A. Mangan also emphasizes, literacy helps to provide a broader perspective for people, to move them out of the relatively enclosed world of oral traditions—just what the CNEI hoped would happen.[19]

Yet literacy is a complex issue, and it is difficult even to establish criteria (just how much must a person be able to read or to write to be considered literate?). Certainly the official figures are impressive. According to the CNEI, by early in the twentieth century there had been a reduction in the percentage of illiterates from 47 percent in 1851 to 14 percent in 1901—apparently 86 percent could both read and write. "This change for the better," it claimed proudly, was "remarkable," especially as two million "of the younger and better educated" had emigrated in the previous half century, "while the majority of the illiterates were persons who were too old to leave their homes." The board further claimed that although in 1871 only 59 percent of children between ten and fifteen years could read and write, in 1901 the percentage had risen to 94 percent. Although critical of the state of education in Ireland, Balfour nevertheless admitted that literacy had improved; yet he claimed in 1903 that still more than 20 percent of the population could not write, and about 13 percent (one-eighth) could neither read nor write. John Coolahan warns us to be suspicious of official statistics, as "they were not obtained in a rigorous manner," but he accepts that illiteracy had declined during the later nineteenth century. David Fitzpatrick believes that almost every young adult could write (or claimed to be able to write) by about 1911.[20]

Few scholars would deny, however, that the CNEI, building upon the work of the hedge schools and other systems existing before and after its founding, made a major contribution to teaching basic skills in reading and writing to perhaps millions of young Irish boys and girls. Fitzpatrick believes that "the general diffusion of reading, writing, and arithmetic has rightly been regarded by historians as the major, indeed the only significant achievement" of the national schools.[21]

Such conclusions invite counterfactual speculation.[22] We can ask an unanswerable question of the CNEI (and, later of the BIA): Had the Irish national schools never existed, would things have been better or worse for Irish people from 1831 to 1922 and after? The government might have continued supporting the Kildare Place Society and other supposedly nondenominational organizations becoming increasingly anathema to Catholics. Such societies, along with Catholic teaching orders and Protestant denominational schools, and the numerous hedge schools—some of which survived well into the period dominated by the CNEI—would have borne the brunt of educating the Irish masses. However, there would have been a huge lacuna for elementary education, and far fewer Irish people would have become literate and proficient even in the three R's. Even if other school systems had taught through English, it is likely that far more people would have been speaking the vernacular in 1900 than was the case. It is also likely that far more emigrants would have left as illiterate and Irish-speaking; possessors of a rich, native oral culture but far less well equipped for life in Britain and its empire or America.[23]

Further, as the National Board's schools multiplied into the thousands, they provided relatively secure employment for many men and women, as monitors, teachers, and even principals; as inspectors and higher officials for a tiny minority. They provided boys and girls with motivation to study and—whatever we may think of the regimentation and rote learning—taught adaptive skills necessary for modern life. Surprisingly, girls may have benefited more than boys from both the literary and vocational sides of the CNEI's curriculum, especially those who intended to emigrate: "With implacable resolve and sometimes with official connivance," writes David Fitzpatrick, "the girls of Ireland manipulated the 'Murder Machine' [national school system] to prepare themselves for life abroad."[24] The CNEI thus massively changed Irish history—and indeed British, Imperial, and American histories too—which had complex social, economic, cultural, and gender implications. A good case can be made that the people would have been worse off in many ways had the national schools never been established.

In absolute assimilationist terms, therefore, the CNEI crusade failed. When we take a less-absolutist view, we can acknowledge that the board had many significant and long-lasting achievements to its credit.

IV

This was also the case for the BIA and its missionary allies. If they failed to destroy Indian tribal identity, and indeed helped stimulate Pan-Indianism, they nevertheless convinced large numbers of Indians of the value of schooling and won them to a sense of loyalty to the United States. Official sources, Indian ex-pupils, and later historians are in broad agreement that by the 1920s the vast majority of Indian children, some of whom would later become leaders in their communities, were attending schools.[25] During summer holidays children often reverted to old ways—thus the BIA's near-paranoia about the supposedly corrupting Indian family environment. As in the Irish case, however, Indian parents were by then also voting with the feet of their children, and the vast majority accepted that there were things the school could teach that were vital to survival.

Many Indians had actually made the schools their own. As early as 1915 the commissioner reported that "the returned student" was "becoming a factor in the life of his people." Eight of the larger boarding schools now had alumni associations, he claimed, "which foster this activity of maintaining a credible interest in school ideals." Indians from all walks of life attended such meetings during the year, one school sent representatives to the Association of Alumni Secretaries of the United States, and a delegation from an Indian school alumni association attended a larger meeting in San Francisco.[26] BIA officials, of course, liked to emphasize every apparent gain for civilization. Historians too, however, some of them Native Americans, and ex-pupils and teachers such as Essie Horne agree that by late in our period of study many Indians had come to regard schools, especially boarding schools explicitly set up to destroy tribal cultures, as central to Indian experiences and identity. This once again demonstrates the adaptability of Native peoples, but it also partly validates the achievement of the educators.

White educators also won over Indians to the importance of the English language and of literacy, both as reading and writing—all these had survival value, and Indian peoples were highly pragmatic in appropriating them. In no autobiographical account did the narrator regret learning English or attaining literacy. Such skills would complement those learned at home. According to the Meriam Report (1928), for Indians between the ages of ten and twenty, in the sixteen states with the largest Indian populations, the illiteracy rate around 1920 had been 17 percent; the illiteracy rate for all Indians of those states was nearly 36 percent; for all Americans it was around 6 percent. This means that the highly critical Meriam group was admitting that over 80 percent of school-age Indians in those states were then literate in some sense. Also, the report admitted that the 1920 figures were an improvement on those of 1910, when Indian illiteracy for that age group was 25 percent. Despite the translation work of some missionaries and the efforts of Indians such as Sequoyah, who invented a way of writing Cherokee, such literacy was, as in the Irish case, almost entirely in English.[27] Much of this improvement was undoubtedly the result of BIA and missionary endeavors. As in the Irish case, the uses made of literacy would vary, and the new skills would at times be exploited to oppose white policies. Yet the government and its allies had again partly won over Indians to the view that English and literacy were vital to survival in modern life. Thus there is much truth in Stearn's claim that "modern education . . . tended to persuade most people of its value, but the definitions of value varied and the extent of persuasion was not uniform."[28]

Not every member of his Tewa-Hopi community, and certainly not every Native American, would have agreed with ex–boarding school student Albert Yava. Yet he spoke for large numbers at that time and since, who saw compromise as the best possible coping strategy. "Some of the old traditional leaders thought we ought to stay the way we used to be"; he continued: "I have always felt that the only way we can save the old traditions is to recognize the new forces at work in our lives, accept that times have changed, and become part of the modern world. That way we can survive and preserve a part of our minds for the old values. If you don't survive you don't have anything."[29]

As in the Irish case, we can again employ counterfactual speculation. It could be argued that missionaries and white teachers not only weakened the faith of many Indians in their own cultural values. They also divided the people, sibling from sibling, and generation from generation. Yet what if treaties had never included educational clauses? What if schools and teachers had never arrived among the tribes, and if Carlisle and such establishments had never been built? The tribes would still have lost lands through those treaties and have been subject to the full onslaught of settlement, escalating in area after area throughout the nineteenth century. Except in isolated cases of cultural brokers or traders, few would have learned English, and fewer still to read and write. More and more white Americans came to accept the idea of the "Vanishing Indian," unfit for survival in the modern world. The BIA, missionaries, and Friends of the Indian, on the other hand, believed in what we might call "the vanishing Indianness." Whatever their ethnocentrism, they tried to defend Indian rights as they saw them. They were buffers between the tribes and settlers, vital sources of adaptive skills, and vital voices for protection.

Some historians argue that the BIA aimed at the "proletarianization" of Indian people; transforming tribal gender roles by providing education, but only to produce a pacified pool of laborers (men) and domestics (women) at the lowest levels in American society. Even if economic exploitation was part of the goal, one could argue that proletarianization is preferable to physical extinction. I am counterfactually arguing, then, that for all their destructive effects, the schools—along with Indian resilience and manipulative creativity, of course—did help Indians survive, thus achieving a major goal of the campaign. Without the schools, I suspect, there would be far fewer Indian people living in the United States today.

To compare both situations, the BIA was even more vital to the survival of (many) Indians than was the CNEI to Irish survival. At no time in the nineteenth century, not even during the most terrible days of the Great Famine, was the actual physical survival of the Irish people in doubt. At no time were tens of millions of foreign settlers rushing in to fill up every piece of supposedly "empty land" in Ireland. Had the CNEI not existed, Irish people in general, and emigrants in particular, would certainly have experienced far greater difficulties then and later. But had the BIA and missionaries not carried their crusade to the Indians, the results might just have been even more catastrophic. White educators were certainly guilty of cultural imperialism, of what I call "culturocide." However, neither they nor the federal government committed genocide against the Indians; indeed, it is my contention that they helped prevent genocide—the physical extermination of Indian peoples in the United States.[30]

A further counterfactual question might be asked of the BIA and CNEI: What might have been achieved had both proceeded with a deeper respect for local cultures and values? Even in a purely pragmatic sense, in order to conquer a culture it may be better to first seek understanding. Although demographic and cultural realities forced a degree of cultural sensitivity upon the CNEI, it is obvious that neither authority was much interested in understanding the "deficient" lifestyles of those they intended to transform. Considering attitudes at the time, then, it is perhaps pointless to further indulge in speculation on this issue.[31]

V

When we move from the national or group level to that of the individual, we get a greater sense of how the schools influenced the lives of Irish and Indian boys and girls as they became men and women. Drawing mostly on autobiographical accounts, I suggest some of the immediate results of national schooling and of BIA and missionary schooling for a few ex-pupils.

According to an Irish folklore informant, there was "no doubt in the world but that the schools were a great boon to the people. Those of them that got good schooling made out well when they went to America." There was scarcely a person in her parish, she believed, who had not spent some time at a national school.[32] Indeed, as historians such as Janet Nolan have shown, the national schools "were an important training ground for emigration"—especially for girls and women, whose other avenues to financial independence were severely restricted in the post-Famine decades. Female teachers became role models for Irish girls, and many of those who emigrated saw their daughters become teachers in the American elementary schools. Irish-American women thus "entered white–collar work at least a generation before their brothers," writes Nolan, and were the largest ethnic group among such teachers in cities with large Irish populations. Although Irish emigrant mothers had often earned their livings as domestic servants of the rich, "their daughters earned salaries as servants of the poor in the overcrowded classrooms of urban America's schools."[33]

Although Peig Sayers did not forsake the Blasket Islands for the emigrant ship, she also greatly enjoyed learning, even doing homework with schoolmates, before being withdrawn for domestic service. So did her son Micheál O'Guiheen, and there is no hint in such accounts of resistance to the assimilatory curriculum, apart from complaints about the difficulty of learning in English. O'Crohan claimed that the island pupils were bright and enthusiastic enough to keep a new teacher on her toes; they understood so quickly that she had to make things harder for them. Whether such memories reflect exactly what happened decades earlier, all communicate well the enjoyment of learning and the belief that schooling mattered.[34]

Dan Breen left school at fourteen: "I had to go out and earn my bread," he wrote simply. He was "a proud boy" the first time he handed the pay-packet to his mother, but perhaps his later role as a guerrilla leader in the War of Independence was partly the result of having a national school teacher who subverted CNEI ideology by teaching Irish nationalism in class. One informant, whose father took him out for seasonal farm work, believed that there were many like him, and many graduated only to seasonal work in England. Their knowledge of English, such as it was, would have helped them there. Patrick MacGowan felt that he learned little at school, yet the English language was obviously of benefit on his many working trips to Scotland and later during the years he spent in America. Most negative was Maurice O'Sullivan, a Blasket Islander who wandered away from school after a few years. Yet O'Sullivan later traveled to Dublin and became a member of the Irish national police force, something he could hardly have done with less or no education.[35]

Patrick Lindsay also remembered fellow pupils being taken from school before they finished, but he was luckier. "Were it not for my father and my mother and the sacrifices they were prepared to make," he wrote, "I would have had to leave too." At the end of the period under review he managed to win one of the ten scholarships for secondary education (high school) offered by the local authority. He was to spend five enjoyable years at the secondary level. Later he became a barrister (lawyer). For him, being able to stay at the national school opened up opportunities that few other children of his time enjoyed.[36]

The same could be said for ex-pupils such as Sean O'Faolain and Frank O'Connor, both of whom were highly critical of many aspects of their national schooling, yet who used it as a stepping stone to further education. O'Connor seems to have enjoyed it far less than O'Faolain. In reference to his schooling O'Connor claimed, "I think that at any time I would have risked an eternity of hell rather than spend a day in that [national] school." O'Connor's mother suddenly withdrew him to attend a Christian Brothers School, not part of the CNEI system, and later he too ended his education for lack of family resources. Yet it is likely that his desire to continue his own education was produced partly through the influence of an idolized national school teacher. O'Connor looked for a job that would allow him to buy books—and he continued on to become a major figure in modern Irish literature. Despite the sometimes dark picture O'Faolain gave of school in Cork, he remembered some inspirational teaching, and how the Presentation Brothers tried to give poor boys a start in life. He too was fortunate because even though his parents were close to poor themselves, they were determined that their children should get as good an education as possible, through and beyond the primary level.[37]

Others also parlayed their national school education into successful careers, by their own accounts. Expelled a number of times, R. B. Robson progressed through the whole national school system to the principalship of a CNEI school. His narrative certainly validates the CNEI in most of its policies, including Anglicization, so natural to an Ulster unionist that it escaped specific comment. Patrick Shea, a Catholic from Southern Ireland also ended up in Ulster, later becoming a senior civil servant in the government of Northern Ireland. He too could criticize the brutality and squalidness of national school life, but he obviously gained immensely from his days at the Athlone School.[38]

So did William O'Malley. Born in the mid-1850s, he was enrolled as soon as he could walk at the local national school in Connemara, western Ireland. He generally enjoyed his education and recalled that one of his schoolmates, forced to emigrate at the age of eighteen or nineteen, later ended up as U.S. ambassador to a European nation. Another schoolmate, the writer claimed, also emigrated to America and became "one of the principal engineers of a great railway company." O'Malley further claimed, perhaps wishfully, that thousands of such emigrants ended up wealthy across the Atlantic. He himself remained at school until he was about fourteen and happily related how the master chose him as a monitor: "and proud I was to be now earning the splendid sum of 10 [shillings] a quarter or £2 a year." He later served as an officer in the British army, and later again as a Member of Parliament for the Irish Parliamentary Party at Westminster, a party dedicated to Irish Home Rule within the Empire. His was a successful exploitation of school for personal gain—but yet again an ironic one in terms of the Union-preserving goals of the CNEI.[39]

We can draw no significant statistical conclusions from a few such recollections, most from men. Yet, Irish girls also benefited massively from CNEI teaching, from education in English literacy, and especially from "domestic" subjects; indeed, by the end of the century they were perhaps more literate and better educated than the boys. Whether in Ireland or abroad, they would exploit that knowledge as domestics, as housewives, or—increasingly—as teachers. Nowhere in forty or so Irish accounts did I come across an ex-pupil, male or female, who regretted having attended a national school. As with Indians, their memories are often highly ambivalent. Yet from the poorest Blasket Islanders to those who attained recognized status in later life, all acknowledged the value of their schooling, sometimes woefully truncated. All to some extent corroborate the broader claims of the CNEI that it was providing an education for the masses, one that helped them achieve some level of literacy and numeracy, and that helped their entry into modern Irish life—and out of it too, if they emigrated. Again we can ask counterfactually: Had there not been a national school system, would Peig Sayers, Frank O'Connor, or R. B. Robson have led more fulfilling lives? Impossible to answer, of course. Yet from their own accounts it is clear that such men and women felt they gained something from the system, even if few of them behaved as the CNEI intended them to. So did perhaps millions of other Irish boys and girls over those nine decades, at home or as emigrants, many of whom might have had no schooling whatsoever but for the CNEI.

VI

In the Indian case things are a little more complicated, again because of the boarding school, and require more space to examine. By the late nineteenth century "the returned student" had become a subject of controversy and anxiety for white educators. Would he or she assume the role of cultural broker, the entering wedge of civilization into the tribe? Or would the student "backslide" and "go back to the blanket"?[40] In general, officials liked to accentuate the positive. "The increasing mass of returned pupils is operating as leaven to the whole mass," claimed the commissioner in 1900. "From the isolation of one or two in a tribe, they have grown in number until they are able to combat successfully hereditary prejudices. As a rule, these pupils are the unconscious, or the conscious, agents who are spreading the desire 'to know' among the younger generations." Yet they faced an uphill battle, and their actions were "frequently nullified by an ancient squaw or ignorant chief."[41]

Indian commissioners and school officials frequently included accounts of returned students in their reports. A Hampton Institute report of 1903 claimed that in terms of progress 673 living ex-students of the school could be thus classified: excellent, 141; good, 333; fair, 149; poor, 42; bad, 8. Similarly in 1908 the commissioner excerpted a Hampton report that provided a long list of 648 ex-students, noting the claimed employment during the past year: the list ran a wide gamut of jobs and careers, including teachers (11), industrial teachers (19), and catechists and other workers (15) at Indian schools. There were 63 agency employees of all kinds, and under the term "professions" were listed physicians (4—possibly including Dr. Susette La Flesche, the sister of Francis and the first female Indian MD); anthropologists (2); one each of editor and lawyer; army and navy employees (8); and various other professions or jobs. There were, as the BIA hoped there would be, 187 "owning farms, ranches, and stock." Similarly gratifying to educators aiming for the "uplift" of supposedly downtrodden Indian girls and women, many female students became wives: there were 164 "girls married and in good homes"; 26 "girls at home" brought up the end of the list. This was followed by short accounts of the later lives of individual ex-students such as Thomas Wildcat Alford (one of the narrators cited in this book); he was by then secretary of the Shawnee General Council—and had sent his three sons to government schools. Ella Alderete, who had received elementary nursing training at Haskell, was head nurse at the Leavenworth (Kansas) Hospital, "with several trained nurses under her charge."[42] David Wallace Adams has compiled a more extensive list of known occupations of living Carlisle and Hampton students from 1912 to 1918. By far the highest number of male ex-students from each school were farmers (769 for Carlisle out of about 3,000 male and females; 269 for Hampton of a total of 852). The highest number of women were housewives (677 for Carlisle; 236 for Hampton).[43]

Many ex-students thus returned to work for the Bureau of Indian Affairs. This phenomenon increased rapidly, and by 1899 about 45 per cent of the personnel in the BIA school service were Indians: 1,106 compared to 1,402 whites. Of these Indians over 500 held "titled positions" with civil service protection, such as teacher or matron; others served throughout the administration of the schools, as disciplinarians, seamstresses, laundresses, cooks, farmers, blacksmiths, industrial teachers, and "assistants." Because reservations were regarded as "nurseries of civilization," writes Wilbert H. Ahern, "the employment of returned students in the Indian Service became an explicit part of the assimilationist policy." Thus for many of these Indian men and women school had also proved useful, both in personal terms—salaries were relatively good—and in providing further opportunities to serve their people. Ahern concludes that it was never easy to balance the many demands of their positions at the schools or afterward when they returned to the reservations. By 1905 the percentage of Indians employed in the BIA school system had dropped to 25 percent. This still meant that over six hundred Indians of both sexes were being employed by the BIA in its schools during the early twentieth century. By 1940 about 60 percent of those employed in the Indian Service (all areas) were Indians.[44]

Therefore during the latter decades of the assimilationist drive, employment in the Indian service, at least below the level of superintendent, and generally below that of teacher, was a reasonable goal for Indian men and women. Ahern sees racism as one major factor obstructing full access to Indians in the BIA. Yet by 1905 one superintendent and one assistant superintendent were Indians; theoretically the sky was the limit, as Ely S. Parker, a Seneca, proved by becoming a high-ranking officer in the army and then commissioner of Indian Affairs (1869–71).[45]

The BIA circulated forms to returned students to ascertain how they were faring in later life, and ex-pupil replies give us some sense of this variety. Around 1911 Lambert Istone told Carlisle authorities that he was then serving as a U.S. scout, and that he had participated in the pursuit of Geronimo to Mexico. His oldest daughter was at school. "I am glad that I attended Carlisle and have received an education," wrote Norman Cassadore, a San Carlos Apache, then engaged in farming: "I can read and understand these things that will help me and my people and I tell them about this." Josephine White, from New York, sounded apologetic about having no occupation "but framing [farming?] and keeping house and taking care of my children"—actually such activities were quite acceptable to the BIA, especially as she had a "bad husband drunkard." She tried to warn her people against using whisky and tobacco, "so many get kill by using strong drink." Wishing she were a young girl again, so she could be back at school, she wrote: "I think Carlisle is the best place for us poor Indians. I thank you for that school[,] a school for every one who wants to learn."[46]

Others also appeared highly pleased with their time at Carlisle, but some were less so. Mrs. Raymond Waterman, an Onondaga from New York, then a housekeeper, sent her best wishes to former classmates and added, "My happiest schooldays were in dear old Carlisle." Michael Burns, an Apache, seemed less pleased. After Carlisle and other experiences he had actually spent one year at Highland University of Kansas, but by 1913 he was "working the hardest kinds of labor; which it requires no education." Asa Daklugie declared himself a farmer and stock raiser and an Indian scout. Despite his dislike of Carlisle he wrote to ask that his two daughters be accepted as students. Festus E. Pelone, apparently an Apache, was then working as a night watchman at Rice Indian School, Arizona, and possessed "about 59 horses and my land." He also spoke well of the school: "I find that I can use to good advantage all the things I learned while at Carlisle," he typed in his form, "and I regret that I did not absorb more." He had earlier "tried to be a medicine man" but "found that to be a losing game, so I went to work."

Many forms contained a general enquiry, "*Tell me something of interest in your present life.*" Luther Standing Bear (whose published books are much quoted in the present work) was by about the same year working as a clerk in a store, having earlier been a teacher. He claimed ownership of 1,120 acres on the Pine Ridge Reservation and defended his earlier employment in Buffalo Bill's Wild West Show. "The schools may not be in favor of the shows," he wrote, "but that is where I learned a good deal from too." Although the traveling exposed him to all kinds of temptations, he declared: "I never forgot what I was taught at Carlisle[:] not to drink not to smoke not chew tobacco or tell lies." And, he added wistfully: "It is easy to be good in school, but it's hard when you get out into the world." Mildred Snow earned her living on the Cattaraugus Reservation in New York doing housework. "I did not graduate from either Carlisle or Hampton," she wrote sadly, "and I regret that more than words can tell." She still hoped that she might get work in government service. Mrs. Paul S. Peters, also a housekeeper, was only two years out of Carlisle; she and her husband each owned 80 acres and "a very happy and comfortable home, and we get along very nicely." She credited much of her success "to Carlisle School in general," as well as to its staff. It was "doing wonders in lifting up the Indians. Long may she live to continue her work." Another student, who owned 180 acres of land, replied simply to the same question: "I am having no interest in my life."

We attain a more detailed—if also more time-distanced—sense of the problems and achievements of returnees from autobiographical accounts. Many ex-pupils, even those who would later value their education, told of the difficulties of re-entry into traditional society.[47] "My homecoming was a bitter disappointment to me," wrote Thomas Alford on his return after graduation from Hampton. He later rose to tribal leadership, but initially his different appearance and manner inspired a cold and suspicious response from his people. "Instead of being eager to learn the new ideas I had to teach them, they gave me to understand that they did not approve of me."[48] Many others received a similarly cold welcome, intensified no doubt by their own arrogant belief that the people needed to be uplifted. In a sense such ex-students had learned too well the BIA's admonition that they become cultural brokers. Later they would regret their hubris, but they frankly recalled it. Polingaysi Qoyawayma also castigated kin for adhering to the old ways, and for not cooking and baking in the proper civilized fashion. Her Hopi parents struggled to accommodate the disdainful returnee, and her mother commented in dismay: "What shall I do with my daughter, who is now my mother?"—again a shocking reversal of the respect due to age in that society.[49]

Much depended on the individual. Those like Essie Horne who cherished both old ways and the new recalled no such traumatic reentry problems. Nor did ex-students Daniel La France or Don Talayesva, who refrained from preaching the new at their people. La France was also imbued with a sense of cultural superiority—"the people had progressed," he noted approvingly. "The past and its traditions were losing their hold on them and the white man's ways were gaining." Apparently he kept such attitudes to himself and generated less friction. Oscar Good Shot frankly recalled how one of the older Sioux men flared up at him, delivering a comment applicable to many return-ees: "you young people who have been to white men's school think you know everything, but you don't know anything."[50] Intergenerational tensions are typical of many societies, but in these situations the returning students were attempting to undermine or even destroy a whole way of life.

Once they had easily or painfully readjusted, young Indian men and women had the rest of their lives to live; here we can but briefly touch on whether individuals considered their schooling useful. Irene Stewart also found return to the old ways difficult, especially having gotten used to the amenities of modern life (to the extent to which they were available at the often woefully equipped schools). Later she would come to enjoy Navajo life again, but in the meantime she moved to another school and became a Christian missionary to white Americans. She returned to the reservation as a missionary worker and later was active in tribal politics. Although critical of many areas of school life, she valued an education that opened different opportunities to her yet also allowed her live among the people. Anna Moore Shaw similarly felt that she and her new husband could not accept the conditions on the Pima reservation: "the education they had strived so hard to give us had prepared us to bring in money from the white man's world; it would be wrong to waste all those years of schooling on a life of primitive farming." Later she, like others mentioned here, would combine her new vision with elements of Pima life. Clearly she valued the years she had spent at a number of American schools.[51]

After thirteen years at different schools, Helen Sekaquaptewa decided to return to Hopiland. She soon clashed with traditional family members, but she married her school sweetheart and lived to her own understanding of Hopi family life. Her autobiography too focuses on the negative sides of schooling, but it also powerfully demonstrates how an Indian girl could value tradition yet simultaneously devour white education. Like many others—indeed more than most—she had managed to fruitfully combine two ways.[52]

The task of reentry was aggravated by the fact that some of the vocational skills learned at school were simply irrelevant to reservation life. In this sense some Indians felt that a major element in their schooling had betrayed them.

Commissioner Parker, a Seneca, was extremely critical of the vocational element in the curriculum. When ex-students returned to the reservation, he
claimed, "[they] found no wagons or carts to be made or mended, no horses
or cattle to be shod, no houses requiring skilled labor, to be built, no fashion-
able clothes to be made, no shoes to make or mend . . . and hence all the time,
money, and patience expended on these people has generally been a dead loss
and has the effect of generally retarding their civilization."[53]

While Parker perhaps exaggerated—many returnees did find use for their
skills—other Indians also noted the problem, as indeed did BIA officials
by attempting to reform its curriculum around 1900 to provide a more "relevant" vocational education. Although Don Talayesva admitted gaining from
school, he also felt that "education had spoiled me for making a living in the
desert," and he feared he would have to face the shame of being unable to support his new wife. Similarly, Standing Bear complained that returnees to the
Lakota reservation were unprepared for the realities there. Hoke Denetsosie,
a Navajo, reinforced the assertions of some later historians that Indian peoples were in fact "proletarianized" and complained that schooling "only half
prepared [pupils] to make a living in the dominant world around us." Other
narrators too found that either they or those whom they knew were victims
of the system. Zitkala-Ša claimed that her brother lost his job as reservation
clerk to a white man. The Mecalero Apache referred to as Chris claimed a
similar problem for Apache returnees, who lost out to whites in competition
for agency jobs.[54]

Although white critics of the BIA, such as those who wrote the Meriam
Report, could also point to the irrelevance of much of its vocational teaching,
obviously there were individual Indians who did find later use for the new
skills.[55] In typically pragmatic fashion, and without irony, a Navajo recalled
how he used English to write down a sacred tribal ritual. Colored crayons
helped him memorize passages: "Thus," he concluded, "from the lessons
taught in reading and writing I learned the singing of ceremonies." Equally
ironic, as we have seen, G. W. Grayson learned the Creek language from fellow pupils—just as O'Sullivan learned Irish at a national school. Hardly what
the authorities wanted in either case, but personally important to each individual. Apaches came to see the wisdom of Geronimo's advice to turn the
white man's schooling to their own advantage. Later many ex-Carlisle students from that tribe employed lawyers, and in 1971, after a series of legal
battles, Apaches succeeded in winning a settlement of $25 million from the
government.[56]

As the BIA hoped, a number of these narrators (besides Essie Horne and
Luther Standing Bear) served for periods as teachers to their own or other

Indian peoples: Lilah Denton Lindsey (Creek), Thomas Wildcat Alford (Shawnee), Lucille Winnie (Iroquois), and Polingaysi Qoyawayma (Hopi), for example. It is not clear whether all men and women attempted to syncretize different cultural traditions in their teaching, as did Horne, Alford, and Standing Bear, but there is every indication that they believed themselves to be productively using their schooling for personal and kin benefit. Chester Yellowhair, a Navajo, learned silversmithing at Albuquerque Indian School. Later he taught this art to pupils at other Indian schools and helped found the Navajo Arts and Crafts Guild. Similarly, Fred Kabotie gained respect and financial reward from white society for his paintings of Hopi ceremonialism; he too returned to his people to teach and helped found the Hopi Cultural Center. Angel DeCora, who illustrated the cover of the first edition of La Flesche's *Middle Five*, emphasized in her curriculum vitae the many white schools she attended. She then secured a job teaching Indian arts and crafts at Carlisle, as the curriculum became slightly less ethnocentric in the early twentieth century.[57]

Apaches who had no interest in farming or sheepherding, took to cattle ranching, and what they learned at Carlisle helped them make the most of the poor land of their reservation. Jim Whitewolf also felt that farming instruction later helped him in his vocation. Ada Damon was one of many ex-pupils who ended up working for the BIA, in her case as a cook at Navajo schools. Jonas Keeble has left a warm account of how he turned the bricklaying skills he learned at the Genoa School into a vocation, and more: he and his son did "some wonderful work—all over, even in North Dakota and around Aberdeen."[58]

Keeble also joined the state militia; many others joined the military: James McCarthy (Papago) and Clinton Rickard (Tuscarora), for example. William Cadman actually served as one of the famous Code Talkers during the Pacific War, using the Navajo language to send secret messages.[59] Even if many ex-pupils remained at lower levels in white society or (more likely) worked among their own peoples, none of them ever claimed that their schooling was useless or, even worse, entirely pernicious or destructive.

A few felt that schooling helped them learn to behave more like a "gentleman" and to feel more equal to white people. Alford believed that he had "learned those little details of toilet that were considered essential to the dress of 'a civilized man.'" Further, and probably because of the sanctioned social activities in the schools, he "no longer felt awkward and self-conscious in the society of the opposite sex. I had learned those outward forms of manner that give one a comfortable feeling in the company of well-bred people."[60]

A few others besides Commissioner Parker made the leap into respectable levels of white society. Dr. Charles Eastman is an obvious example, and he found it difficult being both Indian and American. Yet he never publicly regretted the education that allowed him to progress to the relatively high status of physician. Francis La Flesche worked for the American Bureau of Ethnology, cooperated with the famous anthropologist Alice Fletcher (who later adopted him), and helped produce major studies of his own and other Indian people. His *Middle Five*, which covers only a few years in the early 1860s, is one of the classic accounts of Indian boarding school life; sharp but fair, and at times deeply moving.[61]

Others, such as Thomas Alford, Jason Betzinez, and Anna Moore Shaw, found the Christian God at school. Like them, Howard Whitewolf (Comanche, not to be confused with Jim Whitewolf, Kiowa-Apache) believed that Christianity had transformed his life. He also felt that competence in English helped him gain his position as a mission interpreter. In a highly pragmatic vein Whitewolf too declared that adaptability was crucial to survival. Without education, he believed, Indians were like warriors in the old days who used bows and arrows against firearms. They needed to learn business skills too and to become self-reliant. The new tribal leaders would be ex-school students: "These are the people who will lead us,—men and women who are good Christians, who are educated, and who will fight for the Indians."[62]

In summing up what Haskell had meant to her, Lucille Winnie noted that—as the BIA itself admitted—the program was not slanted toward college entrance, but it was "based on the needs of our people at the time." In a statement like that of O'Faolain about the many things he absorbed at his tough Cork school, Winnie believed that Indians "learned what was to be essential to our future": "No foreign languages were taught, but we got a good basic English foundation. . . . Vocational education . . . was offered to the boys, and the girls were trained in homemaking. During our junior year we chose to specialize in home economics, business, or teaching. No matter what course we chose, our training was thorough; we were qualified to go out and make a living." Winnie went on to enjoy a fascinating life, including a stint working for the magnate Howard Hughes and a period in Hawaii, before helping Cheyenne people organize a craft industry. She obviously gained much from Haskell and other BIA schools.[63]

VII

In absolute terms both organizations failed: miraculously, Irish nationalist identities and Native tribal identities along with complementary Pan-Indian identities survived a century of sustained cultural assault by rich and powerful nations. Yet the BIA and CNEI achieved much, even from their own assimilatory perspectives. By the end of the period under review the vast majority of Irish and Indian children were being schooled, generally with the consent of and even the encouragement of their kin. English had become the language of most Irish people, and many Indian languages were even then under threat. More so than in Ireland, it may be valid to claim that schooling played a crucial role in the very physical survival of Indians.

Indeed, for some individuals the school was more than just a way to survive: for Indians such as La Flesche, Eastman, and Sekaquaptewa, and for O'Faolain, Sayers, and some other Irish children, learning became a joy. They really did find themselves transported into fascinating new universes. Many became adept in more than one culture: "150% men/women," to borrow McFee's term.[64] Some became cultural brokers between peoples. They appeared to be the jewels of the system, proof of both Indian and Irish capacity and of the validity of the crusades. Yet for all their enthusiasm, these individuals did not ever fully accept the assimilatory messages of the BIA or the CNEI, nor did most of their schoolmates or their families or larger communities.

"If the boarding school failed to fulfill the [educational] reformers' expectations," writes Adams in a passage also applicable to Indian day schools and to Irish national schools, "it still had a profound impact on an Indian child's psychological and cultural being."[65] For better or for worse, the BIA and the CNEI educational enterprises massively impacted on millions of Indian and Irish boys and girls and on their communities, and they massively changed Indian and Irish life.

Conclusions

Many people felt that the Government was trying to obliterate our culture by making the children attend school . . . the schooling the children have been getting over the past seventy-five or eighty years has educated them to the [outsider's] ways but made them less knowledgeable about the ways of their own people. A lot of what has been taught is good. It makes them able to understand the way the [outsider] thinks, and to compete in the outside world. But at the same time, they aren't getting as much of their own traditions as they should. Something important is gained, but something important is being lost.

These words could have been uttered by either a Native American or by an Irishman or woman, surveying assimilationist schooling in the period under review. Actually they were spoken by Albert Yava, the Tewa-Hopi quoted in the previous chapter as an advocate of pragmatic compromise; the one who realized that, ultimately, the greatest value is survival.[1] The statement reinforces my contention that there has been much to compare between, on the one hand, the BIA and CNEI assimilationist educational campaigns and, on the other, the responses of Indian and Irish peoples.

I

A number of major, overlapping themes emerge from this study that extend the work of historians of Indian and Irish education, and of mass elementary education. These themes also lend weight to Peter Kolchin's three major claims for the importance of comparative history, introduced earlier: it can show how a particular case fits a broader pattern; it can help historians generate new hypotheses; and it can allow us to account for differences within broader patterns.[2]

The *similarity of government assimiliationist educational programs* is, of course, a dominant theme. Although the Irish and the many Indian societies were very different, leading to differences in specific educational policies and practices, the campaigns were fundamentally similar. They also shared similarities with other systems of colonial, imperial, or government education. Indeed—Kolchin's first claim for comparative history—only by making comparisons can we escape parochialism to see beyond the apparently exceptional quality of a particular case and to establish such broader patterns. Historian J. R. Miller's characterization of the campaigns to school Canadian First Peoples is also highly applicable to BIA and CNEI efforts: the educators believed passionately that they "*knew better* than the native communities and their leaders what was in the best interests of dependent groups" (emphasis in original).[3] This cultural hubris is also well expressed by John Willinsky. Turning "the other" into "us" was the goal: "Colonial schooling presumed a right exercised over those to be educated, a right that is present in every educational act yet that represented a special level of presumption in the colonial context."[4] Mass educational campaigns often enshrine privileged views and act against the local culture, be it "savage," peasant, or proletarian. However, systems such as those presented to the Irish and the Indians sought a near-total obliteration of the "deficient" home culture and the assimilation of its children and, through them, its adults into the dominant culture.

Responses to these programs were also strikingly similar, which brings me to my next major theme, *convergence*. By the early nineteenth century only about two-fifths of all Irish children were enrolled at any kind of school, although far more would have known of the institution. Indians also knew more about schools than might be expected, but far fewer tribal children than Irish children had ever been inside one. The difficulties for educators were greater in the vast areas of the United States, and the "cultural distance" between educator and educated was greater there too. Further, large numbers of Indian families faced the more wrenching decision of whether to release their children for attendance at distant boarding schools and of how to respond if children were removed against kin wishes. By 1930, nevertheless, Indian peoples had generally converged with the Irish in their acceptance of mass education.

Explanations for such convergence lead to further themes. The *pragmatism* of Irish and Indian peoples especially impresses. Individuals in local communities sometimes rejected the new schools as threats to traditional values, but more and more came to see them in terms of personal, kin, and group advantage. Few fully accepted the assimilationist goals of the educators; most responded selectively to the programs offered. Although generally from oral cultures, Irish and Indian adults and children came alive to the advantages of literacy and English and exploited the new skills in ways both supportive of and resistant to the goals of their teachers. Today the death of a language is justifiably seen as tragic loss, equivalent almost to the destruction of national or ethnic identity. Yet Irish people en masse decided they could be Irish—and indeed oppose England's rule—through the English language. Many Indians similarly accepted the new language without loss of tribal or Pan-Indian identity. What Willinsky says about colonial mission schools could be generalized to my study as well. Due to the pragmatic responses of local communities, the Irish and American Indian schools also served "as both buffer [against] and supporter for the larger project of imperialism."⁵

Thus *the attraction of schooling* to colonized and dependent peoples constitutes another closely related theme. In some ways the school was very different from traditional, oral, home-centered education. Yet in other ways it was compatible: all peoples institutionalize the education of their children, so the school was merely a new way of doing this. Indeed, it was a complementary way: Irish and Indian peoples did not necessarily see education in either/or terms; they continued to educate their children to traditional values at home too—much to the chagrin of their "uplifters" in both areas. Nevertheless, by 1930 the school had become a fixture of modern life. Although failing in their absolutist assimilationist goals, the BIA and CNEI had convinced target populations of the value of this institution and of some of its curriculum and thus had partly Americanized and Anglicized them.

Another major theme relates to *empowerment*. Confronting the educational establishments of dominant nations, Indian and Irish peoples managed to negotiate some of the results of the campaigns. We must not "over-empower" native children and their home communities, yet the support of local groups was vital. And empowerment should signify more than just resistance: *accommodating to and manipulating the system also constitute empowerment*. If, on the local level, Indian children and adults did just this, on the national level they were far less empowered than the Irish. White "Friends of the Indian" and later reformers exerted influence in Washington, as did individuals and groups of "civilized" Indians. But during these decades there was no Indian equivalent to the Irish Parliamentary Party, or revolutionary Irish nationalism, forcing their agendas into the very heart of the dominant political establishment.

Empowerment often lead to *symbiosis*, to complicated and changing states of mutual dependence. Teachers needed the cooperation of local communities to fill schools and satisfy CNEI inspectors or BIA superintendents; they, in turn, deferred to central authorities—and ultimately to the British Parliament and Congress. Yet Indians and Irish people also became more and more dependent on schools to teach English, reading, and writing, especially, to their children. Gradually all were tied into a "symbiotic embrace" that authorities certainly dominated, but that neither group completely controlled. As Edward Goodbird suddenly realized when his teacher feared to punish him on his return from the Hidatsa scalp dance, they needed each other.

All of this implies that despite the best efforts of the educators, *influences flowed in more than one direction*. I can only suggest here how the schools had "reflex influences," not only the symbiotic ones relating to the world of education, but influences out into and even beyond the dominant societies. By producing generations of literate and English-speaking Irish men and women, the national schools extended influences into every area of Irish life. Ironically, they also helped bring about the end of the Union for Ireland and the demise of its servant, the CNEI. In a transnational context, the influences of millions of ex-pupils on Britain, the wider empire, America, and other nations were also massive and diverse.

Serving a relatively tiny part of the American population, Indian schools had less obvious reflex effects on the broader society. Yet by the 1920s Native peoples had convinced a minority of Americans of at least the partial validity of tribal ways. "Civilized Indians" such as Charles Eastman and Gertrude Bonnin (Zitkala-Ša), along with generations of literate pupils and ex-pupils, some of whom became leaders in their modernizing communities, affected twentieth-century perceptions of and actions toward "The Indian." Had Native peoples not struggled to retain their identities while simultaneously exploiting the school for its adaptive skills, their positions in the United States, and thus the very texture of American life—especially in western and southwestern areas—would have been different. John Collier's Indian New Deal and the whole 1920s reform movement were responses both to the strengths of tribal values and to the apparent failure of Indian schooling. More recent government policies advocating tribal sovereignty and self-determination, also based on respect for Indian cultures, would have evolved in very different ways had the earlier school crusade not occurred.

A strong degree of *ambivalence* characterized many Indian and Irish responses to schooling. Kin sometimes split bitterly on the issue or pulled their offspring from the classroom whenever it suited family needs. The children's responses were also mixed and even conflicting. Pupils showed dislike for some teachers and lifelong respect for others; expressed hatred of some curricular subjects, enjoyment of others. Even the manual labor demands of the Indian boarding schools could elicit ambivalence, with some pupils reacting positively to the work, payment, and sense of responsibility. Such ambivalence often characterized the responses of individuals—such as Haskell student and teacher Essie Horne or Irish writer Sean O'Faolain.

It would be difficult not to be impressed by *the resilience of children* that emerges explicitly in autobiographical accounts, and even through accounts by BIA and CNEI employees. Few children in modern Western society—with the possible exception of immigrants—are forced to function though an unknown language and to absorb (initially) alien cultural knowledge. Few face the challenges of Indian children carried great distances from home to harsh and often ill-equipped boarding schools. Many children suffered, some died, especially at the Indian boarding schools. Huge numbers in both areas survived the early shocks, "got used to it," and occasionally managed to thrive in the bewilderingly new educational environment.

Some became mediators, actively helping peers and authorities, which brings us to *the importance of school children as cultural brokers*, at times more crucial than adults. The strain on individuals and families was evident in many Indian accounts, especially. From Irish sources the brokering does not emerge as clearly, yet Indian instances alerted me to cases of national school pupils either deliberately or unconsciously acting as mediators between cultures. Presumably this approach can be carried into other areas of assimilationist education. "In the great events of life," writes Thomas E. Jordan, "the young tend to play minor roles." Certainly, they have individually significant crises in their lives, "but they are also participants in larger, stressful events in which their experience tends to be slighted."[6] Not in this book, I hope.

Race lacks the centrality that might have been expected. Whatever British people thought of the Irish, the CNEI was entirely staffed by Irish men and women; the commissioners could not have racially denigrated their clients without compromising themselves. I have also argued that race meant less that might have been expected in the Indian schools. Throughout the period under review, white educators sought Indian citizenship, and the ambitious curriculum at big schools impressively reinforced the BIA's claim that it did not regard Indians as racially inferior. There was a downgrading of ambitions around 1900 when the BIA introduced its more "relevant" and vocationally orientated curriculum. Yet, from ex-pupil accounts I have detected little increase in racist mistreatment by teachers during the early twentieth century. Race did matter to many whites but—compared to how African Americans might have been treated in such an educational system—the BIA and Christian missionaries generally worked to assimilate Indians into something close to equality with white people. Ethnocentrism—contempt for Indian cultures—rather than biological racism impelled the BIA and most missionaries. For pupils at the receiving end, it was staff behavior, rather than skin color or race, that counted.

Class obviously had greater salience in the Irish context. Although the majority of teachers probably sprang from the same socioeconomic level as their pupils, the inspectors and the commissioners obviously saw themselves uplifting the masses into bourgeois modernity—but only to a degree. If a few might rise into secondary and higher levels of education, the vast majority of the boys and girls were destined for modest lives, and the curriculum was designed to elevate Irish children without giving them ideas above their stations.

BIA and missionary educators saw their goals more in cultural and—for some—racial terms. That an Indian such as Charles Eastman might become a university graduate and medical doctor of course validated the effort. In a sense, however, Indians were so culturally different that they existed quite outside of conventional class ideas. Yet like their Irish counterparts, most white American educators also saw the mass of Indians as entering civilization near the bottom: "proletarianized" as farmers, laborers, wives, and domestics, and perhaps teachers, with a few fortunate and gifted individuals rising into more elevated social levels.

A further theme relates to the complicated and indeed ironic role of *gender* in the campaigns. Girls were more carefully supervised at Indian schools, and they probably fled and mitched or played truant less in both areas. They were probably less violent than boys, although female narrators also told of being bullied, sometimes physically, by other girls. Even if they shared some of the BIA and CNEI curriculum—especially academic and religious learning—girls and boys ended up learning different subjects and trades in preparation for supposedly civilized gender roles in later life. Irish girls may have more successfully exploited the CNEI curriculum than the boys—especially those girls who later emigrated to the United States.

In particular ways the acculturation process demanded more of one sex, especially at the Indian boarding schools. Cut off from community women during stressful coming-of-age changes, girls especially must have suffered (although, due no doubt to prevalent conventions of modesty, ex-pupils do not report such suffering). Few Irish girls—except perhaps the small minority who boarded at model schools in their teen years and girls who attended secondary boarding schools—faced such challenges. Used to wandering to the berry fields or to tending crops (in tribes that practiced agriculture), the majority of Indian girls confronted the demand that they become "civilized" housewives working *within* the farmhouse—again a more wrenching change in lifestyle than that experienced by most Irish girls. Indian boys sometimes faced even more radically shocking demands, especially those from hunting-gathering and warrior societies. They were generally schooled to become farmers—women's work in many tribes.

Yet boys and girls shared most of the deeply challenging experiences of the assimilationist assault: the trauma of separation from kin, of enrollment, of instruction in an unintelligible language, of school regimen. Both sexes entered the new universe of the curriculum—and all faced some kind of manual work duties at the Indian boarding schools. Both sexes suffered harsh punishments, and both could record the pleasures they took in learning.

Moreover, traditional Indian societies then, along with traditional Irish ru-

ral society (indeed middle-class and urban Irish society too), assumed without question that males and females would live different lives. In other words,
despite all the new *content* of the gendered education presented by Irish and
American authorities, *the central principle* in each area was compatible: children
should be trained to appropriate gender roles. Ironically, the liberated female
lifestyles promised by both the BIA and CNEI actually replaced traditional
kinds of gender demarcations with new kinds. Tribal Indian and nineteenth-
century Irish children would have been far more shocked had the BIA or CNEI
presented egalitarian gendered education—what twenty-first-century Western
educationalists might insist upon—with no distinction whatsoever between
the curriculum for each sex.[7] Whatever the shocks and stresses involved for
individual boys and girls in both areas, then, the very gendered nature of the
BIA and CNEI educational goals implied a fundamental compatibility between old and new forms of education.

The gender of staff was less important to the assimilatory drive and to pupil responses than might have been expected. The motivation of white wom-
en to become teachers was partly different from that of men. Once at school,
female staff probably had a more difficult time because of discrimination and
even outright sexual harassment. Despite the Victorian ideal of nurturing
femininity, ex-pupils did not generally remember female teachers and staff
as being especially nurturing—and certainly not more culturally sensitive or
more aversive to assimilation than their male counterparts. In terms of teachers in both areas, then, and of those whom they taught, gender counted, but
in complicated and less-than-predictable ways.

All of this suggests a further major theme: *complexity*. The best-laid plans
confronted different kinds of human beings, communities, and different
realities when put into practice and were constantly subject to contingency.
Thus the results in America and Ireland were always changing and complex.
Ultimately, as Peter N. Stearns points out with admirable understatement,
mass education in the modern world "did not automatically create the kind of
uniform political base some policymakers sought."[8]

II

A second major function of comparative history, Kolchin believes, is in the
formation and testing of hypotheses. This whole book involved such a testing. David Wallace Adams, Brenda J. Child, K. Tsianina Lomawaima, Clyde
Ellis, and myself, among other historians of Indian schooling, have all in different ways emphasized similar themes to those above. These themes thus
became the basis of hypotheses when I envisaged the present book. Little had

been written for the period under review about Irish pupil responses to the national schools, or of cultural brokering, or empowerment, or symbiosis in Irish contexts. By illustrating so many similarities and some differences between assimilationist schooling in Ireland and Native America, this study has perhaps returned the debt by providing new perspectives on Indian schooling and has shown its distinct but unexceptional nature. Perhaps the book has also suggested further questions and hypotheses to be posed about tribal experiences. Why, like the Irish language, did some Indian languages collapse, whereas others survived into the twentieth century? To what extent do Indians who lost their tribal languages retain powerful ethnic or national identities, as do many Irish people?

Further potentially instructive hypotheses and questions arise out of my study. To what extent were other supposedly dominant colonial educators forced, like the CNEI on the issue of religion and later on cultural issues, to adapt to local realities? In other words, how do we account for differences—Kolchin's third function of comparative history—within broadly similar assimilationist campaigns? More such studies would warn us against assuming either the passive reception by colonized people of programs passed down from above, or the blind rejection of such programs. Reality, as always, tends to be more messy.

I would especially recommend further studies comparing the experiences of Indians at BIA or missionary schools with those who increasingly attended American state public schools from late in the period under review. Scattered comments in my sources suggested that, for all their negative sides, "Indian schools" cushioned pupils from some forms of racial discrimination. Studies comparing Indian boarding schools with Indian day schools, and especially with Irish, English, Canadian, or other boarding school or residential school situations, would be valuable. Further studies comparing aspects of, say, Native American, Irish, African, and Asian responses to colonial education would also be instructive.[9] Not all scholars would agree with my conclusions on gender—this would constitute a further important area of inquiry.

The present comparative study, then, has shown the similarities and the differences between two century-long campaigns of assimilationist government schooling and the responses they generated. By examining the campaigns together we can get beyond our sense of exceptionalism (be it American or Irish) and can attain a kind of three-dimensional perspective on patterns and developments.[10] Although far less striking than the similarities, the differences alert us to what Frederick Cooper has called the "rootedness" of particular developments and warn us against "unwarranted generalizations."[11]

The CNEI, BIA, and missionary enterprises were carefully planned and executed and were breathtaking in their cultural hubris. The responses of recipient peoples were complex, manipulative, and partly appreciative. Government schooling did change the Indians and the Irish and helped them adapt to the demands of modern life—but never in quite the ways intended by their supremely confident educators.

Notes

Introduction

1. I take the term "resonance" from Nancy Scheper-Hughes, "The Best of Two Worlds, the Worst of Two Worlds: Reflections on Culture and Field Work among the Rural Irish and Pueblo Indians," *Comparative Studies in Society and History* 29 (1987): 58. In 2004 I became a dual citizen of Finland and Ireland.

2. Drawing on a 1980 formulation by Harold J. Abramson, historian Russel A. Kazal notes: "I conceive of assimilation as referring to a process that results in greater homogeneity within a society. Such processes may operate at different levels: among individuals, between groups . . . or between groups and a dominant group in society." This later version is the concern of the present study. Although he warns against assuming "a rather static Anglo-Saxon 'core' American society to which one was presumed to assimilate," Kazal also notes: "Assimilation in America amounts to Americanization if it results in the acquisition of a distinct 'American' culture, behavior, or set of values." Again, this is the usage I employ here. See Kazal, "Revisiting Assimilation: The Rise, Fall, and Reappraisal of a Concept in American Ethnic History," *American Historical Review* 100.2 (April 1995): 437–71, with quotations from 438, 470, 439–40. More recently David Crystal defines "cultural assimilation"—my concern throughout—in a similar way: "one culture is influenced by a more dominant culture and begins to lose its character as a result of its members adopting new behaviour and mores . . . language quickly becomes an emblem of that dominance, typically taking the form of a standard or official language associated with the incoming nation." Crystal, *Language Death* (Cambridge: Cambridge University Press, 2000), 77. On Anglicization, see note 5 below.

3. I summarize and document these developments in Michael C. Coleman, *American Indian Children at School, 1850-1930* (Jackson: University Press of Mississippi, 1993), esp. chap. 3. See also note 16, below, and chap. 2 in the present work.

4. I summarize and document these developments in Michael C. Coleman, "'Eyes Big as Bowls with Fear and Wonder': Children's Responses to the Irish National Schools, 1850–1922," *Proceedings of the Royal Irish Academy* 98C.5 (1998): 177–202. See also chap. 2 in the present work.

5. By "Anglicize" I do not mean that Irish people would become totally English; Scottish and Welsh people enjoyed their own cultural variants and subvariants, while remaining loyal British subjects. "Briticize" might thus be a better term; nevertheless I will use the more common "Anglicize/Anglicization" to describe the assimilatory

goals of the Commissioners of National Education in Ireland (CNEI): Irish people might enjoy some cultural distinctions but would become English-speaking subjects of the monarch, loyal to the Union of Great Britain and Ireland. On the complex development of concepts of British subjecthood, citizenship, and nationality see Rieko Karatani, *Defining British Citizenship: Empire, Commonwealth and Modern Britain* (London: Frank Cass, 2003). Under the Union, the Irish were seen as subjects—rather than citizens, a concept that developed later—of the United Kingdom under the Crown. See also Thomas A. Donoghue, *Bilingual Education in Ireland, 1904–1922: The Case of the Bilingual Programme of Instruction*, Centre of Irish Studies Monograph Series no. 1 (Perth, Australia: Murdoch University, 2000), 1–3, especially.

6. For this figure see *Second Report of the Commissioners of Irish Education Inquiry*, H.C., 1826–27 (400), 12, 4. The reference to "cultural distance" I owe to Aiden Coleman. See also John W. Berry, "Immigration, Acculturation, and Adaptation," *Applied Psychology: An International Review* 46.1 (January 1997): 23: "Greater cultural distance implies the need for greater cultural shedding and culture learning, and perhaps large differences trigger negative intergroup attitudes, and induce greater cultural conflict leading to poorer adaptation." I thank Ulla Riikonen for this reference.

7. Peter N. Stearns, *Schools and Students in Industrial Society: Japan and the West, 1870–1940* (Boston: Bedford, 1998); Edmund Burke III, "The Terror and Religion: Brittany and Algeria," in *Colonialism and the Modern World: Selected Studies*, ed. Gregory Blue et al. (Armonk NY: Sharpe, 2002), 40–50; Ann Laura Stoler, "Tense and Tender Ties: The Politics of Comparison in North America and (Post) Colonial Studies," *Journal of American History* 88.3 (December 2001): 829–65, with the quotation from 865. In his reply to Stoler, Robert J. McMahon worries that there may be "an apples-and-oranges quality" to comparisons of developments too radically different. Yet he too accepts that comparing the seemingly incommensurable may be instructive. McMahon, "Culture of Empire," *Journal of American History* 88.3 (December 2001): 889–90, 892.

8. Rachel Adams, "The Worlding of American Studies," *American Quarterly* 53.4 (December 2001): 720–21. Also see Shelly Fisher Fishkin, "Crossroads of Cultures: The Transnational Turn in American Studies—Presidential Address to the American Studies Association, November 12, 2004," *American Quarterly* 57.1 (March 2005): 17–57, along with replies.

9. Michael Adas, "From Settler Colony to Global Hegemon: Integrating the Exceptionalist Narrative of the American Experience into World History," *American Historical Review* 106.5 (December 2001): 1692–1720, with quotations from 1701, 1703–4. And see Kevin Kenny: "If a single theme has dominated the historiography of the United States in the last decade [to 2003], it is the need to extend the boundaries of inquiry beyond the nation-state, to internationalize the subject [of diaspora studies] and make it more cosmopolitan." Kenny, "Diaspora and Comparison: The Global Irish as a Case Study," *Journal of American History* 90.1 (June 2003): 134.

10. For example, Frank Welsh, *The Four Nations: A History of the United Kingdom* (London: HarperCollins, 2002); Jeremy Black, *A History of the British Isles* (New York: St. Martin's Press, 1997); Stephen Howe, *Ireland and Empire: Colonial Legacies in Irish*

History and Culture (Oxford: Oxford University Press, 2000); Adrian Hastings, *The Construction of Nationhood: Ethnicity, Religion, and Nationalism* (Cambridge: Cambridge University Press, 1997), chap. 3 (Hastings adds America to his four-nation comparison in this chapter and actually begins his book with the words of Irish historian John Hutchinson, which I quote in the following paragraph of my introduction); David Crook and Gary McCulloch, "Introduction: Comparative Approaches to the History of Education," *History of Education* 31.5 (2002): 397.

11. John Hutchinson, "Irish Nationalism," in *The Making of Modern Irish History: Revisionism and the Revisionist Controversy*, ed. D. George Boyce and Alan O'Day (London: Routledge, 1996), 101; Kenny, "Diaspora and Comparison."

12. Joe Cleary, *Literature, Partition, and the Nation State: Culture and Conflict in Ireland, Israel, and Palestine* (New York: Cambridge University Press, 2002); Cormac Ó Gráda, *Black '47 and Beyond: The Great Irish Famine in History, Economy, and Memory* (Princeton NJ: Princeton University Press, 1999); Ian S. Lustick, *Unsettled States, Disputed Lands: Britain and Ireland, France and Algeria, Israel and the West Bank-Gaza* (Ithaca NY: Cornell University Press, 1993).

13. Scheper-Hughes, "Best of Two Worlds," 56–75; David Harding, "Objects of English Colonial Discourse: The Irish and Native Americans," *Nordic Irish Studies* 4 (2005): 37–60; Katie Kane, "'Will Come Forth in Tongues of Fury': Relocating Irish Cultural Studies," *Cultural Studies* 15.1 (January 2001): 98–123; and Kane, "Nits Make Lice: Drogheda, Sand Creek, and the Poetics of Colonial Extermination," *Cultural Critique* 42 (Spring 1999): 81–103; Nicholas P. Canny, "The Ideology of English Colonization: From Ireland to America," *William and Mary Quarterly*, 3rd series, no. 30 (October 1973): 575–98; Michael C. Coleman, "Representations of American Indians and the Irish in Educational Reports, 1850s–1920s," *Irish Historical Studies* 33.129 (May 2002): 33–51; and Coleman, "The Responses of American Indian Children and Irish Children to the School, 1850s–1920s: A Comparative Study in Cross-Cultural Education," *American Indian Quarterly* 23:3/4 (Summer and Fall 1999): 83–112.

14. Lustick, *Unsettled States*, 47, for example, and chap. 2.

15. Peter Kolchin, "The Big Picture: A Comment on David Brion Davis's 'Looking at Slavery from Broader Perspectives,'" *American Historical Review* 105.2 (April 2000): 467–71. See also Crook and McCulloch, "Introduction"; Jurgen Kocka, "Comparison and Beyond," *History and Theory* 42 (February 2003): 39–44.

16. Besides my own work, see, for example, works by David Wallace Adams, John Bloom, Brenda J. Child, David H. DeJong, Clyde Ellis, Frederick E. Hoxie, Donal F. Lindsey, T. Tsianina Lomawaima, Sally McBeth, Joel Pfister, Francis Paul Prucha, S.J., John Rehner and Jeanne Eder, Scott Riney, Ruth Spack, and Margaret Connell Szasz. (These works are repeatedly cited in the present work; see also American Sources: Secondary Sources in the bibliographical note).

17. Again, apart from my own work, see studies by, for example, Donald Akenson, Barry M. Coldrey, John Coolahan, Mary Daly, David Dickson, P. J. Dowling, Sean Farren, Adrian Kelly, John Logan, Mary Peckham Magray, Antonia McManus, Janet Nolan, Thomas A. O'Donoghue, and E. Brian Titley. (These works are cited in later chapters; see also Irish Sources: Secondary Sources in the bibliographical note.)

18. Stearns, *Schools and Students*; David Vincent, *The Rise of Mass Literacy: Reading and Writing in Modern Europe* (Cambridge UK: Polity, 2000); John Willinsky, *Learning to Divide the World: Education of Empire's End* (Minneapolis: University of Minnesota Press, 1998); Andy Green, *Education and State Formation: The Rise of Education Systems in England, France and the U.S.A.* (London: Macmillan, 1990).

19. Willinsky, *Learning to Divide the World*, esp. chap. 5, with quotation from 95.

20. Recent scholarship on Christian missionaries has emphasized the complexity of their relationships not only to non-Western peoples but also to their own variants of Western culture, along with the unpredictability, diversity, and pragmatism of "native" responses to elements of Christianity and modernity. Yet, in my view, the broad picture of missionary educational attempts to transform "deficient" cultures still remains valid. See, for example, Ryan Dunch, "Beyond Cultural Imperialism: Cultural Theory, Christian Missions, and Global Modernity," *History and Theory* 41 (October 2002): 301–25; Andrew Porter, "Church History, History of Christianity, Religious History: Some Reflections on British Missionary Enterprise since the Late Eighteenth Century," *Church History* 71.3 (September 2002): 555–84; and Porter, "'Cultural Imperialism' and Protestant Missionary Enterprise, 1780–1914," *Journal of Imperial and Commonwealth History* 25.3 (September 1997): 367–91; Peggy Brock, "Mission Encounters in the Colonial World: British Columbia and South-West Australia," *Journal of Religious History* 24.2 (June 2000): 159–79; "The Missionary Impulse in United States History," special issue, *Church History* 72.4 (December 2003).

21. See esp. Michael C. Coleman, "The Historical Credibility of American Indian Autobiographical Accounts of Schooling," *Irish Journal of American Studies* 3 (1994): 127–50.

22. Edwin Amenta, "What We Know about the Development of Social Policy: Comparative and Historical Research in Comparative and Historical Perspective," in *Comparative Historical Analysis in the Social Sciences*, ed. James Mahoney and Dietrich Reuschemeyer (Cambridge: Cambridge University Press, 2003), 95; Dietrich Reuschemeyer, "Can One or a Few Cases Yield Theoretical Gains?" in Mahoney and Reuschemeyer, *Comparative Historical Analysis*, 305–36; Kocka, "Comparison and Beyond," 44.

23. George M. Frederickson, *The Comparative Imagination: On the History of Racism, Nationalism, and Social Movements* (Berkeley: University of California Press, 1997), 67.

1. Education in Native America and Ireland to the 1820s

1. *Fourteenth Report of the Commissioners for Inquiring into the State of All Schools, on Public or Charitable Foundations, in Ireland* (1812; hereafter cited as *Fourteenth Report*), appendix A to *Second Report of the Commissioners of National Education in Ireland* (1835), in *Reports of the Commissioners of National Education in Ireland from the Year 1835–1845, Inclusive*, vol. 1 (Dublin: CNEI, 1851): 25.

2. *Second Report of the Commissioners of Irish Education Inquiry*, H.C., 1826–27, vol. 12:4; Graham Balfour, *The Educational Systems of Great Britain and Ireland*, 2nd ed. (Oxford: Clarendon, 1903), 79. A tiny number of these schools may have been of "intermediate"

or secondary level; as late as 1871 there were only 574 such schools in Ireland. John Coolahan, *Irish Education: Its History and Structure* (Dublin: Institute of Government Administration, 1981), 59–60.

3. Michael C. Coleman, *American Indian Children at School, 1850–1930* (Jackson: University Press of Mississippi, 1993), 39.

4. Balfour, *Educational Systems*, 79; Peter N. Stearns, *Schools and Students in Industrial Society: Japan and the West, 1740–1940* (Boston: Bedford, 1998), 1, 10–12.

5. First two quotations from Brenda J. Child, *Boarding School Seasons: American Indian Families, 1900–1940* (Lincoln: University of Nebraska Press, 1998), 74, 78 (Child is a Minnesota Ojibwe); Richard Henry Pratt, *Battlefield and Classroom: Four Decades with the American Indian, 1867–1904*, ed. Robert M. Utley (Lincoln: University of Nebraska Press, 1964), 222.

6. Margaret Connell Szasz, *Indian Education in the American Colonies, 1607–1783* (Albuquerque: University of New Mexico Press, 1988), 17–18.

7. F. Niyi Akinnaso, "Schooling, Language, and Knowledge in Literate and Nonliterate Societies," *Comparative Studies in Society and History* 34.1 (January 1992): 68–109, with quotation from 81. In contrast, Akinnaso sees the following as characteristic of informal education: particularism, contextualization, observation, imitation (78). Ray Willis defines institutions as "patterns of behavior which persist and crytallize . . . to which people become attached as a result of their role in the formation of identity, or through investments of energy and social interests." Such patterns are "always in the course of formation, negotiation, and decline." See "institutions" in Adam Kuper and Jessica Kuper, eds., *The Social Science Encyclopedia*, 2nd ed. (London: Routledge and Kegan Paul, 1996), 417.

8. Akinnaso, "Schooling, Language, and Knowledge," 102.

9. Jean Barman, Yvonne Hebert, and Don McCaskill, "The Legacy of the Past: An Overview," in *Indian Education in Canada*, ed. Jean Barman et al., vol. 1: *The Legacy* (Vancouver: University of British Columbia Press, 1986), 1.

10. I draw especially on the following accounts: Coleman, *American Indian Children at School*, chap. 2; Szasz, *Indian Education in the American Colonies*, chap. 1; George A. Pettitt, *Primitive Education in North America*, Publications in American Archaeology and Ethnology, 43.1 (Berkeley: University of California Press, 1946); Fabio Pittaluga, "Between Two Worlds: Kiowa and Kiowa-Apache Educational Institutions and American Schools, 1880–1900," *European Review of Native American Studies* 16.2 (2002): 11–19. For a useful short account, in the context of the childhoods of other ethnic groups, see Joseph E. Illick, *American Childhoods* (Philadelphia: University of Pennsylvania Press, 2000), esp. chap. 1 on American Indian childhoods.

11. See Szasz, *Indian Education in the American Colonies*, esp. 11–17. Generalizing across Indian tribes, Choctaw historian Devon A. Mihesuah writes that in precontact times (which for many tribes ran into the early nineteenth century) "men and women performed tasks specific to gender. . . . Although the duties were different, none was inferior to the other"—a form of equality changed by white intrusions, she believes. See Mihesuah, *Indigenous American Women: Decolonization, Empowerment,*

Activism (Lincoln: University of Nebraska Press, 2003), 42, and chap. 6. See also Theda Perdue, ed., *Sifters: Native American Women's Lives* (New York: Oxford University Press, 2001): "men and women led remarkably separate lives in most Native societies," yet their different duties were "complementary" (1). The gendered bifurcation of tribal life is apparent from the Indian autobiographies that I have examined from this book. On the "third gender" Berdache or "two-spirited people," see Betty Bell, "Gender in Native America," in *A Companion to American Indian History*, ed. Philip J. Deloria and Neal Salisbury (Malden MA: Blackwell, 2002), 317–18.

12. Donald L. Fixico, *The American Indian Mind in a Linear World: American Indian Studies and Traditional Knowledge* (New York: Routledge, 2003), 92. See esp. chap. 5 in which Fixico compares tribal and school approaches to education, in light of cyclical Indian ways of thought compared to linear Euro-American ways. Fixico was raised in Seminole and Muscogee Creek traditions (xi).

13. Pittaluga, "Between Two Worlds," 12; Henrietta Mann, *Cheyenne-Arapaho Education, 1871–1982* (Niwot: University Press of Colorado, 1997), 13–16.

14. Pettitt, *Primitive Education*, 4; Szasz, *Indian Education in the American Colonies*, 11.

15. Mann, *Cheyenne-Arapaho Education*, 14–16; Luther Standing Bear, *Land of the Spotted Eagle* (1933; rpt., Lincoln: University of Nebraska Press, 1978), 1–2, on relationship with mother; Standing Bear, *My People the Sioux*, ed. E. A. Brininstool (1928; rpt., Lincoln: University of Nebraska Press, 1975), 60–67, 141, on relationship with father; Irene Stewart, *A Voice in Her Tribe: A Navajo Woman's Own Story*, ed. Doris Ostrander Dawdy, with Mary Shepardson, Anthropological Papers no. 17 (Socorro NM: Ballena Press, 1980), 43; Zitkala-Ša, *American Indian Stories* (1921; rpt., Lincoln: University of Nebraska Press, 1986), 18–21.

16. Polingaysi Qoyawayma (Elizabeth Q. White), *No Turning Back: A True Account of a Hopi Indian Girl's Struggle to Bridge the Gap between the World of Her People and the World of the White Man, as Told to Vada F. Carlson* (Albuquerque: University of New Mexico Press, 1964), 90–91; Charles Eastman, *Indian Boyhood* (1930; rpt., NY: Dover, 1971), 11–16; 43–49. See also Raymond Wilson, *Ohiyesa: Charles Eastman, Santee Sioux* (Urbana: University of Illinois Press, 1983); "'Indian for a While': Charles Eastman's Indian Boyhood and the Discourse on Allotment," *American Indian Quarterly* 25.4 (Fall 2001): 604–25.

17. Pittaluga, "Between Two Worlds," 12, 15; James Kaywaykla, *In the Days of Victotio: Recollections of a Warm Springs Apache*, ed. Eve Ball (Tucson: University of Arizona Press, 1970), 8; Eastman, *Indian Boyhood*, 64–69; Allen James, *Chief of the Pomos: Life Story of Allen James*, ed. Ann M. O'Connor (Santa Rosa CA: privately printed, 1972), 15.

18. Jim Whitewolf, *Jim Whitewolf: The Life of a Kiowa Apache Indian*, ed. Charles S. Brant, 48–50 (New York: Dover, 1969); Pittaluga, "Between Two Worlds," 12. Also, Peter LeClair, "Peter LeClair—Northern Ponca: An Autobiographical Sketch with an Introduction and Comments by James H. Howard," *American Indian Tradition* 8 (1961): 18.

19. Anna Moore Shaw, *A Pima Past* (Tucson: University of Arizona Press, 1974), 50–52; Jason Betzinez, with William Sturtevant Nye, *I Fought with Geronimo* (1959; rpt., Lincoln: University of Nebraska Press, 1987), 82–83; Mourning Dove, *Mourning Dove: A Salishan Autobiography*, ed. Jay Miller (Lincoln: University of Nebraska Press, 1990, chap. 2.

20. Pittaluga, "Between Two Worlds," 15–16; Alice C. Fletcher and Francis La Flesche, *The Omaha Tribe*, vol. 2 (1911; rpt., Lincoln: University of Nebraska Press, 1972): chap. 11; E. Adamson Hoebel, *The Cheyennes: Indians of the Great Plains* (New York: Holt, Rinehart and Winston, 1960), chap. 3; Standing Bear, *Land of the Spotted Eagle*, 41–45. Also Albert Yava, *Big Falling Snow: A Tewa-Hopi Indian's Life and Times and the History and Traditions of His People*, ed. Harold Courlander (Albuquerque: University of New Mexico Press, 1978), 1–2, 72.

21. Anonymous, "The Narrative of a Southern Cheyenne Woman," Smithsonian Miscellaneous Collections, ed. Truman Michelson, vol. 8, no. 5 (1932): 9; also, Standing Bear, *Land of the Spotted Eagle*, 147; Mary Little Bear Inkanish, *Dance around the Sun: The Life of Mary Little Bear Inkanish: Cheyenne*, ed. Alice Marriot and Carol H. Rachlin (New York: Crowell, 1977), 9.

22. Francis La Flesche, *The Middle Five: Indian Schoolboys of the Omaha Tribe* (1900; rpt., Madison: University of Wisconsin Press, 1963), xvi. For a study of La Flesche, see Sherry L. Smith, "Francis La Flesche and the World of Letters," *American Indian Quarterly* 25.4 (Fall 2001): 579–603. See also comment by late-twentieth-century Navajo leader Peter McDonald, quoted in Fixico, *American Indian Mind*, 90. Compare the statements of ethnologist La Flesche and McDonald to that quoted in the text below by a Breton anthropologist about his own earlier life, which similarly conveys a sense of how much supposedly "uneducated" children had to learn.

23. "Humility is an important Hopi ideal," writes Peter M. Whitely, "though not all live up to it." Whitely, *Deliberate Acts: Changing Hopi Culture through the Oraibi Split* (Tucson: University of Arizona Press, 1988), 180–81; Yava, *Big Falling Snow*, 3; Charles A. Eastman, *Indian Boyhood* (1902; rpt. New York: Dover), 4 and chap. 5; Eastman, *From Deep Woods to Civilization: Chapters in the Autobiography of an Indian* (1916; rpt., Lincoln: University of Nebraska Press, 1977), 22; Luther Standing Bear, *My Indian Boyhood* (1931; rpt., Lincoln: University of Nebraska Press, 1988), 152–57. Also, for example, on naming: Kaywaykla, *In the Days of Victorio*, 28–29; Whitewolf, *Jim Whitewolf*, 39–41, 71; Pettitt, *Primitive Education*, 50.

24. Thomas Wildcat Alford, *Civilization, and the Story of the Absentee Shawnees, as Told to Florence Drake* (Norman: University of Oklahoma Press, 1936), 21.

25. Kay Bennett, *Kaibah: Recollections of a Navajo Girlhood* (Los Angeles: Westernlore Press, 1964), 124–25; Szasz, *Indian Education in the American Colonies*, 22.

26. Don Talayesva, *Sun Chief: The Autobiography of a Hopi Indian*, ed. Leo W. Simmons (New Haven CT: Yale University Press, 1942), 51; Dorothy Eggan, "Instruction and Effect in Hopi Cultural Continuity," in *Education and Culture: Anthropological Approaches*, ed. George D. Spindler (New York: Holt, Rinehart and Winston, 1964), 331–32.

27. Alford, *Civilization*, 21; John Stands in Timber and Margot Liberty, *Cheyenne Memories* (1967; rpt., Lincoln: University of Nebraska Press, 1972), 63; Shaw, *Pima Past*, 28. Also, Helen Sekaquaptewa, *Me and Mine: The Life Story of Helen Sekaquaptewa, as told to Louise Udall* (Tucson: University of Arizona Press, 1969), 109–17; Bennett, *Kaibah*, 153–54.

28. Whitewolf, *Jim Whitewolf*, 48. Kiowa Apache parents sometimes asked school

authorities to whip their children, another case of calling on outsiders to adminis-
ter discipline. Charles S. Brant, introduction to Whitewolf, *Jim Whitewolf*, 29; Edward
Goodbird, *Goodbird the Indian: His Story*, ed. Gilbert L. Wilson (1914; rpt., St. Paul:
Minnesota Historical Society Press, 1985), 17–18; Talayesva, *Sun Chief*, 79–87.

29. Asa Daklugie et al., *Indeh: An Apache Odyssey*, ed. Eve Ball (Norman: University of
Oklahoma Press, 1988), 144.

30. Two Leggings, *Two Leggings: The Making of a Crow Warrior*, ed. Peter Nabokov
(Lincoln: University of Nebraska Press, 1967), 115, 269–71; Kaywaykla, *In the Days of
Victorio*, 131–32, for example; Mourning Dove, *Mourning Dove*, 79–81; Stands in Timber
and Liberty, *Cheyenne Memories*, 102; Black Eagle, "Xube, a Ponca Autobiography," ed.
William Whitman, *Journal of American Folklore* 52 (April–June 1939): 182.

31. Bennett, *Kaibah*, 133–34. The tribal work ethic is a central theme in the accounts
in Broderick H. Johnson, ed., *Stories of Traditional Navajo Life and Culture*, by Twenty-Two
Navajo Men and Women (Tsaile, Navajo Nation AZ: Navajo College Community Press,
1977); see 184 for slacking off; Shaw, *Pima Past*, 139; Daklugie et al., *Indeh*, 86.

32. Myrtle Begay, in Johnson, *Stories of Traditional Navajo Life*, 59; Kaywaykla, *In the
Days of Victorio*, 76. Also see Daklugie et al., *Indeh*, 146.

33. Anthony F. C. Wallace, *The Death and Rebirth of the Seneca* (New York: Vintage,
1972), 34, plus the entire section "The Ideal of Autonomous Responsibility," 30–39.
Wallace also notes that the Seneca theory of child raising, with its acceptance of per-
missiveness, "was not taken for granted . . . on the contrary, it was very explicitly
recognized, discussed, and pondered" (39).

34. David E. Jones, *Sanapia: Comanche Medicine Woman* (1972; rpt., Prospect Heights
IL: Waveland Press, 1984), xi, 21–22; Rosalio Moisés, Jane Holden Kelley, and William
Curry Holden, *A Yaqui Life: The Personal Chronicle of a Yaqui Indian* (Lincoln: University
of Nebraska Press, 1971), 37; Whitewolf, *Jim Whitewolf*, 46–50; Pittaluga, "Between
Two Worlds," esp. 13–14; Mann, *Cheyenne-Arapaho Education*, 14. On "myth revision"
see also Peter Nabokov, *A Forest of Time: Indian Ways of History* (New York: Cambridge
University Press, 2002), chap. 3.

35. For a brief, recent account of colonial missionary schooling, see Jon Reyner and
Jeanne Eder, *American Indian Education: A History* (Norman: University of Oklahoma
Press, 2004), chap. 1.

36. For an illustration of the Massachusetts seal, see Szasz, *Indian Education in the
American Colonies*, 84. Much of the present section draws on this major study and also
on Richard W. Cogley, *John Eliot's Mission to the Indians before King Philip's War* (Cambridge
MA: Harvard University Press, 1999); James Axtell, *The Invasion Within: The Contest of
Cultures in Colonial North America* (New York: Oxford University Press, 1985).

37. Historians have seen Eliot and other missionaries as cultural aggressors, but
Cogley points to the missionary's relative tolerance of Native lifestyles and his attempts to protect his charges. Cogley claims that "on balance, proselytes were better
off materially after the birth of the mission than they were during the early settlement
period," when they faced the new colonists without a missionary protective barrier.
Cogley, *John Eliot's Mission*, with quotation from 245.

38. See Szasz, *Indian Education in the American Colonies*. For fascinating glimpses into Indian pupil responses to English schooling see James Dow McCullum, ed., *The Letters of Eleazar Wheelock's Indians* (Hanover NH: Dartmouth College, 1932).

39. Axtell, *Invasion Within*, 273–75. Axtell estimates that French Jesuits in Canada may have converted over 10,000 Indian peoples, yet, he concedes, "by no means did they enjoy universal or permanent success in converting the Indians to Christianity" (279); Szasz, 261–62.

40. Kenneth Scott Latourette, *The Great Century in Europe and the United States of America: AD 1800–AD 1914*, vol. 4 of *A History of the Expansion of Christianity* (New York: Harper, 1941).

41. History of the American Board of Commissioners for Foreign Missions (hereafter ABCFM) can be followed in ABCFM, *First Ten Annual Reports . . . 1810–1820* (Boston, ABCFM, 1834), and ABCFM, *Annual Report* (Boston: ABCFM, 1821–40); Coleman, *American Indian Children*, 40–41; and Coleman, "American Indian School Pupils as Cultural Brokers: Cherokee Girls at Brainerd Mission, 1828–1829," in *Between Indian and White Worlds: The Cultural Broker*, ed. Margaret Connell Szasz (Norman: University of Oklahoma Press, 1994). On the Indians' trip to St. Louis in 1831, see Michael C. Coleman, *Presbyterian Missionary Attitudes toward American Indians, 1837–1893* (Jackson: University of Mississippi Press, 1985), 69. See also Albert Furtwangler, *Bringing Indians to the Book* (Seattle: University of Washington Press, 2005).

42. See Fergal McGrath, *Education in Ancient and Medieval Ireland* (Dublin: Studies "Special Publications," 1979); Raymond Gillespie, "Church, State, and Education in Early Modern Ireland," in *O'Connell: Education, Church, and State*, ed. Maurice R. O'Connell (Dublin: Institute of Public Administration, 1992), 40–59.

43. John Logan, "Governesses, Tutors, and Parents: Domestic Education in Ireland, 1700–1880," *Irish Educational Studies* 7.2 (1988): 1–19. Also, Logan, "The Dimensions of Gender in Nineteenth-Century Schooling," in *Gender Perspectives in 19th Century Ireland: Public and Private Perspectives*, ed. Margaret Kelleher and James H. Murphy (Dublin: Irish Academic Press, 1997), 36–49; Antonia McManus, *The Irish Hedge School and Its Books, 1695–1931* (Dublin: Four Courts Press, 2002).

44. I base this statement on the autobiographical accounts and reminiscences I examined for this book; see also, for example, Kelleher and Murphy, *Gender Perspectives in 19th Century Ireland*; David Fitzpatrick, "'A Share of the Honeycomb': Education, Emigration and Irishwomen," in *The Origins of Popular Literacy in Ireland: Language Change and Educational Development*, ed. Mary Daly and David Dickson (Dublin: Department of Modern History, Trinity College, Dublin, and Department of Modern History, University College Dublin, 1990), 167–87.

45. Micheál O'Guiheen, *A Pity Youth Does Not Last: Reminiscences of the Last Blasket Island Poet*, trans. Tim Enright (New York: Oxford University Press, 1982), chaps. 7, 29, with quotations from 25, 104; Colin Heywood, *A History of Childhood: Children and Childhood in the West from Medieval to Modern Times* (Cambridge UK: Polity Press, 2001), 88 (on apprenticeships, for example, see 127–28, 156–60).

46. Patrick Bradley, *While I Remember* (Dublin: Brown and Nolan, n.d.), 62–66;

R. B. Robson, *Autobiography of an Ulster Teacher* (Belfast: n.p., 1935), 20–22; William O'Malley, *Glancing Back: 70 Years' Experiences and Reminiscences of a Press Man, Sportsman and Member of Parliament* (London: Wright and Brown, [1933?]), 152–53.

47. Heywood, *History of Childhood*, 160; David Vincent, *The Rise of Mass Literacy: Reading and Writing in Modern Society* (Cambridge UK: Polity, 2000), 55, for the Breton anthropologist's comment. His name was Pierre-Jakez Hélias. According to Vincent, "his journey through the French education system of the early twentieth century made him sharply aware of the features of his childhood which had remained unchanged since the Middle Ages."

48. Logan, "Governesses," 11.

49. Peter O'Leary, *My Story by Peter O'Leary*, trans. C. T. O'Céirin (Cork: Mercier Press, 1970), 54; Michael McGowan, *The Hard Road to Klondike*, trans. Valentin Iremonger (London: Routledge and Kegan Paul, 1962), 11–12; Irish Folklore Collection, vol. 1506:367–68 (hereafter IFC 1506:367–68). UCD Delargy Centre for Irish Folklore and the National Folklore Collection, University College Dublin. Reproduced with permission of the head of the department. This collection has recently been renamed the National Folklore Collection. But after consultation with the Delargy Centre I have decided to continue with the older, better known, and more specific form, Irish Folklore Collection (IFC). Interviews were conducted in the 1930s, and as the informant is referring to schools of seventy years ago, the passage probably refers to the decades after the mid-nineteenth century. The "first book" probably refers to the first reader of the CNEI.

50. John Coolahan, "Primary Education as a Political Issue in O'Connell's Time," in *O'Connell*, ed. O'Connell, 88.

51. *First Report of the Commissioners of Irish Education Inquiry*, H.C. 1825 (400), vol. 12:3–5, appendix, 14–15 (hereafter cited as *First Report*); Gillespie, "Church, State," 41–42; Donal H. Akenson, *The Irish Education Experiment: The National System of Education in the Nineteenth Century* (London: Routledge and Kegan Paul, 1970), 24–25. For sixteenth- to eighteenth-century contexts, see Tony Crowley, *War of Words: The Politics of Language in Ireland, 1537-2004* (Oxford: Oxford University Press, 2005), chaps. 2–4.

52. *First Report*, 3–4.

53. *First Report*, 4; Gillespie, "Church, State," 46–49; Akenson, *Irish Educational Experiment*, 27–29.

54. McManus, *Irish Hedge School*, 17–22; Gillespie, "Church, State"; Akenson, *Irish Education Experiment*, chap. 2.

55. Goals of Kildare Place Society quoted in Coolahan, "Primary Education," 89; also see the entire chapter. Also see Coolahan, *Irish Education*, 10–12; McManus, *Irish Hedge School*, 47–53, 63–68, and chap. 7; Akenson, *Irish Educational Experiment*, 91; Desmond Bowen, *The Protestant Crusade in Ireland, 1800-70: A Study of Protestant-Catholic Relations between the Act of Union and Disestablishment* (Dublin: Gill and Macmillan, 1978); Kenneth Milne, *The Irish Charter Schools, 1730-1830* (Dublin: Four Courts Press, 1997); Michael C. Coleman, "'The Children Are Used Wretchedly': Pupil Responses to the Irish Charter Schools in the Early Nineteenth Century," *History of Education* 30.4 (July 2001): 339–57.

56. McManus, *Irish Hedge School*, 237.

57. Balfour, *Educational Systems*, 78–82.

58. *First Report*, 4–5; Charles Ivar McGrath, "Securing the Protestant Interest: The Origins and Purpose of the Penal Laws of 1695," *Irish Historical Studies* 30.117 (May 1996): 25–46; Akenson, *Irish Education*, 39–45, with quotation from 40.

59. Akenson, *Irish Education*, 45; McManus, *Irish Hedge School*; J. R. R. Adams, "Swine-Tax and Eat-Him-All-Magee: The Hedge Schools and Popular Education in Ireland," in *Irish Popular Culture, 1650–1850*, ed. James S. Donnelly Jr. and Kerby A. Miller (Dublin: Irish Academic Press, 1998); P. J. Dowling, *The Hedge Schools of Ireland* (Cork: Mercier Press, 1968). Also, *Fourteenth Report*, 29.

60. *First Report*, 4; McManus, *Irish Hedge School*, 131–33; Akenson, *Irish Education*, 51, 377. On literacy, see John Logan, "Sufficient to Their Needs: Literacy and Elementary Schooling in the Nineteenth Century," in *The Origins of Popular Literacy in Ireland: Language Change and Educational Development*, ed. Mary Daly and David Dickson (Dublin: Department of Modern History, Trinity College, Dublin, and Department of Modern History, University College Dublin, 1990), 115; Daly, "Literacy and Language Change in the Late Nineteenth and Early Twentieth Centuries," in *Origins of Popular Literacy*, ed. Daly and Dickson, 154. See also Crowley, *War of Words*, chaps. 4–5.

61. IFC 1194:284–89. For a similar account, IFC 105:237–39. The informant attended a hedge school, sitting on stones around a fire—in a church. See also, for example, IFC 1573:238–40. The informant's father attended a hedge school; IFC 1173:450–51, on the remarkable hedge school teacher, "a man of unsurpassing culture," who later entered the service of the national schools. This man had received from previous hedge school teachers his knowledge of "Classics and Mathematics." Such teachers, the informant believed, "were well able to give instruction in Latin and Greek, Geometry and Algebra, Mensuration, and Bookeeping, Field-surveying and English, History and Astronomy."

62. Dr. Mark F. Ryan, *Fenian Memories* (Dublin: Gill, 1946), 8–9.

63. Lombe Atthil, *Recollections of an Irish Doctor* (London: Religious Tract Society, 1911), 151–52, see also 26.

64. Adams, "Swine Tax," 98, 116; McManus, *Irish Hedge School*, 239–40, and chaps. 3–6. Although McManus is critical of Dowling's noncritical views of the hedge schools (9), her own account is also quite positive.

65. McManus, *Irish Hedge School*, 23–25, 238. She feels that the Great Famine of 1845–48 "put the final nail in the coffin of the hedge schools," although "they lingered on in dwindling numbers until the passing of the Intermediate [education] Act of 1878" (242). Some hedge school teachers later moved into the national system: for example, IFC 1173:450; IFC 616:104.

66. Mary Peckham Magray, *The Transforming Power of the Nuns: Women, Religion, and Cultural Change in Ireland, 1750–1900* (New York: Oxford University Press, 1998), 9; Balfour, *Educational Systems*, 81.

67. Barry M. Coldrey, *Faith and Fatherland: The Christian Brothers and the Development of Irish Nationalism, 1838–1921* (Dublin: Gill and Macmillan, 1988), 22, 89, 109. Also

Coldrey, "'A Most Unenviable Reputation': The Christian Brothers and School Discipline over Two Centuries," *History of Education* 21.3 (1992): 277–89; Balfour, *Educational Systems*, 81.

68. In Ireland, writes Daly, "the spread of literacy generally meant the acquisition of English, in part because both literacy and English were seen as synonymous with modernization, and also because no facilities developed to provide mass literacy through Irish." See Daly, "Literacy and Language Change," in *Origins of Popular Literacy*, ed. Daly and Dickson, 154; Niall Ó Cíosáin, "Printed Popular Literature in Irish, 1750–1850: Presence and Absence," also in *Origins of Popular Literacy*, ed. Daly and Dickson, 45–57. And see comments by McManus, *Irish Hedge Schools*.

69. I use the term "cultural" in the broadest, anthropological sense, implying a whole lifestyle and way of perceiving reality; such a definition also implies that culture is always contested, even within a small population, and always changing.

2. The School as Weapon of State

1. Colin Heywood, *A History of Childhood: Children and Childhood in the West from Medieval to Modern Times* (Cambridge UK: Polity, 2001), 106.

2. John Coolahan, *Irish Education: Its History and Structure* (Dublin: Institute of Public Works, 1981), 3.

3. Assimilation implied a form of citizenship for Indians, as later became explicit in government statements. By about 1820, writes James H. Kettner, "certain central assumptions regularly appeared in discussions of American citizenship," such as the idea of consent and entitlement to certain fundamental privileges and immunities in return for the assumption of duties and responsibilities. There remained much controversy on details, but citizenship basically "constituted membership in a federal community requiring allegiance to nation and state." Kettner, *The Development of American Citizenship, 1608–1870* (Durham: University of North Carolina Press, 1978), 287. See esp. 287–300, on how concepts of dependency and wardship, combined with the idea of separate "national" allegiance to tribe, initially excluded many though not all Native Americans from the status of citizenship. Due to treaty stipulations, congressional acts, the breaking of tribal bonds, or the acceptance of lands in severalty, many Indians became citizens during the nineteenth century (about 3,000 by 1887). The Citizenship Act of 1924 admitted all Indians born within the territorial limits of the United States to citizenship—but by then about two-thirds already possessed this status (300, n. 46). As in the case of African Americans and women, people could be citizens without enjoying full equality with adult white males; see chap. 10, *Development*. Also see U.S. Commissioner for Indian Affairs, *Annual Report of the Commissioner of Indian Affairs* (ARCIA) (Washington DC: Government Printing Office, 1919), 6–8; Jill E. Martin, "'Neither Fish, Flesh, Fowl, nor Good Red Herring': The Citizenship Status of American Indians, 1830–1924," *Journal of the West* 29 (1990): 75–87; David M. Ricci, *Good Citizenship in America* (Cambridge: Cambridge University Press, 2004), parts 1 and 2; Lucy Maddox, *Citizen Indians: Native American Intellectuals, Race, and Reform* (Ithaca NY: Cornell University Press, 2005), esp. 107–14; Devon W.

Carbado, "Racial Naturalization," *American Quarterly* 57.3 (September 2005): 633–58. For an emphasis on the complex rationales for the exclusions of Indians, African Americans, and women from full citizenship, see Rogers M. Smith, *Civic Ideals: Conflicting Visions of Citizenship in U.S. History* (New Haven CT: Yale University Press, 1997). On British ideas of subjecthood see note 5 of the introduction.

4. David Vincent, *The Rise of Mass Literacy: Reading and Writing in Modern Europe* (Cambridge UK: Polity, 2000); Heywood, *History of Childhood*, chap. 9; Peter N. Stearns, *Schools and Students in Industrial Society: Japan and the West, 1870–1940* (Boston: Bedford, 1998); Andy Green, *Education and State Formation: The Rise of Educational Systems in England, France, and the U.S.A.* (London: Macmillan, 1990).

5. Green, *Education and State Formation*, 171, and chap. 5; Barbara Finkelstein, *Governing the Young: Teacher Behavior in Popular Primary Schools in Nineteenth-Century United States* (New York: Falmer Press, 1989), 24; Joel Spring, *The American School: 1642–2000*, 5th ed. (Boston: McGraw-Hill, 2001), 103, and chaps. 6–7.

6. For the text of "this first act of Congress making an appropriation for Indian education," ARCIA (Washington DC: Government Printing Office, 1885), 78–9.

7. Federal Indian policy can be followed in ARCIA. For a critical examination of these developments see, for example, Michael C. Coleman, *American Indian Children at School, 1850–1930* (Jackson: University Press of Mississippi, 1993), esp. 38–41; Margaret Connell Szasz, *Education and the American Indian: The Road to Self-Determination since 1928*, rev. ed. (Albuquerque: University of New Mexico Press, 1999); Francis Paul Prucha, *American Indian Treaties: The History of a Political Anomaly* (Berkeley: University of California Press, 1994); Prucha, *The Great Father: The United States Government and the American Indians*, vols. 1 and 2 (Lincoln: University of Nebraska Press, 1984); Frederick E. Hoxie, *A Final Promise: The Campaign to Assimilate the Indians, 1880–1920* (1984; rpt. with a new preface, Lincoln: University of Nebraska Press, 2001).

8. Theodore Fischbacher, "A Study of the Role of the Federal Government in the Education of the American Indian (PhD diss., Arizona State University, 1967), 89–92, 123–25; ARCIA (Washington DC: Government Printing Office, 1888), xxi–iv. See chap. 5, section III.

9. Fischbacher, "Study of the Role," 68–70. See also Prucha, *Great Father*, 2: appendix D, 1227–29.

10. Prucha, *Great Father*, 1:152–53; ARCIA (1905), H. Doc., vol. 19, 59th Cong., 1st sess., serial 4959, 34–35.

11. Article II of the Constitution states: "He [the President] shall have Power, by and with the Advice and Consent of the Senate, to make Treaties, provided two thirds of the Senators present concur." See Prucha, *American Indian Treaties*, esp. chap. 3, and appendix A, esp. 432–39.

12. Prucha, *American Indian Treaties*, esp. 9–14, with quotations from 226, 9, 12. "The general rule is that a treaty is a formal agreement between two or more sovereign and recognized states operating in an international forum, negotiated by officially designated commissioners and ratified by the governments of the signatory powers" (2).

13. For the full texts of all Indian treaties, see Charles J. Kappler, comp. and ed.,

Indian Affairs: Laws and Treaties, vol. 2 (Washington DC: Government Printing Office, 1904); hereafter cited as Kappler, Laws and Treaties: 764–67, 843–48, 977–82, 1024–25. Available at http://digital.library.okstate.edu/kappler/ (accessed June 23, 2006); ARCIA (1885), H. Exec. Doc., no. 1, part 5, vol. 1, 49th Congress, serial 2378, 80. Of 367 treaties ratified before 1871, there were 120 that contained educational provisions. See John Reyhner and Jeanne Eder, American Indian Education: A History (Norman: University of Oklahoma Press, 2004), 42.

14. Kappler, Laws and Treaties, 2:843–48, 1024–25.

15. On the ending of the process, along with treaty substitutes—bilateral agreements, unilateral statutes, and executive orders—see Prucha, American Indian Treaties, chaps. 12–14, with quotation from 17.

16. On the Cherokees see, for example, ABCFM, Annual Report (1817), in First Ten Annual Reports of the American Board of Commissioners for Foreign Missions (Boston: ABCFM, 1834), 153–58 (hereafter, ABCFM AR, followed by date); William G. McLoughlin, Cherokees and Missionaries, 1789–1839 (New Haven CT: Yale University Press, 1984). On Choctaws see Michael C. Coleman, Presbyterian Missionary Attitudes toward American Indians, 1837–1893 (Jackson: University Press of Mississippi, 1985), 13–14, 58–62.

17. Fischbacher, "Role of the Federal Government," 65–67.

18. McLoughlin, Cherokees and Missionaries, 132.

19. I deal with BIA and CNEI curricula in detail in chap. 5.

20. ABCFM AR (1821), 49; Clyde Ellis, To Change Them Forever: Indian Education at the Rainy Mountain Boarding School, 1893–1920 (Norman: University of Oklahoma Press, 1996), 3. I return to this subject in chap. 8.

21. Cherokee Nation v. Georgia, 1831, in Francis Paul Prucha, ed., Documents of United States Indian Policy (Lincoln: University of Nebraska Press, 2000), 57–59.

22. Coleman, American Indian Children, 40–41. On the education systems built by the Five Civilized Tribes in Oklahoma, which were taken over in 1906 by the federal government, see Report of the Superintendent of Schools for Indian Territory, ARCIA, Reports of the Department of the Interior (Washington DC: Government Printing Office, 1907), 349–55. For an account of an Indian-promoted institution in one of the Five Civilized Tribes see Amanda J. Cobb, Listening to Our Grandmothers' Stories: The Bloomfield Academy for Chickasaw Females, 1852–1949 (Lincoln: University of Nebraska Press, 2000).

23. ARCIA (1870), H. Exec. Doc., no. 1, 41st Cong., 3rd sess., serial 1449, 474; Robert H. Keller Jr., American Protestantism and United States Indian Policy, 1869–82 (Lincoln: University of Nebraska Press, 1983); Prucha, Great Father, vol. 1: chap. 20. See also Elizabeth Tooker, "Ely S. Parker, Seneca, 1828–1895," in American Indian Intellectuals of the Nineteenth and Early Twentieth Centuries, ed. Margot Liberty (1978; rpt. with new preface, Norman: University of Oklahoma Press, 2002), 18–37.

24. ARCIA (1872), H. Exec. Doc., no. 1, part 5, 42nd Cong., 2nd sess., serial 1560, 460–62, with quotation from ARCIA (1870), H. Exec. Doc., no. 1, 41st Congress, 3rd sess., serial 1449, 474.

25. For example, Keller, American Protestantism, 206.

26. ARCIA (1889), in *The American Indian and the United States: A Documentary History*, ed. Wilcomb E. Washburn (New York: Random House: 1973), 1:432–33. I base these broad generalizations upon a wide range of primary and secondary materials, such as ARCIA and appended reports by agents, school staff, and missionaries; correspondence and other material cited throughout this book, held in, esp. RG (Record Group) 75 in the National Archives (see American Sources: Archival Sources, in the bibliographical note); and numerous secondary works by scholars such as Michael C. Coleman, Francis Paul Prucha, Frederick E. Hoxie, David Wallace Adams, Brenda J. Child, Margaret Connell Szasz, K. Tsianina Lomawaima, Clyde Ellis, John Bloom, Sally McBeth, and others (see American Sources: Secondary Sources, in the bibliographical note).

27. See Richard Henry Pratt, *Battlefield and Classroom: Four Decades with the American Indian, 1867–1904*, ed. Robert M. Utley (1964; rpt., Lincoln: University of Nebraska Press, 1987); also Pratt's reports on Carlisle in the yearly ARCIA; autobiographical accounts by ex-students, discussed later in present study; Coleman, *American Indian Children*, 42–44.

28. ARCIA (1900), H. Doc., no. 5, 56th Cong., 2nd sess., serial 4101, 15–16.

29. On "outing" see ibid., 30–32; Pratt, *Battlefield and Classroom*, chap. 27; Robert A. Trennert Jr., "From Carlisle to Phoenix: The Rise and Fall of the Indian Outing System, 1878–1930," *Pacific Historical Review* 52 (August 1983): 267–91. As I demonstrate, many ex-students recalled outing experiences. Last quotation from C. Robinson, *Report of School at Lawrence, Kansas, ARCIA* (Washington DC: Government Printing Office, 1988), 262.

30. Heywood, *History of Childhood*, 72–73; ARCIA (1862), 406, quoted in Reyner and Eder, *American Indian Education*, 123; ARCIA (1863), H. Exec. Doc., no. 1, 38th Cong., 1st sess., serial 1182, 172; ARCIA (1873), H. Exec. Doc., no. 1, part 5, 43rd Cong., 1st session, serial 1601, 376–77.

31. The BIA sought more than assimilation, claims Margaret D. Jacobs. The policy of encouraging and sometimes enforcing the removal of children from their homes "arose from the desire to punish and control Indian people." Jacobs, "A Battle for the Children: American Indian Child Removal in Arizona in the Era of Assimilation," *Journal of Arizona History* 1 (Spring 2004): 32.

32. Hoxie, *Final Promise*, 53–70, with quotation from 69. Jacobs also notes that the BIA campaign was different in the sense that the children of other minority groups were not removed from their families—evidence of a greater white need to control and punish Indians (see note 31, immediately above). A valid point, but the greater "cultural distance" between whites and Indians, along with the actual physical distance of many tribal peoples from the centers of American civilization, even from American small town life, also partly explains the "special" treatment of Indians. Jacobs, "Battle for the Children," 31–62.

33. ARCIA (1900), H. Doc., no. 5, 56th Cong., 2nd sess., serial 4101, esp. 22–23, 13, 28; ARCIA (Washington DC: Government Printing Office, 1909), 3.

34. Prucha, *Great Father*, 2:700–707; Reyner and Eder, *American Indian Education*,

89–92; ARCIA, *Annual Report of the Secretary of the Interior* (Washington DC: Government Printing Office, 1928), 13.

35. ARCIA (1900), *H. Doc.*, no. 5, 56th Cong., 2nd sess., serial 4101, 22; ARCIA (1930), *Annual Report of the Secretary of the Interior* (Washington DC: Government Printing Office, 1930), 26–27. The commissioner noted: "The government is paying tuition for [Indian public school students] in 861 white communities, 23 more than last year. Hundreds of other communities admit Indian children without tuition." See also Szasz, *Education and the American Indian*, chap. 8.

36. ARCIA (1903), *H. Doc.*, no. 5, part 1, 58th Cong., 2nd sess., serial 4645, 2–3. See also comments by R. H. Milroy, agent for the Puyallup, Nesqually, and other Indian tribes of the Washington Territory: school was "a manner of exterminating the Indian tribes" more in accordance with the character and dignity of the American government than "to leave them to be exterminated by the bullets of her soldiers and by whisky, and the poisonous diseases which are brought among them by the lower stratum of our civilization," ARCIA (Washington DC: Government Printing Office, 1876), 137.

37. Spring, *American School*, 150; Coleman, *American Indian Children*, 45; Fischbacher, "Study of the Role," 125–31, with quotation from 127.

38. ARCIA, *Annual Report of the Secretary of the Interior* (Washington DC: Government Printing Office, 1930), 26–27; Fischbacher, "Study of the Role," 130–31; Szasz, *Education and the American Indian*, 2. Szasz also notes ongoing problems then, such as dropout rates, overcrowding, and health conditions. On tribal peoples being possessive of schools see, for example, Essie Burnett Horne and Sally McBeth, *Essie's Story: The Life and Legacy of a Shoshone Teacher* (Lincoln: University of Nebraska Press, 1998); Brenda J. Child, *Boarding School Seasons: American Indian Families, 1900–1940* (Lincoln: University of Nebraska Press, 1998); Ellis, *To Change Them Forever*, esp. 195–200.

39. I summarize this controversy in Coleman, *American Indian Children at School*, 46–50; and see chaps. 5 and 6 of the present study. Reyner and Eder also see little change at the schools. Reyner and Eder, *American Indian Education*, 107. Historians who argue for a significant change in BIA policy include Hoxie, *Final Promise* (the preface to the 2001 edition indicates no change in Hoxie's view on this matter from the 1984 edition), and Scott Riney, *The Rapid City Indian School, 1898–1933* (Norman: University of Oklahoma Press, 1999). K. Tsianina Lomawaima accepts A. Littlefield's use of the term "proletarianization." See Lomawaima, "American Indian Education: Education: By Indians versus For Indians," in *A Companion to American Indian History*, ed. Philip J. Deloria and Neal Salisbury (Malden MA: Blackwell, 2002), 430.

40. ARCIA (Washington DC: Government Printing Office, 1892), 6–7; ARCIA (1905), *H. Doc.*, vol. 19, 54th Cong., 1st sess., serial 4959, 1–13, with quotations from 5. The Indian should be moving from artificial restraints and protection "towards the broad area of individual liberty enjoyed by the ordinary citizen" (4); ARCIA, *Reports of the Department of the Interior* (Washington DC: Government Printing Office, 1908), 11. It was important that the service "pass out of existence in just the right way," he wrote, but "for the next few years it is going to take more men and a higher class of men

to wind up the affairs of the Indian Service"; ARCIA (Washington DC: Government Printing Office, 1909), 4. Also, ARCIA (1930), *Annual Report of the Secretary of the Interior* (Washington DC: Government Printing Office, 1930), 25. On some of the complications inherent in ideas of Indian citizenship, see Adams, *Education for Extinction*, 145–49. Also see note 3 above.

41. Institute for Government Research, *The Problem of Indian Administration* (Meriam Report) (Baltimore: Johns Hopkins University Press, 1828), esp. chap. 9; Coleman, *American Indian Education*, 50–53; Szasz, *Education and the American Indian*, esp. chaps. 1–5.

42. Szasz, *Education and the American Indian*, 6–9; Collier, in ARCIA, *Annual Report of the Secretary of the Interior* (Washington DC: Government Printing Office, 1935), 129. For a recent appraisal of Collier see Joel Pfister, *Individuality Incorporated: Indians and the Multicultural Modern* (Durham NC: Duke University Press, 2004), chap. 4.

43. Szasz, *American Indian Education*, chaps. 10–16; Lomawaima, "American Indian Education," 422–40. Prucha points to the paradox at the center of Indian quests for self-determination: financial support for Indian schools comes from outside the community. Prucha, *Great Father*, 2:1149. As always, government claims and statistics must be treated with caution, but for details on present BIA educational responsibilities see Office of Indian Education Programs (BIA), *2004 Fingertip Facts:* www.oiep.bia. edu/docs/Finger%20Tip%20Fact%202005.pdf (accessed June 23, 2006).

44. *Fourteenth Report of the Commissioners for Inquiring into the State of all Schools, on Public or Charitable Foundations, in Ireland* (1812; hereafter *Fourteenth Report* [1812]), appendix A to *Second Report of the Commissioners of National Education in Ireland* (1835), in *Reports of the Commissioners . . .* (Dublin: CNEI, 1851), with quotations from 25, 29–30; Sean Farren, *The Politics of Irish Education, 1920–65* (Belfast: Institute of Irish Studies, Queens University, 1995), 3–4.

45. *Fourteenth Report* (1812), 30.

46. Donald H. Akenson, *The Irish Education Experiment: The National System of Education in the Nineteenth Century* (London: Routledge & Kegan Paul, 1970), 59.

47. *First Report of the Commissioners of Irish Education Inquiry* (1825; hereafter *First Report* [1825]), 2–3 for the "Petition of the Prelates of the Roman Catholic Church in Ireland"; Akenson, *Irish Educational Experiment*, 95–98; Antonia McManus, *The Irish Hedge School and Its Books, 1695–1831* (Dublin: Four Courts Press, 2002), 56–62; Coolahan, *Irish Education*, 10–12.

48. The text of the famous Stanley letter appears in CNEI, *Reports of the Commissioners of National Education in Ireland from the Year 1834 to 1845, Inclusive* (Dublin: CNEI, 1851), 1–5: "Letter of the Right Hon. E. G. Stanley, Chief Secretary to his Excellency the Lord Lieutenant, Addressed to the Duke of Leinster"; also 6–9.

49. Ibid. For a list of the religion of commissioners from 1831 to 1849, see Akenson, *Irish Educational Experiment*, 129; McManus, *Irish Hedge School*, 63–68. Also Graham Balfour, *The Educational Systems of Great Britain and Ireland* (Oxford: Clarendon, 1903). He claimed that by 1831 all the elements but *one* of the national system were already in place, such as state grants, salaries and gratuities to teachers, normal schools,

requirements for local effort. "There only remained one thing—a guarantee for religious independence" (82). See ibid., chap. 1,B, on Irish elementary education.

50. Aine Hyland argues that despite its image as "a body antagonistic to Irish education," the British Treasury had a much more complicated relationship to the national schools. Its role might be summarized as one of reassuring parliament that its wishes were being carried out. From 1870 to 1920, she writes, "the average [British] government expenditure per pupil in attendance in elementary education in Ireland was consistently higher than in England; on average the per capita grant was 60 per cent higher in Ireland than in England." Hyland, "The Treasury and Irish Education: 1850–1922: The Myth and the Reality," *Irish Educational Studies*, 3.2 (1983), with quotations from 57, 60, 70. Yet see CNEI, *Report* (1905–6), 23–24, in which the board complained about Treasury tightness, despite "tacitly admitting the justice of our claims." And the board contested "the injustice of meting out unequal treatment to the Irish as compared to the British child in all matters appertaining to education."

51. Balfour, *Educational Sytems*, 85; Akenson, *Irish Educational Experiment*, 134–35. For a recent brief but useful account of the National Board, see Janet Nolan, *Servants of the Poor: Teachers and Mobility in Ireland and America* (Notre Dame IN: University of Notre Dame Press, 2004), esp. chaps. 1 and 2.

52. Akenson, *Irish Educational Experiment*, 38–39, 123–39; R. F. Foster, "Knowing Your Place: Words and Boundaries in Anglo-Irish Relationships," *Paddy and Mr Punch: Connections in Irish and English History* (London: Allen Lane, 1993), 82; Stephen Howe, *Ireland and Empire: Colonial Legacies in Irish History and Culture* (Oxford: Oxford University Press, 2000), 69. Also, for example, 36–42, and chap. 5. See also Adrian Hastings, *The Construction of Nationhood: Ethnicity, Religion, and Nationalism* (Cambridge: Cambridge University Press, 1997), 89–95, in which Hastings speculates on why the Union failed for most Irish people. Critiquing the view that Ireland under the Union was a colonial society (and thus that post-1922 Ireland is a postcolonial society) see, as well as Howe (cited above in this note), Bruce Stewart, "Inside Nationalism: A Meditation upon *Inventing Ireland* [by Declan Kiberd]," *Irish Studies Review* 6.1 (1998): 5–16; Liam Kennedy, "Modern Ireland: Post-Colonial Society or Post-Colonial Pretensions?" *Irish Review* 44 (1991): esp. 114–16. Kennedy refers specifically to the degree of *independence* enjoyed by the national school system, to the extent that it quickly fell under (Irish) denominational control. An excellent series of essays is Kevin Kenny, ed., *Ireland and the British Empire* (Oxford: Oxford University Press, 2004).

53. Coolahan, *Irish Education*, 6, 12–14; Balfour, *Educational Systems*, 85–86.

54. Farren, *Politics of Irish Education*, 4–10. Farren accepts the CNEI claim that in 1867, the peak year, 57.4 percent of schools could report some denominational mixes of pupils. By the last year for which such statistics were reported, 1912–13, even the CNEI claimed a figure of only 25 percent; Coolahan, *Irish Education*, 14–19. Coolahan quotes a pastoral letter from the Catholic hierarchy in 1900: by then the national system was "in a great part of Ireland . . . whatever it is in name, as denominational almost as we would desire" (37); E. B. Titley, *Church, State, and the Control of Schooling in Ireland, 1900–1944* (Kingston ON: McGill-Queen's University Press, 1983), chaps. 1–3.

55. Coolahan, *Irish Education*, 15–17. And see breakdown of students according to religious affiliation in 1900, presented later in the text.

56. Ibid., 17–19; McManus sees the Catholic Church availing of the national system in part to destroy the hedge schools. In the eighteenth century, she writes, a symbiotic relationship had existed between the church and the hedge schools. By the 1820s, as the church fought for a share of state aid for Catholic education, "this relationship became strained," *Irish Hedge Schools*, 240–43.

57. Coolahan, *Irish Education*, 23–24, 32–33. On teacher training, see chap. 6 in the present work. John Logan writes: "It may be one of the deeper ironies of nineteenth-century education that it was the abundant funding of the national school system by the state that allowed the church to construct an apparatus with which it would successfully complete the devotional revolution." The schools "became part of the pastoral apparatus" of that church. Logan, "The Dimensions of Gender in Nineteenth-Century Schooling," in *Gender Perspectives in 19th Century Ireland: Public and Private Spheres*, ed. Margaret Kelleher and James H. Murphy (Dublin: Irish Academic Press, 1997), 44.

58. CNEI, *Sixty-Seventh Report . . . for the Year 1900* (hereafter CNEI, *Report*, followed by year in parentheses), 6–13. See also John Coakley, "The Nationality Problem in Irish Primary Education: Political Socialization and the Teaching of History, 1831–1971" (M.A. thesis, University College Dublin, 1974), 46–50, and especially graph, 49, showing declining percentages of pupils attending denominationally mixed schools, 1862–1912.

59. Coolahan, *Irish Education*, 19; Balfour, *Educational Systems*, 83–84; for a list of parliamentary grants, 1870–1900, see Akenson, *Irish Educational Experiment*, 324–25.

60. For the text of the Irish Education Act of 1892 (An Act to Improve National Education in Ireland), with its many reservations as regards compulsion, see CNEI, *Report* (1892), appendix B, 3–13. In 1900 the CNEI referred to some of the difficulties involved in operating the compulsory act, but noted that more recently the act had "a good effect on the school attendance in Dublin and other places where the law has been vigorously enforced." CNEI, *Report* (1990), 17. See also Edel Donohoe, "Compulsory School Attendance Legislation in Ireland (Republic of Ireland and Northern Ireland), 1892–1994," (M.Ed. thesis, University College Dublin, 1994), esp. chap. 1; Michael Quinlivan, "Compulsory Attendance Legislation for Irish Schoolchildren, 1892 and 1926," *Irish Educational Studies* 6.2 (1886–87): 88–105. As with Indian children, compulsory education never became watertight during these decades.

61. Coolahan, *Irish Education*, 8; Donald Herron, "The Christian Brothers' Disconnection from the National Board, 1936 [sic]," *Irish Educational Studies* 3.2 (1983): 37–56; Barry M. Coldrey, *Faith and Fatherland: The Christian Brothers and the Development of Irish Nationalism, 1838-1921* (Dublin: Gill and Macmillan, 1988).

62. CNEI, *Report* (1836), 61–62.

63. CNEI, *Report* (1855), appendix G, 81; (1900), 6–7.

64. CNEI, *Report* (1915–16), 7–8. Such demands, of course, would have been identical for anti–Home Rule Ulster Volunteers (opposing repeal of the Union); apart from

voting, teachers could not participate in any such political activity. Ironically, in terms of its efforts to anglicize the Irish, the CNEI found itself accused in some Irish and British newspapers of having helped instigate the 1916 Rising.

65. Thomas A. O'Donoghue, *Bilingual Education in Ireland, 1904–1922: The Case of the Bilingual Programme of Instruction*, Centre for Irish Studies Monograph no. 1 (Perth, Australia: Murdoch University, 2000), 3. See also Patrick O'Mahony and Gerald Delanty, *Rethinking Irish History: Nationalism, Identity and Ideology* (Houndmills, Basingstoke, Hampshire: Macmillan, 1998), 47: "The Union of Great Britain and Ireland was less an experiment in federalism than the political absorption of the latter by the former."

66. CNEI, *Report* (1879), appendix 1, 151–52; CNEI, *Report* (1885), appendix A, 78; CNEI, *Report* (1904), appendix, section 2, 213–18. Irish could also be taught as an ordinary school subject. The goal of the 1904 Bilingual Programme was that such children would leave school literate and numerate in both languages and would receive a general education in both languages. O'Donoghue, *Bilingual Education in Ireland*, 2, 112. In this study he convincingly shows how a number of separate yet intertwining developments led the CNEI to surrender and to accept a bilingual program for predominantly Irish-speaking areas: for example, the community-centered and pupil-centered ideals of the progressive education movement, the British desire to "kill Home Rule with kindness," the activities of the Gaelic League and other revivalist movements, the support of some of the Catholic clergy and of some teachers in the national schools, and the examples of educational developments elsewhere, especially in Wales. See also Tony Crowley, *War of Words: The Politics of Language in Ireland, 1537–2004* (Oxford: Oxford University Press, 2005), chaps. 5–6.

67. Quotations from John Coolahan, "Education as Cultural Imperialism: The Denial of the Irish Language to Irish Speakers, 1831–1922," *Paedagogica Historica* 37.1 (2001): 31. On the sale of its books outside Ireland see, for example, CNEI, *Report*, 1840, i, 161. Cf. Coakley, "Nationality Problem," 43–44: The CNEI did not attempt to stamp out or even discourage Irish, it simply ignored it until pressure built for its inclusion later in the century. O'Donoghue also accepts this view; see *Bilingual Education in Ireland*, 24. (And see chap. 5 on curriculum).

68. The development of the "payment by results" system can be followed in CNEI, *Report*, for the last three decades of the nineteenth century. See, for example, *Report* (1871), appendix C, 160–62, for the head inspector's response to the new system; see *Report* (1872), appendix E, 229, for comments by another inspector: "It was gratifying to see the increased animation, attention to method, and steadier application to business, brought about by the introduction of the system of payment by results." On the ending of the system, see *Report* (1900), 7–9, 37; Coolahan, *Irish Education*, 28–30.

69. On the dramatic extinction of the CNEI by the government of the Irish Free State in 1922, see CNEI, Minutes of Proceedings, January 31, 1922, 2, MS no. LO 2351, NLI. On the transition from CNEI to separate control of elementary education by the Irish Free State and Northern Ireland, see especially Farren, *Politics of Irish Education*, chaps. 1–5.

70. Wilbert H. Ahearn, "An Experiment Aborted: Returned Indian Students in the Indian School Service, 1881–1908," *Ethnohistory* 44.2 (Spring 1997): 263–304.

71. Michael C. Coleman, "Representation of American Indians and the Irish in Educational Reports, 1850s–1920s," *Irish Historical Studies* 33.129 (May 2002): 33–51. Cf. McManus, *Irish Hedge School*, 231; ARCIA, *Reports of the Department of the Interior* (Washington DC: Government Printing Office, 1920), 12.

3. The Local Community and the School

1. David Vincent, *The Rise of Mass Literacy: Reading and Writing in Modern Europe* (Cambridge UK: Polity, 2000), 48.

2. Mary Peckham Magray, *The Transforming Power of the Nuns: Women, Religion, and Cultural Change in Ireland, 1750–1900* (New York: Oxford University Press, 1998), 83–86, 88. Magray sees this effort as a part of the assault by bourgeois middle-class groups in Ireland on the old, supposedly backward Gaelic culture. Obviously modernization and Anglicization were closely allied, and indeed the CNEI strongly saw its drive to Anglicize as part of the modernization process too.

3. ARCIA (1895), *House Document* no. 5, vol. 2, 54th Cong., 1st sess., serial 3382, 169.

4. Ibid., 189; ARCIA, (1900), *House Document* no. 5, 56th Cong., 2nd sess., serial 4101, 35.

5. ARCIA (Washington DC: Government Printing Office, 1888), 262. Although by then often supplied by white traders, the "Blanket" was a symbol of the old order, summed up in the derogatory phrase "going back to the blanket."

6. In the early twentieth century pupils at Chilocco School were not supposed to go home for five years. See K. Tsianina Lomawaima, *They Called It Prairie Light: The Story of Chilocco Indian School* (Lincoln: University of Nebraska Press, 1994), 24.

7. Margaret D. Jacobs, especially, emphasizes the alienating effects of removal of children to distant boarding schools. Jacobs, "A Battle for the Children: American Indian Child Removal in Arizona in the Era of Assimilation," *Journal of Arizona History* 1 (Spring 2004): 31–62.

8. Marilyn Irvin Holt notes the huge increase in young people taken into institutions in the United States during the decades around the turn of the twentieth century "when families failed to perform within the parameters of white, middle-class expectations." All of this, she believes, "reflected a new level of intervention by outsiders into domestic life." Holt, *Indian Orphanages* (Lawrence: University Press of Kansas, 2001), 3–4.

9. See, for example, Janet Nolan, *Servants of the Poor: Teachers and Mobility in Ireland and America* (Notre Dame IN: University of Notre Dame Press, 2004), esp. 25–27. Nolan writes of the CNEI's "steady usurpation of local autonomy." See chaps. 1 and 2. Tony Fahey has noted the CNEI's appreciation of Catholic nuns in "the embourgeoisment of Irish culture" as they struggled "to raise the tone of Irish life to the civilized standards of metropolitan culture." See Fahey, "Nuns in the Catholic Church in Ireland in the Nineteenth Century," in *Girls Don't Do Honours: Irish Women in Education in the 19th and 20th Centuries*, ed. Mary Cullen (Dublin: Women's Education Bureau, 1987), with quotation from 23.

10. CNEI, *Report* (1861), appendix C, 175; ibid. (1862), appendix D, 222; ibid. (1880), appendix B, 67 ("local vulgarisms"); ibid. (1888), appendix B, 180. Although sharing the above view on pronunciation faults, another inspector took a more tolerant view: "While local vulgarisms and a slovenly pronunciation should, as far as possible, be corrected and guarded against, I think it would be a hopeless, and by no means desirable object, to strive to mould the whole nation into absolute sameness of speech." Ibid. (1877), appendix C, 163.

11. CNEI, *Report* (1892), appendix C, 120.

12. CNEI, *Report* (1884), appendix C, 218–19. See also Michael C. Coleman, "The Representation of American Indians and the Irish in Educational Reports, 1850s–1920s," *Irish Historical Studies* 33.129 (May 2002): 33–51.

13. CNEI, *Report* (1908–9), appendix, sect. 1, 67; CNEI, *Report* (1906–7), appendix, 91.

14. Vincent, *Rise of Mass Literacy*, 7. But see my discussion of the interdependent, symbiotic relationships that grew up between all groups involved, in chap. 7 of the present work.

15. CNEI, *Report* (1870), appendix D, 303.

16. Thomas G. Andrews demonstrates how effectively Indian people could manipulate schools to their own advantage and to help preserve Native cultural values. Andrews, "Turning the Tables on Assimilation: Oglala Lakotas and the Pine Ridge Day Schools, 1889–1920s," *Western Historical Quarterly* 33 (Winter 2002): 407–30. For a good short account see K. Tsianina Lomawaima, "American Indian Education: By Indians versus For Indians," in *A Companion to American Indian History*, ed. Philip Deloria and Neal Salisbury (Malden MA, 2002), 422–40.

17. For an excellent recent account of one tribe's pragmatic and ambivalent responses to schooling, see Jeffrey Ostler, *The Plains Sioux and U.S. Colonialism from Lewis and Clark to Wounded Knee* (New York: Cambridge University Press, 2004), chap. 7.

18. Irish pragmatism is a major theme of Tony Crowley, *War of Words: The Politics of Language in Ireland* (Oxford: Oxford University Press, 2005). Patrick Pearse, later executed as one of the leaders of the 1916 Rising, wrote: "The English thing that is called education in Ireland is founded on a denial of the Irish nation . . . nearly all schools in Ireland teach children to deny their nation. . . . To invent such a system of teaching and to persuade us that it is . . . an Irish education system to be defended by Irishmen against attack, is the most wonderful thing the English have accomplished in Ireland; and the most wicked thing." In *A Significant Educationalist: The Educational Writings of P. H. Pearse*, ed. Séamas Ó Buachalla, ed. (Dublin: Mercier Press, 1980), sect. 6, "The Murder Machine," 374. Also see Sean Farren, *The Politics of Irish Education, 1920-65* (Belfast: Queen's University, Institute of Irish Studies, 1995), 16–17; Thomas O'Donoghue, "Bilingual Education in Ireland in the Late-Nineteenth and Early-Twentieth Centuries," *History of Education* 17.3 (1988): 211–14. See also *An Claidheam Soluis* (The Sword of Light), the publication of the Gaelic league.

19. CNEI, *Report* (1854), appendix G, 87.

20. CNEI, *Report* (1880), appendix B, 66. See photos of barefoot Irish children in this book.

21. Jeremiah Murphy, *When Youth Was Mine: A Memoir of Kerry, 1902–1925* (Dublin: Mentor Press, 1998), 102–3; Peter O'Leary, *My Story*, trans. Cyril T. O Céirin (Cork: Mercier Press, 1980), 53: the children worked on the farm during the day, and then "when the night would come, my mother would light a candle on the table, put us sitting around, give us the books and teach us our lessons"; Michael MacGowan, *The Hard Road to Klondike*, trans. Valentin Iremonger (London: Routledge and Kegan Paul, 1962), 11–12.

22. Tomás O'Crohan, *The Islandman*, trans. Robin Flower (New York: Oxford University Press, 1951), 15; IFC 1157:423; Patrick Shea, *Voices and the Sound of Drums: An Irish Autobiography* (Belfast: Blackstaff Press, 1981), 99; Sean O'Faolain, *Vive Moi! An Autobiography* (London: Rupert Hart-Davis, 1965), 39. Thomas Jordan notes the importance of mothers in stimulating elementary education. Jordan, *Ireland's Children: Quality of Life, Stress, and Child Development in the Famine Era* (Westport CT: Greenwood Press, 1998), 117–18.

23. "As the saying went," writes Crowley, "Irish people loved their language, but they loved their children more." Crowley, *War of Words*, 122. This is a major theme of Crowley's book; see esp. 122–27. Cormac Ó Gráda, *Black '47 and Beyond: The Great Irish Famine in History, Economy, and Memory* (Princeton NJ: Princeton University Press, 1999), 216; O'Donoghue, "Bilingual Education," 209.

24. CNEI, *Report* (1855), appendix G, 75–77; CNEI, *Report* (1856), appendix B, 143–45. See also chap. 5 in the present work. Cf. Vincent, *Rise of Mass Literacy*, 142. In a passage strikingly similar to Keenan's, a Breton speaker told how his parents "were humiliated because they know nothing but their mother tongue. Every time they had to deal with a [French-speaking] city civil servant and every time they ventured into a city, they were exposed to jeers and sly smiles all around."

25. CNEI, *Report* (1884), appendix C, 224–25. Also, Coolahan, *Irish Education*, 21. According to Garrett FitzGerald, the early decades of the nineteenth century saw a sharp decline in the use of Irish by the young in many areas. This occurred not only before the Great Famine "but also, effectively, [before] the introduction of State-aided primary education." FitzGerald, "The Decline of the Irish Language," in *The Origins of Popular Literacy in Ireland: Language Change and Educational Development, 1790–1920*, ed. Mary Daly and David Dickson (Dublin: University College and Trinity College, 1990), 64. On the Catholic Church, see, for example, Adrian Kelly, *Compulsory Irish: Language and Education in Ireland, 1870s–1970s* (Dublin: Irish Academic Press, 2002), 124–28. On the support of clergy for the CNEI bilingual program in some areas, see Thomas A. O'Donoghue, *Bilingual Education in Ireland, 1904–1922: The Case of the Bilingual Programme of Instruction*, Centre for Irish Studies Monograph Series no. 1 (Perth, Australia: Murdoch University, 2000), 89–93. On the collapse of Irish, see also 4–5, 16–18.

26. CNEI, *Report* (1906–7), appendix, 49–50, 95; also 94–99. Again, Dalton was in favor of a bilingual approach and regarded English-only teaching in such areas as "the clumsiest, the most irrational and the most hopelessly ineffective" method (96). Others remembered adults speaking Irish to each other and English to the children. See, for example, IFC 1194:295; my mother mentioned this (personal communica-

tion). In "Bilingual Education," O'Donoghue gives a good account of both the difficulties and the strengths of the CNEI's bilingual program, especially the difficulties faced by teachers.

27. David Crystal, *Language Death* (Cambridge: Cambridge University Press, 2000), 78–79. And see 76–90 esp., in which Crystal develops such views: observers talk of "language murder or linguicide," but he validly claims that sometimes we witness "language suicide" (86), as when groups voluntarily cease to speak their own languages. Perhaps all these terms could be applied to Irish and some Indian cases. Ultimately, he notes, the death of a language is a highly complex thing. On shame about using the "old language," see Crowley, *War of Words*, 125–27. On the complexity of issues relating to language loss, revitalization, and language rights, see, for example, the series of articles in *American Anthropologist* 105.4 (December 2003): 711–81; Bruce E. Johansen, "Back from the (Nearly) Dead: Reviving Indigenous Languages across North America," *American Indian Quarterly* 28.3/4 (Summer and Fall 2004): 566–82; Leena Huss, *Reversing Language Shift in the Far North: Linguistic Revitalization in Northern Scandinavia and Finland* (Uppsala, Sweden: Acta Uralica Upsaliensia 31, 1999).

28. MacGowan, *Hard Road*, 10; IFC 1194:295. This informant went on to note that although later children did learn Irish at school, his generation could not now help them with the language; IFC 495:153. On parents speaking English to children, see also note 26, above.

29. O'Donoghue, "Bilingual Education," 211.

30. O'Donoghue shows how, even in predominantly Irish-speaking areas, Irish people divided on the language issue. Some supported the new CNEI bilingual program of 1904, which encouraged the use of Irish and English in schools, while some strongly opposed it. See O'Donoghue, *Bilingual Education in Ireland*, esp. chap. 6. Ironically, in some Irish-speaking areas the program was forced on local people against their wishes (104). Kevin Kenny writes that the Irish "helped conquer, govern, and evangelize imperial possessions overseas" in Kenny, ed., *Ireland and the British Empire* (Oxford: Oxford University Press, 2004), 16. A major theme of this book is that the Irish were beneficiaries of, as well as victims of, the British Empire.

31. ARCIA (1880), H. *Exec. Doc.* no. 1, part 5, 46th Cong., 3rd sess., serial 1959, 87. As shown in the text below, Luther Standing Bear was one of many Indians encouraged by parents to "go East" to the Carlisle School.

32. Ibid., S. C. Armstrong, principal, Report from the Hampton Normal and Agricultural Institute, 306–7.

33. Child, *Boarding School Seasons*. Example of visit: Luther Standing Bear, *My People the Sioux*, ed. E. A. Brininstool (1928; rpt., Lincoln: University of Nebraska, 1975), 153. Standing Bear's father visited his son's distant school. Cf. Jacobs, "Battle for the Children."

34. Francis La Flesche, *The Middle Five: Indian Schoolboys of the Omaha Tribe* (1900; rpt., Madison: University of Wisconsin Press, 1963), 127–28; Thomas Wildcat Alford, *Civilization and the Story of the Absentee Shawnees, as told to Florence Drake* (Norman: University of Oklahoma Press, 1936), 73–80, 89–90. See also Jacqueline Fear-Segal,

"'Use of the White Man's Wisdom in Defense of Our Customs': White Schools and Native Agendas," *American Studies International* 40.3 (October 2002): 6–32.

35. Lomawaima, *Prairie Light*, 35–36. This incident took place in 1933, just beyond the period covered by the present work.

36. Ellis, *To Change Them Forever*. Also, for example, Child, *Boarding School Seasons*.

37. Helen Sekaquaptewa, *Me and Mine: The Life Story of Helen Sekaquaptewa, as told to Louise Udall* (Tucson: University of Arizona Press, 1969), 120; ARCIA (Washington DC: Government Printing Office, 1877), 93; ARCIA (1899), *House Document* no. 5, 56th Cong., 1st sess., serial 3915, 410–11.

38. Scott Riney, *The Rapid City Indian Boarding School, 1898–1933* (Norman: University of Oklahoma Press, 1999), 73, and chap. 4. See also Wilbert H. Ahern, "An Experiment Aborted: Returned Indian Students in the Indian School Service, 1881–1908," *Ethnohistory* 44.2 (Spring 1997): 263–304.

39. CNEI, *Report* (1851), appendix B, 207–10. McCreedy also blames poor inspection, the lack of interest taken by the local gentry in education, and the failings of teachers for the problems of "irregular attendance."

40. CNEI, *Report* (1855), appendix G, 59–60. Poverty, wrote Keenan, "surrounded the Irish peasant with mud walls; placed a cold roof above his head; covers his shoulders with a tattered garment; weakens or withers the ordinary sensibilities of his manhood; and blinds his eyes against . . . lessons of symmetry, and neatness, and order." Keenan hoped that the growing prosperity of the country along with the national schools would produce a peasantry that was "clean, neat, educated, and comfortable"; CNEI, *Report* (1892), appendix C, 93–94. Significantly, he felt that "The great intercourse with England too, must widen the range of intelligence."

41. CNEI, *Report* (1888), appendix B, 120.

42. Peig Sayers, *Peig: The Autobiography of Peig Sayers of the Great Blasket Island*, trans. Bryan MacMahon (n.p.: Talbot Press, 1974), 63–72; Dan Breen, *My Fight for Irish Freedom* (1924; rpt., Tralee, County Kerry: Anvil Books, 1964), 13; IFC 1573:237–38; IFC 1157:427, 437–38.

43. IFC 1194:493–95.

44. ARCIA (1852), *S. Exec. Doc.*, vol. 3, no. 1, part 3, 32nd Cong., 1st sess., 316–17; I deal with the Omaha buffalo hunt in chap. 8.

45. ARCIA, *Annual Reports of the Department of the Interior, Indian Affairs*, part 1 (Washington DC: Government Printing Office, 1902), 157–58. Jacobs also points to instances of Indians "who openly resisted efforts to enroll their children in boarding school, occasionally resorting to pregnancy, early marriage, or some other subterfuge." Jacobs, "Battle for the Children," 45.

46. ARCIA (1906), *H. Doc.*, vol. 15, 59th Cong., 2nd sess., serial 5118, 216.

47. ARCIA (Washington DC: Government Printing Office, 1887), 234. Cf. CNEI, *Report* (1899–1900), 101: Mr. W. H. Welply complained that with the abolition of attendance fees, "some parents have come to consider it a favour to the teachers to send their children to school at all, where they expect them to be supplied with books, copy-books, and other material gratis."

48. ARCIA (Washington DC: Government Printing Office, 1887), 234; ARCIA (1890), H. Exec. Doc, no. 1, part 5, vol. 2, 51st Cong., 2nd sess., serial 2841. On Indian manipulation see also, for example, Ruth Spack, *America's Second Tongue: American Indian Education and the Ownership of English, 1860–1900* (Lincoln: University of Nebraska Press, 2002); Fear-Segal, "Use of the White Man's Wisdom"; Andrews, "Turning the Tables."

49. ARCIA, *Annual Reports of the Department of the Interior, Indian Affairs*, part 1 (Washington DC: Government Printing Office, 1901), 182. On *chindi* see Irene Stewart, *A Voice in Her Tribe: A Navajo Woman's Own Story*, ed. Dorris Ostrander Dawdy and Mary Shepardson, Anthropological Paper no. 17 (Socorro NM: Ballena Press, 1980), 18–21. Stewart remembered that although she became accustomed to a government boarding school, she feared going near a hospital. "I had been told that lots of children died there, and that there must be a lot of children ghosts."

50. ARCIA (1885), H. Exec. Doc., no. 1, part 5, vol. 2, 49th Cong., serial 2379, 99.

51. Charles Eastman, *From Deep Woods to Civilization: Chapters in the Autobiography of an Indian* (1916; rpt., Lincoln: University of Nebraska Press, 1977), 24–25; Stewart, *Voice in Her Tribe*, 15; Henley in Broderick H. Johnson, ed., *Stories of Traditional Navajo Life and Culture, by Twenty-Two Navajo Men and Women* (Tsaile, Navajo Nation AZ, Navajo Community College Press, 1977), 30–31. Many other instances of similar kin divisions could be cited from the autobiographical literature.

52. ARCIA (Washington DC: Government Printing Office, 1878), 95; ARCIA *Annual Reports of the Department of the Interior, Indian Affairs*, part 1 (Washington DC: Government Printing Office, 1902), 150.

53. ARCIA (1906), H. Doc., vol. 15, 59th Cong., 2nd sess., serial 5118, 118–25.

54. Thomas C. Lemmon, Report of the Superintendent of Moqui [Hopi] School, ibid., 179–82; ARCIA, *Reports of the Department of the Interior* (Washington DC: Government Printing Office, 1907), 80–87. See also Peter M. Whiteley, *Deliberate Acts: Changing Hopi Culture through the Oraibi Split* (Tucson: University of Arizona Press, 1988). Whiteley sees the Oraibi split as primarily the product of internal Hopi needs, but he also accepts that acculturative pressures such as the forced schooling of children were important. "Schooling became a key issue in the factional division of Oraibi," he writes (74). See also Jacobs, "Battle for the Children."

55. Sayers, *Peig*, 14–15.

56. Coleman, *American Indian Children*, 60–61, and chap. 4.

57. James Kaywaykla, *In the Days of Victorio: Recollections of a Warm Springs Apache*, ed. Eve Ball (Tucson: University of Arizona Press, 1970), 199–200; Jason Betzinez, with William Sturtevant Nye, *I Fought with Geronimo* (1959; rpt., Lincoln: University of Nebraska Press, 1987), 149; Fred Kabotie, *Fred Kabotie, Hopi Indian Artist: An Autobiography Told with Bill Belknap* (Flagstaff: Museum of Northern Arizona/Northland Press, 1977), 8–10; Sekaquaptewa, *Me and Mine*, 8–12.

58. Burton to Commissioner of Indian Affairs, February 9, 1903, cited in Whiteley, *Deliberate Acts*, 95–96. See also the corroborating but critical report by teacher Belle Axtell Kolp, notarized affidavit, cited in ibid., 95. In Coleman, *American Indian Children*,

76–77, note 7, I cite further examples of such actions by authorities. On the Wahpeton pageant see Esther Barnett Horne and Sally McBeth, *Essie's Story: The Life and Legacy of a Shoshone Teacher* (Lincoln: University of Nebraska Press, 1998), 99–100.

59. Eastman, *From Deep Woods to Civilization*, 45 and chap. 2; Asa Daklugie et al., *Indeh*, 134–36; Jim Whitewolf, *Jim Whitewolf: The Life of a Kiowa Apache Indian*, ed. Charles S. Brant (New York: Dover, 1969), 83; Edward Goodbird, *Goodbird the Indian: His Story*, ed. Gilbert L. Wilson (1914; rpt., St. Paul: Minnesota Historical Society, 1985), 40–41. I cite other examples in Coleman, *American Indian Children*, chap. 4 (including notes).

60. Don Talayesva, *Sun Chief: The Autobiography of a Hopi Indian*, ed. Leo W. Simmons (New Haven CT: Yale University Press), 89–90, 94; Standing Bear, *My People*, chap. 13. He gives slightly different accounts in his three books, but they are broadly consistent; Coleman, *American Indian Children*, 78, note 26; Zitkala-Ša (Gertrude Bonnin), *American Indian Stories* (1921; rpt., Lincoln: University of Nebraska Press, 1985), chap. 7. For Navajos and work ethic, see account by John Dick, in Johnson, ed., *Stories of Traditional Navajo Life*, 184. The tribal work ethic is a central theme in these stories; Bennett, *Kaibah*, 133–34.

61. Nelson, in Johnson, ed., *Stories of Traditional Navajo Life*, 231–32; Bennett, *Kaibah*, 156–59, 209; Qoyawayma Polingaysi (Elizabeth Q. White), *No Turning Back: A True Account of a Hopi Indian Girl's Struggle to Bridge the Gap between the World of Her People and the World of the White Man*, as told to Vada F. Carlson (Albuquerque: University of New Mexico Press, 1964), 20–26, 51–54 (told in third person).

62. Tsosie, in Johnson, ed., *Stories of Traditional Navajo Life*, 113–15.

4. Regimentation

Chapter epigraph is quoted from "Let the Children Speak," in Gertrude Golden, *Red Moon Called Me: Memoirs of a Schoolteacher in the Government Indian Service* (San Antonio TX: Naylor, 1954), 189. Tribal identity of student not given (possibly Navajo). See 189–205, in which Golden has included essays and letters from pupils she taught: "The letters and compositions are left in the children's own style, with errors and other shortcomings." Many of them simply but powerfully convey the kinds of ambivalent responses to schooling that I examine in the present and following chapters.

1. Susan Douglas Francoza, "Authoring the Educated Self: Educational Autobiography and Resistance," *Educational Theory* 42.4 (Fall 1992): 405.

2. Peig Sayers, *Peig: The Autobiography of Peig Sayers of the Great Blasket Island*, trans. Bryan McMahon (n.p.: Talbot Press, 1974), 26, on the lack of clocks in their houses; on spectacles, Tomás O'Crohan, *The Islandman*, trans. Robin Flower (Oxford: Oxford University Press, 1951), 38–39. In the Irish sections of this chapter I draw on my essay "'Eyes Big as Bowls with Fear and Wonder': Children's Responses to the Irish National Schools, 1850–1922," *Proceedings of the Royal Irish Academy* 98C.5 (1998): 177–202.

3. Coleman, "Eyes Big as Bowls," 13–66, with quotations from 18–19. Indian teachers presenting books to students: Golden, *Red Moon*, 190, for example: "The teacher took me and seat me beside her in a high chair and give me a book with colored pictures in it and told me not to be making any noise" (Esther Perlata, part Mexican); also Joe Beaver, 191.

4. Micheál O'Guiheen, *A Pity Youth Does Not Last: Reminiscences of the Last of the Great Blasket Island's Poets and Storytellers*, trans. Tim Enright (New York: Oxford University Press, 1882), 2–3; Maurice O'Sullivan, *Twenty Years A-Growing*, trans. Moya Llewelyn Davies and George Thomson (New York: Oxford University Press, 1983), 2–3.

5. O'Sullivan, *Twenty Years*, 2; Patrick Shea, *Voices and the Sound of Drums: An Irish Autobiography* (Belfast: Blackstaff Press, 1981), 14. Shea had earlier attended a local convent school; at seven the boys moved on to the all-male national school. Peter O'Leary, *My Story by Peter O'Leary*, trans. Cyril T. O Céirin (Cork: Mercier Press, 1970), 53.

6. IFC 779:171–72 (third-person account). Cf. comments by J. F. Hogan, senior inspector, about schools in his area of responsibility: "a great many infants under six years of age are in attendance but do little or nothing at school; there are no facilities for keeping them employed and they are only in the way," CNEI, *Report* (1904), appendix, 93.

7. IFC 1194:290–91; Shea, *Voices and the Sound of Drums*, 14; Sean O'Faolain, *Vive Moi: An Autobiography* (London: Rupert Hart-Davis, 1965), 40–41.

8. CNEI, *Report* (1870), appendix D, 284; CNEI, *Report* (1900), appendix, 4. To be fair, not many narrators complained that as children they noticed the cold—nor do I recall that, in a later period, it worried me as a pupil. We did have fires, however, and central heating in some schools.

9. CNEI, *Report* (1904), appendix, sect. I, 20; CNEI, *Report* (1898–99), appendix, sect. I, 68.

10. ARCIA (1900), H. Doc. no. 5, 56th Cong., 2nd sess., serial 4100, 22. At that time the BIA ran 153 boarding schools, claiming average attendance of 17,708 pupils, and 154 day schools, with 3,860 pupils. On the importance of the day school as a site for resistance to assimilation, see Thomas G. Andrews, "Turning the Tables on Assimilation: Oglala Lakotas and the Pine Ridge Day Schools, 1889–1920s," *Western Historical Quarterly* 33.4 (Winter 2002): 407–30.

11. Polingaysi Qoyawayma (Elizabeth Q. White), *No Turning Back: A True Account of a Hopi Girl's Struggle to Bridge the Gap between the World of Her People and the World of the White Man, as told to Vada F. Carlson* (Albuquerque: University of New Mexico Press, 1964), 24–25; Don Talayesva, *Sun Chief: The Autobiography of a Hopi Indian*, ed. Leo W. Simmons (New Haven CT: Yale University Press, 1942), 89–90, 96.

12. Fred Provost (no tribal identity), in Golden, *Red Moon*, 191. Provost claimed that his teacher was nice to him, but other children bullied him. When he asked the teacher to complain to the matron, she told him that if he didn't learn to stick up for himself, "she is going to spank us."

13. For accounts of the disorientating and sometimes shocking trip from tribal home to distant boarding school, see Michael C. Coleman, *American Indian Children at School, 1850–1930* (Jackson: University Press of Mississippi, 1993), 72–76.

14. Bertha Sheeply, in Golden, *Red Moon*, 192; quoted in Sally J. McBeth, *Ethnic Identity and the Boarding School Experience of West-Central Oklahoma American Indians* (Lanham MD: University Press of America: 1983), 88. BIA officials could also forthrightly admit problems in the school plants, for example: ARCIA (Washington DC:

Government Printing Office, 1882), xxxviii; ARCIA (1997), H. Doc. no. 5, 55th Cong., 2nd sess., serial 3641, 330–32.

15. Irene Stewart, A Voice in Her tribe: A Navajo Woman's Own Story, ed. Dorris Ostrander Dawdy and Mary Shepardson, Anthropological Paper no. 17 (Socorro NM: Ballena Press, 1980), 15–16.

16. Stinson, in Joseph H. Cash and Herbert T. Hoover, eds., To Be an Indian: An Oral History (New York: Holt, Rinehart & Winston, 1971), 95; Zitkala-Ša (Gertrude Bonnin), American Indian Stories (1921; rpt., Lincoln: University of Nebraska Press, 1985), 49–51; on stairs as boxes, Zitkala-Ša, "Impressions of an Indian Girlhood," in Native American Autobiography: An Anthology, ed. Arnold Krupat (Madison: University of Wisconsin Press, 1994), 288. Despite her bitterly critical memories, Zitkala-Ša later strongly advocated schooling for Indian people; see David L. Johnson and Raymond Wilson, "Gertrude Simmons Bonnin, 1876–1938: 'Americanize the First Americans,'" American Indian Quarterly 12 (Winter 1988): 27–49. Also, Ruth Speck, America's Second Language: American Indian Education and the Ownership of English, 1860–1900 (Lincoln: University of Nebraska Press, 2002), esp. chap. 5. In Spack's view, Zitkala-Ša mastered the English language "to expose the colonizer's power position," 148–49; the Lakota may also have blurred the distinction between fact and fiction in her autobiographical writing (152–53). Her account broadly correlates with other Indian reminiscences I have read.

17. Lucille (Jerry) Winnie, Sah-Gan-De-Oh: The Chief's Daughter (New York: Vantage Press, 1969), 44–47.

18. Esther Burnett Horne and Sally McBeth, Essie's Story: The Life and Legacy of a Shoshone Teacher (Lincoln: University of Nebraska Press, 1998), 31.

19. CNEI, Report (1845), 334–35: "Twelve Practical Rules for the Teachers of National Schools, esp. rules 6 and 7.

20. "Citizen's dress," for example: letter of agent Laurie Tatum, ARCIA (1872), H. Exec. Doc., no. 1, part 5, 42nd Cong., 2nd sess., serial 1560, 633; Commissioner's Report, ARCIA (1875), H. Exec. Doc., no. 1, part 5, 54th Cong., 1st sess., serial 1680, 575. On disciplining the (especially female) body: K. Tsianina Lomawaima, They Called It Prairie Light: The Story of the Chilocco Indian School (Lincoln: University of Nebraska Press, 1994), esp. chap. 4; Sprack, America's Second Tongue, 119–20. See before and after photos in the present book.

21. ARCIA (1871), H. Exec. Doc., no. 1, part 5, 42nd Cong., 2nd sess., serial 1505, 892; ARCIA (Washington DC: Government Printing Office, 1877), 5.

22. Francis La Flesche, The Middle Five: Indian Schoolboys of the Omaha Tribe (1900; rpt., Madison: University of Wisconsin Press, 1963), 27–28. Also, Jim Whitewolf, Jim Whitewolf: The Life of a Kiowa Apache Indian, ed. Charles S. Brant (New York: Dover, 1969), 84. His father took all his former clothes "and rolled them up in a bundle. He said he was going home."

23. Luther Standing Bear, My People the Sioux, ed. J. A. Brininstool (1928; rpt., Lincoln: University of Nebraska Press, 1975), 142; Frank Mitchell, Navajo Blessingway Singer: The Autobiography of Frank Mitchell, 1881–1967, ed. Charlotte J. Frisbie and David

P. McAllester (Tucson: University of Arizona Press, 1978), 58–59, 67–68; Asa Daklugie et al., *Indeh: An Apache Odyssey*, ed. Eve Ball (Norman: University of Oklahoma Press, 1988), 146; Jason Betzinez, with William Sturtevant Nye, *I Fought with Geronimo* (1959; rpt., Lincoln: University of Nebraska Press, 1987), 153.

24. Zitkala-Ša, *American Indian Stories*, 52–56.

25. Standing Bear, *My People*, 141–42. Cf. the account given by Capt. Pratt: Richard Henry Pratt, *Battlefield and Classroom: Four Decades with the American Indians, 1867–1904*, ed. Robert M. Utley (1964; rpt., Lincoln: University of Nebraska Press, 1987), 232; James McCarthy, *A Papago Traveler: Memories of James McCarthy*, ed. John G. Westover (Tucson: Sun Tracks and University of Arizona Press, 1985), 28–29; Albert Yava, *Big Falling Snow: A Tewa-Hopi Indian's Life and the History and Traditions of His People*, ed. Harold Courlander (Albuquerque: University of New Mexico Press, 1978), 12. Also La Flesche, *Middle Five*, 75, on the changing emotions of a new student shorn of his long hair and the acceptance of short hair by more "civilized" boys.

26. La Flesche, *Middle Five*, 28, 74–75. Cf. critical comments in preface, xvii–xviii: the Indian names were difficult to pronounce, concedes La Flesche. "Besides [they] were considered by the missionaries as heathenish, and therefore should be obliterated"; Standing Bear, *My People the Sioux*, 136–38.

27. Yava, *Big Falling Snow*, 3; Daniel La France (Ah-nen-la-de-ni), "An Indian Boy's Story, *Independent* 55 (July 30, 1903): 1783.

28. Andrews, "Turning the Tables," 418–19. At the Irish-speaking schools that I attended in the late 1950s and early 1960s, students were given Irish names (Mícheál Ó Colmáin is mine); we used these names in class, but mostly reverted to the English versions outside class and school.

29. A list of monitors in CNEI, *Report* (1860), appendix G, 130, for example, contains recognizably Irish names such as O'Sullivan, O'Riordan, Connor. Yet these are Anglicized versions of those names. Similarly, inspectors had names such as Fitzgerald and Keenan, but these too were Anglicized version of Irish names. In my research I did not come across references to Irish names as a cultural issue. Cf. Flann O'Brien's fictionalized account of Irish-speaking children being given Anglicized names in national school, *The Poor Mouth (An Béal Bocht): A Bad Story about the Hard Life*, trans. P. C. Power ([1941]; London: Flaminco, 1988), 29–34. All boys received the same name, Jams O'Donnel.

30. O'Crohan, *Islandman*, 15–16, 47. This section draws on my article "'Some Kind of Gibberish': Irish-Speaking Children in the National Schools, 1850–1922," *Studia Anglica Posnaniensia* 33 (1998): 93–103.

31. Sayers, *Peig*, 21, 28–29.

32. Michael MacGowan, *The Hard Road to Klondike*, trans. Valentine Iremonger (London: Routledge and Kegan Paul, 1962), 11–12.

33. O'Sullivan, *Twenty Years*, 207; Shea, *Voices and the Sound of Drums*, 1.

34. IFC 495:219 (first-person account in Irish). Dunce's cap: IFC 657:103–4 (first-person account in Irish). See IFC 495 and 657 and entire file on the *bataí scoir* (tally stick).

35. John Coolahan, "Education as Cultural Imperialism: The Denial of the Irish Language to Irish Speakers, 1831–1922," *Paedagogica Historica* 37.1 (2001): 18–19. Even before 1831, writes Coolahan, parents had internalized a growing contempt for Irish "as inferior and associated with poverty and deprivation," and they were thus willing to operate "the notorious 'tally stick'"; Tony Crowley, *War of Words: The Politics of Language in Ireland, 1537–2004* (Oxford: Oxford University Press, 2005), 122–23; Victor Edward Durkacz, *The Decline of the Celtic Languages: A Study of Linguistic and Cultural Conflict in Scotland, Wales and Ireland from the Reformation to the Twentieth Century* (Edinburgh: John Donald, 1983), 223–34. And see also my discussion of Irish community attitudes in chap. 3 of the present book.

36. O'Leary, *My Story*, 53–54, 97–98.

37. Ibid., 98. The CNEI specifically forbade the humiliation of teachers in front of pupils, see chap. 6 of the present book.

38. Inspector Hugh Hammil, quoted in Coolahan, "Education as Cultural Imperialism," 19–20; CNEI, *Report* (1850), appendix, 135–36.

39. CNEI, *Report* (1855), appendix G, 75. See 73–76.

40. CNEI, *Report* (1857), appendix A, 135.

41. Rev. William Egan to W. Connolly, Inspector of Schools, 16 Nov., 1883, Ed. 9, file 1934, National Archives of Ireland (NAI).

42. In Golden, *Red Moon*, 191–92.

43. For example, Spack, *America's Second Tongue*, 49–52; Jon Reyner and Jeanne Eder, *American Indian Education: A History* (Norman: University of Oklahoma Press, 2004), 74–80; Michael C. Coleman, *Presbyterian Missionary Attitudes toward American Indians, 1837–1893* (Jackson: University Press of Mississippi, 1985), 116–19.

44. ARCIA (Washington DC: Government Printing Office, 1886), xxiii; Spack, *America's Second Tongue*, 7. Also, Francis Paul Prucha, *American Indian Policy in Crisis: Christian Reformers and the Indian, 1865–1900* (Norman: University of Oklahoma Press, 1976), 283–85. After the Civil War, writes Prucha, "English for the Indians became a theoretical principle, and its implementation became almost an obsession . . . with all Indian reformers."

45. Willie Blackbeard in Golden, *Red Moon*, 190.

46. La Flesche, *Middle Five*, xvii; Belle Highwalking, *The Narrative of a Northern Cheyenne Woman*, ed. Katherine M. Weist (Billings: Montana Council for Indian Education, 1979), 3. Not all teachers agreed with this rule. Golden, *Red Moon*, 143.

47. Clyde Ellis, *To Change Them Forever: Indian Education at the Rainy Mountain Boarding School, 1893–1920* (Norman: University of Oklahoma Press, 1996), 105–6. On making Kiowa-speakers put lye soap on their toothbrushes, see McBeth, *Ethnic Identity*, 105.

48. Golden, *Red Moon*, 143.

49. Standing Bear, *My People the Sioux*, 155–56; Anna Moore Shaw, *A Pima Past* (Tucson: University of Arizona Press, 1974), 107–8; La France (Ah-ne-la-den-li), "An Indian Boy's Story," 1781; Charles A. Eastman (Ohiyesa), *From Deep Woods to Civilization: Chapters in the Autobiography of an Indian* (1916; rpt., Lincoln: University of Nebraska Press, 1977), 46, 54.

50. Hailmann, quoted in Spack, *America's Second Tongue*, 25–26. On Hailmann's achievements as superintendent, much influenced by the Froebelian movement in education, see Dorothy W. Hewes, "Those First Good Years of Indian Education: 1894 to 1898," *American Indian Culture and Research Journal* 5.2 (1981): 63–82.

51. O'Sullivan, *Twenty Years*, 33, for example.

52. James Kaywaykla, *In the Days of Victorio: Recollections of a Warm Springs Apache*, ed. Eve Ball (Tucson: University of Arizona Press, 1970), 200. The sign language was initially used at Hampton Institute too; see Paula Fairbanks Molin, "'Training the Hand, the Head, and the Heart': Indian Education at Hampton Institute," *Minnesota History* 51 (Fall 1988): 86; Sam Writer, in Cash and Hoovers, *To Be an Indian*, 210; Horne and McBeth, *Essie's Story*, 32–33.

53. Elsie Allen, *Pomo Basketmaking: A Supreme Art for the Weaver*, ed. Vinson Brown (Healdsburg CA: Naturegraph, 1972), 11–13.

54. Sayers, *Peig*, 21.

55. Ibid., 28, 39, 68.

56. IFC 657:121–22 (in Irish).

57. La Flesche, *Middle Five*, 13; Allan James, *Chief of the Pomos: Life Story of Allen James*, ed. Ann M. Connor (Santa Rosa CA: privately printed, 1972), 19; Refugio Savala, *Autobiography of a Yaqui Poet*, ed. Kathleen M. Sands (Tucson: University of Arizona: 1980), 44–45; Stewart, *Voice in Her Tribe*, 34; Margaret Yeahebah, in Golden, *Red Moon*, 193–94.

58. Whitewolf, *Jim Whitewolf*, 85–86.

59. Daglugie et al., *Indeh*, 144–47, 150–51.

60. CNEI, *Report* (1845), 334–35. Joseph Lancaster, originator of the Lancastrian system, whereby a few monitors, under the eye of a teacher, taught large numbers of students, coined the original version of the motto ("A Time and a Place . . . "). Joel Strong, *The American School: 1642-2000*, 5th ed. (Boston: McGraw-Hill, 2001), 70–71; CNEI *Report* (1849), appendixes H, I, 217–18.

61. CNEI, *Report* (1909–10), appendix, 78–79.

62. ARCIA (1861) S. *Exec. Doc.* no. 137, 48th Cong., 2nd sess., serial 1117, 674; ARCIA (Washington DC: Government Printing Office, 1884), 71. The best results, continued the report, "will never be attained until our roving and lawless Indians are under complete control, and forced not only to stop depredating, but compelled to keep hands off such Indians as desire to work."

63. ARCIA (Washington DC: Government Printing Office, 1876), 136; ARCIA (1881), H. *Exec. Doc.* no. 1, part 5, vol. 2, 47th Cong., 1st sess., serial 2018, 253.

64. Mitchell, *Navajo Blessingway Singer*, 63; Lomawaima, *Prairie Light*, 59 (bell and food), 28 (misses bell); La Flesche, *Middle Five*, 78. A teacher could also get to detest the bell: see Reyner and Eder, *American Indian Education*, 163.

65. R. B. Robson, *Autobiography of an Ulster Teacher* (Belfast: n.p., 1935), chaps. 5, 10–13, 78 (bell).

66. CNEI, *Report* (1855), appendix G, 63; CNEI, *Report* (1880), appendix B, 68.

67. ARCIA (1880), H. *Exec. Doc.* no. 1, part 5, 46th Cong., 3rd sess., serial 1959, 302;

ARCIA (1890), H. Exec. Doc. no. 1, part 5, vol. 2, 51st Cong., 2nd sess., serial 2841, 319. On the education of Indians and African Americans at Hampton see Donal F. Lindsey, *Indians at Hampton Institute, 1877–1923* (Urbana: University of Illinois Press, 1995).

68. Golden, *Red Moon*, 90–91.

69. Horne and McBeth, *Essie's Story*, 33–37.

70. Helen Sekaquaptewa, *Me and Mine: The Life Story of Helen Sekaquaptewa, as told to Louise Udall* (Tucson: University of Arizona Press, 1969), 134–38; Winnie, *Sa-Gan-De-Oh*, chap. 2. See also Lomawaima, *Prairie Light*, chap. 5.

71. Thomas Wildcat Alford, *Civilization, and the Story of the Absentee Shawnees, as told to Florence Drake* (Norman: University of Oklahoma Press, 1936) 99–100; McCarthy, *Papago Traveler*, 26–30. See also Clifford Putney, *Muscular Christianity: Manhood and Sports in Protestant America, 1880–1920* (Cambridge MA: Harvard University Press, 2001).

72. CNEI, *Report* (1890), appendix C, 138–39; CNEI, *Report* (1903), 162. Many of the drills were of an obviously military nature: "Opening and closing of ranks."

73. CNEI, *Report* (1904), sect. 2, appendix K, 198–99.

74. For example, Putney, *Muscular Christianity*. In her study of Irish nuns, Mary Peckham Magray also sees disciplining the body as central. Magray, *The Transforming Power of the Nuns: Women, Religion, & Cultural Change in Ireland, 1750–1900* (New York: Oxford University Press, 1998). See also Patrick F. McDevitt, "Muscular Catholicism: Nationalism, Masculinity and Gaelic Sports, 1884–1916," *Gender and History* 9.2 (August 1997): 262–84.

75. CNEI, *Report* (1855), appendix G, 60.

76. O'Guiheen, *Pity*, 2; Shea, *Voices and the Sound of Drums*, 15, 17–18.

77. Frank O'Connor, *An Only Child* (London: Macmillan, 1961), 139–41.

78. Sean O'Faolain, *Vive Moi! An Autobiography* (London: Rupert Hart-Davis, 1965), 41–42.

79. Ibid., 42–50. O'Faolain remarked on the futility of reporting such brutality to parents or to the board; better to "humbly accept it as the will of God" (49). This is exactly my own recollection of acceptance of occasional outbursts of similar teacher brutality. It was part of life, and grumble though we might, we pupils had no realistic alternative but to accept it. Having experienced regular corporal punishment at school, and having witnessed outbursts of brutality, I have no difficulty in accepting the broad credibility of many such accounts.

80. La Flesche, *Middle Five*, xvii, 121. I return to this issue in chap. 6 and discuss the incident and its implications for autobiographical credibility in Michael C. Coleman, "The Historical Credibility of American Indian Autobiographical Accounts of Schooling, 1850–1930," *Irish Journal of American Studies* 3 (1994): 137–39.

81. Zitkala-Ša, *American Indian Stories*, 57–59; Talayesva, *Sun Chief*, 130.

82. Golden, *Red Moon*, 134.

83. Sekaquaptewa, *Me and Mine*, 136–38; Qoyawayma, *No Turning Back*, 27–28.

84. In Broderick H. Johnson, ed., *Stories of Traditional Navajo Life and Culture by Twenty-Two Navajo Men and Women* (Tsaile, Navajo Nation AZ: Navajo Community College Press, 1977), 175; also Myrtle Begay in ibid., 63; Horne and McBeth, *Essie's Story*, 33–37.

85. In Golden, *Red Moon*, 193.

86. Ibid., 198–99. See also Coleman, *American Indian Children at School*, esp. 157–59, on "getting used to it" and on school becoming a kind of home for some Indian pupils; La Flesche, *Middle Five*, 12; Betzinez, *I Fought with Geronimo*, 202. Also note 91, below.

87. Horne and McBeth, *Essie's Story*, 52–53. In the early and later decades of the twentieth century, the BIA attempted to close schools such as Haskell, Chilocco, or Rainy Mountain. Indian peoples defended them as "our schools" and often fought to keep them open. The government closed Rainy Mountain School in 1920, for example, but over the protests of many Kiowas. For them, writes Clyde Ellis, the boarding school "represented a vital link to the non-Indian world." And even seven decades later in the late 1990s, Ellis believes, "Rainy Mountain remains a powerful force for the Kiowa people." For those who made the break from the tribal home, or for those who perhaps came from difficult home environments or were orphans, the boarding school actually could become a home. See Ellis, *To Change Them Forever*, 183, 199.

5. Curriculum

Chapter epigraph: "Let the Children Speak," in Gertrude Golden, *Red Moon Called Me: Memoirs of a Schoolteacher in the Government Indian Service*, ed. Cecil Dryden (San Antonia TX: Naylor, 1954), 205.

1. M. J. Ashley, "Universes in Collision: Xhosa, Missionaries, and Education in Nineteenth Century South Africa," *Journal of Theology for Southern Africa* 36 (1980): 35. And see Ashley, "Features of Modernity: Missionaries and Educators in South Africa, 1850–1900," *Journal of Theology for Southern Africa* 38.1 (1982): 49–58.

2. David Vincent, *The Rise of Mass Literacy: Reading and Writing in Modern Europe* (Cambridge UK: Polity, 2000), 107.

3. James A. Mangan, "Images for Confident Control: Stereotypes in Imperial Discourse," in *The Imperial Curriculum: Racial Images and Education in the British Colonial Experience*, ed. Mangan (London: Routledge, 1993), 17.

4. Vincent, *Rise of Mass Literacy*, 79.

5. ARCIA (1889), 354.

6. Myrtle Paudlety to Miss Golden, January 4, 1909, in Golden, *Red Moon*, 197; Frank Mitchell, *Navajo Blessingway Singer: The Autobiography of Frank Mitchell, 1881–1967*, ed. Charlotte J. Frisbie and David P. McAllester (Tucson: University of Arizona Press, 1978), 63. During the century under review, huge numbers of letters and reports from BIA and missionary teachers were appended to the ARCIA; I have also consulted original manuscript sources in the National Archives, esp. in Record Group 75 (See American Sources: Archival Sources in the bibliographical note). I base my generalizations on this data and also on work of historians cited in this and other chapters.

7. On the McGuffey readers see John H. Westerhoff III, *McGuffey and His Readers: Piety, Morality, and Education in Nineteenth-Century America* (Nashville TN: Abingdon, 1978). This book contains samples from many levels of the readers. See also Joel Spring, *The American School: 1642–2000*, 5th ed. (Boston: McGraw-Hill, 2001) 156–61.

8. Francis La Flesche, The Middle Five: Indian Schoolboys of the Omaha Tribe (1900; rpt., Madison: University of Wisconsin Press, 1963), 62.

9. ARCIA (Washington DC: Government Printing Office, 1891), 69.

10. This and next four paragraphs: ARCIA (Washington DC: Government Printing Office, 1883), 162–64.

11. This and next two paragraphs: ARCIA (1890), H. Exec. Doc., no. 1, part 5, vol. 2, 51st Cong., 2nd sess., serial 2841, appendix, "Course of Study," clvi–clxii. For a later "new and uniform course of study" see ARCIA (Washington DC: Government Printing Office, 1916), 9–23. The course was planned "with the vocational aims very clear and dominant" (22). On progressive educational ideas see, for example, Jon Reyhner and Joanne Eder, American Indian Education: A History (Norman: University of Oklahoma Press, 2004), 101–4, 210–31; Spack, America's Second Language, esp. 56, 60–61; Margaret Connell Szasz, Education and the American Indian: The Road to Self-Determination since 1928, 3rd ed. (Albuquerque: University of New Mexico Press, 1999), chap. 5. The influences of progressive educational ideas for the CNEI is also a major them of Thomas A. O'Donoghue, Bilingual Education in Ireland, 1904–1922: The Case of the Bilingual Programme of Instruction, Centre for Irish Studies Monograph no. 1 (Perth, Australia: Murdoch University, 2000). I discuss progressive education later in the present chapter.

12. John Logan, "The Dimension of Gender in Nineteenth-Century Schooling," in Gender Perspectives in 19th Century Ireland: Public and Private Spheres (Dublin: Irish Academic Press, 1997), 48. Most of the mixed-gender schools were in the sparsely populated areas of Ireland, and by 1900 three-quarters of the teachers were women.

13. Antonia McManus, The Irish Hedge School and Its Books, 1695–1831 (Dublin: Four Courts Press, 2002), 233–36; Janet Nolan, Servants of the Poor: Teachers and Mobility in Ireland and America (Notre Dame IN: University of Notre Dame Press, 2004), 18–22 and chap. 1, on the CNEI curriculum. On gender see also Logan, "Dimension of Gender," 36–49. The gendered perspective is also apparent in the yearly Report of the CNEI, cited earlier in the text.

14. This and following paragraph: CNEI, Report (1873), appendix A, 56–69.

15. CNEI, Report (1900), 37.

16. This and following three paragraphs: CNEI, Report (1904), appendix, section 2, K, 191–221.

17. In the national schools there was a less clear break than at BIA schools between literary and vocational subjects; many subjects taught to girls in the regular curriculum were obviously of a vocational nature. Logan notes how "the notion of separate though complementary spheres had a powerful manifestation in a curriculum of manual instruction. . . . A vigorous burst of innovation and experimentation in the 1880s and 1890s led to further demarcation of new subject and technical instruction." Needlework and domestic economy "now spawned sewing, dressmaking, cookery, poultry management, laundry work, dairy management and spinning." Irish youth "would be systematically initiated into appropriate and consequently separate occupations." Logan, "Dimensions of Gender," 45–46.

18. Patrick Gallagher, *My Story* (Dungloe, County Donegal: Templecrone Co-operative Society, n.d.), 6, 19; Sean O'Faolain, *Vive Moi! An Autobiography* (London: Rupert Hart-Davis, 1965), 46.

19. Spack, *America's Second Language*, 46, for example. The inadequacy of cultural training for BIA teachers even in the late twentieth century emerges in Reyhner and Eder, *American Indian Education*, 276–81.

20. ARCIA (Washington DC: Government Printing Office, 1887), 249.

21. Zallie Yulow in ARCIA (Washington DC: Government Printing Office, 1885), 250; ARCIA (1896), H. Doc., no. 5, vol. 1, 54th Cong., 2nd sess., serial 3489, 23. "It is hard to realize the magnitude of the task which confronts the Indian woman," continued the commissioner. "With the change of domicile [from tipi to modern cabin] is implied a new way of eating, sleeping, and dressing, new occupations, even new hygiene." See also discussions of gender in chap. 1 of the present book and, for example, Michael C. Coleman, *Presbyterian Missionary Attitudes toward American Indians, 1837–1893* (Jackson: University Press of Mississippi, 1985), 92–97; David Smits, "The 'Squaw Drudge': A Prime Index of Heathenism," *Ethnohistory* 29 (1982): 281–306.

22. Margaret D. Jacobs has shown how individual BIA female employees who strongly advocated such changes could, through their own independent and even anti-male attitudes, subvert many of the goals of the campaign. Jacobs, *Engendered Encounters: Feminism and Pueblo Cultures, 1879–1934* (Lincoln: University of Nebraska Press, 1999), esp. chaps. 1 and 2.

23. ARCIA (1853), S. Exec. Doc., no. 1, 35th Cong., 2nd sess., serial 658, 348–49; ARCIA (Washington DC: Government Printing Office, 1877), 136–37.

24. ARCIA (Washington DC: Government Printing Office, 1887), xvii–iii; see also Coleman, *American Indian Children*, 43; Robert A. Trennert Jr., "From Carlisle to Phoenix: The Rise and Fall of the Indian Outing System, 1878–1930," *Pacific Historical Review* 52 (August 1983): 267–91. Student files give details of each boy's or girl's "outing" experience. See School Records, Records of the Carlisle Indian Industrial School, Records of Non-Reservation Schools, RG 75, NA.

25. ARCIA, *Annual Reports of the Department of the Interior* (Washington DC: Government Printing Office, 1903), part 1, 381–84. Also, ARCIA (1905), H. Doc., vol. 19, 59th Cong., sess. 1, serial 4959, 1–13; Coleman, *American Indian Children*, 46–50. On the "new and uniform course of study" of 1915, see ARCIA (Washington DC: Government Printing Office, 1916), 9–23. The economic needs of Indians, especially, "demand . . . instruction along eminently practical lines" (10).

26. Hoxie, *Final Promise*, 210; the words are from the 1984 text, but in his preface to the 2001 reprint he has not changed his views on these major issues. K. Tsianina Lomawaima, *They Called It Prairie Light: The Story of the Chilocco Indian School* (Lincoln: University of Nebraska Press, 1994), 87.

27. ARCIA, *Annual Reports of the Department of the Interior* (Washington DC: Government Printing Office, 1898), 381.

28. ARCIA (Washington DC: Government Printing Office, 1906), 206; ARCIA, *Reports of the Department of the Interior* (Washington DC: Government Printing Office, 1907), 351.

29. ARCIA (1906), H. Doc., vol. 15, 59th Cong., 2nd sess., serial 5118, 179–80.

30. Irene Stewart, A Voice in Her Tribe: A Navajo Woman's Own Story, ed. Dorris Ostrander Dawdy and Mary Shepardson, Anthropological Paper no. 17 (Socorro NM: Ballena Press, 1980), 17; Kay Bennett, Kaibah: Recollections of a Navajo Girlhood (Los Angeles: Westernlore Press, 1964), 218, 227.

31. Haskell exam answers, in Examination Papers, 1915 (Haskell Institute), Records of the Education Division, RG 75, NA; Luther Standing Bear, My People the Sioux, ed. E. A. Brininstool (1928; rpt., Lincoln: University of Nebraska Press, 1975), 147, 175–90, and chaps. 16–18; Jason Betzinez, with William Sturtevant Nye, I Fought for Geronimo (1959; rpt., Lincoln: University of Nebraska Press, 1987), 154–59; Daniel La France, "An Indian Boy's Story," Independent 55 (July 30, 1903): 1783–84.

32. Helen Sekaquaptewa, Me and Mine: The Life Story of Helen Sekaquaptewa, as told to Louise Udall (Tucson: University of Arizona Press, 1969), 124, 138, 183, and 188 (on Hopi work ethic).

33. Don Talayesva, Sun Chief: The Autobiography of a Hopi Indian, ed. Leo W. Simmons (New Haven CT: Yale University Press, 1942), 109; James McCarthy, A Papago Traveler: The Memories of James McCarthy, ed. John G. Westover (Tucson: Sun Tracks and University of Arizona Press, 1985), 43, 45; Lucille (Gerry) Winnie, Sah-gan-de-oh: The Chief's Daughter (New York: Vantage Press, 1969), 50. Also, Kabotie, Hopi Indian Artist, 30, 32; Sekaquaptewa, Me and Mine, 139.

34. CNEI, Report (1840), in Reports to the Commissioners . . . 1834 to 1845, 160; CNEI, Report (1890), appendix C, 39; CNEI, Report (1893), appendix C, 95.

35. CNEI, Report (1842), in Reports of the Commissioners . . . 1834 to 1845, 184; CNEI, Report (1845), 307; CNEI, Report (1847), 139.

36. John Coolahan, Irish Education: Its History and Structure (Dublin: Institute of Public Administration, 1981), 7.

37. Coolahan, Irish Education, 7–8, 23–24. With the ending of the "payments by results" system in 1900, and responding to criticism that its curriculum was "too 'bookish,'" the board accepted recommendations that "Manual Instruction should be introduced and should be continued through all the classes," CNEI, Report (1900), 7–9, 57.

38. See also, for example, Stearns, Schools and Students, 156–57. He generalizes on the United States, France, and Japan.

39. CNEI, Report (1884), appendix C, 221–22; CNEI, Report (1889), appendix B, 8.

40. IFC 1194:533–34.

41. Eamon Kelly, The Apprentice (Dublin: Merino Press, 1996), 69–70; IFC 1157:426; R. B. Robson, Autobiography of an Ulster Teacher (Belfast: n.p., 135), chap. 16.

42. Peter N. Stearns, Schools and Students in Industrial Society: Japan and the West, 1870-1940 (Boston: Bedford, 1998), 63. Stearns notes that by the 1850s middle-class Americans were moving from earlier ideas of children as sinful to a belief in them as innocent. Yet a major goal of the new school systems was to keep them this way. For broader contexts, see Colin Heywood, A History of Childhood: Children and Childhood in the West from Medieval to Modern Times (Cambridge UK: Polity, 2001).

43. ARCIA, *Annual Reports of the Department of the Interior* (Washington DC: Government Printing Office, 1899), part 1, 29; ARCIA, *Annual Reports of the Department of the Interior* (1903), part 1, 7; ARCIA (1890), *H. Exec. Doc.*, no. 1, part 5, vol. 2, 51st Cong., 2nd sess., serial 2841, appendix, "Course of Study," clix.

44. Standing Bear, *My People the Sioux*, 144–45, 203; ARCIA (Washington DC: Government Printing Office, 1882), 180. Also, M. Friedmann, Annual Report, *The Red Man* 3 (1910): 63; Report of School at Hampton, Va., ARCIA, *Report of the Secretary of the Interior* (Washington DC: Government Printing Office, 1895), vol. 2:414. On the struggle of the BIA to accommodate both Protestant and Catholic demands for Indian schooling, see Francis Paul Prucha, *The Churches and the Indian Schools, 1888–1912* (Lincoln: University of Nebraska Press, 1979).

45. ARCIA (Washington DC: Government Printing Office, 1892), 212; ARCIA, *Report of the Secretary of the Interior* (Washington DC: Government Printing Office, 1896), 198. Also ARCIA, *Reports of the Department of the Interior* (Washington DC: Government Printing Office, 1920), vol. 2:12, quoted in chap. 2 of this book.

46. Zitkala-Ša (Gertrude Bonnin), *American Indian Stories* (1921; rpt., Lincoln: University of Nebraska Press), 62–64, 73; Sekaquaptewa, *Me and Mine*, 129, 222–44. She became a Mormon.

47. Mitchell, *Navajo Blessingway Singer*, 65–66. Like Sekaquaptewa he blended at least two spiritual traditions: he was both a traditional "singer" and a Catholic; Talayesva, *Sun Chief*, 96, 116–17, 119–34.

48. La Flesche, *Middle Five*, 14; Mary Little Bear Inkanish, *Dance around the Sun: The Life of Mary Little Bear Inkanish: Cheyenne*, ed. Alice Marriot and Carol K. Rachlin (New York: Crowell, 1977), 50–51, 53; David E. Jones, *Sanapia: Comanche Medicine Woman* (Prospect Heights IL: Waveland Press, 1972), 24.

49. La Flesche, *Middle Five*, 62–63; Betzinez, *I Fought with Geronimo*, 156; Howard Whitewolf, "A Short Story of My Life," *American Indian Magazine* 5 (January–March 1917): 29, 31.

50. Alford, *Civilization*, 76–77, 104–7.

51. The complex motivations for religious and cultural changes, along with the equally complex manipulations of Western cultures and religions by non-Western peoples, are a major concern of writers cited throughout the present work, such as David W. Adams, John Bloom, Clyde Ellis, Sally McBeth, Scott Riney, and the present writer; also a concern of Native American historians such as Brenda J. Child, K. Tsianina Lomawaima, and Devon A. Mihesuah. See also Jeffrey Ostler, *The Plains Sioux and U.S. Colonialism from Lewis and Clark to Wounded Knee* (New York: Cambridge University Press, 2004), chap. 8; Bonnie Sue Lewis, *Creating Indian Christians: Native Clergy in the Presbyterian Church* (Norman: University of Oklahoma Press, 2003), esp. chap. 1; Neal Salisbury, "Embracing Ambiguity: Native Peoples and Christianity in Seventeenth-Century North America," *Ethnohistory* 50.2 (Spring 2003): 247–59.

52. The diversity of tribal spiritual beliefs emerges from many Indian autobiographies. A recent synthesis is Joel Martin, *The Land Looks after Us: A History of Native*

American Religion (New York: Oxford University Press, 2001). Also, for example, H. L. Harrod, *Becoming and Remaining a People: Native American Religions on the Northern Plains* (Tucson: University of Arizona Press, 1995); R. J. DeMallie and Douglas R. Parks, eds., *Sioux Indian Religion: Tradition and Innovation* (Norman: University of Oklahoma Press, 1987); J. D. Loftin, *Religion and Hopi Life in the Twentieth Century* (Bloomington IN: Indiana University Press, 1991).

53. Coleman, *American Indian Children*, 118–19; see also chap. 4, section 3, on the seven "clusters" of influences I suggest for examining pupil motivations.

54. Edward Goodbird, *Goodbird the Indian: His Story*, ed. Gilbert L. Wilson (1914; rpt., St. Paul: University of Minnesota Press, 1985), esp. chap. 5, quotation from 44.

55. Malcolm McFee, "The 150% Man, a Product of Blackfeet Acculturation," *American Anthropologist* 70 (December 1968): 1096–1103.

56. CNEI, *Report* (1845), *Reports of the Commissioners . . . 1834 to 1825*, 385; CNEI, *Report* (1836), 62.

57. CNEI, *Report* (1845), 318–19; CNEI, *Report* (1915–16), appendix, Rules and Regulations, 7–8.

58. CNEI, *Report* (1900), 6; CNEI, *Report* (1915–16), Rules and Regulations, chap. 3 (Religious Instruction), 1–11 (paginated separately). On clashing Protestant and Catholic views on religious instruction and services at BIA schools, see Prucha, *Churches and Indian Schools*, chaps. 12 and 13.

59. Statistic: CNEI, *Report* (1900), 16; Robert Briscoe with Alden Hatch, *For the Life of Me* (Boston: Little, Brown, 1958).

60. Robson, *Autobiography*, 13; IFC 1057:482–83. See also IFC 1762:412–17; O'Leary, *My Story*, 54.

61. Frank O'Connor, *An Only Child* (London: Macmillan, 1961), 147; Shea, *Voices and the Sound of Drums*, 16.

62. For a recent synthesis, see Spring, *America's Schools*.

63. For example, Scott Riney, *The Rapid City Indian School, 1893–1923* (Norman: University of Oklahoma Press, 1999), 122–24. Many of these performances, writes Riney, "played on white stereotype and misrepresentations of Indian cultures."

64. Angel DeCora, "Angel DeCora—An Autobiography," *Red Man* 5 (May 1913): 279–85. For an excellent recent account of her pedagogy and many contributions to Indian art, see Anne Ruggles Gere, "The Art of Survivance: Angel DeCora at Carlisle, *American Indian Quarterly* 28.3/4 (Summer and Fall 2004): 649–84; Fred Kabotie, *Fred Kabotie: Hopi Indian Artist: An Autobiography Told with Bill Belknap* (Flagstaff: Museum of Northern Arizona/Northland Press, 1977), 27–29; Thomas G. Andrews, "Turning the Tables on Assimilation: Oglala Lakotas and the Pine Ridge Day Schools, 1889–1920s," *Western Historical Quarterly* 33 (Winter 2002): 421–25.

65. Talayesva, *Sun Chief*, 95.

66. Standing Bear, *My People the Sioux*. For his more critical view, see *Land of the Spotted Eagle* (1933; rpt., Lincoln: University of Nebraska Press, 1978), for example, 235–36, 242.

67. This and the following paragraph: Examination Papers, 1915 (Haskell

Institute), Records of the Education Division, RG 75, NA. In Ireland the CNEI gave detailed requirements for its courses, suggesting what was to be asked in examinations. See, for example, CNEI, Report (1873), appendix A, Programme of Instruction and Examination for National Schools, and Scale of Results Fees, 56–69; CNEI, Report (1904), appendix, section 2, K, schedule 18, Programme, 191–21.

68. U.S. Statutes at Large 43 (June 2, 1924): 253. See John R. Wunder, "Retained by the People": A History of American Indians and the Bill of Rights (New York: Oxford University Press, 1994), 44–51.

69. Institute for Government Research, The Problem of Indian Administration (Meriam Report) (Baltimore: Johns Hopkins University Press, 1928). I summarize the Meriam Report's criticisms in Coleman, American Indian Children, 50–53.

70. The goal of the 1904 Bilingual Programme was that such children would leave school literate and numerate in both languages and would receive a general education also in both languages. O'Donoghue, Bilingual Education in Ireland, 2, 112.

71. Sixth Reading Book (Dublin: CNEI, 1897), 165–66. Copies of some of these texts and others used in the national schools are available in the National Library of Ireland and the Early Printed Books Library of Trinity College, University of Dublin. I consulted, along with the Sixth Reading Book, the following: The Third Book of Lessons for the Use of the Irish National Schools (1836); The Second Book of Lessons (1861); The Third Book of Lessons (1863); The Third Reading Book (1867); The Fifth Reading Book (1869); Selections from the British Poets . . . (1875, 1898). Readers also contained passages about famous beauty spots such as the lakes of Killarney, Glendalough, or the Giant's Causeway; or from work by other Irish poets (from Oliver Goldsmith's "The Deserted Village" or Patrick Campbell's "The Harper and His Dog"—along with "Ye Mariners of England"); or about the "Christian Antiquities of Ireland" and the "Pagan Antiquities of Ireland." And see J. P. (Lorcan) Walsh, "A Comparative Analysis of the Reading Books of the Commissioners of National Education and of the Christian Brothers, 1831–1900" (M.A. thesis, National University of Ireland, Dublin, 1983), 92. Walsh depicts the inclusion of more—but uncontroversial—material on Ireland in the later nineteenth century.

72. CNEI, Report (1904), appendix, section 2, K, 194, 204.

73. CNEI, Report (1888), appendix B, 128–29; CNEI Report (1891), appendix B, 173; CNEI Report, (1893), appendix C, 177.

74. CNEI, Report (1908), appendix, Section 18, Programmes, 88, 92; David Fitzpatrick, "The Futility of History: A Failed Experiment in Irish Education," in Ideology and the Historians, ed. Ciaran Brady (Dublin: Lilliput Press, 1991), 173. Also see John Coolahan, "The Irish and Others in Nineteenth-Century Textbook," in The Imperial Curriculum, ed. J. A. Mangan, 54–63; Coolahan, "Imperialism and the Irish National School System," in "Benefits Bestowed": Education and British Imperialism, ed. J. A. Mangan (Manchester UK: University of Manchester Press, 1988), esp. 84–91; Gabriel Doherty, "National Identity and the Study of Irish History," English Historical Review 111 (1996): 324–49, with quotation from 329; Walsh, "Comparative Analysis of the Reading Books."

75. For an excellent examination of sanctioned history readers, spanning a spectrum from moderate nationalist to moderate unionist ideologies, see Karin Fischer, "Another Irish Nation: Historiographical Variations as Found in Late-Nineteenth-Century and Early Twentieth-Century Schools," *Canadian Journal of Irish Studies* 30.1 (2004): 41–47. I thank the author for sending me a copy. I examined R. Barry O'Brien, *The Children's Study: Ireland* (1897); P. W. Joyce, *A Child's History of Ireland* (1897); P. W. Joyce, *A Concise History of Ireland from the Earliest Times to 1908* (1912); H. Kingsmill Moore, *Irish History for Young Readers* (1915).

76. Minutes of board meetings of the Commissioners of National Education in Ireland, 1831–1900 (National Library of Ireland [NLI], M.S.S.); also, Minutes of the Proceedings of the Commissioners of National Education in Ireland, 1900–1922 (private and confidential), (NLI). Also Fitzpatrick, "Futility of History."

77. CNEI, *Report* (1885), appendix C, 181; CNEI, *Report* (1895), appendix B, 179.

78. CNEI, *Report* (1895), appendix B, 136. Contemporaneously in England, elementary school books and curricula explicitly foregrounded Englishness and Britishness and distinguished English education and history from those of Germany or France. One could facetiously claim that the CNEI also foregrounded Britishness. See Stephen Heathorn, *For Home, Country, and Race: Constructing Gender, Class, and Englishness in the Elementary School* (Toronto: University of Toronto Press, 2000).

79. W. J. M. Starkie, *Recent Reforms in Irish Education* (1902), 10, quoted in John Coolahan, "Education as Cultural Imperialism: The Denial of the Irish Language to Irish Speakers, 1831–1922," *Paedagogica Historica* 37.1 (2001): 28. On Starkie's concern about books, see Fitzpatrick, "Futility of History," esp. 178–81 (quotations from Starkie's diary).

80. Of the many studies examining Indian policy reform, see Reyhner and Eder, *American Indian Education*, chaps. 4–7; Szasz, *Education and the American Indian*, esp. chaps. 2 and 3; Hoxie, *Final Promise*; Lucy Maddox, *Citizen Indians: Native Americans Intellectuals, Race, and Reform* (Ithaca NY: Cornell University Press, 2005).

81. On "voice," see Jacqueline Fear-Segal, commentary (manuscript) on Michael C. Coleman, "Assimilating the Irish and the Indians: A Comparative Study in Cross-Cultural Education," paper presented to the Annual Meeting of the Organization of American Historians (OAH), St. Louis MO, March 30, 2000.

82. CNEI, *Report* (1856), appendix B, 4, 170; Report of Special Agent in Indian Service, ARCIA (Washington DC: Government Printing Office, 1889), 345.

83. CNEI, *Report* (1895), appendix B, 179.

84. CNEI, *Report* (1865), appendix C, 167.

85. CNEI, *Report* (1877), appendix C, 91; CNEI *Report* (1890), appendix C, 73. These criticisms are corroborated by my own memory of Irish elementary and secondary school to 1964. Poetry, Shakespeare, religious catechism—parts were learned by heart. "You—the next sixteen lines": this is my memory of the approach of many, though not all, teachers.

86. O'Connor, *Only Child*, 141; O'Faolain, *Vive Moi!* 46 (so can I—almost fifty years

later!); IFC 1572.242 (first-person account). Also, on corporal punishment during religious class: IFC 1573:242, and IFC 1057:396–97.

87. Kelly, Apprentice, 77–78.

88. O'Connor, Only Child, 140.

89. Peig Sayers, Peig: The Autobiography of Peig Sayers of the Great Blasket Island, trans. Bryan MacMahon (n.p.: Talbot, 1974), 19.

90. Charles Hutchins to Hon. W. P. Dole, Oct. 15, 1864, Letters received 1824–81, Schools 1824–73, M659, reel 794, 96–97, RG 75, NA; ARCIA (1897) H. Doc., no. 5, 55th Cong., 2nd sess., serial 3641, 336–37. On the mechanical nature of "recitation," see Spack, America's Second Language, 62–63.

91. La Flesche, Middle Five, xviii (language), 50–52 (history).

92. La Flesche, Middle Five, 45; Standing Bear, My People the Sioux, 239.

93. Anna Moore Shaw, A Pima Past (Tucson: University of Arizona Press, 1974), 126–27.

94. Sprack, America's Second Language, esp. 60–61.

95. ARCIA, Annual Reports of the Department of the Interior (Washington DC: Government Printing Office, 1903), part I, 384.

96. Spack, America's Second Language, esp. chap. 2, with quotations from 61, 71, 75. Spack's comments on the unwillingness of Indian pupils to speak the new language, for fear of public embarrassment (64–65), strikes a chord with someone like myself who has tried for decades to activate Finnish university students "to use" English.

97. CNEI, Report (1884), 161–62, 230; CNEI, Report (1903), 161–62. On the direct method (modh díreach) in Ireland, and some of its inadequacies for bilingual teaching, see also O'Donoghue, Bilingual Education Ireland, esp. 63–66 and chap. 5.

98. Kelly, Apprentice, 70–71.

99. Fitzpatrick, "Futility of History," esp. 182–83; Vincent, Rise of Mass Literacy, esp. chap. 5. "What the newly literate thought they were doing as they took up a book or a pen was neither controlled by nor independent of the purposes designated by authors and educators" (145). Also see Stearns, Schools and Students, 163, for example.

100. ARCIA (1892), 699; Charles A. Eastman (Ohiyesa), From the Deep Woods to Civilization: Chapters in the Autobiography of an Indian (1916; rpt., Lincoln: University of Nebraska Press, 1977), 47, 54; Goodbird, Goodbird the Indian, 43; Standing Bear, My People the Sioux, 155, on the shock when a teacher accurately predicted an eclipse.

101. Thomas Wildcat Alford, Civilization, and the Story of the Absentee Shawnees, as told to Florence Drake (Norman: University of Oklahoma Press, 1936), 80; Asa Daklugie et al., Indeh: An Apache Odyssey, ed. Eve Ball, (Norman: University of Oklahoma Press, 1988), 141, 144–45.

102. John Willinsky, Learning to Divide the World: Education at Empire's End (Minneapolis: University of Minnesota Press, 1998), 137, and chap. 7. See also Declan Kiberd, Inventing Ireland: The Literature of the Modern Nation (London: Vintage, 1996), 619–20.

103. Sayers, Peig, 26; O'Sullivan, Twenty Years A-Growing, trans. Moya Llewelyn Davies and George Thomson (Oxford: Oxford University Press, 1983), 3–4; Micheál

O'Guiheen, *A Pity Youth Does Not Last: Reminiscences of the Last of the Great Blasket Island's Poets and Storytellers*, trans. Tim Enright (Oxford: Oxford University Press, 1982), 3.

104. Patrick Shea, *Voices and the Sound of Drums: An Irish Autobiography* (Belfast: Blackstaff, 1981), 15. Compare with early-twentieth-century science curriculum (for boys), CNEI, *Report* (1904), appendix, section 2, K, 199–201.

105. O'Faolain, *Vive Moi!* 45–46.

106. This is the major theme of Nolan's *Servants of the Poor*: how the national schools stimulated girls, especially through the role model effects of female teachers. Many Irish girls emigrated to become domestics (servants of the rich); later generations of Irish American women rose in class status to become elementary school teachers (servants of the poor). With women's decreasing prospects of marriage or a cash job in post-Famine Ireland, "the national school increasingly served as a training ground for emigration, equipping girls [especially] with the necessary skills to seek their fortunes outside the country" (27). Further, the schools did offer "a wider worldview" that served emigrants especially well.

107. On French policy in Brittany see Vincent, *Rise of Mass Literacy*, 142–43; Helias Pierre-Jakez, "A Breton Peasant Remembers the 1920s," in Stearns, *Schools and Students*, 101–106.

6. School Staff

1. CNEI, *Report* (1857), appendix A, section 1, 6.

2. CNEI, *Report* (1913–14), appendix, section 1, 114.

3. Boarding school matrons were to be surrogate mothers for Indian children, especially girls by taking care of, disciplining, and training them to proper health, hygiene, and gender roles. See T. Tsianina Lomawaima, *They Called it Prairie Light: The Story of Chilocco Indian School* (Lincoln: University of Nebraska Press, 1994), 45–46. On "field matrons," see Lisa E. Emmerich, "'Right in the Midst of My Own People': Native American Women and the Field Matron Program," in *American Nations: Encounters in Indian Country, 1850 to the Present*, ed. Frederick E. Hoxie, Peter N. Mancall, and James H. Merrell (New York: Routledge, 2001), 143–55.

4. John Coolahan, *Irish Education: Its History and Structure* (Dublin: Institute of Public Administration, 1981), 30. Oliver Goldsmith, "Deserted Village" (1770), lines 193–216, can be found at http://etext.virginia.edu/toc/modeng/public/GolDese.html (accessed June 15, 2006).

5. ARCIA (Washington DC: Government Printing Office, 1877), 134.

6. ARCIA (Washington DC: Government Printing Office, 1888), 256–57.

7. Quoted in Clyde Ellis, *To Change Them Forever: Indian Education at the Rainy Mountain Boarding School, 1893–1920* (Norman: University of Oklahoma Press, 1996), 43; Minnie Braithwaite Jenkins, *Girl from Williamsburg* (1951), 33, in Patricia A. Carter, "'Completely Discouraged': Women Teachers' Resistance in the Bureau of Indian Affairs Schools, 1900–1910," *Frontiers* 15.3 (1995): 53, and see whole article, 53–86.

8. Gertrude Golden, *Red Moon Called Me: Memoirs of a Schoolteacher in the Government Indian Service*, ed. Cecil Dryden (San Antonio TX: Naylor, 1954), 90.

9. Institute for Government Research, *The Problem of Indian Administration* (Meriam Report) (Baltimore: Johns Hopkins University Press, 1928), 368.

10. Carter, "'Completely Discouraged,'" 53–86, with quotations from 79.

11. Ibid., esp. 58–68, with quotation from 65 (from Estelle Audrey Brown's autobiography, *Stubborn Fool* [1952]); David Wallace Adams, *Education for Extinction: American Indians and the Boarding School Experience, 1875–1928* (Lawrence: University Press of Kansas, 1994), 82–94. From my own research I strongly agree with these broad generalizations on BIA teacher motivations.

12. Golden, *Red Moon*, xi.

13. Michael C. Coleman, *Presbyterian Missionary Attitudes toward American Indians, 1837–1893* (Jackson: University Press of Mississippi, 1985), 23–27.

14. R. B. Robson, *Autobiography of an Ulster Teacher* (Belfast: n.p., 1935), with quotation from 54.

15. John Logan, "The Dimensions of Gender in Nineteenth-Century Education," in *Gender Perspectives in 19th-Century Ireland: Public and Private Spheres*, ed. Margaret Kelleher and James H. Murphy (Dublin: Irish Academic Press, 1997), 46–49. By 1901 CNEI female teachers received about 80 percent of what males received. Although in 1900 about 55 per cent of teachers were women, only 28 per cent of principals were female.

16. By the beginning of the twentieth century, the term "profession" meant a dignified vocation practiced by "professionals," who professed selfless contractual service, membership of a strong association, and functional expertise modeled on the natural sciences. Bruce Kimball, *The "True Professional Ideal" in America: A History* (Cambridge MA: Harvard University Press, 1992), 303. On "normal" teacher training departments, see Jon Reyhner and Jeanne Eder, *American Indian Education: A History* (Norman: University of Oklahoma Press, 2004), 138; Anne Ruggles Gere, "Indian Heart/White Man's Head: Native-American Teachers in Indian Schools, 1880–1930," *History of Education Quarterly* 45.1 (Spring 2005): 47–48.

17. Theodore Fischbacher, "A Study of the Role of the Federal Government in the Education of the American Indian" (PhD diss., Arizona State University, 1967), 55–59, 89–92, 123–25.

18. ARCIA (1890), H. *Exec. Doc.*, no. 1, part 5, vol. 2, 51st Congress, 2nd sess., serial 2841, cxlvi–cxlvii.

19. Fischbacher, "Study," 89–92, 123–25; ARCIA (Washington DC: Government Printing Office, 1888), xxi–xxiv; ARCIA (1890), H. *Exec. Doc.*, no. 1, part 5, vol. 2, 51st Cong., 2nd sess., serial 2841, xvii.

20. ARCIA (1890), H. *Exec. Doc.*, no. 1, part 5, vol. 2, 51st Cong., 2nd sess., serial 2841, cxlviii. See cxlvi, on the conditions of appointment for an agent, esp. "that the education and proper training of Indian children . . . receive your constant and careful attention."

21. On civil service status, ARCIA (1897), H. *Doc.*, no. 5, 55th Cong., 2nd sess., serial 2641, 322: "The effect of placing the employees of the Indian schools in the classified service has been quite salutary," declared the superintendent of Indian schools. "There has been a marked increase in stability of tenure, efficiency, and real devotion

to the work on the part of the [Indian] service as a whole." Also see Reyhner and Eder, *American Indian Education*, esp. 89–97; cf. Dorothy W. Hewes, "Those First Good Years of Indian Education, 1894–1898," *American Indian Culture and Research Journal* 5.2 (1981): 75–76, on the development a more relevant civil service examination. Hewes does not cite a source on this.

22. ARCIA (1897), H. Doc., no. 5, 55th Cong., 2nd sess., serial 2641, 327–29.

23. ARCIA (1906), H. Doc., vol. 15, 59th Cong., 2nd sess., serial 5118, 69.

24. Esther Burnett Horne and Sally McBeth, *Essie's Story: The Life and Legacy of a Shoshone Teacher* (Lincoln: University of Nebraska Press, 1998), 71–79, 94. Beyond the period covered by this study, she graduated as a qualified teacher from the Normal Training Department of the Haskell Institute. Her ongoing training was through BIA inservice summer schools.

25. ARCIA, *Reports of the Department of the Interior* (Washington DC: Government Printing Office, 1913), 25–26.

26. Because they were far more isolated than teachers in white communities, teachers at Indian schools had less opportunity to organize themselves for employee solidarity: "the absence of sympathetic colleagues limited the possibility of unified worker action against the BIA." See Carter, "'Completely Discouraged,'" 79. The decade between 1900 and 1910 was "one of transition for the BIA, as policy-makers struggled to increase professionalization and stability amid exponential growth of schools and workers" (54). On the Irish National Teachers Organization (INTO) and its growing bargaining power, see Coolahan, *Irish Education*, 31–32; Síle Chuinneghǎin, "Women Teachers and INTO Policy, 1905–16," *Irish Educational Studies* 14 (Spring 1995): 221–25.

27. Institute for Government Research, *Indian Administration* (Meriam Report), 360, 367, 359. See 359–70.

28. CNEI, Report (1835), in *Reports of the Commissioners . . . 1834 to 1845, Inclusive*, 18–20.

29. CNEI, Report (1845), in ibid., 334–35, 321.

30. Coolahan, *Irish Education*, 31; Marienne A. Larsen, "Pedagogic Knowledge and the Victorian Era Anglo-American Teacher," *History of Education* 31.5 (2002): 457–74. In Britain, the United States, and Canada, Larsen writes, "School inspectors, educational reformers and teacher-trainers all agreed on the importance or moral training in the education of the working classes. Above all, the teacher was to be a moral trainer, instilling Christian virtues into the hearts and minds of his/her pupils" (465).

31. CNEI, Report (1835), in *Reports of the Board . . . 1834 to 1842, Inclusive*, 20; Coolahan, *Irish Education*, 23.

32. Coolahan, *Irish Education*, 23; CNEI, Report (1846), 10–12.

33. Coolahan, *Irish Education*, 23, 32–33. Tony Fahey notes that by the 1870s, although three-quarters of female lay teachers were formally untrained, "a large proportion of them had received an unofficially and largely informal training as monitors in convent schools." See "Nuns in the Catholic Church in Ireland in the Nineteenth Century," in *Girls Don't Do Honours: Irish Women in Education in the 19th and 20th Centuries* (Dublin: Women's Education Bureau, 1987), 24–26. Fahey also notes that the nuns who participated in such training of monitors were themselves often untrained,

"keen amateurs [rather] than professionals in the strict sense of the term." They then made no important contributions to the science of pedagogy. Mary Peckham Magray also points to the important role of nuns, through their senior schools, in providing some form of teacher training for Catholics until the changes of the 1880s. Indeed, one of their training schools was to become the first of the Catholic teacher-training colleges in 1883. See Magray, *The Transforming Power of the Nuns: Women, Religion, and Cultural Change in Ireland, 1750–1900* (New York: Oxford University Press, 1998), 81–82.

34. CNEI, *Report* (1903), 2; CNEI, *Report* (1919–20), 28.

35. CNEI, *Report* (1911–12), 44. See also Thomas A. O'Donoghue, *Bilingual Education in Ireland, 1904–1922: The Case of the Bilingual Programme of Instruction*, Centre for Irish Studies Monograph no. 1 (Perth, Australia: Murdoch University, 2000), chap. 4, on related teacher training problems.

36. Robson, *Autobiography*, chaps. 10–13, with quotations from 79, 82, 94.

37. CNEI, *Report* (1877), appendix C, 159. Also, Janet Nolan, *Servants of the Poor: Teachers and Mobility in Ireland and Irish America* (Notre Dame IN: University of Notre Dame Press, 2004), chap. 2.

38. IFC 1057:396–97; IFC 1157:434.

39. ARCIA (1895), H. Doc., no. 5, vol. 2, 54th Cong., 1st sess., serial 3382, 249; Horne and McBeth, *Essie's Story*, 64. On abuses at Canadian Indian schools see J. R. Miller, *Shingwauk's Vision: A History of Native Residential Schools* (Toronto: University of Toronto Press, 1996), chap. 11.

40. Education 9, file 14357, NAI. It is doubtful whether better screening and training would have reduced such mistreatment of children in both areas. By the 1960s in Ireland teachers had gone through or were going through training. This did not prevent the occasional outbursts of brutality and endemic corporal punishment that I observed at school.

41. Helen Sekaquatewa, *Me and Mine: The Life Story of Helen Sekaquaptewa, As told to Louise Udall* (Tucson: University of Arizona Press, 1969), 104–7; John Bloom, *To Show What an Indian Can Do: Sports at Native American Boarding Schools* (Minneapolis: University of Minnesota Press, 2000), 94. On Canada, through and beyond the period covered by the present study, see Miller, *Shingwauk's Vision*, esp. 328–37. On later twentieth-century developments in Ireland see Mary Raftery and Eoin O'Sullivan, *Suffer the Little Children: The Inside Story of Ireland's Industrial Schools* (Dublin: New Island Book, 1999), esp. chap. 10, "The Evil Within: Child Sexual Abuse."

42. Carter, "'Completely Discouraged,'" 76–79; Adams, *Education for Extinction*, 90–93.

43. Eastman, *Deep Woods*, 48; Francis La Flesche, *The Middle Five: Indian Schoolboys of the Omaha Tribe* (1900; rpt., Madison: University of Wisconsin Press, 1963), 14.

44. Horne and McBeth, *Essie's Story*, 41–45.

45. Robson, *Autobiography*, 13; Frank O'Connor, *An Only Child* (London: Macmillan, 1961), 145; IFC 1676:330.

46. Jim Whitewolf, *Jim Whitewolf: The Life of a Kiowa Apache Indian*, ed. Charles S. Brant (New York: Dover, 1969), 90; Fred Kabotie, *Fred Kabotie, Hopi Indian Artist: An*

Autobiography Told with Bill Belknap (Flagstaff: Museum of Northern Arizona/Northland Press, 1977), 11, 27–29, 65; La Flesche, *Middle Five*, chap. 6.

47. Shea, *Voices and the Sound of Drums*, 17–18.

48. See, for example, Reyhner and Eder, *American Indian Education*, 94; Carter, "'Completely Discouraged,'" 70; Sally J. McBeth, *Ethnic Identity and the Boarding School Experience of West-Central Oklahoma American Indians* (Lanham MD: University Press of America, 1983), 94, 97. On motivation see also Adams, *Education for Extinction*, 82–94.

49. Tomás O'Crohan, *The Islandman*, trans. Robin Fowler (1937; rpt., New York: Oxford University Press, 1951), chap. 7; IFC 1157:440–41.

50. Asa Daklugie et al., *Indeh: An Apache Odyssey*, ed. Eve Ball (Norman: University of Oklahoma Press, 1988), 125–27, for example; Wilbert H. Ahern, "An Experiment Aborted: Returned Indian Students in the Indian School service, 1881–1908," *Ethnohistory* 44.2 (Spring 1997): 263–304.

51. On possibly non-Western forms of racial thinking see, however, Jonathan Glassman, "Slower Than a Massacre: The Multiple Sources of Racial Thought in Colonial Africa," *American Historical Review* 109.3 (June 2004): 720–54.

52. See, for example, George M. Fredrickson, *Race: A Short History* (Princeton NJ: Princeton University Press, 2002); Audrey Smedley, *Race in North America: Origin and Devolution of a Worldview* (Boulder CO: Westview, 1993). See "Contemporary Issues Forum: Race and Racism," special section of *American Anthropologist* 100.3 (September 1998), 609–715. Also in this issue, "American Anthropological Association Statement on Race" declares: "Historical research has shown that the idea of race has always carried more meaning than physical differences; indeed, physical variations in the human species have no meaning except the social ones that humans put on them," 712. See also "Exchanges across a Difference: The Status of the Race Concept," special section of *American Anthropologist* 105.1 (March 2003): 110–24.

53. Frederick E. Hoxie, *A Final Promise: The Campaign to Assimilate the Indians, 1880–1920* (1984; rpt., Lincoln: University of Nebraska Press, 2002). In the preface to the new, otherwise unchanged edition Hoxie does not modify his earlier views. Michael C. Coleman, *American Indian Children at School, 1850–1893* (Jackson: University of Mississippi press, 1993), 46–50. "Relevant" education was in the air then; see K. J. King, *Pan-Africanism and Education: A Study of Race, Philanthropy and Education in the Southern States of America and East Africa* (Oxford UK: Clarendon Press, 1971).

54. But see, for example, Ruth Spack, *America's Second Tongue: American Indian Education and the Ownership of English, 1860-1900* (Lincoln: University of Nebraska Press, 2002), 70–76.

55. Mary McDaniel, in Earl Shorris, *Death of the Great Spirit: An Elegy for the American Indian* (New York: Signet, 1971), 158; Luther Standing Bear, *My People the Sioux*, ed. E. A. Brininstool (1928; rpt., Lincoln: University of Nebraska Press, 1975), 189.

56. See Coleman, *American Indian Children*, 99–100. A number of narrators reported prejudice by parents; others mentioned how they were treated well by fellow pupils and other whites.

57. ARCIA (1900), *Annual Reports of the Department of the Interior* (Washington DC:

Government Printing Office: 1900), 14–15; ARCIA (1905), H. Doc., vol. 19, 54th Cong., 1st sess., serial 4959, 5.

58. Patrick Bradley, While I Remember (Dublin: Brown and Nolan, n.d.), 38–39; Antonia McManus, The Irish Hedge School and Its Books, 1695–1831 (Dublin: Four Courts Press, 2002), 91, for example: "It was vital for the master's reputation that he should impress parents, so that they might spread his name." The supposedly best master would attract the most scholars. "This meant that the hedge schoolmaster lived with a profound sense of insecurity."

59. Adams, Education for Extinction, 82; CNEI, Report (1900), 22. See also note 14 above.

60. ARCIA (Washington DC: Government Printing Office, 1889), 374; Adams, Education for Extinction, 82–83; CNEI, Report (1904), 10. For a ringing praise of female teachers, see Report of inspector Dr. Moran, CNEI Report (1882), appendix B, 26–27.

61. I discuss this whole affair in Michael C. Coleman, "The Historical Credibility of American Indian Autobiographical Accounts of Schooling, 1850–1930," Irish Journal of American Studies 3 (1994): 137–38. See also Maurice O'Sullivan, Twenty Years A-Growing, trans. Moya Llewelyn Davis and George Thomson (1933, rpt., New York: Oxford University Press, 1983), 8–9.

62. Lucille (Jerry) Winnie, Sah-gan-de-oh: The Chief's Daughter (New York: Vantage, 1969), 45–49, 58; Horne and McBeth, Essie's Story, 33–37; Golden, Red Moon, 12–13.

63. CNEI, Report (1866), 29–30; CNEI, Report (1815–16), 7–8.

64. An Claidheamh Soluis, December 2, 1899, 605.

65. O'Connor, Only Child, 142–46; Sean O'Faolain, Vive Moi! An Autobiography (London: Rupert Hart-Davis, 1965), 50.

66. Patrick Shea, Voices and the Sound of Drums: An Irish Autobiography (Belfast: Blackstaff Press, 1981), 14–15; Dan Breen, My Fight for Irish Freedom (1924; rpt., Tralee, County Kerry: Anvil, 1964), 13. By the time Breen attended school the "happy English child" passage had long since been deleted from the CNEI curriculum, but it obviously had left a deep mark on Irish folk memory—I remember being told of it in the 1950s and 1960s.

67. ARCIA (1868), H. Exec. Doc., no. 1, 40th Cong., 3rd sess., serial 1366, 700–701.

68. Carter, "'Completely Discouraged.'"

69. ARCIA, Annual Reports of the Department of the Interior (Washington DC: Government Printing Office, 1900), 30; Ahern, "Experiment Aborted." By 1940 about 60 percent of those employed in the Indian Service (all areas) were Indians. ARCIA, Annual Report of the Secretary of the Interior (Washington DC: Government Printing Office, 1941), 439.

70. Anne Ruggles Gere, "An Art of Survivance: Angel DeCora at Carlisle," American Indian Quarterly 28.3/4 (Summer and Fall 2004): 649–84. On Indian teachers as purveyors of tribal values, see also Gere, "Indian Heart/White Head."

71. Horne and McBeth, Essie's Story, 41–44.

72. Ibid., 58–59, 67, 21. On Horne as a cultural broker, see the introduction by McBeth, xxxviii–xl. Thomas G. Andrews also shows the importance of an Indian teacher in "Turning the Tables on Assimilation: Oglala Lakotas and the Pine Ridge Day Schools, 1889–1920s," Western Historical Quarterly 33.4 (Winter 2002): 421–25 esp.

73. Lomawaima, *They Called It Prairie Light*, 130, 167, xiv.

74. I have developed this argument at greater length in Michael C. Coleman, "The Symbiotic Embrace: American Indians, White Educators and the School, 1820s–1920s," *History of Education* 25.1 (March 1996): 1–18. The Indian part of the present section draws on this article.

75. M. Friedman, Annual Report, *Red Man* 3 (1910): 62.

76. ARCIA, *Reports of the Department of the Interior* (Washington DC: Government Printing Office, 1908), 11.

77. Coleman, "Symbiotic Embrace," 8. Such developments can be followed in ARCIA.

78. ARCIA (1861), S. Exec. Doc., no. 1, 37th Cong., 2nd sess., serial 1117, 674.

79. Charles Hutchins to Hon. W. P. Dole, October 15, 1864, Letters Received, 1824–81, Schools, 1824–73, M659, reel 794, 96–97, RG 75, NA; Nathan Tinson to Mahlon Stubbs, December 12 (?), 1870, Letters Received, 1824–81, Schools, 1824–73, M234, reel 798: 130, RG 75, NA; ARCIA (1881), H. Exec. Doc., no. 1, part 5, vol. 2, 47th Cong., 1st sess., serial 2100, 243–44. Larger boarding schools also faced inspections, apart from those regularly organized by the BIA. In 1881, for example, a committee made up of the president of Dickinson College, along with clergymen and laymen, sent in a glowing report on the Carlisle School, ARCIA (1881), H. Exec. Doc., no. 1, part 5, vol. 2, 47th Cong., 1st sess., serial 2100, 243–44.

80. Golden, *Red Moon*, 13, 16,19, 209.

81. ARCIA (Washington DC: Government Printing Office, 1889), 357.

82. Standing Bear, *My People the Sioux*, 161.

83. Janet Nolan does not use the concept of "symbiosis." Yet the struggle of Irish national schoolteachers and of Irish American teachers in American elementary schools for recognition, security, and mobility is also a major theme of *Servants of the Poor*. See esp. chap. 2 on the situation in the CNEI-run schools.

84. CNEI Report (1861), 263. In American context: "Their habits and feelings must not be disregarded," acknowledged the ABCFM in 1823 of southern Indians. They "must be led kindly and cautiously to understand the reason and utility of missionary proceedings." See ABCFM, *Annual Report* (1823), 101.

85. Coolahan, *Irish Education*, 22.

86. CNEI, Report (1836), *Reports of the Commissioners . . . 1834 to 1845, Inclusive*, 108–11.

87. Coolahan, *Irish Education*, 24–30.

88. CNEI, Report (1871), appendix C, 160–61.

89. Robson, *Autobiography*, chap. 21.

90. Nolan also mentions the "teacher's nervousness in the face of the inspector's visit," which was "increased by the occasional arbitrary dismissal in spite of reforms [in the system]." *Servants of the Poor*, 39.

91. IFC 1157:431–32. This informer's recollection of pupil cooperation recalls my own experience in teacher training almost a century later in 1981, when otherwise uncontrollable teenage boys and girls became model students at the arrival of the inspector. "Were we good, sir?" one student asked after the inspector had left. "You were great!" I told them. Then things reverted to normal.

92. O'Crohan, *Islandman*, 39–40; IFC 1057:402–03. Patrick Gallagher told how a teacher, who had earlier seemed nervous, actually assaulted an inspector, and the pupils threw turf at him; the next day, however, the pupils found out that the teacher was going to America. Gallagher, *My Story* (Dungloe: Templecrone Co-operative Society, n.d.), 18–19. On the inspectorate see P. F. O'Donavan, "The National School Inspectorate and Its Administrative Context in Ireland, 1870–1962" (PhD thesis, National University of Ireland, Dublin, 1992).

93. IFC 1194: 295–96.

94. David Vincent, *The Rise of Mass Literacy: Reading and Writing in Modern Europe* (Cambridge UK: Polity, 2000), 29.

95. CNEI, *Report* (1865), appendix C, 165.

96. CNEI, *Report* (1882), appendix B, 12; CNEI, *Report* (1890), appendix C, 39: "I wish I could say that falsification does not exist," wrote Mr. Hamilton, "but I have had too many proofs to the contrary." CNEI Report (1898–99), 69: "I cannot close this report," wrote head inspector A. Purser, "without referring to the careless and even dishonest manner in which the school accounts continue to be kept."

97. Michel Foucault, "The Eye of Power: Conversation with Jean-Pierre Barou and Michelle Perrot," in *Power/Knowledge: Selected Interviews and Other Writings, 1972–1977*, ed. Colin Gordon, trans. Colin Gordon et al. (Brighton, Sussex: Harvester Press, 1980), 156. Foucault notes, and I concur, that "certain positions preponderate and permit an effect of supremacy to be produced."

7. Peers and Mediation

1. Maurice O'Sullivan, *Twenty Years A-Growing*, trans. Moya Llewelyn Davies and George Thomson (1933; rpt., Oxford: Oxford University Press, 1983), 2. See similar passage in Peig Sayers, *Peig: The Autobiography of Peig Sayers of the Great Blasket Island*, trans. Bryan MacMahon (n.p.: Criterion, 1974), 21.

2. Esther Burnett Horne and Sally McBeth, *Essie's Story: The Life and Legacy of a Shoshone Teacher* (Lincoln: University of Nebraska Press, 1998), 51–52. Ultimately her sister failed to adjust and after three years left school.

3. Charles A. Eastman (Ohiyesa), *From Deep Woods to Civilization: Chapters in the Autobiography of an Indian* (1916; rpt., Lincoln: University of Nebraska Press, 1977), 18–25.

4. IFC 1057:392–93.

5. Patrick Shea, *Voices and the Sound of Drums: An Irish Autobiography* (Belfast: Blackstaff Press, 1981), 18–19.

6. IFC 1157:432–33. In the 1950s a boy from Cork gave us Dublin children his version of these rhymes: "Tell-tale, piggy snail, hanging outa cow's tale."

7. R. B. Robson, *Autobiography of an Ulster Teacher* (Belfast: n.p., 1935), 47–48.

8. Francis La Flesche, *The Middle Five: Indian Schoolboys of the Omaha Tribe* (1900; rpt., Madison: University of Wisconsin Press, 1963), 11, 134.

9. Clinton Rickard, *Fighting Tuscarora: The Autobiography of Chief Clinton Rickard*, ed. Barbara Graymont (Syracuse NY: Syracuse University Press, 1973, 9; Rogers, John,

Red World and White: Memoirs of a Chippewa Boyhood (1957; rpt., Norman: University of Oklahoma Press, 1974), 69–72.

10. Kay Bennett, *Kaibah: Recollections of a Navajo Girlhood* (Los Angeles: Westernlore Press, 1964), 245–47.

11. Helen Sekaquaptewa, *Me and Mine: The Life Story of Helen Sekaquaptewa, as Told to Louise Udall* (Tucson: University of Arizona Press, 1969), esp. 93–95, 104–04, 125–27.

12. Quoted in Sally J. Mcbeth, *Ethnic Identity and the Boarding School Experience of West-Central Oklahoma American Indians* (Lanham MD: University Press of America, 1983), 131; K. Tsianina Lomawaima, *They Called It Prairie Light: The Story of the Chilocco Indian School* (Lincoln: University of Nebraska Press, 1994), 149–50.

13. Through pupil essays, written in English, a teacher might come to know of bullying. See "Let the Children Speak," essays appended to Gertrude Golden, *Red Moon Called Me: Memoirs of a Schoolteacher in the Government Indian Service* (San Antonio TX: Naylor, 1954), 189, for example. "I didn't talk to anyone," wrote one pupil of her first days at school. "Some of them is mean to me sometime, too, and make me cry." On Canada see J. R. Miller, *Shingwauk's Vision: A History of Residential Schools* (Toronto: University of Toronto Press, 1996), 9: "The boys' dormitory was conducted under a reign of terror and violence by the big boys." At the present the problem of bullying at school has become a major concern of educationalists in Europe. See, for example, "Beating the Bullies," *Time Magazine*, January 24, 2005: 32–35.

14. Margaret Connell Szasz, *Indian Education in the American Colonies, 1607–1783* (Albuquerque: University of New Mexico Press, 1988), 23. Szasz refers specifically to colonial times, but her insight is relevant to the period under review in the present study. And see Michael C. Coleman, "American Indian School Pupils as Cultural Brokers: Cherokee Girls at Brainerd Mission, 1828–1829," in *Between Indian and White Worlds: The Cultural Broker*, ed. Margaret Connell Szasz (Norman: University of Oklahoma Press, 1994), 122–35. A recent analysis of the phenomenon, stressing the need for complex understandings of both "culture" and "brokering" is Eric Hindraker, "Translation and Cultural Brokering," in *A Companion to American Indian History*, ed. Philip Deloria and Neal Salisbury (Malden MA: Blackwell: 2002), 356–75.

15. Mildred Stinson, in *To Be an Indian: An Oral History*, ed. Joseph H. Cash and Herbert T. Hoover (New York: Holt, Rinehart, and Winston, 1971), 95; James McCarthy, *A Papago Traveler: Memoirs of James McCarthy*, ed. John G. Westover (Tucson: Sun Tracks and University of Arizona Press, 1985), 38–39; Don Talayesva, *Sun Chief: The Autobiography of a Hopi Indian*, ed. Leo W. Simmons (New Haven CT: Yale University Press, 1942), 96–97, 102.

16. Asa Daklugie et al., *Indeh: An Apache Odyssey*, ed. Eve Ball (Norman: University of Oklahoma Press, 1988), 144–49; Anna Moore Shaw, *A Pima Past* (Tucson: University of Arizona Press, 1974), 126, 131.

17. This theme dominates La Flesche, *Middle Five*. Quotations are from 13, 151.

18. O'Sullivan, *Twenty Years*, 33.

19. Tomás O'Crohan, *The Islandman*, trans. Robin Flower (1937; rpt., Oxford: Oxford University Press, 1951), 20; Micheál O'Guiheen, *A Pity Youth Does Not Last: Reminiscences*

of the Last of the Great Blasket Island's Poets and Storytellers (Oxford: Oxford University Press, 1982), 2.

20. IFC 1573:241–42; IFC 1194:532.

21. O'Crohan, *Islandman*, 35.

22. Shaw, *Pima Past*, 126, 131; Lucille (Jerry) Winnie, *Sah-gan-de-oh: The Chief's Daughter* (New York: Vantage Press, 1969), 46; La Flesche, *Middle Five*, for example, 21–22, 28, with quotation from 75.

23. Jim Whitewolf, *Jim Whitewolf: The Life of a Kiowa Apache Indian*, ed. Charles S. Brant (New York: Dover, 1969), chap. 3; quotation from 89.

24. Horne and McBeth, *Essie's Story*, 56.

25. Winnie, *Sah-gan-de-oh*, 45–49, 58; Narcissa Owen, *Memoir of Narcissa Owen, 1831–1907* (1907; rpt., Owenboro KY: McDowell, 1980), 53; Talayesva, *Sun Chief*, 130; Hoke Denetsosie, in *Stories of Traditional Navajo Life and Culture, by Twenty-Two Navajo Men and Women*, ed. Broderick H. Johnson (Tsaile, Navajo Nation AZ: Navajo Community College Press, 1977), 94.

26. Shea, *Voices and the Sound of Drums*, 16–17.

27. Sean O'Faolain, *Vive Moi! An Autobiography* (London: Rupert Hart-Davis, 1965), 46.

28. Peter O'Leary, *My Story*, trans. Cyril T. O Céirin (Cork: Mercier Press, 1970), 53–54, 60. On occasion pupils could teach the teacher. Sayers claimed that a new master sometimes stood behind pupils, trying to pick up Irish from their conversation. See Sayers, *Peig*, 29–30. The teacher of Irish at Jeremiah Murphy's school felt inadequate to the task and "needed a little help from myself and another boy" to ensure the class achieved a pass mark in the language (as an extra subject). The inspector was also impressed. See Murphy, *When Youth Was Mine: A Memoir of Kerry, 1902–1925* (Dublin: Mentor Press, 1998), 84.

29. ARCIA (Washington DC: Government Printing Office, 1892), 705.

30. CNEI, *Report* (1881), appendix B, 102.

31. ARCIA (Washington DC: Government Printing Office, 1892), 705. The reference here was to specifically religious education but typified the BIA's attitude on the issue of mediation; ARCIA (Washington DC: Government Printing Office, 1877), 3; ARCIA (1873), H. Exec. Doc., no. 1, part 5, 43rd Cong., 1st sess., serial 1601, 556; ARCIA (Washington DC: Government Printing Office, 1889), 379. Also see ARCIA (1875), H. Exec. Doc., no. 1, part 5, 44th Cong., 1st sess., serial 1860, 821.

32. George Webb, *A Pima Remembers* (1959; rpt., Tucson: University of Arizona Press, 1982), 85; Luther Standing Bear, *My People the Sioux*, ed. E. A. Brininstool (1828; rpt., Lincoln: University of Nebraska Press, 1975), chaps. 13, 16.

33. La Flesche, *Middle Five*, 61; Whitewolf, *Jim Whitewolf*. See also Coleman, "American Indian School Pupils."

34. See photos of Chiricahua Apaches in this book, for example.

35. Thomas Wildcat Alford, *Civilization and the Story of the Absentee Shawnees*, as told to Florence Drake (Norman: University of Oklahoma Press, 1936), 107–09.

36. Standing Bear, *My People the Sioux*, 167; Richard Henry Pratt, *Battlefield and*

Classroom: Four Decades with the American Indian, 1867–1904, ed. Robert M. Utley (Lincoln: University of Nebraska Press, 1987), 294 and all chap. 26.

37. Daniel La France (Ah-nen-la-de-ni), "An Indian Boy's Story," *Independent* 55 (July 30, 1903), 1784–85.

38. IFC 1194:532–33; IFC 52:141: *biodh na sean daoine ar a ndicheall focail Bearla a pio-cadh suas ó's na p'paistibh nuar a tagaidais abhaile ó'n scoil*"; CNEI *Report* (1908–09), appendix, section I, 142.

39. CNEI, *Report* (1908–09), appendix, section I, 144.

40. "Let the Children Speak," in Golden, *Red Moon,* 194–95.

41. The remainder of this section draws on Coleman, "American Indian School Pupils." This study was based on a collection of letters in the John Howard Payne Papers (JHPP), vol. 8:1–62, Newberry Library, Chicago. As all letters were from the same one-year period, I merely cited MS page numbers in the notes, which I also do here. The late William G. McLoughlin alerted me to this collection, *Cherokees and Missionaries, 1789–1839* (New Haven CT: Yale University Press, 1984), 141, n. 37.

42. JHPP, 48, 22.

43. Ibid., 43.

44. Ibid., 22, 36.

45. Ibid., 13–14. Shame in face of the failure of one's own people to modernize is a major theme in the Irish section of my "Representations of American Indians and the Irish in Educational Reports, 1850s–1920s, *Irish Historical Studies* 33.129 (May 2002): 42–51, esp.

46. JHPP, 48.

47. This is a major theme of McLoughlin, *Cherokees and Missionaries.* A more recent work is Izumi Ishi, "Alcohol and Politics in the Cherokee Nation before Removal, *Ethnohistory* 50.4 (Fall 2003): 671–96, on tribal efforts to control alcohol and to defend Cherokee sovereignty vis-à-vis the U.S. government.

48. JHPP, 31.

49. See, for example, Joel Strong, *The American School, 1642–2000,* 5th ed. (Boston: McGraw-Hill, 2001), 261–65; Amanda J. Cobb, *Listening to Our Grandmothers' Stories: The Bloomfield Academy for Chickasaw Females, 1852-1949* (Lincoln: University of Nebraska Press, 2000), 96–99, on extracurricular activities as a form of "social literacy."

50. Bennett, *Kaibah,* 244–47. Despite the goal of quarantining children from the supposedly corrupting home environment, many schools allowed visits from kin or periodic holidays home. See, for example, Thomas Klani, in Broderick, ed., *Stories of Traditional Navajo Life,* 244. Kay Bennett also enjoyed visits home, yet by the end of the summer she and her siblings were anxious to return to school. See Bennett, *Kaibah,* 233. See also Talayesva, *Sun Chief,* 100. A. A. Spencer, superintendent of the Montana Indian School, claimed that such visits were "highly prized." The pupils "returned at the end of the vacation, and they seemed more cheerful and contented than ever before during the last school year." ARCIA (1895), H. Doc., no. 5, vol. 2, 54th Cong., 1st sess., serial 3381, 188.

51. Michael C. Coleman, *American Indian Children at School, 1850–1930* (Jackson: University Press of Mississippi, 1993), 94–95.

52. ARCIA (1897), H. Doc., no. 5, 55th Cong., 2nd sess., serial 3641, 325–27. In describing the ambitious extracurricular activities at "more advanced schools," the superintendent argued in favor of literary and scientific clubs that "should be seekers after truth," not debating societies where mere oratory or casuistry could carry the audience.

53. ARCIA, *Annual Reports of the Department of the Interior* (Washington DC: Government Printing Office, 1901), 291.

54. O'Faolain, *Vive Moi!* 40.

55. IFC 1194:511; O'Sullivan, *Twenty Years*, 3; Murphy, *When Youth Was Mine*, 39. Sports were often important at Irish secondary schools, and Daniel Murphy notes how Irish Holy Ghost missionary schools in West Africa "placed strong emphasis on games and athletics in the tradition of the schools the priests themselves had come from in Ireland." Murphy, *A History of Irish Emigrant and Missionary Education* (Dublin: Four Courts Press, 2000), 454. Obviously, much depended on the facilities of each school. In addition, the later nineteenth century saw the growth of many sports organizations. The Gaelic Athletic Association (GAA) began to organize in almost every community throughout the country. Its activities were highly ideological as well as sports related: Neal Garnham, "Accounting for the Early Success of the Gaelic Athletic Association," *Irish Historical Studies* 34.133 (May 2004): 65–78; Patrick F. McDevitt, "Muscular Catholicism: Nationalism, Masculinity and Gaelic Team Sports, 1884–1916," *Gender and History* 9.2 (August 1997): 262–84. McDevitt's title obviously plays upon the more well-known association of "muscular Christianity" and Protestantism. See Clifford Putney, *Muscular Christianity: Manhood and Sports in America, 1880-1920* (Cambridge MA: Harvard University Press, 2001).

56. Shea, *Voices and the Sound of Drums*, 17–18.

57. IFC 1194:512–16: "is deacair liúm-sa an méis sin a creideamhaint" (that's a hard thing for me to believe), one of them would continually say, looking into the fire.

58. Eamon Kelly, *The Apprentice* (Dublin: Mercier, 1996), 69–70, 73–74.

59. See Beth A. Haller, "Cultural Voices or Pure Propaganda? Publications of the Carlisle Indian School, 1879–1918," *American Journalism* 19.2 (2002): 65–85, on the changing nature of these publications. They remained, Haller believes, heavily controlled and heavily assimilationist throughout.

60. ARCIA, *Annual Reports of the Department of the Interior* (Washington DC: Government Printing Office, 1901), 182; ARCIA (Washington DC: Government Printing Office, 1918), 21.

61. Irene Stewart, *A Voice in Her Tribe: A Navajo Woman's Own Story*, ed. Dorris Ostrander Dawdy and Mary Shepardson, Anthropological Paper no. 17 (Socorro NM: Ballena Press, 1980), 32; Polingaysi Qoyawayma (Elizabeth Q. White), *No Turning Back: A True Account of a Hopi Girl's Struggle to Bridge the Gap Between the World of Her People and the World of the White Man, as Told to Vada F. Carlson* (Albuquerque: University of New Mexico Press, 1964), 59–61. Jean A. Keller notes how, partly to improve student

health, Sherman Institute began to inaugurate recreational programs and facilities in the early twentieth century. See Keller, *Empty Beds: Indian Student Health at Sherman Institute, 1902-1922* (East Lansing: Michigan State University Press, 2002), 33–35; Standing Bear, *My People the Sioux*, 147–49, 171–72.

62. Horne and McBeth, *Essie's Story*, 45. Haskell attendance figure: ARCIA, *Reports of the Secretary of the Interior* (Washington DC: Government Printing Office, 1920),150; Stewart, *Voice*, 30. On Christmas, see also Edward Goodbird, *Goodbird the Indian: His Story*, ed. Gilbert L. Wilson (1914; rpt., St. Paul: Minnesota Historical Society Press, 1985), 39–40; also, for example, Standing Bear, *My People the Sioux*, 146–47.

63. John Bloom, *To Show What an Indian Can Do: Sports at Native American Boarding Schools* (Minneapolis: University of Minnesota Press, 2000), with quotations from xvi, xvii, 129, xx; David Wallace Adams, "More Than a Game: The Carlisle Indians Take to the Gridiron, 1893–1917, *Western Historical Quarterly* 32 (Spring 2001): 25–53; for the broader American context see Putney, *Muscular Christianity*.

64. ARCIA (1881), H. Exec. Doc., no. 1, part 5, vol. 2, 48th Cong., 1st sess., serial 2018, 247; Pratt, *Battlefield and Classroom*, 317–18.

65. Adams, "More Than a Game," 27, 42–43 (passage by Thorpe). See also Bill Crawford, *All American: The Rise and Fall of Jim Thorpe* (Hoboken NJ: Wiley, 2005); Daklugie et al., *Indeh*, 146–47.

66. McCarthy, *Papago Traveler*, 40–41, 47, 49–52, 61–67.

67. In Bloom, *To Show What an Indian Can Do*, 36. See also Putney, *Muscular Christianity*, chap. 6.

68. Winnie, *Sah-gan-de-oh*, 53–55; Horne and McBeth, *Essie's Story*, 46–47.

69. Institute for Government Research, *The Problem of Indian Administration* (Meriam Report) (Baltimore: Johns Hopkins University Press, 1928), 394–96. Haskell Institute, Essie Horne's school, was specifically singled out for criticism; Bloom, *To Show What an Indian Can Do*, xvii. See also McCarthy, *Papago Traveler*, 61–67.

70. Bloom, *To Show What an Indian Can Do*, quotation from 121; 37–50, on the stadium. The Meriam Report also singled out this stadium-building venture for criticism (see note 69, above).

71. In Bloom, *To Show What an Indian Can Do*, 72–73.

72. Robson, *Autobiography*, chaps. 10–12.

73. In 1900, for example, Carlisle claimed an average attendance of 981 students. ARCIA (1900), H. Doc., no. 5, 56th Cong., 2nd sess., serial 4101, 16. In 1900 there were about 1,000 pupils on the rolls at the Dublin college, but far fewer teacher trainees (about 800 in thirty model schools). CNEI, *Report* (1900), 18–19, 36; Institute for Government Research, *Problem of Indian Administration*, 395–96.

74. Paul E. Willis, *Learning to Labour: How Working Class Kids Get Working Class Jobs* (Aldershot, Hampshire: Gower, 1977); Celia Haig-Brown, *Resistance and Renewal: Surviving the Indian Residential School* (Vancouver BC: Tillicum Library, 1988), chap. 4, with quotations from 88, 103; Lomawaima, *Prairie Light*; see also Coleman, *American Indian Children*, 154–57.

75. Willis, *Learning to Labour*, 19; Rosalie Wax, "The Warrior Dropouts," in *Native*

America Today: Sociological Perspectives, ed. Howard M. Bahr et al. (New York: Harper and Row, 1972), with quotation from 147.

76. Winnie, *Sah-gan-de-oh*, 52; Horne and McBeth, *Essie's Story*, 32. On such developments among Indian orphans, see Marilyn Irvin Holt, *Indian Orphanage* (Lawrence: University Press of Kansas, 2001).

77. Anonymous Choctaw in *Nations Remembered: An Oral History of the Five Civilized Tribes, 1865–1907*, ed. Theda Purdue (Westport CT: Greenwood Press, 1980), 131–32. On boarding school student tribunals, see, for example, report from the Hampton Institute, ARCIA (1890), H. *Exec. Doc.*, no. 1, part 5, vol. 2, 51st Cong., 2nd sess., serial 2841, 319–20. Go-betweens: Rogers, *Red World and White*, 69–72.

78. La Flesche, *Middle Five*, esp. chaps. 1–4; on cake as currency, 71.

79. Allen James, *Chief of the Pomos: Life Story of Allen James*, ed. Ann M. Connor (Santa Rosa CA: privately printed, 1972), 40–42; Stewart, *Voice in Her Tribe*, 29–30. For *Presbyterian Missionary Attitudes toward American Indians, 1837–1893* (Jackson: University Press of Mississippi, 1985), I read letters from Presbyterian missionaries serving at the Omaha school during the early 1860s, when La Flesche was a pupil. These missionaries at a small school expressed no awareness of such pupil subcultures.

80. Reyhner and Eder, *American Indian Education*, 199–200; Lomawaima, *Prairie Light*, xiii.

81. McCarthy, *Papago Traveler*, 29, 45; Talayesva, *Sun Chief*, 107.

82. Horne and McBeth, *Essie's Story*, 32.

83. La France, "Indian Boy's Story," 1782.

84. Eastman, *Deep Woods*, 41–42; Standing Bear, *My People the Sioux*, 57.

85. This is a major theme of Eastman, *Deep Woods*; with quotation from 195. See also Raymond Wilson, *Ohiyesa: Charles Eastman, Santee Sioux* (Urbana: University of Illinois Press, 1983), 154–58. Zitkala-Ša for a time served as the secretary of this Pan-Indian association before founding her own National Council for American Indians. See Dexter Fisher, foreword to Zitkala-Ša, *American Indian Stories*, xv–xvi. Also see Lucy Maddox, *Citizen Indians: Native American Intellectuals, Race, and Reform* (Ithaca NY: Cornell University Press, 2005).

86. ARCIA (Washington DC: Government Printing Office, 1891), 70; Friedman, Annual Report, in *Red Man* 3 (October 1910), 63–64. Cf. Africa: schools that took pupils from different parts of individual countries and from other parts of Africa broadened their national and political horizons. See Magnus O. Bassey, *Western Education and Political Domination in Africa* (Westport CT: Bergin and Garvey, 1999), 63–65.

8. Resistance and Rejection

1. IFC 1194:509–11.

2. Peter N. Stearns, *Schools and Students in Industrial Society: Japan and the West, 1870–1940* (Boston: Bedford, 1998), 61.

3. Francis La Flesche, *The Middle Five: Indian Schoolboys of the Omaha Tribe* (1900; rpt., Madison: University of Wisconsin Press, 1963), 97–98, 66–68.

4. See also Michael C. Coleman, *American Indian Children at School, 1850-1930* (Jackson: University Press of Mississippi, 1993), chaps. 8,9.

5. K. Tsianina Lomawaima, *They Called It Prairie Light: The Story of Chilocco Indian School* (Lincoln: University of Nebraska Press, 1994), xi, 130, 167; David Wallace Adams, *Education for Extinction: American Indians and the Boarding School Experience, 1875–1928* (Lawrence: University Press of Kansas, 1995), 210, and chap. 7.

6. La Flesche, *Middle Five*, 74–75; Frank Mitchell, *Navajo Blessingway Singer: The Autobiography of Frank Mitchell, 1881–1967*, ed. Charlotte J. Frisbie and David P. McAllester (Tucson: University of Arizona Press, 1978), 66; Adams, *Education for Extinction*, 232.

7. Lomawaima, *Prairie Light*, 94–98; Luther Standing Bear, *My People the Sioux*, ed. E. A. Brininstool (1928; rpt., Lincoln: University of Nebraska Press, 1975), 144, 154.

8. K. Tsianina Lomawaima, "Oral Histories from Chilocco Indian Agricultural School, 1920–1940," *American Indian Quarterly* 11 (Summer 1987): 248.

9. W. Roger Buffalohead and Paulette Fairbanks Molin, "'A Nucleus of Civilization': American Indian Families at Hampton Institute in the Late Nineteenth Century," *Journal of American Indian Education* 33.3 (Spring 1996): 59–94.

10. Ironically, Helen Sekaquatewa's Hopi mother complained of such affairs as they brought unmarried youths of both sexes together. See Sekaquatewa, *Me and Mine: The Life Story of Helen Sekaquaptewa, as told to Louise Udall* (Tucson: University of Arizona Press, 1969), 117–19. Also see Margaret D. Jacobs, *Engendered Encounters: Feminism and Pueblo Cultures, 1879–1934* (Lincoln: University of Nebraska Press, 1999), 140–41. Indian adults from other tribes also made such complaints. See Adams, *Education for Extinction*, 219.

11. La Flesche, *Middle Five*, 49, 52–53; Lilah Denton Lindsey, "Memoirs of the Indian Territory Mission Field," *Chronicles of Oklahoma* 36 (1958): 182; Anna Moore Shaw, *A Pima Past* (Tucson: University of Arizona Press, 1974), 137; Esther Burnette Horne and Sally McBeth, *Essie's Story: The Life and Legacy of a Shoshone Teacher* (Lincoln: University of Nebraska Press, 1998), 34.

12. Don Talayesva, *Sun Chief: The Autobiography of a Hopi Indian*, ed. Leo W. Simmons (New Haven CT: Yale University Press, 1942), 97–99, 111–18.

13. Adams, *Education for Extinction*, 232.

14. Quoted in John Bloom, *To Show What an Indian Can Do: Sports at Native American Boarding Schools* (Minneapolis: University of Minnesota Press, 2000), 26–27.

15. Brenda J. Child, *Boarding School Seasons: American Indian Families* (Lincoln: University of Nebraska Press, 1998), 93–94.

16. Mourning Dove (Christine Quintasket), *Mourning Dove: A Salishan Autobiography*, ed. Jay Miller (Lincoln: University of Nebraska Press, 1990), 27; Zitkala-Ša (Gertrude Bonnin), *American Indian Stories* (1912; rpt., Lincoln: University of Nebraska Press, 1985), 59–61; Adams, *Education for Extinction*, 209–10.

17. Lindsey, "Memories," 186; Asa Daklugie et al., *Indeh: An Apache Odyssey*, ed. Eve Ball (Norman: University of Oklahoma Press, 1980), 150–51; Richard Henry Pratt, *Battlefield and Classroom: Four Decades with the American Indians, 1867–1904*, ed. Robert M. Utley (1964; rpt., Lincoln: University of Nebraska Press, 1987), 274–75.

18. I have not seen a study of pupils' responses to CNEI schooling earlier than my own: Michael C. Coleman, "'Eyes Big as Bowls with Fear and Wonder': Children's Responses to the Irish National Schools, 1850–1922," *Proceedings of the Royal Irish Academy* 98C.5 (1998): 177–202. For an earlier, broader study, see T. O. McCoolam, "The Hard Old Bench: A Study of School Life as Portrayed in the Autobiographical and Fictional Works of a Number of Anglo-Irish Writers"(M.A. thesis, University of Ulster, 1985), which focuses on primary and secondary education to portray generally negative memories. See also A. Norman Jeffares and Anthony Kamm, eds., *An Irish Childhood* (London: Collins, 1987). A recent study drawing on pupil reminiscences is Janet Nolan, *Servants of the Poor: Teachers and Mobility in Ireland and America* (Notre Dame IN: University of Notre Dame Press, 2004), esp. chaps. 1 and 2.

19. Maurice O'Sullivan, *Twenty Years A-Growing*, trans. Moya Llewelyn Davies and George Thomson (Oxford: Oxford University Press, 1983), 34; IFC 1057:406–7.

20. IFC 1506:366; IFC 1057:385–86, 293–94.

21. Michael MacGowan, *The Hard Road to Klondike*, trans. Valentin Iremonger (London: Routledge and Kegan Paul, 1962), 23.

22. Tomás O'Crohan, *The Islandman*, trans. Robin Flower (Oxford: Oxford University Press, 1951), 21–22; IFC 1157:429.

23. R. B. Robson, *Autobiography of an Ulster Teacher* (Belfast: n.p., 1935), 35. This incident reminds me of a similar experience of my own (c. 1960), when I refused to present my hand to a Christian Brother to strap me for what, I felt, was unjust punishment. The teacher also backed down, but my father had to visit the school and discuss matters with him. See Patrick Withers, "My Schooldays: Downstairs and Upstairs," *Ireland's Own*, October 18, 1952, 6.

24. IFC 1157:428; Jeffares and Kamm, *Irish Childhood*, 13.

25. IFC 1194:503–4. See also Patrick Shea, *Voices and the Sound of Drums* (Belfast: Blackstaff Press, 1981), 16–17.

26. IFC 1057:386–86.

27. Ibid., 386; Withers, "My Schooldays," 6; Robson, *Autobiography of an Ulster Teacher*, 14.

28. Robson, *Autobiography of an Ulster Teacher*, 14; William O'Malley, *Glancing Back: 70 Years' Experiences and Reminiscences of Press Man, Sportsman and Member of Parliament* (London: Wright & Brown, 1933 [?]), 152–53.

29. Susan Douglas Franzosa, "Authoring the Educated Self: Educational Autobiography and Resistance," *Educational Theory* 42.4 (Fall 1992): 395–96.

30. See Michael C. Coleman, "The Historical Credibility of American Indian Autobiographical Accounts of Schooling, 1850–1930," *Irish Journal of American Studies* 3 (1994): 127–50. My arguments could, of course, be extended to Irish accounts.

31. Kay Bennett, *Kaibah: Recollections of a Navajo Girlhood* (Los Angeles: Westernlore Press, 1964), 226–27; Mitchell, *Navajo Blessingway Singer*, 66; La Flesche, *Middle Five*, 112. I recall a similar sense of thrill when, at an Irish-speaking summer camp during the late-1950s, we surreptitiously spoke English out of earshot of "the authorities."

32. Clyde Ellis, *To Change Them Forever: Indian Education at the Rainy Mountain Boarding School, 1893–1920* (Norman: University of Oklahoma Press, 1996), 105–6.

33. Amy Goodburn, "Literacy Practices at the Genoa Industrial School," *Great Plains Quarterly* 19 (Winter 1999): 35–52, esp. 46–48, on pupils' letters.

34. Ruth Spack, *America's Second Tongue: American Indian Education and the Ownership of English, 1860–1900* (Lincoln: University of Nebraska Press, 2002), esp. chaps. 3, 4, and 5, with quotations from 7, 11, 111. How Indian pupils and ex-pupils "performed" and manipulated both "Indianness" and American individuality is a major theme of Joel Pfister, *Individuality Incorporated: Indians and the Multicultural Modern* (Durham NC: Duke University Press, 2004), esp. part 1.

35. Irene Stewart, *A Voice in Her Tribe: A Navajo Woman's Own Story*, ed. Dorris Opstrander Dawdy and Mary Shepardson, Anthropological Paper no. 17 (Socorro NM: Ballena Press, 1980, 18–21; Chris (pseudonym), *Apache Odyssey: A Journey between Two Worlds*, ed. Morris E. Opler (New York: Holt, Rinehart & Winston, 1969), 87–89, 122–24; La Flesche, *Middle Five*, 58–64.

36. Jim Whitewolf, *Jim Whitewolf: The Life of a Kiowa Apache Indian*, ed. Charles S. Brant (New York: Dover, 1969), 96; Lomawaima, *Prairie Light*, 137–40.

37. Horne and McBeth, *Essie's Story*, 33.

38. Lomawaima, *Prairie Light*, 115.

39. La Flesche, *Middle Five*, chap. 10. I discuss this in Coleman, "Credibility of American Indian Autobiographical Accounts," 136–37. Significantly, missionaries writing forty years earlier, contemporaneously with the hunt, corroborated La Flesche's recall; Chris, *Apache Odyssey*, 87–88.

40. Edward Goodbird, *Goodbird the Indian: His Story*, ed. Gilbert L. Wilson (1914; rpt., St. Paul: Minnesota Historical Society Press, 1985), 41.

41. ARCIA (Washington DC: Government Printing Office: 1892), 693. The Ghost Dance was actually a heavily syncretic blend of many tribal and Christian beliefs. A recent study of the Ghost Dance is Rani-Henrik Andersson, *Wanági Wachípi Ki: The Ghost Dance among the Lakota Indians in 1890* (Tampere, Finland: Tampere University Press, 2003). Jeffrey Ostler does not see the Ghost Dance as syncretic. See Ostler, *The Sioux Indians and U.S. Colonialism from Lewis and Clark to Wounded Knee* (New York: Cambridge University Press, 2004), 255, and all part 3.

42. Adams, *Education for Extinction*, 331. Such comments recall my own frustration at the unwillingness of Finnish university students, decades ago, to participate during "discussion classes" in English. These often became either teacher monologues or one-on-one question sessions between the teacher and each pupil in his or her turn. Students—and perhaps teacher—have improved significantly in more recent times.

43. La Flesche, *Middle Five*, chap. 14, with quotation from 122.

44. IFC 657:118–19 (in Irish).

45. Frank O'Connor, *An Only Child* (London: Macmillan, 1961), all chap. 13.

46. Education 2, 15:154, NAI; CNEI, Minutes (1905), NLI. See Parliamentary Questions, 383: "The Commissioners have decided that membership of an [Unionist]

Orange Lodge is a direct violation of their rules." A teacher was dismissed for membership (456).

47. Interestingly, when the smoke of the fire began to distort the faces of onlookers, some of the children began, either seriously or in jest, to scream that they were seeing fairies. See IFC 517:362–67. Dan Breen was very young at the time of the Boer War, but he also remembered the local adults' "exultation over the victories gained by the Boer generals . . . and how thrilled they were by the British defeat at Spion Kop." See Breen, *My Fight for Irish Freedom* (1924; rpt., Tralee, County Kerry: Anvil Books, 1964), 12.

48. Institute for Government Research, *The Problem of Indian Administration* (Meriam Report) (Baltimore: Johns Hopkins University Press, 1928), 392–94. Also 314–39. A major recent study is Jean A. Keller, *Empty Beds: Indian Student Health at Sherman Institute, 1902–1922* (East Lansing: Michigan State University Press, 2002).

49. Scott Riney claimed that during the influenza pandemic of 1918–19, mortality at the Rapid City Indian School in South Dakota was comparable to mortality among other Indians and white people in the area. See Riney, *The Rapid City Indian School, 1898–1933* (Norman: University of Oklahoma Press, 1999), 69, and all chap. 2. "The school's greatest failing," he concludes, "was its inability to provide adequate healthcare for students, a problem directly attributable to inadequate appropriations," rather than to failings of the staff (72–73). On the possible efficacy of tribal medical practices see Paul Kelton, "Avoiding the Smallpox Spirits: Colonial Epidemics and Southeastern Indian Survival," *Ethnohistory* 51.1 (Winter 2004): 45–71.

50. Lisa E. Emmerich notes the hostility of white BIA field matrons to traditional medicine. Native American BIA field matrons appeared more reticent in this area. See Emmerich, "'Right in the Midst of My Own People': Native American Women and the Field Matron Program," in *American Nations: Encounters in Indian Country, 1850 to the Present*, ed. Frederick E. Hoxie, Peter C. Mancall, and James H. Merrell (New York: Routledge, 2001), 148–49; originally published in *American Indian Quarterly* 3.2 (1992): 219–37.

51. ARCIA (Washington DC: Government Printing Office, 1885), 235, 243; Standing Bear, *My People the Sioux*, 162–66. Standing Bear blamed the local Indian agent who failed to pass communications from the school to the people, rather than Superintendent Pratt, for such insensitivity.

52. Whitewolf, *Jim Whitewolf*, 96–97; Chris, *Apache Odyssey*, 46–47; Stewart, *Voice in Her Tribe*, 16.

53. Keller, *Empty Beds*, with quotation from 12. For an example of concern see La Flesche, *Middle Five*, 145–52.

54. CNEI *Report* (1884), 238–39; CNEI *Report* (1899), 140.

55. ARCIA (Washington DC: Government Printing Office, 1885), 244.

56. ARCIA (1993–94), H. Exec. Doc., no. 1, part 5, vol. 1, 53rd Cong., 2nd sess., serial 3210, 7; ARCIA, *Annual Reports of the Department of the Interior* (Washington DC: Government Printing Office, 1899), 26–27; ARCIA (Washington DC: Government Printing Office, 1905), 14, 43. Also see Adams, *Education for Extinction*, 229–31.

57. Gertrude Golden, *Red Moon Called Me: Memoirs of a Schoolteacher in the Government Indian Service*, ed. Cecil Dryden (San Antonio TX: Naylor), 91–92. The account is characteristic of Golden in two senses: her bitter resentment of a particular colleague and her sensitivity to Indian children's needs, as she perceived them.

58. Narcissa Owen, *Memoirs of Narcissa Owen, 1831–1907* (Siloan Springs AR: Siloan Springs Museum, 1980), 53; Elsie Allen, *Pomo Basketmaking: A Supreme Art for the Weaver*, ed. Vinson Brown (Healdsburg CA: Naturegraph, 1972), 8–9. Perhaps the most shocking case of violence was reported in 1896. Mary J. Platt of the Pechanga School in California was raped and murdered, allegedly by a group of Indians, who burned the school down with the body inside. They were later caught and tried. It is unclear whether the perpetrators had been students of that or any school, but the crime suggests the real dangers BIA teachers could face. See ARCIA, *Report of the Secretary of the Interior* (Washington DC: Government Printing Office, 1896), 22–23.

59. In Child, *Boarding School Seasons*, 94–94; Adams, *Education for Extinction*, 237–38.

60. James Kaywaykla, *In the Days of Victorio: Recollections of a Warm Springs Apache*, ed. Eve Ball (Tucson: University of Arizona Press, 1970), 200; Standing Bear, *My People the Sioux*, 153; Horne and McBeth, *Essie's Story*, 48.

61. ARCIA (1880), H. Exec. Doc., no. 1, part 5, 46th Cong., 3rd sess., serial 1959, 301; ARCIA (Washington DC: Government Printing Office, 1882), 8; E. J. Bost to Commissioner, December 4, 1914, and Commissioner to E. J. Bost, December 15, 1914, both in Central Classified Files (CCF), File 821 for Wittenberg, RG 75, NA.

62. IFC 1194:493.

63. CNEI, *Report* (1878), appendix B, 82–84. Don Talayesva, Hopi, was embarrassed at being placed in class with younger pupils. See Talayesva, *Sun Chief*, 96.

64. CNEI, *Report* (1899–1900), 140. The act itself, he reported being told, was "defective in regard to truants, as we [in Ireland] have not similar powers to those in England. I have had letters from various [local] committees complaining of this."

65. Max Henley, in Broderick H. Johnson, ed., *Stories of Traditional Navajo Life and Culture, by Twenty-Two Navajo Men and Women* (Tsaile, Navajo Nation AZ: Navajo Community College Press, 1977), 32; Adams, *Education for Extinction*, 228; E. J. Bost to Commissioner, March 18, 1908, CCF, File 821 for Wittenberg, RG 75, NA.

66. Lomawaima, *Prairie Light*, 120–21, and 131 on more careful surveillance of girls.

67. Mitchell, *Navajo Blessingway Singer*, 67–69; Whitewolf, *Jim Whitewolf*, 87–90. See also, for example, Coleman, *American Indian Children*, 166–70, for other such accounts.

68. Sekaquaptewa, *Me and Mine*, 137; Bennett, *Kaibah*, 227–28.

69. ARCIA (Washington DC: Government Printing Office, 1888), 248; ARCIA (Washington DC: Government Printing Office, 1905), 250. And see ARCIA, *Annual Reports of the Department of the Interior* (Washington DC: Government Printing Office, 1903–4, 41–42. The farmer in charge of the San Xavier School for the Papagos told how the parents, when requested by the Phoenix Indian School to help bring about the return of some runaways and absentees, refused to cooperate. When the BIA em-

ployee placed some of the recalcitrant adults under arrest, one of them brought a writ of habeas corpus (another example of Indians learning to use modern methods to defeat the modernizers), claiming that the children were being held against their will. In the end the Indian lost his case in an American court.

70. Minnie Braithwaite Jenkins, *Girl from Williamsburg* (Richmond VA: Dietz Press, 1951), 283.

71. G. W. Grayson, *A Creek Warrior for the Confederacy: The Autobiography of Chief G. W. Grayson*, ed. W. David Baird (Norman: University of Oklahoma Press, 1988), 42; Annie Lowry, *Karnee: A Piute Narrative*, ed. Lalla Scott (Greenwich CT: Fawcett, 1966), 61–64, 67–68; Daklugie et al., *Indeh*, 151. Also see Chester Yellowhair, "I Was Born in the Dark Ages," *Desert Magazine* 23 (November 1960): 18.

72. IFC 1057:397.

73. IFC 517:368. It is unclear whether this account refers to a national school. Compare another informant's account of similarly harsh punishment, including the hoisting of the "culprit" on another boy's back. Then "the master would let down his trousers and flail him with a stick." See IFC 1194:518.

74. James McCarthy, *A Papago Traveler: The Memoirs of James McCarthy*, ed. John G. Westover (Tucson: Sun Tracks and University of Arizona Press, 1967), 68; Rosalio Moisés, Jane Holden Kelley, and William Curry Holden, *A Yaqui Life: The Personal Chronicle of a Yaqui Indian* (1971; rpt., Lincoln: University of Nebraska Press, 1977), 43; Refugio Savala, *Autobiography of a Yaqui Poet*, ed. Kathleen M. Sands (Tucson: University of Arizona Press, 1980), 45; Myrtle Begay, in Johnson, ed. *Stories of Traditional Navajo Life*, 65–66; Sekaquaptewa, *Me and Mine*, 142–44, 153–56; Talayesva, *Sun Chief*, 117, 119–34; Savala, *Autobiography*, 45.

75. Jason Betzinez, with William Sturtevant Nye, *I Fought with Geronimo* (1959; rpt., Lincoln: University of Nebraska Press, 1987), 159; Standing Bear, *My People the Sioux*, 190.

76. O'Sullivan, *Twenty Years*, 183.

9. Results

1. David Vincent, *The Rise of Mass Literacy: Reading and Writing in Modern Europe* (Cambridge UK: Polity, 2000), 146–47.

2. Philip Bull, *Land, Politics, and Nationalism: A Study of the Irish Land Question* (Dublin: Gill and Macmillan, 1996), 55, chap. 5; David Hempton, *Religion and Political Culture in Britain and Ireland: From the Glorious Revolution to the Decline of Empire* (Cambridge: Cambridge University Press, 1996), 86.

3. Adrian Hastings, *The Construction of Nationhood: Ethnicity, Religion and Nationalism* (Cambridge: Cambridge University Press, 1997), 89–95. On the changing and complex nature of Irish-British relationships, see also Kevin Kenny, ed., *Ireland and the British Empire* (Oxford: Oxford University Press, 2004).

4. Simplistically believing that the national schools had almost alone destroyed the Irish language, the new Irish Free State/Republic of Ireland threw most of the responsibility for restoring Irish onto the educational system but failed to reverse the

process of language loss. See Adrian Kelly, *Compulsory Irish: Language and Education in Ireland 1870s–1970s* (Dublin: Irish Academic Press, 2002).

5. Vincent, *Rise of Literacy*, 145. See also Daniel Heath Justice, introduction to "Empowerment through Literature," special issue, *American Indian Quarterly* 28.1/2 (Winter–Spring 2004): 4. "Native peoples in North America have a long and often vexed relationship with the often unpredictable power of the written word. Those marks on paper, hide, bark, and canvas have served as both tools of liberation for indigenous communities and as weapons of devastation against them."

6. John Willinsky, *Learning to Divide the World: Education at Empire's End* (Minneapolis: University of Minnesota Press, 1998), 89–90. Alvin Jackson also sees the national schools, along with new technologies such as printing and the railway, as having helped the cause of nationalism. See Jackson, *Home Rule: A History of Ireland* (London: Phoenix, 2003), 25–26.

7. On British Protestant identity see, for example, Hastings, in note 4 above; Hempton, *Religion and Political Culture*.

8. Rev. J. A. Lippincott, in the Carlisle publication the *Red Man* (March 1898, 7), quoted in David Wallace Adams, *Education for Extinction: American Indians and the Boarding School Experience, 1875–1928* (Lawrence: University Press of Kansas, 1995), 274.

9. Esther Burnett Horne and Sally McBeth, *Essie's Story: The Life and Legacy of a Shoshone Teacher* (Lincoln: University of Nebraska Press, 1998), xxxiii.

10. In 2006 there are 561 federally recognized tribal governments in the United States. See the Bureau of Indian Affairs Web site at www.doi.gov/bureau-indian-affairs.html (accessed June 30, 2006). For a recent account of contemporary Indian peoples see Peter Iverson, *"We Are Still Here": American Indians in the Twentieth Century* (Wheeling IL: Harlan-Davidson: 1998).

11. See 1990 Census, "American Indian Languages Spoken at Home by American Indian Persons 5 Years and Over in Households"; over 280,000 then spoke tribal languages. In the 2000 census 4.1 million (1.5 percent) reported American Indian and Alaska Native ancestry. This included 2.5 million who reported only American Indian and Alaska Native ancestry. See www.factfinder.census.gov/home/aian/index. html (accessed June 30, 2006). For a pessimistic view of tribal language survival, see William Bright, "Native North American Languages," in *The Native North American Almanac*, ed. Duane Champagne (Detroit: Gale Research, 1994), esp. 445–46. See also Bruce E. Johansen, "Back from the (Nearly) Dead: Reviving Indigenous Languages Across North America," *American Indian Quarterly* 28.3/4 (Summer and Fall 2004): 566–82. For details on the Indian educational situation in the early twenty-first century, see "Fingertip Facts," www.oiep.bia.edu/body.html (accessed June 30, 2006).

12. For a recent account of the persistence of Indian spiritual values, along with syncretic blendings with Christianity, see Joel W. Martin, *The Land Looks After Us: A History of Native American Religion* (New York: Oxford University Press, 2001). See also, for example, Vine Deloria Jr. and Thomas R. Wildcat, *Power and Place: Indian Education in America* (Golden CO: American Indian Graduate Center and Fulcrum Resources: 2001).

13. Adams, *Education for Extinction*, 336.

14. Graham Balfour, *The Educational Systems of Great Britain and Ireland* (Oxford UK: Clarendon Press, 1903), 110.

15. Charles Townsend, *Ireland in the Twentieth Century* (London: Arnold, 1998), esp. 68–70. See also, for example, Alvin Jackson, *Ireland, 1798-1998* (Oxford UK: Blackwell, 1999), chap. 5. This is also a major theme of Jackson, *Home Rule*.

16. Vincent, *Rise of Mass Literacy*. In his final chapter (5) Vincent points to the differences between plans and results.

17. See Kelly, *Compulsory Irish*, 125–28. Some Catholic clergy supported the Irish language: Thomas A. O'Donoghue, *Bilingual Education in Ireland, 1904–1922: The Case of the Bilingual Programme of Instruction*, Centre for Irish Studies Monograph no. 1 (Perth, Australia: Murdoch University, 2000), 89–93. The pragmatic acceptance of the English language by Irish people is a major theme of Tony Crowley, *War of Words: The Politics of Language in Ireland 1537–2004* (Oxford: Oxford University Press, 2005).

18. On many of these developments in Finland see, for example, Aira Kemiläinen, *Finns in the Shadow of the 'Aryans': Race Theories and Racism* (Helsinki: Finnish Historical Society, 1998), 41–46, 107–28; Fred Singleton, *A Short History of Finland* (Cambridge: Cambridge University Press, 1998), 73–80.

19. Tomás O'Crohan, *The Islandman* (Oxford: Oxford University Press, 1951), 223; J. A. Mangan, *The Imperial Curriculum: Racial Images and Education in the British Colonial Experience* (London: Routledge, 1993), 20.

20. CNEI, *Report* (1903), 2; Balfour, *Educational Systems*, 110; John Coolahan, *Irish Education: Its History and Structure* (Dublin: Institute of Public Administration, 1981), 29–30; David Fitzpatrick, "'A Share of the Honeycomb': Education, Emigration, and Irishwomen," in *The Origins of Popular Literacy in Ireland: Language Change and Educational Development 1700-1920*, ed. Mary Daly and David Dickson (Dublin: Trinity College, Dublin, and University College Dublin, 1990), 168.

21. Fitzpatrick, "Share of the Honeycomb," 168.

22. For recent critical discussions of "what if" counterfactual speculation, see the forum essay by Martin Bunzl, "Counterfactual History: A User's Guide," *American Historical Review* 109.4 (June 2004): 245–58; with this essay the AHR hoped to provoke discussion on the issue. See also Gary McCulloch, "Virtual History and the History of Education," *History of Education* 32.2 (2003): 145–56. I have further developed the ideas expressed here in my text in Michael C. Coleman, "Counterfactuals I'd Rather Not Contemplate: What If the Nineteenth-Century Educational Campaigns to Americanize the Indians and to Anglicize the Irish Had Never Taken Place?" Endnote lecture presented at Tenth Maple Leaf and Eagle Conference on North American Studies, University of Helsinki, Finland, May 7, 2004.

23. I have always cherished the fact that most of my school learning, to the age of sixteen, was in Irish, so I do not argue that the decline of the vernacular was a positive thing. Yet considering the fact that we gained the world language, and that vast numbers emigrated to English-speaking countries and the British Empire during and after the period under review, I merely suggest that for many Irish people the acquisi-

tion of English was a gain—as they themselves demonstrated by rejecting Irish. See also Kenny, *Ireland and the British Empire*.

24. Fitzpatrick, "Share of the Honeycomb," 167–87, with quotation from 178. By late in the nineteenth century, Fitzpatrick writes, Irish girls and women "were slightly better educated and more migratory than men" (175). However, this "superior performance" at elementary schools "reflected not only their [girls'] possibly stronger desire to better themselves, but also their declining importance in the labor market" (170). Also, see Janet Nolan, *Servants of the Poor: Teachers and Mobility in Ireland and Irish America* (Notre Dame IN: University of Notre Dame Press, 2004).

25. Jon Reyhner and Jeanne Eder, *American Indian Education: A History* (Norman: University of Oklahoma Press, 2004), 201, on later leaders.

26. ARCIA, *Reports of the Secretary of the Interior* (Washington DC: Government Printing Office, 1915), 6–7.

27. On Indian literacy/illiteracy see the Institute for Government Research, *The Problem of Indian Administration* (Meriam Report) (Baltimore: Johns Hopkins University Press, 1928), 357–58.

28. Peter N. Stearns, *Schools and Students in Industrial Society: Japan and the West, 1870–1940* (Boston: Bedford, 1998), 163.

29. Albert Yava, *Big Falling Snow: A Tewa-Hopi Indian's Life and Times and the History and Traditions of His People*, ed. Harold Courlander (Albuquerque: University of New Mexico Press, 1978), 133.

30. By "genocide" I mean the actual or attempted *physical extermination* of a people. The United Nations Convention on the Prevention and Punishment of the Crime of Genocide (1951) has a much broader definition than mine. See Article II, available at www.hrweb.org/legal/genocide.html (accessed June 30, 2006). On this issue compare my view with Lilian Friedberg, "Dare to Compare: Americanizing the Holocaust," *American Indian Quarterly* 24.3 (Spring 2000): 353–80. Reyhner and Eder use the term "cultural genocide" in *American Indian Education*, 107.

31. I broadly concur with Jon Reyner and Jeanne Eder: it is difficult to imagine how a more enlightened and culturally relativistic policy could have been followed in the nineteenth century. See Reyner and Eder, *American Indian Education*, 166. That is, unless, as happened in Ireland, demographic or other circumstances forced the educational authority to exhibit greater sensitivity to local cultural and religious values.

32. IFC 1194:493.

33. Nolan, *Servants of the Poor*, with quotations from 3.

34. Peig Sayers, *Peig: The Autobiography of Peig Sayers of the Great Blasket Island*, trans. Bryan MacMahon (Belfast: Talbot Press, 1974), 26; O'Crohan, *Islandman*, 35.

35. Dan Breen, *My Fight for Irish Freedom* (1924; rpt., Tralee, County Kerry: Anvil, 1964), 13; IFC 1573:237–38; Maurice O'Sullivan, *Twenty Years A-Growing*, trans. Moya Llewelyn Davies and George Thomson (1933; rpt., Oxford: Oxford University Press, 1983), chaps, 24–26, and see postscript, xi: after some years he left the Guards to settle "among the Connemara peasantry."

36. Patrick Lindsay, *Memories* (Dublin: Blackwater Press, 1993), 17, 30–31.

37. Frank O'Connor, *An Only Child* (London: Macmillan, 1961), 140–41, chap. 13; Sean O'Faolain, *Vive Moi! An Autobiography* (London: Rupert Hart-Davis, 1965), chap. 3, and 52.

38. Patrick Shea, *Voices and the Sound of Drums: An Irish Autobiography* (Belfast: Blackstaff Press, 1981), esp. 102–3.

39. William O'Malley, *Glancing Back: 70 Years' Experiences and Reminiscences of Press Man, Sportsman, and Member of Parliament* (London: Wright & Brown, [1933?]), 150–53.

40. A full-scale study was undertaken by the Board of Indian Commissioners (not part of the BIA), leading to a detailed "Returned Student Survey" of 1916–17. Copy available to me at the Newberry Library, Chicago.

41. ARCIA (1900), H. Doc., no. 5, 56th Cong., 2nd sess., serial 4101, 34–35.

42. ARCIA, *Annual Reports of the Department of the Interior* (Washington DC: Government Printing Office, 1903), 437; ARCIA, *Reports of the Department of the Interior* (Washington DC: Government Printing Office, 1908), 138–40.

43. Adams, *Education for Extinction*, 289. And see 287, where he presents the Hampton criteria for placing ex-students into one of five categories: excellent, good, fair, poor, bad. See all chap. 9.

44. Wilbert H. Ahern, "An Experiment Aborted: Returned Indian Students in the Indian School Service, 1881–1908," *Ethnohistory* 44.2 (Spring 1997): 263–303, with quotations from 267, 273; ARCIA, *Annual Report of the Secretary of the Interior* (Washington DC: Government Printing Office, 1941), 439.

45. Ahern, "An Experiment Aborted," 290. See also 282, for job listings.

46. Material in this and next two paragraphs: School Records, Records of Graduates and Returned Students, Records of the Carlisle Indian Industrial School, RG 75, NA. There is a folder each for many ex-pupils, and I examined about 200 such folders, but I have no way of knowing how representative they were. Although not all ex-pupils gave positive answers, many did, so the folders may have been selected out by the Carlisle authorities. Each folder contained a variety of materials—official forms containing student answers, along with letters (and copies) to and from the school.

47. For a more detailed examination of "the return home," see, for example, Coleman, *American Indian Children*, chap. 10; Adams, *Education for Extinction*, chap. 9.

48. Thomas Wildcat Alford, *Civilization and the Story of the Absentee Shawnees, as Told to Florence Drake* (Norman: University of Oklahoma Press, 1936), 111. See also Jacqueline Fear-Segal, "'Use the Club of the White Man's Wisdom in Defense of Our Customs': White Schools and Native Agendas," *American Studies International* 40.3 (October 2002): 6–32.

49. Jim Whitewolf, *Jim Whitewolf: The Life of a Kiowa Apache Indian*, ed. Charles S. Brant (New York: Dover, 1969), 95; Polingaysi Qoyawayma (Elizabeth Q. White), *No Turning Back: A True Account of a Hopi Girl's Struggle to Bridge the Gap between the World of Her People and the World of the White Man*, as told to Vada F. Carlson (Albuquerque: University of New Mexico Press, 1969), 67–75, chaps. 10–15 (and see note 51 below). Such a sense of superiority often developed while pupils were still at school. See Jim Whitewolf, *Jim Whitewolf: The Life of a Kiowa Apache Indian*, ed. Charles S. Brant (New York: Dover, 1969), 95.

50. Daniel La France (Ah-nen-la-de-ni), "An Indian Boy's Story," *Independent* 55 (July 1903), 1786–87; Don Talayesva, *Sun Chief: The Autobiography of a Hopi Indian,* ed. Leo W. Simmons (New Haven CT: Yale University Press, 1942), 135–36; Oscar Good Shot, "Oscar Good Shot: The Narrative of a Sioux Visitor," in Thomas Marquis, *The Cheyennes of Montana* (Algonac MI: Reference, 1978), 269–70.

51. Irene Stewart, *A Voice in Her Tribe: A Navajo Woman's Own Story,* ed. Dorris Ostrander Dawdy and Mary Shepardson, Anthropological Paper no. 17 (Socorro NM: Ballena Press, 1980), 33–36; Anna Moore Shaw, *A Pima Past* (Tucson: University of Arizona Press, 1974), 146–50, 199–234.

52. Helen Sekaquaptewa, *Me and Mine: The Life Story of Helen Sekaquaptewa, as Told to Louise Udall* (Tucson: University of Arizona Press, 1969), 144–46, 151–66, 197–98, 224–49. Margaret D. Jacobs sees Hopis such as Sekaquaptewa and Polingaysi as being influenced by white women and schooling but also drawing upon their own cultures "to shape a unique, multicultural view of womanhood." See Jacobs, *Engendered Encounters: Feminism and Pueblo Cultures, 1879–1934* (Lincoln: University of Nebraska Press, 1999), 47–55, with quotation from 54.

53. Ely S. Parker, "General Parker's Autobiography," in "Writings of General Parker," *Publications of the Buffalo Historical Society* 8 (1905): 529–31.

54. Talayesva, *Sun Chief,* 234; Luther Standing Bear, *Land of the Spotted Eagle* (1933; rpt., Lincoln: University of Nebraska Press, 1978), 239–40; Hoke Denetsosie in Broderick H. Johnson, ed., *Stories of Traditional Navajo Life and Culture, by Twenty-Two Navajo Men and Women* (Tsaile, Navajo Nation NM: Navajo Community College Press, 1977), 102; Zitkala-Ša (Gertrude Bonnin), *American Indian Stories* (1921; rpt., Lincoln: University of Nebraska Press, 1985), 90–91, 109–25; Chris (pseudonym), *Apache Odyssey: A Journey between Two Worlds,* ed. Morris E. Opler (New York: Holt, Rinehart & Winston, 1969), 68, 138, 189.

55. Institute for Government Research, *Problem of Indian Administration* (Meriam Report), esp. 382–92.

56. In Johnson, ed., *Stories of Traditional Navajo Life,* 241 ; G. W. Grayson, *A Creek Warrior for the Confederacy: The Autobiography of Chief G. W. Grayson,* ed. W. David Baird (Norman: University of Oklahoma Press, 1988), 41–42; on the Apache claim, comments by Eve Ball, in Asa Daklugie et al., *Indeh: An Apache Odyssey,* ed. Eve Ball (Norman: University of Oklahoma Press, 1988), 290–91.

57. Chester Yellowhair, "I was Born in the Dark Ages," *Desert Magazine* 23 (November 1960): 17–18; Kabotie, *Fred Kabotie,* 65–68, 106–14; Angel DeCora, "Angel DeCora—An Autobiography," *Red Man* 3 (1910): 167–95; Anne Ruggles Gere, "An Art of Survivance: Angel DeCora at Carlisle," *American Indian Quarterly* 28.3/4 (Summer and Fall 2004): 649–84.

58. Whitewolf, *Jim Whitewolf,* 96; Daklugie et al., *Indeh,* 84, 274; Ada Damon, "'That's the Way We Were Raised': An Oral Interview with Ada Damon," ed. Yvonne Ashley, *Frontiers* 2 (1977): 62; Jonas Keeble, in *To Be an Indian: An Oral History,* ed. Joseph H. Cash and Herbert T. Hoover (New York: Holt, Rinehart & Winston, 1969), 60–61.

59. Keeble, in Cash and Hoover, *To Be an Indian,* 61; James McCarthy, *A Papago Traveler: Memories of James McCarthy,* ed. John G. Westover (Tucson: Sun Tracks and

University of Arizona Press, 1985), 68–98; Shaw, *Pima Past*, 140–51; Clinton Rickard, *Fighting Tuscrora: The Autobiography of Chief Clinton Rickard*, ed. Barbara Graymont (Syracuse NY: Syracuse University Press, 1973), chap. 2; Cadman, in Johnson, ed., *Stories of Traditional Navajo Life*, 213.

60. Alford, *Civilization*, 108–109.

61. For treatments of both see David J. Carlson, "'Indian for a While': Charles Eastman's *Indian Boyhood* and the Discourse of Allotment," *American Indian Quarterly* 25.4 (Fall 2001): 604–25; Sherry L. Smith, "Francis La Flesche and the World of Letters," ibid., 579–603. See also Joan Mark, *A Stranger in Her Native land: Alice Fletcher and the American Indians* (Lincoln: University of Nebraska Press, 1988).

62. Howard Whitewolf, "A Short Story of My Life," *American Indian Magazine* 5 (January–March 1917): 31.

63. Lucille (Jerry) Winnie, *Sah-gan-de-oh: The Chief's Daughter* (New York: Vantage Press, 1969), 53, 58.

64. Malcolm McFee, "The 150% Man, a Product of Blackfeet Acculturation," *American Anthropologist* 70 (December 1968): 1096–1103.

65. Adams, *Education for Extinction*, 336.

Conclusions

1. Albert Yava, *Big Falling Snow: A Tewa-Hopi Indian's Life and the History and Traditions of His People*, ed. Harold Courlander, quoted in *Native American Autobiography: An Anthology*, ed. Arnold Krupat (Madison: University of Wisconsin Press, 1994), 482. I have altered the text slightly to disguise its origin.

2. Peter Kolchin, "The Big Picture: A Comment on David Brion Davis's 'Looking at Slavery from Broader Perspectives,'" AHR Forum, *American Historical Review* 105.2 (April 2000): 467–71.

3. J. R. Miller, *Shingwauk's Vision: A History of Native Residential Schools* (Toronto: University of Toronto Press, 1996), 436. Miller sees this hubris springing mainly from the educators' sense of racial superiority over Aboriginal peoples. I have shown that even where racism did not apply, teaching authorities in the United States and Ireland exhibited such ethnocentric attitudes.

4. John Willinsky, *Learning to Divide the World: Education at Empire's End* (Minneapolis: University of Minnesota Press, 1998), 90–91.

5. Willinsky, *Learning to Divide*, 94.

6. Thomas E. Jordan, *Ireland's Children: Quality of Life, Stress, and Child Development in the Famine Era* (Westport CT: Greenwood Press, 1998), 1.

7. See Willinsky, *Learning to Divide*, 106, on the possibly liberating nature of schooling for women in India. Also see Stearns, *Schools and Students*, 162: in the West and Japan, schools "encouraged women to have fewer children by giving them a sense of new goals and an awareness of alternatives." Cf. Magnus O. Bassey, *Western Education and Political Domination in Africa: A Study in Critical and Dialogical Pedagogy* (Westport CT: Bergin and Garvey, 1999), 91–98, on the virtual exclusion of girls from colonial missionary education and on continuing gender inequalities on that continent. Further,

I want to suggest that twenty-first-century Western campaigns for female equality in the non-Western world—which I support—might take pause. The also confident advocates of these campaigns might consider more carefully the nature of the cultures they hope to change in order to produce "correct" and modern forms of gender relations in such (also supposedly deficient) non-Western societies.

8. Peter N. Stearns, *Schools and Students in Industrial Society: Japan and the West, 1870–1940* (Boston: Bedford, 1998), 162.

9. See, for example, Michael C. Coleman, "Western Education, American Indian and African Children: A Comparative Study of Pupil Motivation through Published Reminiscences, 1860s–1960s," *Canadian and International Education* 18.1 (1989): 36–53.

10. I owe the three-dimensional idea to Donagh Coleman.

11. On the importance of comparison to establish both "the rootedness of history in place and time and the connections in places and times across the world," see Frederick Cooper, "Race, Ideology, and the Perils of Comparative History," *American Historical Review* 101.4 (October 1996): 1135.

Bibliographical Note

This bibliographical note indicates the major sources, primary and secondary, that I relied upon for the present study. For secondary sources on Indian history I generally confined myself to books and to material published since 1993. For earlier studies see my *American Indian Children at School, 1850–1930* (Jackson: University Press of Mississippi, 1993), Bibliography, B: Secondary Sources (211–22). Further sources are referred to in the endnotes to the text of the present study, as are suggestions for additional reading.

The bibliographical note is divided into the following sections (with some unavoidable overlap between sections):

American Sources
Autobiographies and Reminiscences
Other Published Primary Sources
Archival
Secondary Sources

Irish Sources
Autobiographies and Reminiscences
Other Published Primary Sources
Archival
Secondary Sources

Comparative Studies
Mass Education, Imperialism, Colonialism
§
American Sources
Autobiographies and Reminiscences
I provide a full listing of approximately one hundred autobiographies and autobiographical fragments by American Indians in my *American Indian Children at School*, Bibliography, A, 1 (203–08). Published since then, and highly useful for the present work in that it is the autobiography of an ex-student and ex-teacher at Indian schools: Esther Burnett Horne and Sally McBeth, *Essie's Story: The Life and Legacy of a Shoshone Teacher* (Lincoln: University of Nebraska Press, 1998). Containing autobiographical passages by Indians from the eighteenth century to the present: Arnold Krupat,

ed., *Native American Autobiography: An Anthology* (Madison: University of Wisconsin Press, 1994). Also, Herbert Lewis, ed., *Oneida Lives: Long-Lost Voices of Wisconsin Oneidas* (Lincoln: University of Nebraska Press, 2005), esp. chap. 7.

A number of autobiographies by white teachers at BIA and missionary schools also proved useful, such as Gertrude Golden, *Red Moon Called Me: Memoirs of a School Teacher in the Government Indian Service*, ed. Cecil Dryden (San Antonio TX: Naylor, 1954); Minnie Braithwaite Jenkins, *Girl from Williamsburg* (Richmond VA: Dietz Press, 1951); Janett Woodruff, as told to Cecil Dryden, *Indian Oasis* (Caldwell ID: Caxton, 1939); Richard Henry Pratt, *Battlefield and Classroom: Four Decades with the American Indian, 1867–1904*, ed. Robert M. Utley (1964; rpt., Lincoln: University of Nebraska Press, 1987).

Other Published Primary Sources

If read critically, much of the history of Indian schooling can be followed in U.S. Commissioner for Indian Affairs, *Annual Report of the Commissioner of Indian Affairs* (ARCIA), 1851–1941. (These reports were available to me in different publications, or sometimes as a separate publication; in the notes I fully cite the specific publication). As well as containing the Commissioner's Report and statistical materials, voluminous numbers of reports from superintendents, teachers, and others were appended to the ARCIA. Catholic and Protestant missionary societies also reported to the BIA, and letters from these organizations are also appended. Comparison of published letters from field operatives with many originals contained in the archives (see below), suggests that generally correspondence from the field was not greatly altered in approach to assimilation before publication in ARCIA.

Other published reports provide further angles on the education of Indians: American Board of Commissioners for Foreign Missions, *First Ten Annual Reports of the American Board of Commissioners for Foreign Missions, 1810–20* (Boston: ABCFM, 1834); *Annual Report of the American Board of Commissioners for Foreign Missions* (Boston: 1821–41); *Memorial Volume of the First Fifty Years of the American Board of Commissioners for Foreign Missions* (Boston: ABCFM, 1861). Also consulted: Board of Foreign Missions of the Presbyterian Church in the USA, *Annual Report of the Board of Foreign Missions of the Presbyterian Church in the USA* (New York: Board of Foreign Missions, 1838–1893). A crucial study, often cited in my text, was the famous and controversial Meriam Report: Institute for Government Research, *The Problem of Indian Administration* (Baltimore: Johns Hopkins Press, 1928).

Internet sources also proved useful for locating U.S. government material on Indian affairs. For the full texts of all Indian treaties see Charles J. Kappler, comp. and ed., *Indian Affairs: Laws and Treaties*, vol. 2 (Washington DC: Government Printing Office, 1904). Available at http://digital.library.okstate.edu/kappler. Also useful is the current BIA website: www.doi.gov./bureau-indian-affairs.html. Contemporary information is available at www.oiep.bia.edu/body.html (all most recently accessed June 26, 2006).

Archival Sources

Individual letters, reports, student materials, and other documents are cited in my notes. From the vast archival sources available in the U.S. National Archives (www. archives.gov/index.html; accessed June 26, 2006), I utilized material in the following collections:

Records of the Bureau of Indian Affairs, Record Group 75 (RG 75)

Central Classified Files, 1907–1919; File 821 for Fort Shaw and Wittenberg

Letters Received, 1824–1881 (M234); Schools, 1824–1873

Records of the Education Department; Examination papers, 1915 (Haskell Institute)

Records of Non-Reservation Schools; Records of the Carlisle Indian Industrial School; School Records

Reports of Inspection and Field Jurisdictions of the Office of Indian Affairs, 1873–1900 (Microfilm1070)

Superintendents' Annual Narrative and Statistical Reports from Field Jurisdictions Of the Bureau of Indian Affairs, 1907–1938

I also utilized material from other American archives, especially:

National Anthropological Archives, Smithsonian Institution, Washington DC (www.nmnh.si.edu/naa/; accessed June 26, 2006), Alice C. Fletcher and Francis la Flesche Papers

Newberry Library, Chicago (www.newberry.org/newberryhome.html; accessed June 26, 2006), Board of Indian Commissioners, Returned Student Survey, Bulletin no. 24, 1916–17 (copy)

Newberry Library, Chicago; John Howard Payne Papers, vol. 8

Presbyterian Historical Society, Philadelphia (www.history.pcusa.org/; accessed June 26, 2006)

American Indian Correspondence. This whole collection, along with Indian sections of the BFM Annual Report, has been microfilmed: American Indian Correspondence: The Presbyterian Historical Society's Collection of Missionaries' Letters, 1833–1893 (Westport CT: Greenwood Press, 1979).

Secondary Sources

I have drawn on many of my own publications for the present work, especially American Indian Children at School, 1850–1930 (Jackson: University Press of Mississippi, 1993). I also used my more recent studies citing material published since 1993: "Treaties and American Indian Schools in the Era of Assimilation, 1794–1930," Encyclopedia of Native American Treaties, ed. Donald Fixico (New York: ABC-CLIO, forthcoming); "The Symbiotic Embrace: American Indians, White Educators, and the School, 1820s–1920s," History of Education (Great Britain) 25 (March 1996): 1–18; "American Indian School Pupils as Cultural Brokers: Cherokee Girls at Brainerd Mission, 1828–29," Between American Indian and White Worlds: The Cultural Broker, ed. Margaret Connell Szasz (Norman: University of Oklahoma Press, 1994), 123–39; "The Historical Credibility of American Indian Autobiographical Accounts of Schooling, 1850–1930," Irish Journal of American Studies 3 (1994): 127–50. I have also written a number of studies explicitly comparing Irish and Indian education: see Comparative Studies, below.

Many important books on aspects of Indian education and history have appeared since 1993. Some focus on broad areas, some on individual schools. Some are by Native American scholars, such as the following: Donald J. Fixico, *The American Indian Mind in a Linear World: American Indian Studies and Traditional Knowledge* (New York: Routledge, 2003), especially chap. 5; Vine Deloria Jr. and Daniel Wildcat, *Power and Place: Indian Education in America* (Golden CO: American Indian Graduate Center and Fulcrum Resources, 2001); Amanda J. Cobb, *Listening to Our Grandmothers' Stories: The Bloomfield Academy for Chickasaw Females, 1852–1949* (Lincoln: University of Nebraska Press, 2000); Brenda J. Child, *Boarding School Seasons: American Indian Families, 1900–1914* (Lincoln: University of Nebraska Press, 1998); Henrietta Mann, *Cheyenne-Arapaho Education, 1871–1982* (Niwot: University Press of Colorado, 1997); K. Tsianina Lomawaima, *They Called It Prairie Light: The Story of the Chilocco Indian School* (Lincoln: University of Nebraska Press, 1994); and more recently by Lomawaima, "American Indian Education: By Indians versus For Indians," in *A Companion to American Indian History*, ed. Philip Deloria and Neal Salisbury (Malden MA: Blackwell, 2002), 422–40; Devon A. Mihesuah, *Cultivating the Rosebuds: The Education of Women at the Cherokee Female Seminary, 1851–1909* (Urbana: University of Illinois Press, 1993).

Non-Indian scholars besides myself have also devoted books to these and related issues: Lucy Maddox, *Citizen Indians: Native American Intellectuals, Race, and Reform* (Ithaca NY: Cornell University Press, 2005); Bill Crawford, *All American: The Rise and Fall of Jim Thorpe* (Hoboken NJ: Wiley, 2005); Jon Reyhner and Jeanne Eder, *American Indian Education: A History* (Norman: University of Oklahoma Press, 2004); Joel Pfister, *Individuality Incorporated: Indians and the Multicultural Modern* (Durham NC: Duke University Press, 2004); Jeffrey Ostler, *The Plains Sioux and U.S. Colonialism from Lewis and Clark to Wounded Knee* (New York: Cambridge University Press, 2004), esp. chaps. 7 and 8; Ruth Spack, *America's Second Tongue: American Indian Education and the Ownership of English, 1860–1900* (Lincoln: University of Nebraska Press, 2002); Jean A. Keller, *Empty Beds: Indian Student Health at Sherman Institute, 1902–22* (East Lansing: Michigan State University Press, 2002); John Bloom, *To Show What an Indian Can Do: Sports at Native American Boarding Schools*, Sports and Culture Series, vol. 2 (Minneapolis: University of Minnesota Press, 2000); Scott Riney, *The Rapid City Indian School, 1893–1933* (Norman: University of Oklahoma Press, 1999); Clyde Ellis, *To Change Them Forever: Indian Education at the Rainy Mountain Boarding School, 1893–1920* (Norman: University of Oklahoma Press, 1996); David Wallace Adams, *Education for Extinction: American Indians and the Boarding School Experience, 1875–1928* (Lawrence: University Press of Kansas, 1995). On a closely related subject is Marilyn Irvin Holt, *Indian Orphanages* (Lawrence: University Press of Kansas, 2001).

A number of other studies are important: Frederick E. Hoxie, *A Final Promise: The Campaign to Assimilate the Indians, 1880–1920* (1984; rpt., with new preface by author, Lincoln: University of Nebraska Press, 2001); Margaret Connell Szasz, *Education and the American Indian: The Road to Self-Determination since 1928*, rev. ed. (Albuquerque: University of New Mexico Press, 1999), especially chaps. 1–8; also by Szasz, *Indian Education in the American Colonies, 1607–1783* (Albuquerque: University of New Mexico

Press, 1988); Margaret Jacobs, *Gendered Encounters: Feminism and Pueblo Cultures, 1879–1934* (Lincoln: University of Nebraska Press, 1999), Francis Paul Prucha, *American Indian Treaties: The History of a Political Anomaly* (Berkeley: University of California Press, 1994); and Prucha's monumental *The Great Father: The United States Government and the American Indians*, vols. 1 and 2 (Lincoln: University of Nebraska Press, 1984); Peter Nabokov, *A Forest of Time: American Indian Ways of History* (New York: Cambridge University Press, 2002). For a broader context on Indian schooling see Joel Spring, *The American School, 1642–2000*, 5th ed. (Boston: McGraw-Hill, 2001).

Useful collections of essays are the following: Philip J. Deloria and Neal Salisbury, eds., *A Companion to American Indian History* (Malden MA: Blackwell, 2002); Frederick E. Hoxie, Peter C. Mancall, and James H. Merrell, *American Nations: Encounters in Indian Country, 1850 to the Present* (New York: Routledge, 2001); Russell Thornton, ed. *Studying Native America: Problems and Prospects* (Madison: University of Wisconsin Press, 1998).

Also providing context and information are the following: David Ricci, *Good Citizenship in America* (Cambridge: Cambridge University Press, 2004); Theda Perdue, ed., *Sifters: Native American Women's Lives* (New York: Oxford University Press, 2001); Joel W. Martin, *The Land Looks After Us: A History of Native American Religion* (New York: Oxford University Press, 2001); Margot Liberty, ed., *American Indian Intellectuals of the Nineteenth and the Early Twentieth Centuries* (1978; rpt., Norman: University of Oklahoma Press, 2002); Joseph Illick, *American Childhoods* (Philadelphia: University of Pennsylvania Press, 2000); Clifford Putney, *Muscular Christianity: Manhood and Sports in Protestant America, 1880–1920* (Cambridge MA: Harvard University Press, 2001); Rogers M. Smith, *Civic Ideas: Conflicting Visions of Citizenship in U.S. History* (New Haven CT: Yale University Press, 1997); James H. Kettner, *The Development of American Citizenship, 1608–1870* (Chapel Hill: Published for the Institute of Early American History and Culture, Williamsburg VA, by the University of North Carolina Press, 1978).

Irish Sources
Published Primary Sources: Autobiographies and Reminiscences
Interpretations of pupil responses and other aspects of Irish educational history are based partly on about forty autobiographies and autobiographical fragments and reminiscences (some unpublished, from the Irish Folklore Collection—see Primary Sources below). These narratives are cited in notes to the present work. For a more compact citation of these narratives see notes to my "'Eyes as Big as Bowls with Fear and Wonder': Children's Responses to the Irish National Schools, 1850–1922," *Proceedings of the Royal Irish Academy* 98C.5 (1998): 177–202. Autobiographies examined since then include the following: Loombe Atthill, *Recollections of an Irish Doctor* (London: Religious Tract Society, 1911); William O'Malley, *Glancing Back: 70 Years' Experiences and Reminiscences of Press Man, Sportsman and Member of Parliament* (London: Wright and Brown, n.d. [1933?]); Jeremiah Murphy, *When Youth Was Mine: A Memoir of Kerry, 1902–1925* (Dublin: Mentor, 1998); Eamon Kelly, *The Apprentice* (Dublin: Marion, 1996); Mark F. Ryan, *Fenian Memories* (Dublin: Gill and Son, 1946); Patrick J. Lindsay, *Memories* (Dublin: Blackwater, 1993); Patrick Gallagher ("Paddy the Cope"), *My Story* (Dungloe: Templecrone Co-Operative Society, n.d.).

Other Published Primary Sources
The history of the National Board can be critically followed in Commissioners of
National Education in Ireland, [Annual] *Report of the Commissioners of National Education
in Ireland* (Dublin: CNEI, 1834 to 1919–20), and in the voluminous accompanying yearly appendixes. Available separately or in bound volumes at the National Library of
Ireland (NLI). On events leading up to the establishment of the National Board and
later developments, see the following: *Fourteenth Report of the Commissioners for Inquiring
into the State of All Schools, on Public or Charitable Foundations, in Ireland* (1812); Reports
from Commissioners, *First Report of the Commissioners of Irish Education Inquiry*, H.C.
1825; *Second Report of the Commissioners of Irish Education Inquiry*, H.C. 1826–27; *Royal
Commission of Inquiry into Primary Education (Ireland)*, H.C. 1870 (Powis Commission).

For critical perspectives on the CNEI see *Claidheamh Soluis* [Sword of Light], publication of the Gaelic League; [Patrick H. Pearse], *A Significant Irish Nationalist: The Educational
Writings of P. H. Pearse*, ed. Séamas Ó Buachalla (Dublin: Mercier Press, 1980).

Archival Sources
National Library of Ireland (www.nli.ie; accessed June 23, 2006); Minutes of Board
Meeting of the Commissioners of National Education in Ireland, 1831–1900 (Feb.
1837–June 1940 missing) (Manuscript Section, NLI)

National Library of Ireland; Minutes of the Proceedings of the Commissioners of
National Education in Ireland, 1900–1921 (private and confidential), MS, No. LO 2351
(NLI)

National Archives of Ireland (www.nationalarchives.ie); Irish Education Schools
Index (organized by county)

UCD Delargy Centre for Irish Folklore and the National Folklore Collection,
University College Dublin (www.ucd.ie/irishfolklore; accessed June 26, 2006), Irish
Folklore Collection (cited in text as IFC); recently changed to National Folklore
Collection; in my notes I retained the older, more common name, Irish Folklore
Collection

Secondary Sources
A number of works are useful in part or in their entirety. In *The Irish Hedge School and Its
Books, 1695–1831* (Dublin: Four Courts Press, 2002), Antonia Fraser helps set the scene
for the establishment of the CNEI and continues some distance into the period of its
existence. Adrian Kelly, *Compulsory Irish: Language and Education in Ireland 1870s–1970s*
(Dublin: Irish Academic Press, 2002), in a sense goes the other way. His study begins
with CNEI attitudes to language and shows how the new Irish Free State/Republic
misconstrued the role of the CNEI in the collapse of Irish and then tried to use the
educational institutions of the new state to revive the language. Also on language is
Tony Crowley, *War of Words: The Politics of Language in Ireland 1537–2000* (Oxford: Oxford
University Press, 2005), esp. chaps. 5–6. Janet Nolan shows in *Servants of the Poor:
Teachers and Mobility in Ireland and Irish America* (Notre Dame IN: University of Notre
Dame Press, 2004) the importance of the national schools for the mobility of women,

especially, in both Ireland and in the United States, to which huge numbers of them emigrated. See also Thomas A. O'Donoghue, *Bilingual Education in Ireland, 1904–1922: The Case of the Bilingual Programme of Instruction*, Centre for Irish Studies Monograph Series no. 1 (Perth, Australia: Murdoch University, 2000); Sean Farren, *The Politics of Irish Education, 1920–1965* (Belfast: Queen's University, 1995); Mary Cullen, ed., *Girls Don't Do Honours: Irish Women in Education in the 19th and 20th Centuries* (Dublin: Women's Education Bureau, 1987); E. Brian Titley, *Church, State, and the Control of Education in Ireland, 1900–1944* (Kingston ON: McGill-Queen's University Press, 1983).

John Coolahan, *Irish Education: Its History and Structure* (Dublin: Institute of Public Education, 1980), chap. 1, on primary school education, is still an excellent short history of the CNEI. See also articles by Coolahan cited in the notes of the present study, including "Education as Cultural Imperialism: The Denial of the Irish Language to Irish Speakers, 1831–1922," *Paedagogica Historica* 37.1 (2001): 17–33. Donald Akenson, *The Irish Education Experience: The National System of Education in the Nineteenth Century* (London: Routledge and Kegan Paul, 1970), remains highly useful.

Little, to my knowledge, had been written on pupil responses to national schools until my own article "'Eyes Big as Bowls with Fear and Wonder': Children's Responses to the Irish National Schools, 1850–1922," *Proceedings of the Royal Irish Academy* 98C.5 (1998): 177–202. However, for a broader study of responses to primary and secondary education see T. O. McCollam, "The Hard Old Bench: A Study of School Life as Portrayed in the Autobiographical and Fictional Works of a Number of Anglo-Irish Writers" (M.A. thesis, University of Ulster, 1985). See also Janet Nolan, *Servants of the Poor: Teachers and Mobility in Ireland and Irish America* (Notre Dame IN: University of Notre Dame Press, 2004); A. Norman Jeffares and Anthony Kamm, eds., *An Irish Childhood* (London: Collins, 1987).

Other works giving broader contexts on the national schools include, for example, Kevin Kenny, ed., *Ireland the British Empire* (Oxford: Oxford University Press, 2004); Alvin Jackson, *Home Rule: An Irish History, 1800–2000* (London: Phoenix, 2003); Jim Mac Laughlin, *Reimagining the Nation State: The Contested Terrains of Nation-Building* (London: Pluto, 2001); Stephen Howe, *Ireland and Empire: Colonial Legacies and Irish History* (New York: Oxford University Press, 2000); Bernadette Cunningham and Máire Kennedy, eds., *The Experience of Reading: Irish Historical Perspectives* (Dublin: Rare Books Group of the Library Association of Ireland/Economic and Social History Society of Ireland, 1999); Patrick O'Mahony and Gerard Delanty, *Rethinking Irish History: Nationalism, Identity and Ideology* (Houndmills, Basingstoke, Hampshire: Macmillan, 1998); Mary Peckham Magray, *The Transforming Power of the Nuns: Women, Religion, and Cultural Change in Ireland, 1750–1900* (New York: Oxford University Press, 1998); Thomas E. Jordan, *Ireland's Children: Quality of Life, Stress, and Child Development in the Famine Era* (Westport CT: Greenwood Press, 1998); James S. Donnelly Jr., and Kerby A. Miller, eds., *Irish Popular Culture, 1650–1850* (Dublin: Irish Academic Press, 1998); Kenneth Milne, *The Irish Charter Schools, 1730–1830* (Dublin: Four Courts Press, 1997); Margaret Kelleher and James H. Murphy, eds., *Gender Perspectives in 19th Century Ireland: Private and Public Spheres* (Dublin: Irish Academic Press, 1997); Maurice R. O'Connell, ed., O'Connell: Education, Church and State, Proceedings of the Second Annual Daniel O'Connell Workshop (Dublin: Institute of Public Administration, 1992); David Hempton, Religion and Culture in Britain and Ireland: From the Glorious Revolution to the Decline of Empire (Cambridge: Cambridge University Press, 1996); Mary Daly and David Dickson, eds., The Origins of Popular Literacy in Ireland: Language Change and Educational Development, 1700–1920 (Dublin: Department of Modern History, Trinity College, Dublin/Department of Modern Irish History, University College, Dublin, 1990); Barry M. Coldrey, Faith and Fatherland: The Christian Brothers and the Development of Irish Nationalism, 1838–1921 (London: Gill and Macmillan, 1988); P. J. Dowling, The Hedge Schools of Ireland, rev. ed. (Cork: Mercier, 1968).

Comparative Studies

A number of scholars have explicitly compared American Indian and Irish experiences, thus comforting me in my venture: David Harding, "Objects of English Colonial Discourse: The Irish and Native Americans," Nordic Irish Studies 4 (2005): 37–60; Katie Kane, "'Will Come Forth in Tongues of Fury': Relocating Irish Cultural Studies," Cultural Studies 15.1 (January 2001): 98–123; and Kane, "Nits Make Lice: Drogheda, Sand Creek, and the Poetics of Colonial Extermination," Cultural Critique 42 (Spring 1999): 81–103; Nancy Scheper-Hughes, "The Best of Two Worlds, the Worst of Two Worlds: Reflections on Culture and Field Work among the Rural Irish and Pueblo Indians," Comparative Studies in Society and History 29 (1987): 56–75; Nicholas P. Canny, "The Ideology of English Colonization: From Ireland to America," William and Mary Quarterly, 3rd series, no. 30 (October 1973): 575–98.

Partly stimulated by such work, I have written two Irish-Indian comparative studies: Michael C. Coleman, "Representations of American Indians and the Irish in Educational Reports, 1850s–1920s," Irish Historical Studies 33.129 (May 2002): 33–51; Coleman, "The Responses of American Indian Children and Irish Children to the School, 1850s–1920s: A Comparative Study in Cross-Cultural Education," American Indian Quarterly 23.3/4 (Summer and Fall 1999): 83–112. For a further comparative perspective see Michael C. Coleman, "Western Education, American Indian and African Children: A Comparative Study of Pupil Motivation through Published Reminiscences, 1860s–1960s," Canadian and International Education 18 (1989): 36–53.

Comparative studies relating Irish experiences with those of (unlikely) other peoples proved instructive: Joe Cleary, Literature, Partition, and the Nation State: Culture and Conflict in Ireland, Israel, and Palestine (New York: Cambridge University Press, 2002); Cormac Ó Gráda, Black '47 and Beyond: The Great Irish Famine in History, Economy, and Memory (Princeton NJ: Princeton University Press, 1999); Ian S. Lustick, Unsettled States, Disputed Lands: Britain and Ireland, France and Algeria, Israel and the West Bank-Gaza (Ithaca NY: Cornell University Press, 1993).

Recent comparative interest in the different yet connected histories of the peoples of the so-called British Isles is evidenced by such books as the following: Frank Welsh, The Four Nations: A History of the United Kingdom (London: HarperCollins, 2002); Jeremy Black, A History of the British Isles (New York: St. Martin's Press, 1997); Adrian

Hastings, *The Construction of Nationhood: Ethnicity, Religion, and Nationalism* (Cambridge: Cambridge University Press, 1997), chap. 3. Hasting adds America to his four-nation comparison in this chapter. Over a century old but still highly useful is Graham Balfour, *The Educational Systems of Great Britain and Ireland* (Oxford: Clarendon, 1903).

A major comparative study that proved greatly helpful in placing Irish and Indian experiences in broader contexts and in suggesting the value of comparison of similar educational processes in very different cultural and historical contexts is Peter N. Stearns, *Schools and Students in Industrial Society: Japan and the West, 1870–1940* (Boston: Bedford, 1998). Many of the essays in the following collection are also thought-provoking: James Mahoney and Dietrich Reuschmeyer, eds., *Comparative Historical Analysis in the Social Sciences* (Cambridge: Cambridge University Press, 2003). In addition, a number of recent articles also argued for the potential of comparative study, such as David Crook and Gary McCulloch, "Introduction: Comparative Approaches to the History of Education," *History of Education* 31.5 (2002): 397; Rachel Adams, "The Worlding of American Studies," *American Quarterly* 53.4 (December 2001): 720–21; Michael Adas, "From Settler Colony to Global Hegemon: Integrating the Exceptionalist Narrative of the American Experience into World History," *American Historical Review* 106.5 (December 2001); Edmund Burke III, "The Terror and Religion: Brittany and Algeria," in *Colonialism and the Modern World: Selected Studies*, ed. Gregory Blue et al. (Armonk NY: Sharpe, 2002), 40–50; Ann Laura Stoler, "Tense and Tender Ties: The Politics of Comparison in North America and (Post) Colonial Studies," *Journal of American History* 88.3 (December 2001): 829–65.

A number of recent United States/Canadian comparative studies influenced my thinking: Jill St. Germain, *Indian Treaty-Making Policy in the United States and Canada, 1867–1877* (Lincoln: University of Nebraska Press, 2001); C. L. Higham, *Noble, Wretched, and Redeemable: Protestant Missionaries to the Indians in Canada and the United States, 1820–1900* (Albuquerque: University of New Mexico Press; Calgary AB: University of Calgary Press, 2000); Roger L. Nichols, *Indians in the United States and Canada: A Comparative Study* (Lincoln: University of Nebraska Press, 1998).

Mass Education, Imperialism, Colonialism

In this section I note a number of important studies in overlapping areas such as the rise of mass education and the related spread of imperial/colonial education; also, works on developments in Britain and the United States that influenced and were influenced by such complex and century-long developments: Steve Attidge, *Nationalism, Imperialism and Identity in Late Victorian Culture: Civil and Military Worlds* (Houndmills, Hampshire UK: Palgrave, 2003); Colin Heywood, *A History of Childhood: Children and Childhood in the West from Medieval to Modern Times* (Cambridge UK: Polity, 2001); David Vincent, *The Rise of Mass Literacy: Reading and Writing in Modern Europe* (Cambridge UK: Polity, 2000); David Crystal, *Language Death* (Cambridge: Cambridge University Press, 2000); Matthew Frye Jacobson, *Barbarian Virtues: The United States Encounters Foreign Peoples at Home and Abroad, 1876–1917* (New York: Hill and Wang, 2000); Stephen Heathorn, *For Home, Country, and Race: Constructing Gender, Class, and Englishness in the Elementary School,*

1880–1914 (Toronto: University of Toronto Press, 2000); John Willinsky, *Learning to Divide the World: Education at Empire's End* (Minneapolis: University of Minnesota Press, 1998); Kathryn Castle, *Britannia's Children: Reading Colonialism through Children's Books and Magazines* (Manchester UK: Manchester University Press, 1996); J. A. Mangan, ed., *The Imperial Curriculum: Racial Images and Education in the British Colonial Experience* (London: Routledge, 1993); Andy Green, *Education and State Formation: The Rise of Education Systems in England, France and the USA* (London: Macmillan, 1990).

Index

In the Indigenous Education series

American Indians, the Irish, and Government Schooling
A Comparative Study
by Michael C. Coleman

CPSIA information can be obtained
at www.ICGtesting.com
Printed in the USA
LVHW091617310119
605955LV00001B/87/P

9 780803 224858